W9-AXK-582

# PROPERTY MANAGEMENT

## DWIGHT E. NORRIS

ASHLEY CROWN SYSTEMS, INC.

2002

This publication is designed to provide accurate and current information regarding the subject matter covered. The principles and conclusions presented are subject to local, state and federal laws and regulations, court cases and revisions of same. If legal advice or other expert assistance is required, the reader is urged to consult a competent professional in that field.

Project Managers: Charli Hislop/Mary Achenbach
Cover/Book Design: Mary Achenbach
Editor: Cynthia Simone


Some images copyright www.arttoday.com
Some forms courtesy of David Tennan, Broker, GRI, CRS
                        Re/Max Calabasas Centre, Calabasas, CA

Published by Ashley Crown Systems, Inc.
22952 Alcalde Drive
Laguna Hills, CA 92653-1311

PRINTED IN THE UNITED STATES OF AMERICA

ISBN #0-934772-10-X

# Table of Contents

## HOTEL BUSINESS OPERATIONS . . . . . . . . . . . 395

## CURRENT ISSUES IN HOTEL/MOTEL MANAGEMENT . . . . . . . . . . . 423

## LEGAL ISSUES IN PROPERTY MANAGEMENT . . . . . . 447

# About the Author

Dwight E. Norris holds a Bachelor of Arts and a Masters Degree in Communications from Pepperdine University, and has been involved in the real estate business since 1979. As broker, appraiser, instructor and author, his experiences in real estate are diverse.

Dwight is a skilled writer and a people person. In this book Dwight presents in-depth knowledge of a complex field in a lively, entertaining way. His love for people permeates a subject that is sometimes handled in a mundane, impersonal manner. Dwight brings each chapter alive with stories and examples to animate and accompany sound principles of property management.

Dwight offers his best wishes to all who embark on this study.

*Dwight E. Norris*

Dwight E. Norris

# Preface

Society has gotten more and more complex in the last several decades. Laws have been passed that govern everything from how we dispose of waste by-products to how we deal with one another in the leasing, sale and financing of real property.

In the management of real property for others, there is more accountability and more paperwork then ever. Objectives and management plans have to be more precise. More is at stake for ownership and management. Computers and software programs have become necessary tools that must be employed in the task of property management.

Consequently, today's property manager must function at a high level of professionalism. They must be people-oriented, have knowledge of applicable laws, regulations, environmental issues, contracts, taxes and accounting procedures, as well as be well-schooled in state-of-the-art tools that will help accomplish their goals quickly and efficiently.

This text is intended to be on the cutting edge of the property management profession for the 21st Century. It addresses legal and technical issues of both today and tomorrow while, at the same time, deals with the human element—which never changes.

The style of this book is user-friendly. While technical in part and up-to-date, it's written in a down-to-earth manner that will bring a smile to the face of the reader and make the most esoteric concepts understandable. This book is designed to help the introductory student connect with an exciting and fast-moving profession, as well as help each student grow toward their full potential.

It is hoped that interested students will tap the extensive resources of this text and reach high in the attainment of their professional objectives.

# Overview of Property Management

- The Evolution Of Property Management
- Property Types Requiring Professional Property Management Services
- Educational Opportunities In Property Management
- Organizations And Certifications In Property Management
- The Delivery Of Property Management Services
- Positions Available In Property Management
- Benefits Of A Career In Property Management
- Future Trends In Property Management

CHAPTER 1

# THE EVOLUTION OF PROPERTY MANAGEMENT

The profession of property management has evolved with the times and changed with the waves of history. Join us for an historical and innovative perspective on the development of this important profession.

## In the Beginning

In early times, only those in power could own land. In most societies, that meant that the king or the emperor owned the land. Hence, the term *real estate; real* referring to *regal* or *royal,* and *estate* referring to *land.*

Sometimes subjects of the king could rise to a higher status due to military service or other distinguishing contributions to the kingdom. If they could emerge from *serfdom* to *freedmen*, they too could own land, subject to the king's authority.

Today all in the United States are *freedmen*, and are entitled to own as much property as they can acquire. The day property management became an important task was the day someone acquired more property than he or she could effectively manage, or perhaps just didn't have the interest or the expertise. That day the manager of real property assets was born.

In biblical times, the *keeper* of the vineyard had to give account of his stewardship. In medieval times, *vassals* received *fiefs* from regional *lords* serving at the pleasure of the king. These *fiefs* were rights in the land that soon became heritable. They were more than the land itself. They represented political power and position as the vassal had to raise a military force, collect taxes and build bridges and fortifications. He also had to ensure that the land would be agriculturally productive. This was accomplished through a hierarchy of servants and managers, ending at the bottom with the local peasants who tilled the land and harvested the crops.

From Europe to the United States, the private ownership of real property was enshrined as one of the hallmarks of a free society. In colonial times, estates were large and required management help to ensure the maximum productivity of the land.

John Jacob Astor (1763-1848), at one time the richest man in America from his real estate holdings on Manhattan Island, needed help collecting the rents and managing his properties. About the same time, European investors became absentee owners of land on the East Coast of the United States. They needed help finding tenants and collecting rents for their commercial and residential properties, as well as performing required maintenance to insure their properties did not deteriorate nor their values decline.

## Technological Advances

At the beginning of the 20th Century, rapid technological advances swept society into the new era of urbanization. People had already begun to cluster around the big cities as the ports of Boston, New York and others attracted ships from the east and stimulated trade and business.

Now, however, engineers and architects would build steel-frame commercial office buildings, hotels and apartments the likes of which had never before been seen on the face of the earth! *Skyscrapers* they were called, and no other name would more aptly describe the wonder felt in the hearts of most who gazed upon them. They would lift thousands of workers above the street level of the city to work in offices of trade and commerce. They would increase tremendously the density possible in an extremely limited area.

But how could workers climb 30 and 40 stories day after day just to get to their offices? Enter technological advancement Number 2, *high-speed electric elevators*. Now workers would be delivered to their offices quickly, safely and conveniently. Elevators like these made skyscrapers practical.

Since skyscrapers were owned jointly by investors who participated in stock and bond issues, their efficient management was an absolute necessity. If space were not rented promptly and rents collected on time, financial disaster could result. Investors demanded effective property management.

Additionally, they invested more capital than ever before in larger apartment houses, office buildings and high-rises of all types. With properties of greater value and massive investment capital at stake, quality property management was essential.

The advent of the *automobile* was another technological advance that changed forever the way people lived in this country. With the automobile, the work force was introduced to suburbia. People could get out of the city and into the country. They did not have to live in the city to work in the city. They could commute. This enabled them to live some distance from real estate they may have owned in the city, and again made property management necessary. In addition to housing in the suburbs, commercial properties and support facilities had to be constructed. At first these consisted of small stores and shopping centers, as well as some office space. These properties, too, required property management.

## From the 1930s Forward

The stock market crash of 1929 and the depression that followed into the '30s also brought about changes in real estate that had an impact on property management. Banks became the owners of record numbers of properties on which they had to foreclose. Those banks needed professional property management services because they did not have the time or expertise to provide it themselves, and to neglect the properties would be to further jeopardize assets.

World War II ended in 1945. The Federal Housing Administration (FHA) loan had been instituted in 1934, making available low down payment loans for the purchase of homes, helping to stimulate the economy and bring the depression to an end. Now thousands of returning servicemen and women would also have available to them the Veterans Administration (VA) loan, requiring no down payment and making housing readily available. This further increased suburban sprawl and caused the building of more commercial properties and support facilities.

The automobile continued to advance and people were commuting record distances. By now the *airplane* had become a routine part of the transportation of society and people were traveling farther and farther from any property they may have owned. All of this increased the demand for quality property management services.

Today commercial support facilities take the form of one-stop shopping centers, air conditioned malls, and elaborate developments as well as the familiar smaller strip centers offering numerous convenience stores. Business travel by air is literally a daily occurrence and an ample supply of hotels and motels are everywhere.

The savings and loan crisis of the late '80s marked another time in the history of our nation when record numbers of foreclosure properties were owned by the lenders. The Resolution Trust Corporation (RTC) was formed to liquidate the inventory. Again, so the assets did not lose value, expert property management services were needed.

Into the '90s with the general recession and the downturn in the economy, many homes declined in value below the level of their indebtedness. Many "upside down" homeowners walked away from their homes. Others could not make their payments, due to unemployment and business reversals. Again, record numbers of foreclosure properties required professional property management services.

Such demand for these services arises from economic crises and from times of healthy growth and expansion. Whatever the reason, at the time they are needed, property management services are extremely important to protect the investment of owners and lenders, and to ensure that the purpose for which the property was produced can be offered productively to the end users. Professional property management services protect the value of real property assets and safeguard a very important part of the nation's economy.

# PROPERTY TYPES REQUIRING PROFESSIONAL PROPERTY MANAGEMENT SERVICES

## Agricultural Land

Farms of various types are a unique specialty among property managers. These properties offer challenges different from any other. Some aspects of the farm business are dependent on factors that are beyond our control: weather, national and international economic policies and conditions, government restrictions on exports or marketing and foreign tariffs. Other aspects are important and have to be managed carefully, such as soil conditions, crop rotation, administering pesticides and environmental protection.

To keep the farming industry as stable as possible, the federal government is heavily involved with special funding programs. A property manager would have to be knowledgeable in this area as well as in all elements important to the successful operation of the farm. Specialized training is required for competence in this field and is available from selected colleges and universities.

## Industrial Property

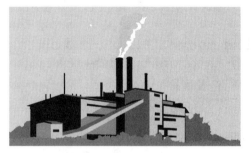 Industrial property refers to those where goods are manufactured or processed and prepared for distribution. Some businesses, like steel mills and oil refineries, still operate their own plants separate from other properties. They are involved in heavy manufacturing. Many other businesses, however, are part of an industrial park, a highly developed community within a community zoned for these specific purposes. They are involved in light manufacturing and assembly. These parks could be owned by a company that rents various units to the tenant occupants, owned outright by government agencies, or joint ventured between the two. They also can be set up as condominium projects where the tenant occupant owns the airspace inside his or her unit and has an undivided interest in the common areas. Other types of industrial properties include warehouses for the storage or distribution of goods.

Businesses that produce a product in this type of development want to be certain there is an available labor force in the area, that transportation is readily available to ship their product and that environmental and other governmental regulations are sufficiently favorable to allow them to conduct their business.

## Commercial Property

Commercial property includes office buildings and retail shopping centers, the places where *commerce* is conducted. These proper-

ties can range in value from several hundred thousand dollars to many millions. Office buildings can be relatively small walk-up structures or elaborate high-rises. Shopping centers, such as strip centers, can be small and less expensive, serving the local market. They also can be large regional centers with diverse tenants drawing customers from many miles around.

All commercial properties are income-producing businesses. Their stream of income is the key to their value. Although privately owned, these properties are considered *public accommodation* properties and the public has certain rights to them. A manager responsible for such properties must be well trained and highly professional.

## Residential Properties

Residential properties are those where people live. These properties are as diverse as the people that occupy them. A **Single Family Residence (SFR)** is a house that is intended to be occupied by one family. Some investors like SFRs because of their increased liquidity over other investment properties. Others find themselves with an SFR rental unit they cannot sell at a particular time, possibly because of a job transfer.

**Condominiums** are another type of residential property, usually individually owned. They are desirable to tenants as rental units because they are generally larger than apartments and have greater amenities. A property manager overseeing condominiums also will have to deal with a homeowner's association; a set of bylaws; and Covenants, Conditions, and Restrictions (CC&Rs) for the development.

**Multi-Family Units** are another type of residential property. Multi-family units range from duplexes to apartment complexes containing hundreds of units. Apartment complexes can be in the style of garden apartments, walk-up or high-rise buildings.

Increased building costs have led to the proliferation of apartments, resulting in a lower cost per family unit when compared to other types of housing.

Apartments comprise approximately 40% of all residential housing. These properties constitute a large part of the responsibilities of residential property managers and are emphasized in this book.

## Special Purpose Properties

These properties are specially designed to meet unique purposes within the community. Effective management in this category requires a specialized knowledge of the particular business involved in these properties. Special purpose properties include mini-storage facilities, mobile home parks, hotels/motels, automobile service stations, recreational resorts, theaters and nursing homes.

Management opportunities exist in all of these types of properties. A solid property management education should be obtained as a foundation. Then the peculiarities of a special property type can be learned through focused research and guided work experience.

## Common Interest Developments

Common Interest Developments (CIDs) include community apartment projects, stock cooperatives, condominiums, and Planned Unit Developments (PUDs). The following definitions are useful to a property manager.

***Community apartment project***—A development in which the owner has an undivided interest in the land with the exclusive right to occupy a particular unit. Owners are usually tenants in common in the building and have one mortgage and one tax bill for the entire building.

***Condominium project***—A development in which the owners have an undivided interest with each other in common areas and the interior airspace in a particular unit. The owner does not own the land and performs no exterior maintenance. Interest is usually fee simple and individual mortgages and tax bills are issued on each individual unit. Condominium projects may exist for residential, commercial and industrial property.

***Stock cooperative***—A development in which a corporation is formed for the purpose of holding title to improved real property. Stockholders in the corporation receive the right of exclusive occupancy of one of the units. Right of occupancy must be transferred with the stock.

***Planned Unit Development (PUD)***—A development in which each owner owns his or her own housing unit and land, and has an undivided interest in common areas with other owners. The care and maintenance of the common areas usually require the administration of an association and regular dues paid by the owners.

Management of CIDs requires interfacing with homeowners associations and an awareness of the unique problems facing such developments. While these properties can be self-managed, most associations function through an on-site manager or a property management company.

The on-site manager works solely for the association, working under the requirements of the community board of directors and carrying out its policies. The manager hires additional staff members and contracts for major services.

# EDUCATIONAL OPPORTUNITIES IN PROPERTY MANAGEMENT

Those interested in careers in property management may receive education in a number of ways.

- Formal education from a college or university
- Membership and certification in professional organizations
- On-the-job training

Some states require that property management services be offered under the authority of a real estate broker's license. Studies that meet the requirements to obtain a real estate agent's license will also broaden one's knowledge of real estate as it relates to the property manager's responsibilities. Real property is land, whatever is growing or built on it, the rights and interests associated with ownership, and even the airspace above it. The broader one's knowledge of real estate principles, the better equipped one is as a property manager.

The minimum educational requirement to enter the apartment and property management career field is a high school diploma or its equivalent. A 1986 survey of property managers found that more than 90% of respondents had education beyond high school. Basic skills in math and accounting as well as communications and computer can be obtained during high school, but further study is desirable.

In today's markets, advanced education is becoming essential for apartment and property managers. While many schools offer degrees in real estate, there are no college degrees in property management. Some colleges and universities, however, do provide certification in property management. To locate these schools, see the listing in *Barron's Index of College Majors,* published by Barron's Educational Series, Inc., New York.

Psychology, business and economics courses are useful for the property manager. Speaking more than one language can be invaluable and is sometimes the key to being hired. In a survey conducted by the Institute of Real Estate Management (part of the National Association of Realtors), 28% of those surveyed had some college experience and 49% were college graduates, while 18% had advanced degrees.

Community involvement is another factor the property manager should not overlook. There is no substitute for having one's finger on the pulse of the community to better understand and solve the particular problems related to the property for which one is responsible.

# ORGANIZATIONS AND CERTIFICATIONS IN PROPERTY MANAGEMENT

Information and opportunities abound for the property manager in the following organizations.

## Building Owners and Managers Association International (BOMA)

1201 New York Avenue NW
Washington, D.C. 20005
(202) 408-2662

Web site address: **http://www.boma.org**

BOMA is perhaps the earliest organization related to property management to be formed in the 20th Century. It began in Chicago in 1907 as building managers met to exchange information. It held its first national meeting in 1908 and has since expanded to international status.

BOMA offers the *Real Property Manager (RPM)* designation to its members.

## Building Owners and Managers Institute (BOMI)

1521 Ritchie Highway
Arnold, MD 21012
(410) 974-1410

Web site address: **http://www.bomi-edu.org**

BOMI is an educational institution offering courses and designations for commercial property professionals. The American Institute of Architects (AIA) uses BOMI courses to meet continuing education requirements. The Institute for Real Estate Management

(IREM) also recognizes BOMI courses by crediting elective points toward the CPM designation and also continuing education requirements. The following designations are available from BOMI.

- *Real Property Administrator (RPA)*
- *Facilities Management Administrator (FMA)*
- *Systems Maintenance Technician (SMT)*
- *Systems Maintenance Administrator (SMA)*

## Institute of Real Estate Management (IREM)

National Headquarters
430 North Michigan Avenue
Chicago, IL 60611-4090
(312) 661-1930

Web site address: **http://www.irem.org**

IREM is part of the National Association of Realtors (NAR). It was formed in 1933 to establish ethical standards and a high degree of professionalism in property management. IREM established strict educational, experience and ethical requirements for membership.

IREM offers the *Accredited Residential Manager (ARM)* designation. This designation requires certain experience and education standards and the successful completion of a one-week course.

IREM also offers the *Certified Property Manager (CPM)* designation. The CPM is the most advanced designation offered by IREM with only about 9,000 CPMs nationwide. Candidates must successfully complete required course work, have experience in managing a minimum number of apartment units or square feet of retail space, and have five years of experience as a property manager.

IREM also offers the *Accredited Management Organization (AMO)* designation to property management companies that meet prescribed high standards.

# Community Associations Institute (CAI)

1630 Duke Street
Alexandria, VA 22314
(703) 548-8600

Web site address: **http://www.caionline.org**

CAI is a national nonprofit association formed in 1973 to educate and represent America's residential community association industry. Its members include condominium and homeowner associations, cooperatives, association-governed planned communities, property managers and firms, individual homeowners, attorneys, accountants, engineers, builders/developers and other service providers for community associations. CAI's purpose is to provide education and legislative advocacy. It also acts as a clearinghouse for ideas and practices that encourage successful operation and management of all types of residential common-interest housing.

CAI offers the *Certified Manager of Community Associations (CMCA)* designation. More than 1,600 managers have met the educational and competency requirements to hold this designation.

CAI also offers the *Professional Community Association Manager (PCAM)* designation. To earn the PCAM, a manager must complete more than 70 hours of formal classroom study, passing a written exam for each of seven courses, and then complete a case study demonstrating the ability to integrate theory and practice. Also, the manager must have at least three years of work experience in association management and agree to abide by the PCAM Code of Ethics.

# National Board of Certifications for Community Association Managers (NBC-CAM)

P. O. Box 25037
Alexandria, VA 22313
(703) 836-6902

The independent NBC-CAM was formed in 1996 by the Community Management Association for developing a new community managers certification program. The Professional Community Association Manager (PCAM) and other recognized certifications will be *grand parented* into the new Certified Manager of Community Associations (CMCA) designation. One goal in this self-regulated certification program is an attempt to avoid licensing requirements. Without contending with license requirements a CMCA could display his or her professional management credential in any state. A future NBC-CAM prospect will designate "A" and "B" certification levels. The "A" certification would apply to fundamental community association property management requirements, while the "B" certification would apply to a specific state's laws and requirements.

## International Real Estate Institute (IREI)

1224 North Nokomis
Alexandria, MN 56308
(320) 763-4648

Web site address: **http://iami.org/irei.html**

The IREI offers education opportunities to real estate professionals in all stages of real estate production in the international arena. One essential ingredient on the international real estate scene is the professional property manager. For property managers who meet educational and experience requirements, IREI offers the *Registered Property Manager (RPM)* designation.

## FIABCI-USA

2030 Clarendon Blvd., Suite 400
Arlington, VA 22201
(703) 524-4279

Web site address: **http://www.fiabci-usa.com**

FIABCI was founded in 1949 and stands for Federation Internationale des Administrateurs de Biens Conseils Immobiliers. It is an affiliate of the National Association of Realtors (NAR). It is headquartered in Paris and brings together real estate professionals in a multi-disciplinary approach to solve real estate problems around the world. Seventeen percent of its specialties practiced are comprised of property management professionals. Upon meeting educational and experience requirements, FIABCI offers the *Certified International Property Specialist (CIPS)* designation.

## International Council of Shopping Centers (ICSC)

665 Fifth Avenue
New York, NY 10022
(212) 421-8181

Web site address: **http://www.icsc.org**

ICSC was established in 1957 and brings together some 33,000 members from the U.S. and more than 60 other countries. ICSC offers courses, conferences and study tours related to the marketing and managing of shopping centers throughout the world. ICSC offers the following designations.

- *Certified Shopping Center Manager (CSM)*
- *Certified Marketing Director (CMD)*
- *Certified Leasing Specialist (CLS)*
- *Senior level designation for CSM and CMD (SCSM/SCMD)*

## National Apartment Association (NAA)

201 N. Union Street, Suite 200
Alexandria, VA 22314
(703) 518-6141

NAA has been in existence for more than 50 years and has grown to a federation of nearly 150 state and local associations throughout the country. NAA provides legislative monitoring, lobbying and educational programs for property managers of apartments.

NAA offers the following designations:

- *Certified Apartment Property Supervisor (CAPS)*
- *Certified Apartment Manager (CAM)*
- *Certified Apartment Maintenance Technician (CAMT)*
- *National Apartment Leasing Professional (NALP)*

## Society of Industrial Office Realtors (SIOR)

700 11th Street, NW, Suite 510
Washington, DC 20001-4511
(202) 737-1150
(202) 737-8796 fax

SIOR members specialize in meeting the needs of corporate clients. They perform all duties related to commercial and industrial property transactions including maximizing the performance of investment property and portfolios, negotiating leases and purchases, and providing essential industrial and office real estate brokerage services. SIOR exists to provide an information network, professional development and legislative awareness. SIOR offers the prestigious *Society of Industrial Office Realtors (SIOR)* designation.

## Urban Land Institute (ULI)

1025 Thomas Jefferson Street NW, 500W
Washington, D.C. 20007-5201
(202) 624-7000

Web site address: **http://www.uli.org**

The ULI was established in 1936 as a nonprofit education and research institute. Its mission is to provide responsible leadership in the use of lands in order to enhance the total environment. ULI conducts research on land use, provides forums for the open exchange of ideas and experience, and produces books and periodicals. ULI has 26 councils devoted to subjects such as commercial and retail development, residential development, and residential multifamily. ULI may serve as a resource for the professional property manager.

# THE DELIVERY OF PROPERTY MANAGEMENT SERVICES

Professional property management services may be delivered in a number of ways, depending on the property characteristics and the needs of the owners.

## Employed by Owner

Large corporations that own overseas facilities may employ a property manager to work from headquarters or be on site. Associations responsible for residential, commercial or industrial developments may hire a property manager to work for them exclusively. Syndicates with considerable real estate holdings will sometimes want to hire their own property manager. In this arrangement the employer considers having the property manager as an employee of its own company to be advantageous from the standpoint of communication, planning and the accomplishment of its objectives.

## Professional Property Management Company

The professional property management company today is a sophisticated amalgam of talent and expertise to get the job done. Such a company will have state-of-the-art computers and software for tracking, record keeping, bookkeeping and reports. Diversified abilities of staff members will include people skills, speaking the required languages for the area, performing maintenance, and expertise that relates to the laws of fair housing and landlord/tenant relations. These companies may have at least one Certified Property Manager (CPM) on staff and be able to deal with the full spectrum of property management services. Some companies, however, become highly specialized, dealing exclusively with certain types of properties, i.e. medical buildings or malls, each having its own peculiar set of requirements and problems. Other property management companies might deal only with multi-family apartment complexes over a certain minimum size (100 units or more). The requirements for these properties would be different from a

15-unit building or a number of scattered four-plexes. Professional property management companies are usually paid a fee based on a percentage of the rents collected.

## Real Estate Companies

Real estate companies sometimes develop a property management function under the umbrella of their marketing activities. An agent sells a small income-producing property to a client, but no planning has been put into who will manage the property. Frequently property management is an overlooked task and expense until the burden on the owner becomes unbearable. To keep their clients happy, real estate companies often have been forced into the property management business.

# POSITIONS AVAILABLE IN PROPERTY MANAGEMENT

However professional property management services are delivered, certain positions in the specialty need to be filled. These positions are based on the functions that need to be performed in service to the owners. Any of the positions listed may have assistants, as required. Anyone aspiring to a career in property management probably can find a niche compatible with his or her talents and abilities.

## Executive Management Positions

A number of executive positions are available within the property management profession. These positions require extensive experience, the broadest technical real estate and property management education possible, and all of the skills and abilities expected of any business executive.

### EXECUTIVE MANAGER

This manager oversees the entire operation of the property management company. He or she is responsible for the performance of supervisors and on-site managers, maintenance and accounting. The Certified Property Manager (CPM) designation is recommended for this position.

## ASSET MANAGER

Also called a portfolio manager, the asset manager may work for a large corporation with significant real estate holdings or a professional property management company. This job is to develop corporate strategy and measures of performance regarding shareholder value, debt-equity ratio and market share in the management of a corporation's real estate resources.

The asset manager acts in place of the owner by making decisions about how a property should be operated and when it should be bought, renovated or sold. The portfolio manager is responsible for managing the complete property portfolio, which means preserving the asset value of property.

The portfolio manager can oversee a group or a portfolio of properties that are frequently of different types. The portfolio is most often owned by a bank, pension fund, corporation, insurance company or group of foreign investors. The portfolio manager makes most of the daily property management decisions and has oversight of the property managers to ensure compliance with the management plan. Nevertheless, the portfolio manager reports to the owner on overall performance. The portfolio manager must have company approval before selling or buying properties, or committing to major property expenditures. The portfolio manager studies market trends to make recommendations to the owner.

In addition to analyzing financial requirements for each property, developing management policy and procedures, and approving rental rates and budgets, the portfolio manager also can:

- Provide final approval on all leases, even participating in negotiations for very large leases

- Arrange property financing when needed

- Compile alternative property uses for increased income, such as converting apartments to condominiums

- Determine and approve major renovations

- Supervise the work of company-hired in-house or third-party property supervisors

### RISK MANAGER

A risk manager is employed in any situation where the protection of the real property assets is a complex issue. This is particularly true in the area of global properties.

Risk management includes evaluation of the financial situation, political atmosphere, environmental conditions and corporate takeover vulnerability. Currency value changes, for example, can be affected by any one of a number of conditions including country profiles, site selection, environmental compliance, corporate tax requirements and leasing policies that influence foreign real estate.

Global properties encounter many environmental risks. These can include air pollution, asbestos insulation, air and noise pollution, and the disposal of chlorofluorocarbon (CFC) material, waste water and nuclear waste. Those created by atmospheric and

geological conditions can be mitigated by well-engineered buildings designed to withstand earthquakes, monsoons, hurricanes or tornadoes. Lack of adequate water supply and waste water treatment can be a serious problem, along with the supply of energy resources. Methods for insulating against the cold of the polar regions and the heat of the equator are important. Another factor is that construction risks might require importation of experienced labor. The prior investigation of environmental impact rests with the risk manager who should be prepared to work with officials to relieve the effects of any deleterious conditions.

The risk manager handles political risk by developing contract enforcement systems and seeking government approval of land-use changes. In the area of financial risk management, the manager maintains oversight of interest rates and rate hedging, price controls, inflation and currency exchange rates, and repatriation funds in conformance with a government's foreign capital and profit repatriation control.

## Middle Management Positions

Middle management positions involve more hands-on activities related to property management. While executive managers of various types are involved in decision making and policy setting, middle managers are more concerned with implementing the decisions of ownership and upper management.

Middle managers should have good people skills, be likeable and personable, yet firm. They need to relate to both owners and tenants. They must be able to understand management objectives and know what it takes to achieve them. They should have good financial and accounting skills, and be able to assemble and understand financial reports. They should be trustworthy, hard-working and honest. They must have a serious acceptance of the responsibilities entrusted to them.

### REGIONAL MANAGER

The regional manager works for a large property management company and oversees the work of property supervisors or on-site managers. He or she sees to it that the policies of upper management are carried out. The individual must have good people skills and the ability to delegate in order to accomplish management objectives through the work force.

### PROPERTY SUPERVISOR

The property supervisor is responsible for several properties and supervises the on-site managers of those properties. He or she handles budgets, monthly statements and other reports, on-site inspections, and supervision of all aspects of building operation. The property supervisor also seeks to maximize net operating income by minimizing expenditures and being efficient at lowering vacancies and collecting rent. This position reports directly to the owner.

### ON-SITE MANAGER

The on-site manager is in the trenches, living or maintaining an office on the property and interacting with tenants on a daily basis. He or she is responsible for most of the hands-on duties including taking applications and screening prospective tenants, collecting rents, completing all paperwork correctly, bookkeeping, handling other records, and overseeing maintenance and supervision of the tenants and the building. The on-site manager must have a unique combination of traits including likeability and tact, but not excluding firmness, salesmanship and the ability to say *No!*

# Specialty Property Management Positions

The requirements to effectively manage a large residential, commercial or industrial property are so all-encompassing that many specialty tasks must be performed. Below are some of the specialty positions available within property management.

### LEASING AGENT

The leasing agent may work on-site or from an off-site office location. This agent must secure qualified tenants for leases on residential, commercial and industrial property. He or she must be knowledgeable of the legalities involved in all types of leases, as well as the financial implications of the terms of the lease as they relate to overall management objectives.

### ACCOUNTANT/BOOKKEEPER

The accountant/bookkeeper must supervise the keeping of financial records pertaining to the properties being managed. This is important for tax purposes, financing, buying and selling, renovation and knowledge of whether or not financial objectives are being met.

### ADMINISTRATIVE ASSISTANT

The administrative assistant would assist any of the executive or middle management personnel in the achievement of their job objectives. The administrative assistant should be familiar with the overall management and property operation, standard operating procedures, policies and controls. This person should be detail oriented and be able to facilitate management operations.

### MAINTENANCE SUPERVISOR

The maintenance supervisor would be responsible for maintenance of the buildings in his or her charge. This usually would involve hiring competent maintenance workers, supervising all maintenance activities to insure quality, overseeing the cost of expenditures, complying with city and county regulations, inspecting properties to plan for preventive maintenance and ensuring the safety of all properties.

### GENERAL MAINTENANCE

Plumbers, electricians, landscapers, window-washers, janitors, carpenters, masons and others are all needed from time to time to keep a building operating smoothly. Handymen and general maintenance workers of all types may be hired by owners and managers of large residential, commercial, industrial and special purpose properties.

### BUILDING ENGINEER

The building engineer inspects the structural components of a building and the permanent systems such as electrical, heating and air conditioning, waste removal, security, plumbing, elevators, escalators, stairwells, loading docks and fire safety systems. He or she ensures compliance with local government regulatory agencies. This position is concerned with all factors that affect safe operation of the building, thus ensuring the safety of the occupants and protecting the owner from litigation. These efforts also help preserve the value of the real property.

# BENEFITS OF A CAREER IN PROPERTY MANAGEMENT

The perceived benefits of a career in property management are as diverse as the people who enter the field.

## Excellent Earning Potential

Compensation can range from free rent and a small percentage of rents collected, to six-figure incomes and stock options for top level executives.

## Travel

Travel is afforded to those who take on a national or international scope in their work.

## Fast Pace

A fast-paced, fast-moving work environment requiring diverse skills and ever-changing demands is an appeal to many.

## Professional Growth

Property management offers an opportunity to attain levels of professional accomplishment and to grow in knowledge and ability in a field that is in a constant state of flux. The professional property manager has the opportunity to become as competent and as valuable to owners as he or she wants to be.

## Job Satisfaction

Property management also offers tremendous job satisfaction. Tenants benefit from the living or work environment property managers provide, and owners have their valuable assets protected and maximized for earning potential. These are essential services that benefit all of society.

## Job Security

No one person is indispensable, but until all property owners want to manage their properties themselves, job security for competent professionals in property management should be a certainty.

# FUTURE TRENDS IN PROPERTY MANAGEMENT

Management of residential, commercial and industrial properties continues to grow as a profession as reflected in the variety of opportunities discussed in this chapter. As the global economy grows and the world becomes smaller through various technological advances, the opportunities for well-educated property managers will continue. At the same time, the demand will include higher entry requirements.

Among other things, the professional property manager of the 21st Century could contend with fluctuations in development, new building materials and fittings, increased power exercised by foreign and institutional owners, more operation of global properties, and continuing electronic and other technological advances. Property management is an attractive and diverse career field for those who have the interest to keep themselves abreast of the advances in their particular specialty.

# SUMMARY

Property management is as old as recorded history. During the 20th Century, the property manager evolved from merely collecting rent and showing properties to much more comprehensive duties. A number of inventions and economic changes led to the creation of a professional designation for various kinds of property management. This is turn led to managers instituting professional organizations to establish ethical and professional standards.

Some major property management specialties include residential, commercial, industrial, agricultural, retail center and common interest developments. These are all property management disciplines that require specialized education to carry out management duties effectively. Each specialty has at least one association that provides training and certification.

Another category connected to property management is that of asset or portfolio manager. This management profession generally does not require a real estate license. However, those managers who specialize in real estate frequently acquire licenses. The property manager needs to be aware of the services asset managers can provide. No matter what type of property, owners want managers with the education, training, certification and experience to perform the job.

# QUESTIONS

1. The earliest role of the property manager was to:

   a. collect the rents
   b. oversee fields
   c. find vacancies for prospective tenants
   d. develop management plans

2. All of the following contributed to the escalation of property management as a profession during the first 40 years of the 20th Century except:

    a. inventions like the telephone, elevator and automobile

    b. the Great Depression and mortgage foreclosures

    c. development of large shopping center malls

    d. building of multi-family apartments and skyscrapers

3. Specialized property management may require knowledge about:

    a. fair housing laws

    b. employment laws

    c. computers

    d. all of the above

4. Demand for property management services can arise from:

    a. economic crises

    b. times of healthy growth and expansion

    c. both a and b

    d. none of the above

5. The management of agricultural land can be affected by which of the following:

    a. weather

    b. embargo

    c. tariffs

    d. all of the above

6. Over which of the following factors in the management of farm lands would the property manager have some measure of control:

    a. weather

    b. crop rotation

    c. prevailing interest rate

    d. international economic conditions

7. Light manufacturing and assembly plants would be included in which type of property:

    a. residential
    b. commercial
    c. industrial
    d. none of the above

8. Heavy manufacturing plants would include:

    a. strip centers
    b. steel mills
    c. warehouses
    d. garment factories

9. Commercial properties include all of the following except:

    a office buildings
    b. retail shopping centers
    c. air conditioned malls
    d. warehouses

10. A public accommodation is:

    a. a complimentary restroom in a gas station
    b. a commercial building in which the public has certain rights
    c. an industrial park zoned for assembly
    d. a bond issue for special assessments

11. The owner of an industrial park would want to be certain that:

    a. there was an available labor force in the area
    b. transportation corridors were nearby
    c. governmental regulations were reasonably favorable
    d. all of the above

12. The term CC&Rs stands for:

    a. Codes, Covenants and Restrictions
    b. Covenants, Conditions and Regulations
    c. Customers, Clients and Regulars
    d. Covenants, Conditions and Restrictions

13. All of the following are types of residential housing except:

    a. multi-family units

    b. stock cooperatives

    c. office buildings

    d. four-plexes

14. Apartments comprise approximately what percentage of all residential housing:

    a. 10%

    b. 25%

    c. 40%

    d. 60%

15. Common Interest Developments (CIDs) include the following types of properties:

    a. community apartment project

    b. stock cooperative

    c. planned unit development

    d. all of the above

16. A condominium project is what kind of development:

    a. a planned unit development

    b. a less than freehold estate

    c. a common interest development

    d. a community property development

17. The Certified Property Manager (CPM) designation is offered through which of the following organizations:

    a. IREM

    b. AZTEC

    c. BOMA

    d. CAI

18. The term that is synonymous with asset manager is:

    a. regional manager

    b. money manager

    c. on-site manager

    d. portfolio manager

19. Risk managers are:

    a. managers who have not yet proven
       their professional competence
    b. managers who analyze the financial,
       political, environmental and other
       components of a highly complex situation
    c. managers who work in unsafe areas
    d. managers who prescribe capitalization
       rates for investors

20. All of the following are potential benefits of a
    property management career except:

    a. excellent earning potential
    b. slow pace, steady environment
    c. room for professional growth
    d. job security

# ANSWERS

1. *b*
2. *c*
3. *d*
4. *c*
5. *d*
6. *b*
7. *c*
8. *b*
9. *d*
10. *b*
11. *d*
12. *d*
13. *c*
14. *c*
15. *d*
16. *c*
17. *a*
18. *d*
19. *b*
20. *b*

# The Economics of Property Management

- **A Word About Economics**
- **The Business Cycle**
- **The Real Estate Cycle**
- **Supply And Demand**
- **Pulling It All Together**
- **Further Investigation**

C H A P T E R

2

# A WORD ABOUT ECONOMICS

Webster says that "economics" is the science that deals with the production, distribution and consumption of wealth and with the various related problems of labor, finance, taxation and other factors.

> ## "ECONOMICS"
>
> The science that deals with the production, distribution and consumption of wealth and with the various problems of labor, finance, taxation and other factors.

The study of economics can be a frustrating endeavor. It can get as sophisticated and theoretical as one could wish. Countless hours can be spent considering the meaning and effect of *X-inefficiency*, *equi-productive effort points*, *separability hypotheses*, *residual impactees* or *carte-blanche reference variables*. Add to that the esoteric theories of *Pareto-optimality*, *Gresham's Law*, *Giffen's Paradox* and *Slutsky's Proposition* and what do you have? Disagreement and confusion! Students and scholars at the most sophisticated level of the discipline disagree on what the simplest action means.

At this level the study of economics loses something. It loses the ability to be applied practically to the local situation. It becomes fodder for the machinations of intellectuals and pseudo-intellectuals, but it does not help the property manager or the investor in the trenches who is trying to figure out how to survive in this business. It takes on a life of its own: a system of words, symbols, models and theories; an end in itself. But it rarely projects into the real world in a meaningful, understandable way.

The design of this book is to keep the discussion of economics to a basic, practical level. We want to notice the principles that have proven to have a certain impact on the economy, particularly the local real estate markets. We want to understand what various statistics mean from the standpoint of our management decisions. We want to pick up on trends which are series of events heading in a certain direction and apt to produce a predictable result. In this way a basic understanding of economics will help us be more effective property managers and more valuable to our clients.

# THE BUSINESS CYCLE

The first thing to understand about the business cycle is that it *is* a cycle. Levels of income, employment and unemployment, the success of various industries and the amount of goods and services produced in a fiscal year are always in a state of flux. They are never static.

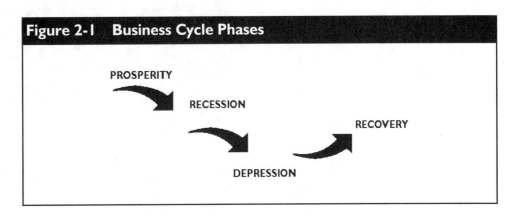

**Figure 2-1    Business Cycle Phases**

Stages in the business cycle are generally considered to be prosperity, recession, depression and recovery. Following is a description of these stages.

## Business Cycle Phases

### PROSPERITY

In times of prosperity unemployment is very low and consumers have more income. With more buying power, demand for goods and services increases and prices increase. Inflation may increase, decreasing the purchasing power of the dollar. Credit is available to expand the production of goods to meet the increasing demand.

### RECESSION

In times of recession increased production has caught up with increasing demand and surpassed it. With supply now exceeding demand, industry has cut back on production and business is oversupplied with goods. Layoffs occur and unemployment rises. Consumers have less confidence in the economy and less money to spend. Prices decline as business tries to attract customers and credit is more difficult to obtain. Production activity has slowed down and only necessities are being purchased. The recession bottoms out when surplus supplies of goods have been exhausted and buyers come back to the marketplace.

## DEPRESSION

Depression in a society is a rare economic event characterized by extremely high unemployment, no confidence in the economy and no ability to purchase. It would follow a recession as a matter of degree if consumers had absolutely no way to re-enter the marketplace and purchase the goods and services they needed. Since the Great Depression (1929-1934) certain safeguards have been put in place to ensure that such an event does not occur again. One such safeguard was the establishment of the Federal Deposit Insurance Corporation (FDIC) which insures depositors in banks and savings and loan associations against the possibility of losing their money should the bank fail.

## RECOVERY

In the early stages of recovery, consumers venture out into the marketplace and buy goods and services at reduced prices. As demand exceeds supply of goods, production heats up, employing more people and making more money available for consumers to spend. Commercial and industrial real estate reduce their vacancy rate, and the economy is headed for prosperity once again.

The following tables offer information reflecting on the business cycle.

## Figure 2-2   Unemployment Rates by State

### Total Unemployed and Insured Unemployed—States: 1980 to 1994

[For civilian noninstitutional population 16 years old and over. Annual averages of monthly figures. Total unemployment estimates based on the Current Population Survey (CPS); see text, section 1, and Appendix III. U.S. totals derived by independent population controls; therefore State data may not add to U.S. totals]

| STATE | TOTAL UNEMPLOYED | | | | | | | | INSURED UNEMPLOYED [3] | | | |
|---|---|---|---|---|---|---|---|---|---|---|---|---|
| | Number (1,000) | | | | Percent [1] | | | | Number (1,000) | | Percent [4] | |
| | 1980 | 1985 | 1990 [2] | 1994 [2] | 1980 | 1985 | 1990 [2] | 1994 [2] | 1993 | 1994 | 1993 | 1994 |
| **United States** | **7,637** | **8,312** | **7,047** | **7,996** | **7.1** | **7.2** | **5.6** | **6.1** | **[5]2,751** | **[5]2,670** | **[5]2.6** | **[5]2.5** |
| Alabama | 147 | 160 | 130 | 122 | 8.8 | 8.9 | 6.9 | 6.0 | 33.4 | 31.0 | 2.1 | 1.9 |
| Alaska | 18 | 24 | 19 | 24 | 9.7 | 9.7 | 7.0 | 7.8 | 12.2 | 13.6 | 5.5 | 6.0 |
| Arizona | 83 | 96 | 99 | 126 | 6.7 | 6.5 | 5.5 | 6.4 | 28.0 | 27.4 | 1.9 | 1.8 |
| Arkansas | 76 | 91 | 78 | 64 | 7.6 | 8.7 | 7.0 | 5.3 | 27.1 | 24.9 | 3.0 | 2.6 |
| California | 790 | 934 | 874 | 1,329 | 6.8 | 7.2 | 5.8 | 8.6 | 478.6 | 485.9 | 3.9 | 4.0 |
| Colorado | 88 | 101 | 89 | 84 | 5.9 | 5.9 | 5.0 | 4.2 | 23.9 | 23.4 | 1.6 | 1.5 |
| Connecticut | 94 | 83 | 95 | 97 | 5.9 | 4.9 | 5.2 | 5.6 | 49.5 | 47.8 | 3.3 | 3.2 |
| Delaware | 22 | 17 | 19 | 19 | 7.7 | 5.3 | 5.2 | 4.9 | 6.8 | 6.5 | 2.1 | 1.9 |
| District of Columbia | 24 | 27 | 22 | 24 | 7.3 | 8.4 | 6.6 | 8.2 | 9.8 | 8.9 | 2.3 | 2.1 |
| Florida | 251 | 320 | 390 | 446 | 5.9 | 6.0 | 6.0 | 6.6 | 122.5 | 99.5 | 2.3 | 1.8 |
| Georgia | 163 | 188 | 182 | 185 | 6.4 | 6.5 | 5.5 | 5.2 | 45.1 | 40.0 | 1.6 | 1.3 |
| Hawaii | 21 | 27 | 16 | 35 | 4.9 | 5.6 | 2.9 | 6.1 | 12.7 | 14.8 | 2.5 | 2.9 |
| Idaho | 34 | 37 | 29 | 33 | 7.9 | 7.9 | 5.9 | 5.6 | 13.4 | 13.2 | 3.3 | 3.1 |
| Illinois | 459 | 513 | 369 | 340 | 8.3 | 9.0 | 6.2 | 5.7 | 136.9 | 119.4 | 2.7 | 2.3 |
| Indiana | 252 | 215 | 149 | 151 | 9.6 | 7.9 | 5.3 | 4.9 | 33.6 | 30.0 | 1.4 | 1.2 |
| Iowa | 82 | 112 | 62 | 57 | 5.8 | 8.0 | 4.3 | 3.7 | 22.4 | 18.6 | 1.9 | 1.5 |
| Kansas | 53 | 62 | 57 | 70 | 4.5 | 5.0 | 4.5 | 5.3 | 20.1 | 18.6 | 1.9 | 1.7 |
| Kentucky | 133 | 161 | 104 | 98 | 8.0 | 9.5 | 5.9 | 5.4 | 29.1 | 31.6 | 2.1 | 2.2 |
| Louisiana | 121 | 229 | 117 | 156 | 6.7 | 11.5 | 6.3 | 8.0 | 32.1 | 29.4 | 2.1 | 1.9 |
| Maine | 39 | 30 | 33 | 45 | 7.8 | 5.4 | 5.2 | 7.4 | 14.2 | 15.5 | 2.9 | 3.1 |
| Maryland | 140 | 104 | 122 | 138 | 6.5 | 4.6 | 4.7 | 5.1 | 47.2 | 45.8 | 2.5 | 2.4 |
| Massachusetts | 162 | 120 | 195 | 190 | 5.6 | 3.9 | 6.0 | 6.0 | 78.7 | 80.1 | 2.9 | 2.9 |
| Michigan | 534 | 433 | 350 | 281 | 12.4 | 9.9 | 7.6 | 5.9 | 108.4 | 92.0 | 2.9 | 2.4 |
| Minnesota | 125 | 133 | 117 | 103 | 5.9 | 6.0 | 4.9 | 4.0 | 39.1 | 37.1 | 1.9 | 1.7 |
| Mississippi | 79 | 116 | 90 | 83 | 7.5 | 10.3 | 7.6 | 6.6 | 20.4 | 19.1 | 2.2 | 2.0 |
| Missouri | 167 | 158 | 151 | 132 | 7.2 | 6.4 | 5.8 | 4.9 | 51.5 | 47.5 | 2.3 | 2.1 |
| Montana | 23 | 31 | 24 | 22 | 6.1 | 7.7 | 6.0 | 5.1 | 9.2 | 9.7 | 3.2 | 3.2 |
| Nebraska | 31 | 44 | 18 | 25 | 4.1 | 5.5 | 2.2 | 2.9 | 8.4 | 7.2 | 1.2 | 1.0 |
| Nevada | 27 | 41 | 33 | 48 | 6.2 | 8.0 | 4.9 | 6.2 | 17.8 | 16.0 | 2.9 | 2.4 |
| New Hampshire | 22 | 21 | 36 | 29 | 4.7 | 3.9 | 5.7 | 4.6 | 7.0 | 6.8 | 1.5 | 1.4 |
| New Jersey | 260 | 217 | 206 | 273 | 7.2 | 5.7 | 5.1 | 6.8 | 109.9 | 106.8 | 3.3 | 3.2 |
| New Mexico | 42 | 57 | 46 | 49 | 7.5 | 8.8 | 6.5 | 6.3 | 11.8 | 11.5 | 2.2 | 2.0 |
| New York | 597 | 544 | 467 | 593 | 7.5 | 6.5 | 5.3 | 6.9 | 223.8 | 227.6 | 3.0 | 3.0 |
| North Carolina | 187 | 168 | 144 | 157 | 6.6 | 5.4 | 4.2 | 4.4 | 41.5 | 44.3 | 1.4 | 1.4 |
| North Dakota | 15 | 20 | 13 | 13 | 5.0 | 5.9 | 4.0 | 3.9 | 4.1 | 3.9 | 1.7 | 1.5 |
| Ohio | 426 | 455 | 310 | 307 | 8.4 | 8.9 | 5.7 | 5.5 | 96.3 | 87.3 | 2.1 | 1.8 |
| Oklahoma | 66 | 112 | 86 | 90 | 4.8 | 7.1 | 5.7 | 5.8 | 18.9 | 16.7 | 1.6 | 1.4 |
| Oregon | 107 | 116 | 83 | 89 | 8.3 | 8.8 | 5.6 | 5.4 | 46.3 | 45.4 | 3.8 | 3.6 |
| Pennsylvania | 425 | 443 | 315 | 360 | 7.8 | 8.0 | 5.4 | 6.2 | 164.0 | 169.4 | 3.4 | 3.5 |
| Rhode Island | 34 | 25 | 35 | 35 | 7.2 | 4.9 | 6.8 | 7.1 | 16.4 | 18.9 | 4.0 | 4.6 |
| South Carolina | 96 | 107 | 83 | 115 | 6.9 | 6.8 | 4.8 | 6.3 | 30.5 | 29.3 | 2.1 | 2.0 |
| South Dakota | 16 | 18 | 13 | 12 | 4.9 | 5.1 | 3.9 | 3.3 | 2.4 | 2.1 | 0.9 | 0.7 |
| Tennessee | 152 | 180 | 126 | 127 | 7.3 | 8.0 | 5.3 | 4.8 | 42.8 | 41.4 | 2.0 | 1.9 |
| Texas | 352 | 565 | 544 | 605 | 5.2 | 7.0 | 6.3 | 6.4 | 137.5 | 128.7 | 2.0 | 1.8 |
| Utah | 40 | 43 | 35 | 36 | 6.3 | 5.9 | 4.3 | 3.7 | 9.5 | 8.4 | 1.4 | 1.1 |
| Vermont | 16 | 13 | 15 | 15 | 6.4 | 4.8 | 5.0 | 4.7 | 7.9 | 7.7 | 3.3 | 3.1 |
| Virginia | 128 | 160 | 141 | 166 | 5.0 | 5.6 | 4.3 | 4.9 | 30.8 | 31.0 | 1.2 | 1.2 |
| Washington | 156 | 170 | 125 | 174 | 7.9 | 8.1 | 4.9 | 6.4 | 83.9 | 94.4 | 3.9 | 4.3 |
| West Virginia | 74 | 100 | 64 | 70 | 9.4 | 13.0 | 8.4 | 8.9 | 18.9 | 18.2 | 3.2 | 3.0 |
| Wisconsin | 167 | 171 | 114 | 132 | 7.2 | 7.2 | 4.4 | 4.7 | 53.9 | 49.8 | 2.4 | 2.2 |
| Wyoming | 9 | 18 | 13 | 13 | 4.0 | 7.1 | 5.5 | 5.3 | 3.6 | 3.7 | 1.9 | 1.9 |

[1] Total unemployment as percent of civilian labor force.   [2] See footnote 2, table 614.   [3] Source: U.S. Employment and Training Administration, *Unemployment Insurance, Financial Handbook*, annual updates.   [4] Insured unemployment as percent of average covered employment in the previous year.   [5] Includes 57,600 in Puerto Rico and the Virgin Islands in 1993 and 62,100 in 1994.

This table, produced by the U.S. Bureau of Labor Statistics as reported in the *Statistical Abstract of the U.S., 1996*, shows the relative strength of the states regarding unemployment rates for periods ranging from 1980 to 1994. This will reveal, for these periods of time, one important factor in the business cycle.

## Figure 2-3    State Ranking for Unemployment: 1995

### B-12  Unemployed And Unemployment Rate, 1995

| State | unemployed (000) | unemployment rate % | Rank by % |
|---|---|---|---|
| Alabama | 129 | 6.3 | 7 |
| Alaska | 21 | 6.9 | 5 |
| Arizona | 113 | 5.3 | 17 |
| Arkansas | 57 | 4.7 | 34 |
| California | 1,216 | 7.9 | 2 |
| Colorado | 83 | 4.0 | 40 |
| Connecticut | 92 | 5.3 | 18 |
| Delaware | 15 | 4.0 | 41 |
| Florida | 357 | 5.2 | 21 |
| Georgia | 188 | 5.1 | 26 |
| Hawaii | 31 | 5.2 | 22 |
| Idaho | 32 | 5.3 | 19 |
| Illinois | 308 | 5.1 | 27 |
| Indiana | 151 | 4.8 | 32 |
| Iowa | 47 | 3.1 | 47 |
| Kansas | 64 | 4.7 | 35 |
| Kentucky | 96 | 5.1 | 28 |
| Louisiana | 139 | 7.1 | 4 |
| Maine | 40 | 6.2 | 8 |
| Maryland | 140 | 5.1 | 29 |
| Massachusetts | 180 | 5.7 | 14 |
| Michigan | 242 | 5.1 | 30 |
| Minnesota | 95 | 3.7 | 44 |
| Mississippi | 72 | 5.7 | 15 |
| Missouri | 145 | 5.2 | 23 |
| Montana | 23 | 5.3 | 20 |
| Nebraska | 22 | 2.5 | 50 |
| Nevada | 48 | 5.8 | 13 |
| New Hampshire | 25 | 3.9 | 43 |
| New Jersey | 280 | 6.8 | 6 |
| New Mexico | 47 | 5.9 | 12 |
| New York | 533 | 6.2 | 9 |
| North Carolina | 147 | 4.0 | 42 |
| North Dakota | 10 | 3.0 | 48 |
| Ohio | 270 | 4.9 | 31 |
| Oklahoma | 75 | 4.8 | 33 |
| Oregon | 78 | 4.6 | 36 |
| Pennsylvania | 316 | 5.4 | 16 |
| Rhode Island | 35 | 7.2 | 3 |
| South Carolina | 95 | 5.2 | 24 |
| South Dakota | 10 | 2.7 | 49 |
| Tennessee | 140 | 5.2 | 25 |
| Texas | 578 | 6.0 | 11 |
| Utah | 33 | 3.3 | 45 |
| Vermont | 13 | 4.2 | 39 |
| Virginia | 157 | 4.5 | 38 |
| Washington | 174 | 6.2 | 10 |
| West Virginia | 66 | 8.3 | 1 |
| Wisconsin | 94 | 3.3 | 46 |
| Wyoming | 12 | 4.6 | 37 |
| **50 States** | 7,336 | n/a | |
| DC | 26 | 9.0 | |
| **United States** | 7,362 | (unweighted) 5.7 | |

### Rank in order

**By %**

1. West Virginia
2. California
3. Rhode Island
4. Louisiana
5. Alaska
6. New Jersey
7. Alabama
8. Maine
9. New York
10. Washington
11. Texas
12. New Mexico
13. Nevada
14. Massachusetts
15. Mississippi
16. Pennsylvania
17. Arizona
18. Connecticut
19. Idaho
20. Montana
21. Florida
22. Hawaii
23. Missouri
24. South Carolina
25. Tennessee
26. Georgia
27. Illinois
28. Kentucky
29. Maryland
30. Michigan
31. Ohio
32. Indiana
33. Oklahoma
34. Arkansas
35. Kansas
36. Oregon
37. Wyoming
38. Virginia
39. Vermont
40. Colorado
41. Delaware
42. North Carolina
43. New Hampshire
44. Minnesota
45. Utah
46. Wisconsin
47. Iowa
48. North Dakota
49. South Dakota
50. Nebraska

Source: Congressional Quarterly

## Figure 2-4   Gross Domestic Product: 1960 –1995

### No. 685. GDP in Current and Real (1992) Dollars: 1960 to 1995

[**In billions of dollars.** For explanation of gross domestic product and chained dollars, see text, section 14]

| ITEM | 1960 | 1970 | 1980 | 1981 | 1982 | 1983 | 1984 | 1985 | 1986 |
|---|---|---|---|---|---|---|---|---|---|
| **CURRENT DOLLARS** | | | | | | | | | |
| **Gross domestic product (GDP)** | **526.6** | **1,035.6** | **2,784.2** | **3,115.9** | **3,242.1** | **3,514.5** | **3,902.4** | **4,180.7** | **4,422.2** |
| Personal consumption expenditures | 332.2 | 648.1 | 1,760.4 | 1,941.3 | 2,076.8 | 2,283.4 | 2.492.3 | 2,704.8 | 2,892.7 |
| Durable goods | 43.3 | 85.0 | 213.5 | 230.5 | 239.3 | 279.8 | 325.1 | 361.1 | 398.7 |
| Nondurable goods | 152.9 | 272.0 | 695.5 | 758.2 | 786.8 | 830.3 | 883.6 | 927.6 | 957.2 |
| Services | 136.0 | 291.1 | 851.4 | 952.6 | 1,050.7 | 1,173.3 | 1,283.6 | 1.416.1 | 1,536.8 |
| Gross private domestic investment | 78.8 | 150.2 | 465.9 | 556.2 | 501.1 | 547.1 | 715.6 | 715.1 | 722.5 |
| Fixed investment | 75.5 | 148.1 | 473.5 | 528.1 | 515.6 | 552.0 | 648.1 | 688.9 | 712 9 |
| Nonresidential | 49.2 | 106.7 | 350.3 | 405.4 | 409.9 | 399.4 | 468.3 | 502.0 | 494.8 |
| Residential | 26.3 | 41.4 | 123.2 | 122.6 | 105.7 | 152.5 | 179.8 | 186.9 | 218.1 |
| Change in business inventories | 3.2 | 2.2 | -7.6 | 28.2 | -14.5 | -4.9 | 67.5 | 26.2 | 9.6 |
| Net exports of goods and services | 2.4 | 1.2 | -14.9 | -15.0 | -20.5 | -51.7 | -102.0 | -114.2 | -131.5 |
| Exports | 25.3 | 57.0 | 278.9 | 302.8 | 282.6 | 277.0 | 303.1 | 303.0 | 320.7 |
| Imports | 22.8 | 55.8 | 293.8 | 317.8 | 303.2 | 328.6 | 405.1 | 417.2 | 452.2 |
| Government consumption expenditures and gross investment | 113.2 | 236.1 | 572.8 | 633.4 | 684.8 | 735.7 | 796.6 | 875.0 | 938.5 |
| Federal | 65.6 | 115.9 | 248.4 | 284.1 | 313.2 | 344.5 | 372.6 | 410.1 | 435.2 |
| National defense | 54.9 | 90.6 | 174.2 | 202.0 | 230.9 | 255.0 | 282.7 | 312.4 | 332.4 |
| State and local | 47.6 | 120.2 | 324.4 | 349.2 | 371.6 | 391.2 | 424.0 | 464.9 | 503.3 |
| **CHAINED (1992) DOLLARS** | | | | | | | | | |
| **Gross domestic product (GDP)** | **2,261.7** | **3,388.2** | **4,611.9** | **4,724.9** | **4,623.6** | **4,810.0** | **5,138.2** | **5,329.5** | **5,489.9** |
| Personal consumption expenditures | 1,432.6 | 2,197.8 | 3,009.7 | 3,046.4 | 3,081.5 | 3,240.6 | 3,407.6 | 3,566.5 | 3,708.7 |
| Durable goods | 105.2 | 187.0 | 282.6 | 285.8 | 285.5 | 327.4 | 374.9 | 411.4 | 448.4 |
| Nondurable goods | 615.4 | 859.1 | 1,065.1 | 1,074.3 | 1,080.6 | 1,112.4 | 1,151.8 | 1,178.3 | 1,215.9 |
| Services | 717.4 | 1,155.4 | 1,670.7 | 1,696.1 | 1,728.2 | 1,809.0 | 1,883.0 | 1,977.3 | 2,041.4 |
| Gross private domestic investment | 270.5 | 419.5 | 626.2 | 689.7 | 590.4 | 647.8 | 831.6 | 829.2 | 813.8 |
| Fixed investment | 269.2 | 432.1 | 648.4 | 660.6 | 610.4 | 654.2 | 762.4 | 799.3 | 805.0 |
| Nonresidential | 155.9 | 282.8 | 461.1 | 485.7 | 464.3 | 456.4 | 535.4 | 568.4 | 548.5 |
| Residential | 121.8 | 149.1 | 186.1 | 171.2 | 140.1 | 197.6 | 226.4 | 229.5 | 257.0 |
| Change in business inventories | 10.6 | 5.7 | -10.0 | 33.1 | -15.6 | -5.9 | 74.8 | 29.8 | 10.9 |
| Net exports of goods and services | -21.3 | -65.0 | 10.1 | 5.6 | -14.1 | -63.3 | -127.3 | -147.9 | -163.9 |
| Exports | 86.8 | 158.1 | 331.4 | 335.3 | 311.4 | 303.3 | 328.4 | 337.3 | 362.2 |
| Imports | 108.1 | 223.1 | 321.3 | 329.7 | 325.5 | 366.6 | 455.7 | 485.2 | 526.1 |
| Government consumption expenditures and gross investment | 617.2 | 866.8 | 941.4 | 947.7 | 960.1 | 987.3 | 1,018.4 | 1,080.1 | 1.135.0 |
| Federal | 349.4 | 427.2 | 399.3 | 415.9 | 429.4 | 452.7 | 463.7 | 495.6 | 518.4 |
| National defense | 301.3 | 349.0 | 280.7 | 296.0 | 316.5 | 334.6 | 348.1 | 374.1 | 393.4 |
| State and local | 267.2 | 440.0 | 543.6 | 532.8 | 531.4 | 534.9 | 555.0 | 584.7 | 616.9 |

| ITEM | 1987 | 1988 | 1989 | 1990 | 1991 | 1992 | 1993 | 1994 | 1995 |
|---|---|---|---|---|---|---|---|---|---|
| **CURRENT DOLLARS** | | | | | | | | | |
| **Gross domestic product (GDP)** | **4,692.3** | **5,049.6** | **5,438.7** | **5,743.8** | **5,916.7** | **6,244.4** | **6,550.2** | **6,931.4** | **7,245.8** |
| Personal consumption expenditures | 3,094.5 | 3,349.7 | 3,594.8 | 3,839.3 | 3,975.1 | 4,219.8 | 4,454.1 | 4,698.7 | 4,924.3 |
| Durable goods | 416.7 | 451.0 | 472.8 | 476.5 | 455.2 | 488.5 | 530.7 | 580.9 | 606.4 |
| Nondurable goods | 1,014.0 | 1,081.1 | 1,163.8 | 1,245.3 | 1,277.6 | 1,321.8 | 1,368.9 | 1,429.7 | 1,486.1 |
| Services | 1,663.8 | 1,817.6 | 1,958.1 | 2,117.5 | 2,242.3 | 2,409.4 | 2,554.6 | 2,688.1 | 2,831.8 |
| Gross private domestic investment | 747.2 | 773.9 | 829.2 | 799.7 | 736.2 | 790.4 | 871.1 | 1,014.4 | 1,065.3 |
| Fixed investment | 722.9 | 763.1 | 797.5 | 791.6 | 738.5 | 783.4 | 850.5 | 954.9 | 1,028.2 |
| Nonresidential | 495.4 | 530.6 | 566.2 | 575.9 | 547.3 | 557.9 | 598.8 | 667.2 | 738.5 |
| Residential | 227.6 | 232.5 | 231.3 | 215.7 | 191.2 | 225.6 | 251.7 | 287.7 | 289.8 |
| Change in business inventories | 24.2 | 10.9 | 31.7 | 8.0 | -2.3 | 7.0 | 20.6 | 59.5 | 37.0 |
| Net exports of goods and services | -142.1 | -106.1 | -80.4 | -71.3 | -20.5 | -29.5 | -64.9 | -96.4 | -102.3 |
| Exports | 365.7 | 447.2 | 509.3 | 557.3 | 601.8 | 639.4 | 660.0 | 722.0 | 804.5 |
| Imports | 507.9 | 553.2 | 589.7 | 628.6 | 622.3 | 669.0 | 724.9 | 818.4 | 906.7 |
| Government consumption expenditures and gross investment | 992.8 | 1,032.0 | 1,095.1 | 1,176.1 | 1,225.9 | 1,263.8 | 1,289.9 | 1,314.7 | 1,358.5 |
| Federal | 455.7 | 457.3 | 477.2 | 503.6 | 522.6 | 528.0 | 522.1 | 516.3 | 516.7 |
| National defense | 350.4 | 354.0 | 360.6 | 373.1 | 383.5 | 375.8 | 362.2 | 352.0 | 345.7 |
| State and local | 537.2 | 574.7 | 617.9 | 672.6 | 703.4 | 735.8 | 767.8 | 798.4 | 841.7 |
| **CHAINED (1992) DOLLARS** | | | | | | | | | |
| **Gross domestic product (GDP)** | **5,648.4** | **5,862.9** | **6,060.4** | **6,138.7** | **6,079.0** | **6,244.4** | **6,383.8** | **6,604.2** | **6,739.0** |
| Personal consumption expenditures | 3,822.3 | 3,972.7 | 4,064.6 | 4,132.2 | 4,105.8 | 4,219.8 | 4,339.7 | 4.471.1 | 4,578.5 |
| Durable goods | 454.9 | 483.5 | 496.2 | 493.3 | 462.0 | 488.5 | 524.1 | 562.0 | 580.8 |
| Nondurable goods | 1,239.3 | 1,274.4 | 1,303.5 | 1,316.1 | 1,302.9 | 1,321.8 | 1,348.9 | 1,390.5 | 1.422.5 |
| Services | 2,126.9 | 2,212.4 | 2,262.3 | 2,321.3 | 2,341.0 | 2,409.4 | 2,466.8 | 2,519.4 | 2,576.1 |
| Gross private domestic investment | 820.5 | 826.0 | 861.9 | 817.3 | 737.7 | 790.4 | 857.3 | 979.6 | 1,011.3 |
| Fixed investment | 799.4 | 818.3 | 832.0 | 805.8 | 741.3 | 783.4 | 836.4 | 921.1 | 976.9 |
| Nonresidential | 542.4 | 566.0 | 588.8 | 585.2 | 547.7 | 557.9 | 593.6 | 652.1 | 715.0 |
| Residential | 257.6 | 252.5 | 243.2 | 220.6 | 193.4 | 225.6 | 242.7 | 268.9 | 262.8 |
| Change in business inventories | 26.2 | 11.6 | 33.3 | 10.4 | -3.0 | 7.3 | 19.1 | 58.9 | 33.7 |
| Net exports of goods and services | -156.2 | -114.4 | -82.7 | -61.9 | -22.3 | -29.5 | -74.4 | -108.1 | -114.2 |
| Exports | 402.0 | 465.8 | 520.2 | 564.4 | 599.9 | 639.4 | 660.6 | 715.1 | 774.8 |
| Imports | 558.2 | 580.2 | 603.0 | 626.3 | 622.2 | 669.0 | 735.0 | 823.3 | 888.9 |
| Government consumption expenditures and gross investment | 1,165.9 | 1,180.9 | 1,213.9 | 1,250.4 | 1,258.0 | 1,263.8 | 1,260.5 | 1,259.9 | 1,260.7 |
| Federal | 534.4 | 524.6 | 531.5 | 541.9 | 539.4 | 528.0 | 508.7 | 489.7 | 472 7 |
| National defense | 409.2 | 405.5 | 401.6 | 401.5 | 397.5 | 375.8 | 354.9 | 336.9 | 320.0 |
| State and local | 631.8 | 656.6 | 682.6 | 708.6 | 718.7 | 735.8 | 751 8 | 770.5 | 788.6 |

Source: U.S. Bureau of Economic Analysis as cited in *Statistical Abstract of the U.S., 1996.*

The GDP for chained dollars reached a record $6.7 trillion in 1995. *Chained dollars* means factors are weighted to account for annual changes in price levels.

# THE REAL ESTATE CYCLE

The second thing to remember about the business cycle is that it always precedes the real estate cycle. Another way to say that is that the real estate cycle always follows the business cycle.

It makes sense that when the business cycle is allowing consumers a time of prosperity, increased earnings and purchasing power, available credit and confidence in the economy, that this is the time when they will step out and make the largest purchase of their lifetimes.

The real estate cycle mirrors the business cycle. It goes through a time of prosperity, a time when consumers have high levels of employment and high purchasing power. Consumer confidence in the economy is high, interest rates are favorable, and credit is available. Buyers abound and sellers are in the minority, but loving every minute of it. It is a *seller's market*. Prices rise. Developers respond to the increased demand by building more housing units, from single family units to multi-family.

Eventually, production once again catches up with demand and surpasses it. The construction industry cuts back on production and workers are laid off. There is an oversupply of housing units on the market. Consumers have less confidence in the economy and less money to spend. Housing prices decline but few people can buy. For those who can, it is now a *buyer's market*.

The real estate recession bottoms out when consumers regain confidence in the economy and the real estate market. They must believe they will have a job in the future and that real estate values will not continue to drop. Anyone buying at current appraised value in the contraction phase of a recession will find their down payment evaporating into thin air. As confidence and demand increase, values begin to rebound and we are on our way again into recovery and prosperity in the real estate cycle.

But how does this affect the rental market? When real estate is expanding and there are new housing starts, the residential rental market is usually good. More people are employed. Families that have been doubling up to save on rent no longer need to do that and seek their own rental space. Multi-family units are built in response to increased demand, favorable interest rates and willingness of investors to buy them. Commercial and industrial vacancies are reduced due to increased manufacturing and business activity.

## Figure 2-5 Vacancy Rates for Housing Units: 1990 –1995

### No. 1201. Vacancy Rates for Housing Units—Characteristics: 1990 to 1995

[In percent. Annual averages. Based on Current Population Survey and Quarterly Household Survey. Rate is relationship between vacant housing for rent or for sale and the total rental and homeowner supply, which comprises occupied units, units rented or sold and awaiting occupancy, and vacant units available for rent or sale. For composition of regions, see table 27. See also *Historical Statistics. Colonial Times to 1970*, series N 249-2]

| CHARACTERISTIC | RENTAL UNITS | | | | | HOMEOWNER UNITS | | | | |
|---|---|---|---|---|---|---|---|---|---|---|
| | 1990 | 1992 | 1993 [1] | 1994 | 1995 | 1990 | 1992 | 1993 [1] | 1994 | 1995 |
| Total units. . . . | 7.2 | 7.4 | 7.3 | 7.4 | 7.6 | 1.7 | 1.5 | 1.4 | 1.5 | 1.5 |
| Inside MSA's . . . . . . | 7.1 | 7.4 | 7.5 | 7.3 | 7.6 | 1.7 | 1.6 | 1.4 | 1.5 | 1.5 |
| Outside MSA's . . . . . | 7.6 | 7.0 | 6.5 | 7.7 | 7.9 | 1.8 | 1.5 | 1.5 | 1.5 | 1.6 |
| Northeast . . . . . . . . | 6.1 | 6.9 | 7.0 | 7.1 | 7.2 | 1.6 | 1.3 | 1.3 | 1.5 | 1.5 |
| Midwest . . . . . . . . . | 6.4 | 6.7 | 6.6 | 6.8 | 7.2 | 1.3 | 1.2 | 1.1 | 1.1 | 1.3 |
| South. . . . . . . . . . | 8.8 | 8.2 | 7.9 | 8.0 | 8.3 | 2.1 | 1.7 | 1.7 | 1.7 | 1.7 |
| West . . . . . . . . . . | 6.6 | 7.1 | 7.4 | 7.1 | 7.5 | 1.8 | 1.9 | 1.4 | 1.6 | 1.7 |
| Units in structure: | | | | | | | | | | |
| 1 unit . . . . . . . . | 4.0 | 3.8 | 3.7 | 4.5 | 5.4 | 1.4 | 1.3 | 1.2 | 1.3 | 1.4 |
| 2 units or more. . . | 9.0 | 9.4 | 9.4 | 9.0 | 9.0 | 7.1 | 5.8 | 5.3 | 5.1 | 4.8 |
| 5 units or more. . . | 9.6 | 10.0 | 10.2 | 9.7 | 9.5 | 8.4 | 7.4 | 6.8 | 5.3 | 5.1 |
| Units with— | | | | | | | | | | |
| 3 rooms or less . . | 10.3 | 11.4 | 10.7 | 11.1 | 11.4 | 10.2 | 8.6 | 6.9 | 9.7 | 9.2 |
| 4 rooms . . . . . . | 8.0 | 7.9 | 8.1 | 7.9 | 8.2 | 3.2 | 2.6 | 2.5 | 3.0 | 2.8 |
| 5 rooms . . . . . . . | 5.7 | 5.3 | 5.7 | 5.7 | 5.8 | 2.0 | 1.9 | 1.7 | 1.8 | 1.8 |
| 6 rooms or more. . . | 3.0 | 3.1 | 3.2 | 3.4 | 3.8 | 1.1 | 1.1 | 1.0 | 0.9 | 1.1 |

[1] Beginning 1993. based on 1990 population census controls.
Source: U.S. Bureau of the Census. *Current Housing Reports*, series H111/95 and prior reports.

Source: U.S. Bureau of the Census as reported in the *Statistical Abstract of the U.S., 1996.*

This table offers information about vacancies for residential units regionally throughout the United States according to characteristics of the units. This is useful information when combined with demographics for the area, such as family unit size. In the West, during the years 1990 to 1995, the lowest vacancy rate occurred in units of six rooms or more. The vacancy rate rises as the number of rooms decreases, indicative of larger family sizes due to greater immigrant population in the West.

## Figure 2-6 New Apartments Completed and Rented in 3 Months: 1980 –1994

### No. 1188. New Apartments Completed and Rented in 3 Months, by Region: 1980 to 1994

[Structures with five or more units, privately financed, nonsubsidized, unfurnished apartments. Based on sample and subject to sampling variability. For composition of regions, see table 27]

| YEAR AND RENT | NUMBER (1.000) | | | | | PERCENT RENTED IN 3 MONTHS | | | | |
|---|---|---|---|---|---|---|---|---|---|---|
| | U.S. | North-east | Mid-west | South | West | U.S. | North-east | Mid-west | South | West |
| 1980 . . . . . . . . . . . . . . . . . . | 196.1 | 14.2 | 43.8 | 91.5 | 46.6 | 75 | 77 | 77 | 74 | 75 |
| 1981 . . . . . . . . . . . . . . . . . . | 135.3 | 4.9 | 36.9 | 68.4 | 25.1 | 80 | 85 | 86 | 78 | 75 |
| 1982 . . . . . . . . . . . . . . . . . . | 117.0 | 4.6 | 21.9 | 66.8 | 23.7 | 72 | 74 | 79 | 70 | 72 |
| 1983 . . . . . . . . . . . . . . . . . . | 191.5 | 3.5 | 41.1 | 115.1 | 31.8 | 69 | 73 | 86 | 63 | 69 |
| 1984 . . . . . . . . . . . . . . . . . . | 313.2 | 3.8 | 41.2 | 194.4 | 73.9 | 67 | 64 | 79 | 63 | 70 |
| 1985 . . . . . . . . . . . . . . . . . . | 365.2 | 8.1 | 54.0 | 166.1 | 137.0 | 65 | 69 | 72 | 59 | 68 |
| 1986 . . . . . . . . . . . . . . . . . . | 407.6 | 16.9 | 64.5 | 171.7 | 154.5 | 66 | 70 | 70 | 62 | 67 |
| 1987 . . . . . . . . . . . . . . . . . . | 345.6 | 11.3 | 66.0 | 124.5 | 143.9 | 63 | 73 | 65 | 59 | 64 |
| 1988 . . . . . . . . . . . . . . . . . . | 284.5 | 8.7 | 60.4 | 91.7 | 123.8 | 66 | 52 | 73 | 58 | 69 |
| 1989 . . . . . . . . . . . . . . . . . . | 247.8 | 13.4 | 45.8 | 86.3 | 102.3 | 70 | 74 | 74 | 68 | 69 |
| 1990 . . . . . . . . . . . . . . . . . . | 214.3 | 12.7 | 44.3 | 77.2 | 80.0 | 67 | 66 | 75 | 64 | 65 |
| 1991 . . . . . . . . . . . . . . . . . . | 165.3 | 6.8 | 37.9 | 63.6 | 57.0 | 70 | 83 | 78 | 65 | 68 |
| 1992 . . . . . . . . . . . . . . . . . . | 110.2 | 10.9 | 34.0 | 37.4 | 28.0 | 74 | 75 | 80 | 72 | 70 |
| 1993 . . . . . . . . . . . . . . . . . . | 77.2 | 3.7 | 25.3 | 27.7 | 20.5 | 75 | 37 | 81 | 76 | 73 |
| **1994** . . . . . . . . . . . . . | **104.0** | **3.7** | **32.2** | **44.5** | **23.6** | **80** | **96** | **78** | **78** | **85** |
| Less than $350 . . . . . . . . . . | 6.7 | 0.1 | 2.0 | 3.6 | 1.0 | 81 | 95 | 90 | 74 | 89 |
| $350-$549 . . . . . . . . . . | 39.5 | 0.7 | 14.5 | 16.2 | 8.1 | 79 | 95 | 75 | 78 | 86 |
| $350-$449 . . . . . . . . . . | 14.5 | 0.7 | 3.8 | 6.1 | 3.9 | 83 | 99 | 78 | 83 | 87 |
| $450-$549 . . . . . . . . . | 25.1 | (Z) | 10.7 | 10.1 | 4.2 | 76 | (Z) | 74 | 75 | 85 |
| $550-$749 . . . . . . . . . . | 37.1 | 2.6 | 14.2 | 12.5 | 7.8 | 83 | 97 | 80 | 82 | 87 |
| $550-$649 . . . . . . . . . | 21.9 | 1.6 | 8.9 | 7.6 | 3.7 | 83 | 100 | 80 | 81 | 84 |
| $650-$749 . . . . . . . . . | 15.2 | 1.0 | 5.3 | 4.8 | 4.1 | 84 | 93 | 80 | 82 | 90 |
| $750 or more . . . . . . . . . . | 20.7 | 0.2 | 1.5 | 12.3 | 6.7 | 79 | 90 | 70 | 78 | 82 |
| Median asking rent . . . . . . . | $576 | $614 | $546 | $582 | $621 | (X) | (X) | (X) | (X) | (X) |

X Not applicable.   Z Less than 50 units.

Source: U.S. Bureau of the Census. *Current Housing Reports*, series H130 and H131, and unpublished data.

Source: U.S. Bureau of the Census as reported in the *Statistical Abstract of the U.S., 1996.*

This table shows the relative strength of the rental market region by region throughout the United States. In the Northeast, 96% were completed and rented within three months in 1994 as compared to only 37% in the same area for 1993. A property manager concerned with the area would want to search out other economic and demographic information to understand the dynamics of what was occurring there.

## Figure 2-7 Vacancy Rates—Industrial Buildings: 1995

### No. 1208. Industrial Buildings—Floorspace and Vacancy Rates for Major Cities: 1995

| CITY | FLOORSPACE (sq. ft.) | | | VACANCY RATES (percent) | | |
|---|---|---|---|---|---|---|
| | Total | General warehouse | Office warehouse [1] | Total | General warehouse | Office warehouse [1] |
| Atlanta. GA . . . . . . . . . . . . . . . . . . . . | (NA) | 138.327.298 | 111.040.435 | (NA) | 4.5 | 5.6 |
| Baltimore. MD . . . . . . . . . . . . . . . . . . | (NA) | 96.071.812 | 24.442.980 | (NA) | 11.3 | 14.6 |
| Boston. MA . . . . . . . . . . . . . . . . . | 46.907.777 | (NA) | (NA) | 21.2 | (NA) | (NA) |
| Charlotte. NC . . . . . . . . . . . . . . . . | (NA) | 15.629.816 | 5.047.755 | (NA) | 14.2 | 8.5 |
| Dallas. TX . . . . . . . . . . . . . . . . . . | (NA) | 284.922.831 | 65.379.388 | (NA) | 7.5 | 8.3 |
| Denver. CO . . . . . . . . . . . . . . . . . . | (NA) | 108.102.500 | 14.986.800 | (NA) | 4.0 | 13.0 |
| Detroit. MI . . . . . . . . . . . . . . . . . . | 263.643.540 | (NA) | (NA) | 8.6 | (NA) | (NA) |
| Houston. TX . . . . . . . . . . . . . . . . . | (NA) | 127.126.065 | 20.665.401 | (NA) | 14.0 | 19.0 |
| Indianapolis. IN . . . . . . . . . . . . . . . | (NA) | 43.500.000 | 25.100.000 | (NA) | 2.5 | 10.0 |
| Kansas City. MO . . . . . . . . . . . . . . | (NA) | 123.212.825 | (NA) | (NA) | 13.4 | (NA) |
| Los Angeles. CA . . . . . . . . . . . . . | 775.000.000 | (NA) | (NA) | 12.0 | (NA) | (NA) |
| Miami. FL . . . . . . . . . . . . . . . . . . | (NA) | 130.000.000 | 10.000.000 | (NA) | 7.5 | 9.5 |
| Milwaukee . WI . . . . . . . . . . . . . . . | (NA) | (NA) | 191.244.500 | (NA) | (NA) | 4.2 |
| New Orleans. LA . . . . . . . . . . . . . . | (NA) | (NA) | (NA) | (NA) | (NA) | (NA) |
| New York. NY . . . . . . . . . . . . . . . . | (NA) | (NA) | (NA) | (NA) | (NA) | (NA) |
| Philadelphia. PA . . . . . . . . . . . . . . | (NA) | 99.000.000 | 37.000.000 | (NA) | 18.0 | 6.0 |
| Pittsburgh. PA . . . . . . . . . . . . . . . . | (NA) | 12.600.000 | 6.700.000 | (NA) | 18.7 | 11.1 |
| San Diego. CA . . . . . . . . . . . . . . . | (NA) | 17.776.729 | (NA) | (NA) | 11.0 | (NA) |
| San Francisco. CA . . . . . . . . . . . . | (NA) | (NA) | (NA) | (NA) | (NA) | (NA) |
| Seattle. WA . . . . . . . . . . . . . . . . . | (NA) | 62.350.096 | 9.453.841 | (NA) | 4.3 | 2.8 |
| St. Louis. MO . . . . . . . . . . . . . . . . | 198.918.000 | (NA) | (NA) | 4.0 | (NA) | (NA) |
| Washington. DC . . . . . . . . . . . . . . | 70.242.369 | (NA) | (NA) | 13.4 | (NA) | (NA) |

NA Not available.   [1] Space is between 10 - 50 percent used for office.

Source: ONCOR International. Houston. TX. *Market Data Book*, 1995 (copyright).

Source: ONCOR International as reported in the *Statistical Abstract of the U.S., 1996.*

This table **(Figure 2-7)** shows the vacancy rates and floor space for industrial buildings in major cities throughout the United States for 1995. Some data is not available. One of the drawbacks of U.S. Government reports is that they can be sporadic and greatly delayed. Sometimes the most recent information available is several years old. Other times, studies and analyses may be discontinued for budgetary reasons, creating gaps in the continuity of the report, or simply ending it prematurely.

## Figure 2-8 Vacancy Rates for Office Buildings by Major Cities: 1980 –1995

**No. 1204. Office Buildings—Vacancy Rates for Major Cities, 1980 to 1995. and Status of Supply, 1995**

[**As of December.** Excludes government owned and occupied, owner-occupied, and medical office buildings]

| CITY | VACANCY RATE FOR EXISTING SPACE (percent) | | | | | | | | | SUPPLY STATUS, December 1995 (mil. sq. ft.) | | |
|---|---|---|---|---|---|---|---|---|---|---|---|---|
| | | | | | | | | | | Existing space | | Space under construction |
| | 1980 | 1985 | 1989 | 1990 | 1991 | 1992 | 1993 | 1994 | 1995 | Total | Available for lease | |
| Total [1] | 4.6 | 16.9 | 19.5 | 20.0 | 20.2 | 20.5 | 19.4 | 16.2 | 14.3 | 2,834.1 | 441.2 | 12.2 |
| Atlanta, GA | 10.0 | 21.0 | 19.9 | 19.1 | 19.5 | 19.4 | 16.8 | 13.0 | 10.4 | 88.8 | 9.2 | 2.1 |
| Baltimore, MD | 7.2 | 11.5 | 16.4 | 20.0 | 21.0 | 20.6 | 17.3 | 15.5 | 17.0 | 41.0 | 7.0 | 0.2 |
| Boston, MA | 3.8 | 13.1 | 15.3 | 19.6 | 19.1 | 17.5 | 17.7 | 13.3 | 10.4 | 136.3 | 14.2 | 0.1 |
| Charlotte, NC | (NA) | 16.7 | 14.3 | 16.5 | 19.4 | (NA) | (NA) | 10.0 | 8.9 | 21.2 | 1.9 | 0.7 |
| Chicago, IL | 7.0 | 16.5 | 17.0 | 18.6 | 20.0 | 22.1 | 21.4 | 18.7 | 15.5 | 188.8 | 29.3 | 0.0 |
| Dallas, TX | 8.6 | 23.0 | 26.9 | 25.8 | 26.0 | 31.3 | 29.5 | 21.7 | 18.7 | 116.4 | 21.8 | 0.2 |
| Denver, CO | 6.6 | 24.7 | 26.1 | 24.8 | 23.0 | 21.5 | 15.9 | 12.8 | 12.1 | 68.5 | 8.3 | 0.4 |
| Detroit, MI | (NA) | (NA) | (NA) | (NA) | (NA) | (NA) | 21.4 | 19.7 | 16.9 | 67.2 | 11.4 | 0.0 |
| Houston, TX | 4.0 | 27.6 | 27.5 | 24.9 | 27.3 | 27.0 | 25.1 | 24.7 | 21.9 | 157.6 | 34.5 | 0.0 |
| Indianapolis, IN | (NA) | (NA) | 20.0 | 21.2 | 21.4 | 22.4 | 18.8 | 18.4 | 14.3 | 26.0 | 3.7 | 0.2 |
| Kansas City, MO. | 4.2 | 16.2 | 15.8 | 14.1 | 16.9 | 15.2 | 13.9 | 11.5 | 9.1 | 30.7 | 2.8 | 0.1 |
| Los Angeles, CA. | 0.9 | 15.3 | 19.7 | 16.8 | 20.2 | 21.2 | 21.0 | 19.6 | 23.2 | 220.5 | 51.2 | 0.5 |
| Miami, FL | 2.4 | 20.9 | 22.0 | 23.4 | 22.6 | 18.5 | 19.0 | 15.4 | 13.8 | 40.6 | 5.6 | 0.7 |
| Milwaukee, WI | (NA) | (NA) | 20.4 | 22.9 | 19.5 | 18.4 | 21.0 | 17.6 | 16.3 | 24.0 | 3.9 | 0.3 |
| New Orleans, LA | (NA) | 21.8 | 25.7 | 29.0 | 25.0 | (NA) | (NA) | (NA) | (NA) | (NA) | (NA) | (NA) |
| New York, NY [2] | 3.1 | 7.9 | 15.1 | 16.0 | 18.8 | 18.3 | 17.9 | 16.3 | 17.0 | 319.2 | 54.2 | 0.0 |
| Philadelphia, PA | 6.3 | 14.5 | 16.3 | 18.2 | 17.3 | 19.0 | 17.8 | 16.3 | 16.2 | 70.9 | 11.5 | 0.1 |
| Pittsburgh, PA | 1.2 | (NA) | 16.3 | 16.3 | 14.2 | (NA) | 17.0 | 15.8 | 14.5 | 36.6 | 5.3 | 0.1 |
| San Diego, CA | (NA) | 24.7 | 17.6 | 19.5 | 23.7 | 23.8 | 22.1 | 18.8 | 17.4 | 37.5 | 6.5 | 0.3 |
| San Francisco, CA | 0.4 | 13.7 | 15.7 | 14.7 | 13.3 | 12.5 | 13.7 | 11.7 | 10.2 | 53.4 | 5.4 | 0.0 |
| Seattle, WA | (NA) | (NA) | 12.4 | 12.3 | 12.8 | 15.9 | 17.6 | 14.7 | 7.1 | 24.8 | 1.8 | 0.0 |
| St. Louis, MO | (NA) | (NA) | 22.6 | 21.0 | 20.5 | 21.8 | 19.1 | 18.1 | 12.7 | 32.3 | 4.1 | 0.1 |
| Washington, DC | 2.5 | 9.0 | 14.4 | 19.0 | 17.6 | 15.4 | 14.1 | 13.4 | 10.8 | 220.8 | 23.9 | 1.7 |

NA Not available. [1] Includes other cities not shown separately. In 1993, 51 cities were covered. [2] Refers to Manhattan

Source: ONCOR International, Houston, TX, 1980-1985, *National Office Market Report*, semi-annual; 1986-1990, *International Office Market Report*, semi-annual; thereafter, *Market Data Book* (copyright).

Source: ONCOR International as reported in the *Statistical Abstract of the U.S., 1996.*

Notice in the supply status column for 1995, the city of Los Angeles has over 23% of its total space in office buildings vacant, the highest of all of the major cities listed. This is valuable information for managers of this type of property. They would know that they would have to be very competitive in the price per square foot and possibly offer incentives in the form of extra services or discounts in order to reduce the vacancy rate.

# SUPPLY AND DEMAND

Supply and demand is the most basic of market principles. A marketplace is any place or entity where buyers and sellers want to exchange a commodity for another commodity—usually cash for something. The greater the supply with little demand, the less valuable the commodity is at the time. The scarcer the supply with growing demand, the more valuable it is. It works for any commodity in existence.

If some virus swept through the dairy farms of our country and eliminated 70% of all milk producing cows, our supply of milk would be hit hard. Demand probably would not increase or decrease, but in relation to the now limited supply of milk, it would have the effect of an increase. Demand is up in relation to the supply, so prices go up. They have to. People start showing up at the grocery stores early, even waiting in line outside to pay twice what they used to, just so they can be assured of getting the milk they want. That is the way supply and demand works.

Supply and demand is what runs the business and real estate cycles. The business cycle is prospering when demand is high for consumer goods, supply has fallen behind and must catch up, and prices are rising. In the real estate market, the same scenario exists. Prices rise when supply is scarce and buyers are eager and plentiful. Developers gear up production of new housing units and eventually supply catches up with demand. When supply catches or exceeds demand, prices will come down again. And so it goes.

Due to the nature of real estate, however, there are some peculiarities in supply and demand in the real estate market.

## Real Estate Supply

Real estate supply is relatively inelastic. Producing livable housing units takes more time than the production of any other consumable commodity. Real estate supply is slow to change. Once demand for additional housing units is anticipated or recognized, developers have to buy the land, get final permits approved, arrange for financing, build the units and have them sold. This process can easily take 18 months or longer. In the meantime, demand has continued to grow.

## Real Estate Demand

Though real estate supply is slow to respond to demand for real estate, demand can change much more quickly. Favorable interest rates can bring buyers to the marketplace. While it may not be the only factor, there are times when it is the most important factor. A large source of employment moving into a limited market area can create tremendous demand almost overnight. In a little town called Delta, Utah, the Intermountain Power Plant, which supplies electrical power to places as far away as Southern California, was doubling its capacity and calling for many more workers. The population of Delta would increase from 2,000 to 4,000 in a very short time. Increased demand for housing units had to be accommodated.

Another factor related to demand for real estate is that it must be accompanied by the ability to pay. This is true also for demand for household commodities, but the ability to pay for these is more easily attainable by the average consumer. With real estate demand, the ability to pay cannot be assumed. And it is not enough to *need* housing accommodations or admire them. Everyone needs to live somewhere, but for the demand to be viable in the marketplace, the ability to pay must be present.

Since ability to pay is a critical component of demand, unemployment rates for a particular area should be checked. This will help the property manager to forecast particular rent levels and project the future income of the building he or she manages.

Population is another issue that needs to be considered by the property manager; not only numbers, but characteristics and trends. How much of the population owns its own home and how many are candidates for renting? **Figure 2-9** shows the percentage of homes per state that are owner occupied, leaving the balance of the population to rent their housing units.

What about the demographics of the population? Considerations such as the age of the occupants and the languages spoken and composition of family units can be valuable in meeting community needs. **Figure 2-10** as reported in the *Statistical Abstract of the U.S., 1996*, offers some of this information.

What about trends in projected population changes? **Figure 2-11** from the *Congressional Quarterly* offers projections for state population changes through the year 2005.

## Figure 2-9   Home Ownership by State: 1990

| B-31 Home Ownership, 1990 | | |
|---|---|---|
| State | % of homes owner occupied % | Rank |
| Alabama | 70.5 | 6 |
| Alaska | 56.1 | 46 |
| Arizona | 64.2 | 38 |
| Arkansas | 69.6 | 13 |
| California | 55.6 | 47 |
| Colorado | 62.3 | 42 |
| Connecticut | 65.6 | 33 |
| Delaware | 70.3 | 8 |
| Florida | 67.2 | 27 |
| Georgia | 64.9 | 36 |
| Hawaii | 53.9 | 49 |
| Idaho | 70.1 | 10 |
| Illinois | 64.2 | 39 |
| Indiana | 70.2 | 9 |
| Iowa | 70.0 | 11 |
| Kansas | 67.9 | 22 |
| Kentucky | 69.6 | 14 |
| Louisiana | 65.9 | 32 |
| Maine | 70.5 | 7 |
| Maryland | 65.0 | 35 |
| Massachusetts | 59.3 | 45 |
| Michigan | 71.0 | 4 |
| Minnesota | 71.8 | 2 |
| Mississippi | 71.5 | 3 |
| Missouri | 68.8 | 16 |
| Montana | 67.3 | 26 |
| Nebraska | 66.5 | 29 |
| Nevada | 54.8 | 48 |
| New Hampshire | 68.2 | 17 |
| New Jersey | 64.9 | 37 |
| New Mexico | 67.4 | 25 |
| New York | 52.2 | 50 |
| North Carolina | 68.0 | 20 |
| North Dakota | 65.6 | 34 |
| Ohio | 67.5 | 24 |
| Oklahoma | 68.1 | 18 |
| Oregon | 63.1 | 40 |
| Pennsylvania | 70.7 | 5 |
| Rhode Island | 59.5 | 44 |
| South Carolina | 69.9 | 12 |
| South Dakota | 66.1 | 31 |
| Tennessee | 68.0 | 21 |
| Texas | 60.9 | 43 |
| Utah | 68.1 | 19 |
| Vermont | 69.0 | 15 |
| Virginia | 66.3 | 30 |
| Washington | 62.6 | 41 |
| West Virginia | 74.1 | 1 |
| Wisconsin | 66.7 | 28 |
| Wyoming | 67.8 | 23 |
| **50 States** | n/a | |
| DC | 38.9 | |
| **United States** | 64.2 | |

Rank in order

By %

1. West Virginia
2. Minnesota
3. Mississippi
4. Michigan
5. Pennsylvania
6. Alabama
7. Maine
8. Delaware
9. Indiana
10. Idaho
11. Iowa
12. South Carolina
13. Arkansas
14. Kentucky
15. Vermont
16. Missouri
17. New Hampshire
18. Oklahoma
19. Utah
20. North Carolina
21. Tennessee
22. Kansas
23. Wyoming
24. Ohio
25. New Mexico
26. Montana
27. Florida
28. Wisconsin
29. Nebraska
30. Virginia
31. South Dakota
32. Louisiana
33. Connecticut
34. North Dakota
35. Maryland
36. Georgia
37. New Jersey
38. Arizona
39. Illinois
40. Oregon
41. Washington
42. Colorado
43. Texas
44. Rhode Island
45. Massachusetts
46. Alaska
47. California
48. Nevada
49. Hawaii
50. New York

## Figure 2-10 Population Characteristics by Cities: 1990

### Table C. Cities — **Population Characteristics**

[Cities include incorporated places with 1990 population of 25,000 or more in all States except Hawaii which has no incorporated places recognized by the Bureau of the Census. For Hawaii, census designated places (CDP's) with a 1990 population of 25,000 or more are included.]

| City | Hispanic origin[1] Total[2] | Mexican | Puerto Rican | Percent of total | Under 5 years | 5 to 17 years | 18 to 20 years | 21 to 24 years | 25 to 34 years | 35 to 44 years | 45 to 54 years | 55 to 64 years | 65 to 74 years | 75 years and over | Median age (Years) | Males per 100 females | Percent foreign born | Language other than English | Spanish |
|---|---|---|---|---|---|---|---|---|---|---|---|---|---|---|---|---|---|---|---|
| | 15 | 16 | 17 | 18 | 19 | 20 | 21 | 22 | 23 | 24 | 25 | 26 | 27 | 28 | 29 | 30 | 31 | 32 | 33 |
| CALIFORNIA—Con. | | | | | | | | | | | | | | | | | | | |
| Livermore city | 5 587 | 3 817 | 287 | 9.8 | 8.4 | 18.8 | 4.1 | 5.3 | 20.4 | 17.1 | 11.9 | 6.9 | 4.3 | 2.8 | 31.7 | 99.3 | 6.6 | 9.4 | 4.6 |
| Lodi city | 8 766 | 7 773 | 94 | 16.9 | 7.9 | 17.3 | 3.9 | 5.8 | 18.2 | 14.2 | 9.1 | 7.9 | 7.7 | 8.0 | 33.3 | 96.2 | 10.5 | 19.2 | 11.7 |
| Lompoc city | 10 100 | 8 362 | 174 | 26.8 | 9.7 | 19.3 | 3.6 | 5.6 | 21.3 | 15.5 | 9.4 | 7.2 | 5.5 | 3.0 | 30.7 | 111.5 | 13.4 | 22.8 | 16.8 |
| Long Beach city | 101 419 | 80 523 | 2 063 | 23.6 | 8.8 | 16.7 | 5.1 | 8.2 | 21.2 | 14.7 | 8.2 | 6.4 | 6.1 | 4.8 | 30.0 | 101.9 | 24.3 | 32.8 | 19.1 |
| Los Altos city | 795 | 363 | 29 | 3.0 | 5.1 | 15.5 | 2.7 | 2.7 | 9.5 | 17.4 | 16.2 | 12.2 | 11.8 | 6.9 | 43.4 | 93.8 | 13.2 | 15.4 | 1.7 |
| Los Angeles city | 1 391 411 | 936 507 | 14 367 | 39.9 | 8.1 | 16.7 | 5.2 | 7.9 | 20.7 | 15.0 | 9.2 | 7.2 | 5.8 | 4.2 | 30.7 | 100.8 | 38.4 | 49.9 | 35.3 |
| Los Gatos town | 1 367 | 859 | 58 | 5.0 | 5.1 | 13.6 | 3.2 | 4.6 | 16.8 | 17.9 | 15.8 | 10.3 | 6.6 | 6.1 | 38.9 | 91.5 | 10.9 | 12.0 | 2.8 |
| Lynwood city | 43 565 | 36 750 | 272 | 70.3 | 11.6 | 25.9 | 6.0 | 8.3 | 19.1 | 13.1 | 6.8 | 4.1 | 3.0 | 2.1 | 24.1 | 102.0 | 43.9 | 67.6 | 65.3 |
| Madera city | 15 759 | 14 765 | 88 | 53.8 | 10.0 | 23.8 | 5.1 | 6.3 | 15.7 | 12.8 | 7.7 | 6.9 | 6.2 | 5.3 | 27.9 | 94.4 | 21.8 | 43.3 | 40.5 |
| Manhattan Beach city | 1 645 | 952 | 53 | 5.1 | 5.7 | 10.7 | 2.5 | 5.7 | 23.1 | 20.6 | 14.0 | 9.0 | 5.9 | 2.7 | 36.1 | 104.4 | 8.1 | 9.3 | 4.0 |
| Manteca city | 7 241 | 5 707 | 314 | 17.8 | 9.5 | 22.9 | 4.2 | 5.4 | 18.8 | 16.2 | 8.8 | 6.0 | 5.0 | 3.2 | 29.5 | 100.8 | 7.1 | 13.8 | 9.1 |
| Marina city | 2 837 | 1 364 | 692 | 10.7 | 10.6 | 18.6 | 6.1 | 10.8 | 24.0 | 13.6 | 6.4 | 5.6 | 3.2 | 1.1 | 26.5 | 111.8 | 18.3 | 28.2 | 7.3 |
| Martinez city | 2 676 | 1 651 | 117 | 8.4 | 7.0 | 15.8 | 3.6 | 5.1 | 20.1 | 19.7 | 12.1 | 7.5 | 4.4 | 3.6 | 34.2 | 98.2 | 9.2 | 13.1 | 5.1 |
| Maywood city | 25 931 | 21 633 | 113 | 93.1 | 12.0 | 24.6 | 6.6 | 9.8 | 19.7 | 12.5 | 6.2 | 4.0 | 2.4 | 2.1 | 23.7 | 107.3 | 58.1 | 89.6 | 88.3 |
| Menlo Park city | 2 710 | 1 910 | 31 | 9.7 | 6.5 | 12.3 | 2.4 | 4.6 | 19.4 | 17.2 | 10.5 | 9.0 | 9.8 | 8.1 | 37.6 | 90.5 | 16.0 | 16.8 | 7.5 |
| Merced city | 16 786 | 15 198 | 160 | 29.9 | 11.2 | 23.3 | 4.6 | 6.8 | 18.3 | 13.0 | 7.6 | 6.2 | 5.2 | 3.8 | 27.1 | 97.6 | 18.9 | 34.7 | 20.6 |
| Milpitas city | 9 434 | 7 172 | 355 | 18.6 | 8.3 | 18.2 | 4.2 | 6.5 | 23.7 | 18.1 | 10.0 | 6.1 | 3.3 | 1.6 | 30.6 | 112.8 | 30.8 | 41.0 | 10.4 |
| Mission Viejo city | 5 615 | 3 518 | 201 | 7.7 | 7.8 | 19.9 | 4.1 | 4.4 | 17.1 | 20.1 | 12.5 | 6.3 | 5.1 | 2.8 | 33.4 | 98.2 | 12.5 | 14.6 | 5.0 |
| Modesto city | 26 920 | 22 406 | 593 | 16.3 | 9.0 | 21.2 | 4.1 | 5.4 | 18.0 | 15.6 | 9.3 | 6.3 | 6.1 | 4.4 | 30.8 | 94.2 | 12.7 | 21.2 | 10.7 |
| Monrovia city | 10 177 | 8 166 | 167 | 28.5 | 8.9 | 16.7 | 4.3 | 6.6 | 21.5 | 15.5 | 8.7 | 6.8 | 6.0 | 4.9 | 31.2 | 94.4 | 19.8 | 28.3 | 21.0 |
| Montclair city | 10 649 | 8 988 | 195 | 38.2 | 10.1 | 21.0 | 5.2 | 7.0 | 19.1 | 14.0 | 8.9 | 6.9 | 4.7 | 3.1 | 28.4 | 99.5 | 20.7 | 35.4 | 27.2 |
| Montebello city | 40 263 | 35 599 | 253 | 67.6 | 8.4 | 18.8 | 4.9 | 7.5 | 18.3 | 12.7 | 8.9 | 8.6 | 7.0 | 4.9 | 30.4 | 93.7 | 39.0 | 68.6 | 49.5 |
| Monterey city | 2 495 | 1 264 | 140 | 7.8 | 7.0 | 11.2 | 7.3 | 8.0 | 24.1 | 14.5 | 7.9 | 7.1 | 7.3 | 5.6 | 31.6 | 102.8 | 14.7 | 20.1 | 4.8 |
| Monterey Park city | 19 031 | 15 958 | 242 | 31.3 | 6.4 | 16.1 | 4.5 | 6.9 | 17.8 | 14.2 | 9.9 | 10.4 | 8.8 | 5.0 | 34.0 | 95.0 | 51.8 | 73.0 | 21.8 |
| Moorpark city | 5 613 | 4 906 | 83 | 22.0 | 11.5 | 22.0 | 3.5 | 4.8 | 22.9 | 19.7 | 7.9 | 4.0 | 2.6 | 1.2 | 29.2 | 103.7 | 15.4 | 24.7 | 16.3 |
| Moreno Valley city | 27 165 | 21 788 | 1 090 | 22.9 | 11.5 | 25.5 | 3.9 | 4.9 | 21.6 | 16.7 | 7.5 | 4.5 | 2.9 | 1.1 | 27.2 | 99.2 | 12.3 | 21.5 | 14.3 |
| Mountain View city | 10 821 | 7 255 | 384 | 16.0 | 6.6 | 11.2 | 3.1 | 7.1 | 28.0 | 17.6 | 9.5 | 7.1 | 5.8 | 4.0 | 32.8 | 104.0 | 23.0 | 27.4 | 11.5 |
| Napa city | 9 425 | 8 026 | 144 | 15.2 | 7.5 | 17.1 | 4.0 | 5.4 | 16.6 | 16.0 | 10.4 | 8.2 | 7.9 | 6.9 | 34.7 | 94.2 | 10.9 | 16.0 | 11.2 |
| National City city | 26 914 | 24 460 | 578 | 49.6 | 9.1 | 18.9 | 7.9 | 11.3 | 19.3 | 11.6 | 6.4 | 6.2 | 5.4 | 4.0 | 26.4 | 112.5 | 35.7 | 56.5 | 41.0 |
| Newark city | 8 672 | 6 424 | 407 | 22.9 | 8.9 | 19.3 | 4.4 | 5.9 | 20.8 | 16.3 | 11.8 | 7.2 | 3.6 | 1.7 | 30.6 | 101.7 | 21.0 | 30.3 | 12.6 |
| Newport Beach city | 2 648 | 1 538 | 93 | 4.0 | 3.9 | 9.4 | 3.4 | 6.7 | 19.5 | 16.4 | 13.9 | 11.3 | 9.5 | 6.0 | 39.4 | 97.5 | 9.1 | 10.6 | 3.9 |
| Norwalk city | 45 118 | 38 691 | 539 | 47.9 | 8.9 | 20.9 | 5.1 | 6.8 | 19.1 | 14.0 | 8.9 | 7.7 | 5.7 | 2.9 | 29.3 | 100.7 | 28.3 | 47.2 | 35.0 |
| Novato city | 3 460 | 1 703 | 185 | 7.3 | 7.8 | 17.1 | 3.3 | 5.3 | 17.9 | 18.4 | 12.2 | 8.2 | 6.2 | 3.6 | 34.2 | 94.5 | 11.4 | 14.7 | 5.8 |
| Oakland city | 51 711 | 38 797 | 2 367 | 13.9 | 8.1 | 16.8 | 4.2 | 6.4 | 19.0 | 17.2 | 9.3 | 7.0 | 6.6 | 5.5 | 32.7 | 92.5 | 19.8 | 27.3 | 11.4 |
| Oceanside city | 28 982 | 24 380 | 1 066 | 22.6 | 9.6 | 16.7 | 4.2 | 7.3 | 20.6 | 13.5 | 7.0 | 7.1 | 8.7 | 5.3 | 30.8 | 98.4 | 15.7 | 24.2 | 17.0 |
| Ontario city | 55 542 | 48 261 | 709 | 41.7 | 10.8 | 22.1 | 4.9 | 7.4 | 20.8 | 14.7 | 7.7 | 5.2 | 3.9 | 2.5 | 27.3 | 101.5 | 22.8 | 37.1 | 31.7 |
| Orange city | 25 278 | 21 376 | 261 | 22.8 | 7.7 | 16.7 | 5.3 | 7.4 | 20.0 | 15.5 | 10.7 | 8.1 | 5.2 | 3.5 | 31.5 | 101.8 | 20.1 | 27.1 | 17.8 |
| Oxnard city | 77 320 | 72 789 | 530 | 54.4 | 9.3 | 21.4 | 5.3 | 7.4 | 19.1 | 13.9 | 8.7 | 7.2 | 5.0 | 2.8 | 28.3 | 104.7 | 31.4 | 51.8 | 44.5 |
| Pacifica city | 5 099 | 2 259 | 282 | 13.5 | 7.8 | 16.9 | 4.0 | 5.2 | 19.1 | 19.6 | 11.7 | 8.2 | 5.0 | 2.4 | 33.5 | 97.8 | 14.7 | 19.7 | 7.0 |
| Palmdale city | 15 154 | 11 246 | 426 | 22.0 | 13.0 | 22.3 | 3.6 | 5.4 | 24.1 | 15.3 | 7.1 | 4.6 | 3.1 | 1.6 | 27.6 | 101.8 | 13.4 | 21.5 | 15.4 |
| Palm Springs city | 7 504 | 5 939 | 98 | 18.7 | 5.2 | 11.2 | 3.0 | 4.8 | 14.4 | 13.0 | 10.8 | 11.8 | 13.8 | 12.0 | 43.7 | 96.0 | 20.2 | 22.6 | 14.8 |
| Palo Alto city | 2 792 | 1 519 | 95 | 5.0 | 4.8 | 12.9 | 2.9 | 5.2 | 18.8 | 17.8 | 13.0 | 9.1 | 8.8 | 6.7 | 38.0 | 95.6 | 18.1 | 17.5 | 3.9 |
| Paradise town | 874 | 617 | 24 | 3.4 | 5.7 | 15.0 | 2.7 | 2.6 | 10.7 | 13.8 | 8.7 | 10.2 | 16.1 | 14.5 | 44.6 | 87.4 | 4.1 | 5.3 | 2.0 |
| Paramount city | 28 998 | 25 693 | 255 | 60.8 | 11.5 | 23.6 | 5.5 | 8.2 | 19.9 | 12.7 | 7.2 | 5.1 | 3.9 | 2.4 | 25.6 | 100.8 | 37.6 | 59.4 | 52.6 |
| Pasadena city | 35 912 | 26 126 | 484 | 27.3 | 7.4 | 14.6 | 4.3 | 7.1 | 21.2 | 15.3 | 9.4 | 7.4 | 6.6 | 6.6 | 32.7 | 95.3 | 27.5 | 35.8 | 22.9 |
| Petaluma city | 3 985 | 2 454 | 101 | 9.2 | 7.9 | 17.9 | 3.8 | 4.8 | 17.8 | 18.7 | 10.7 | 6.8 | 6.5 | 5.1 | 33.9 | 94.6 | 8.7 | 11.9 | 5.0 |
| Pico Rivera city | 49 237 | 44 635 | 203 | 83.2 | 8.7 | 21.4 | 6.5 | 7.3 | 17.0 | 12.9 | 8.9 | 8.7 | 6.4 | 3.3 | 29.1 | 98.5 | 29.3 | 64.1 | 60.5 |
| Pittsburg city | 11 288 | 8 459 | 637 | 23.7 | 10.2 | 20.9 | 4.3 | 6.2 | 20.8 | 15.7 | 8.2 | 5.9 | 4.7 | 3.1 | 29.0 | 99.4 | 18.7 | 28.5 | 17.0 |
| Placentia city | 10 174 | 8 677 | 120 | 24.7 | 7.1 | 18.6 | 5.5 | 8.0 | 17.4 | 15.3 | 12.6 | 8.4 | 4.5 | 2.7 | 31.0 | 101.1 | 19.1 | 27.3 | 18.3 |
| Pleasant Hill city | 2 099 | 1 124 | 111 | 6.6 | 6.8 | 13.8 | 3.3 | 4.9 | 20.7 | 19.3 | 11.1 | 8.4 | 7.3 | 4.4 | 35.2 | 94.9 | 11.0 | 12.5 | 3.6 |
| Pleasanton city | 3 383 | 1 976 | 140 | 6.7 | 7.3 | 18.5 | 4.1 | 5.2 | 18.1 | 20.4 | 14.5 | 6.5 | 3.2 | 2.2 | 33.3 | 98.4 | 7.4 | 9.3 | 2.7 |
| Pomona city | 67 533 | 59 621 | 639 | 51.3 | 11.1 | 21.7 | 5.2 | 8.1 | 20.5 | 13.9 | 7.3 | 5.2 | 3.9 | 3.0 | 26.8 | 105.4 | 31.6 | 49.6 | 41.9 |
| Porterville city | 10 299 | 9 584 | 90 | 34.8 | 9.5 | 23.3 | 4.5 | 5.3 | 16.4 | 13.8 | 8.0 | 6.4 | 6.7 | 6.1 | 29.7 | 92.2 | 16.4 | 32.7 | 25.7 |
| Poway city | 3 023 | 2 301 | 144 | 6.9 | 7.6 | 22.4 | 4.1 | 4.4 | 15.8 | 19.9 | 12.4 | 6.5 | 4.4 | 2.5 | 32.6 | 99.7 | 9.5 | 11.6 | 4.4 |
| Rancho Cucamonga city | 20 298 | 16 158 | 486 | 20.0 | 9.3 | 22.3 | 4.2 | 5.6 | 20.3 | 18.7 | 9.4 | 5.1 | 3.3 | 1.7 | 29.5 | 97.7 | 11.1 | 19.1 | 11.9 |
| Rancho Palos Verdes city | 2 215 | 1 279 | 73 | 5.3 | 4.7 | 16.7 | 3.6 | 4.1 | 10.6 | 15.7 | 18.0 | 14.7 | 8.5 | 3.5 | 41.9 | 96.7 | 23.2 | 27.9 | 3.6 |
| Redding city | 2 632 | 1 703 | 89 | 4.0 | 8.3 | 18.6 | 4.2 | 5.2 | 16.3 | 15.0 | 9.8 | 8.3 | 8.3 | 6.2 | 33.5 | 92.7 | 3.8 | 6.3 | 1.9 |
| Redlands city | 11 450 | 10 114 | 190 | 19.0 | 7.6 | 19.4 | 4.8 | 6.0 | 16.8 | 16.2 | 10.1 | 7.2 | 6.4 | 5.5 | 32.3 | 91.8 | 10.4 | 17.6 | 11.5 |
| Redondo Beach city | 6 917 | 4 613 | 239 | 11.5 | 5.8 | 10.4 | 3.0 | 6.7 | 29.7 | 19.4 | 10.7 | 7.0 | 4.6 | 2.6 | 33.0 | 104.8 | 12.4 | 15.9 | 7.9 |
| Redwood City city | 15 935 | 11 139 | 279 | 24.1 | 7.9 | 14.2 | 3.7 | 6.5 | 22.2 | 16.7 | 10.1 | 7.3 | 6.8 | 4.7 | 33.0 | 101.6 | 23.8 | 30.8 | 20.2 |
| Rialto city | 22 787 | 19 336 | 557 | 31.5 | 10.8 | 24.9 | 4.5 | 5.2 | 18.6 | 15.2 | 8.2 | 6.0 | 4.3 | 2.4 | 27.7 | 95.8 | 13.0 | 24.0 | 20.2 |
| Richmond city | 12 690 | 9 516 | 323 | 14.5 | 8.7 | 17.7 | 4.2 | 5.9 | 18.2 | 16.1 | 10.1 | 7.6 | 6.9 | 4.4 | 32.4 | 91.2 | 15.6 | 22.4 | 10.8 |
| Ridgecrest city | 2 198 | 1 624 | 76 | 7.9 | 9.4 | 20.3 | 3.9 | 5.9 | 19.8 | 15.6 | 10.8 | 7.4 | 4.5 | 2.4 | 30.2 | 103.5 | 7.2 | 10.2 | 4.9 |
| Riverside city | 58 826 | 50 152 | 1 320 | 26.0 | 9.0 | 19.9 | 6.1 | 7.2 | 19.4 | 14.5 | 8.4 | 6.4 | 5.3 | 3.6 | 29.0 | 98.9 | 15.5 | 25.0 | 18.7 |
| Rohnert Park city | 3 247 | 1 854 | 140 | 8.9 | 8.5 | 18.4 | 6.3 | 7.9 | 21.0 | 17.0 | 8.1 | 5.3 | 4.5 | 3.0 | 29.1 | 95.2 | 8.7 | 11.4 | 4.5 |
| Rosemead city | 25 641 | 22 168 | 213 | 49.7 | 6.8 | 21.6 | 5.4 | 7.2 | 18.4 | 14.1 | 8.6 | 7.1 | 5.1 | 3.8 | 28.8 | 98.3 | 46.4 | 72.0 | 38.9 |
| Roseville city | 4 825 | 3 752 | 132 | 10.8 | 8.0 | 19.2 | 3.6 | 4.4 | 18.1 | 17.9 | 10.2 | 7.2 | 6.2 | 5.0 | 33.3 | 93.4 | 6.5 | 10.0 | 5.1 |
| Sacramento city | 60 007 | 48 673 | 1 607 | 16.2 | 8.2 | 18.0 | 4.2 | 6.3 | 19.3 | 15.6 | 8.9 | 7.4 | 6.9 | 5.2 | 31.8 | 93.8 | 13.7 | 23.8 | 9.7 |
| Salinas city | 55 084 | 50 190 | 580 | 50.6 | 10.2 | 21.8 | 5.0 | 7.3 | 19.7 | 13.7 | 7.7 | 6.1 | 4.8 | 3.5 | 27.8 | 100.1 | 26.4 | 47.2 | 40.6 |
| San Bernardino city | 56 755 | 50 567 | 866 | 34.6 | 10.8 | 20.8 | 4.8 | 7.1 | 19.6 | 13.1 | 7.6 | 6.4 | 5.7 | 4.3 | 28.2 | 98.0 | 15.5 | 29.0 | 24.1 |

[1]Persons of Hispanic origin may be of any race.   [2]Includes other Hispanic origin groups, not shown separately.   [3]Persons 5 years old and over.

## Figure 2-11    Projected Population Changes by State: 1993 – 2005

| A-4  Projected Population 2005 and Projected Population Change 1993-2005 | | | | Rank in order |
| --- | --- | --- | --- | --- |
| State | Projected Population 2005 (000) | % change in population 1993-2005 % | Rank by % change | By % |
| Alabama | 4,516 | 0.6 | 38 | 1. Nevada |
| Alaska | 694 | 1.3 | 7 | 2. Utah |
| Arizona | 4,881 | 1.8 | 3 | 3. Arizona |
| Arkansas | 2,655 | 0.8 | 25 | 4. Florida |
| California | 36,657 | 1.3 | 7 | 5. Colorado |
| Colorado | 4,273 | 1.5 | 5 | 6. Washington |
| Connecticut | 3,564 | 0.7 | 31 | 7. Alaska |
| Delaware | 793 | 1.1 | 17 | 8. California |
| Florida | 16,900 | 1.7 | 4 | 9. Georgia |
| Georgia | 8,033 | 1.3 | 7 | 10. Hawaii |
| Hawaii | 1,354 | 1.3 | 7 | 11. New Mexico |
| Idaho | 1,277 | 1.2 | 12 | 12. Idaho |
| Illinois | 12,677 | 0.7 | 31 | 13. Montana |
| Indiana | 6,133 | 0.6 | 38 | 14. North Carolina |
| Iowa | 2,949 | 0.4 | 45 | 15. Oregon |
| Kansas | 2,772 | 0.7 | 31 | 16. Texas |
| Kentucky | 4,086 | 0.6 | 38 | 17. Delaware |
| Louisiana | 4,611 | 0.6 | 38 | 18. New Hampshire |
| Maine | 1,352 | 0.7 | 31 | 19. South Carolina |
| Maryland | 5,598 | 1.0 | 20 | 20. Maryland |
| Massachusetts | 6,523 | 0.7 | 31 | 21. Tennessee |
| Michigan | 9,927 | 0.4 | 45 | 22. Vermont |
| Minnesota | 4,998 | 0.8 | 25 | 23. Virginia |
| Mississippi | 2,819 | 0.5 | 43 | 24. South Dakota |
| Missouri | 5,728 | 0.8 | 25 | 25. Arkansas |
| Montana | 968 | 1.2 | 12 | 26. Minnesota |
| Nebraska | 1,747 | 0.7 | 31 | 27. Missouri |
| Nevada | 1,839 | 2.4 | 1 | 28. New Jersey |
| New Hampshire | 1,276 | 1.1 | 17 | 29. Wisconsin |
| New Jersey | 8,638 | 0.8 | 25 | 30. Wyoming |
| New Mexico | 1,895 | 1.3 | 7 | 31. Connecticut |
| New York | 18,654 | 0.2 | 50 | 32. Illinois |
| North Carolina | 8,006 | 1.2 | 12 | 33. Kansas |
| North Dakota | 661 | 0.3 | 48 | 34. Maine |
| Ohio | 11,677 | 0.5 | 43 | 35. Massachusetts |
| Oklahoma | 3,517 | 0.7 | 31 | 36. Nebraska |
| Oregon | 3,493 | 1.2 | 12 | 37. Oklahoma |
| Pennsylvania | 12,682 | 0.4 | 45 | 38. Alabama |
| Rhode Island | 1,070 | 0.6 | 38 | 39. Indiana |
| South Carolina | 4,116 | 1.1 | 17 | 40. Kentucky |
| South Dakota | 794 | 0.9 | 24 | 41. Louisiana |
| Tennessee | 5,771 | 1.0 | 20 | 42. Rhode Island |
| Texas | 20,734 | 1.2 | 12 | 43. Mississippi |
| Utah | 2,336 | 1.9 | 2 | 44. Ohio |
| Vermont | 647 | 1.0 | 20 | 45. Iowa |
| Virginia | 7,284 | 1.0 | 20 | 46. Michigan |
| Washington | 6,237 | 1.4 | 6 | 47. Pennsylvania |
| West Virginia | 1,884 | 0.3 | 48 | 48. North Dakota |
| Wisconsin | 5,518 | 0.8 | 25 | 49. West Virginia |
| Wyoming | 520 | 0.8 | 25 | 50. New York |
| **50 States** | 287,734 | n/a | | |
| DC | 554 | -0.4 | | |
| **United States** | 288,286 | 0.9 | | |

# Mitigating Factors

If real estate were a perfect market, supply and demand would completely control all of its activities and levels. There are other factors, however, that can make an impact on the real estate market.

### INTERNATIONAL FACTORS

First, people continue to immigrate to the United States for reasons of freedom and opportunity which are lacking in their country of origin. This increases demand for housing units. Second, from an economics standpoint, the value of the dollar in relation to foreign currency has an impact on the real estate market. When the dollar loses value, many people invest in real estate as a hedge against inflation. Having many buyers in the marketplace drives the price of real estate up. This prices some out of the housing market, increasing the demand for rental properties. Rising values of real estate coupled with increased demand for rental units drives up rental rates. An astute property manager raises the rents when the demand is greater than the supply of available rental units and the tenants can afford the increase. This is called an ***economic rent increase.***

### MONEY AND INTEREST RATES

If interest rates are high and money is difficult to borrow, real estate activity will be slow. The overall strength of the real estate market will not be good. If interest rates are high, capitalization rates will be high, thus lowering the value of income producing residential property. Some buyers for such properties will be in the marketplace at those times, but most will be kept away by foreboding interest rates. An economic ceiling will be kept on rental rates as most tenants will not be able to afford an increase.

### LOCAL CONDITIONS

Many different local conditions can have an impact on the area's rental market.

*Rent control*—Some areas have rent control ordinances. This will prohibit rent increases on certain types of property. Single family residences and specific commercial properties are usually exempt from rent control. Properties affected will be residential apartments, mobile home parks and some hotels. Vacancies should be less of a problem in these areas, but the ability to raise the value of the property by increasing the income has been taken away. The property manager needs to go to the local city or county agency governing such regulations and understand exactly how the ordinance applies.

*Moratoriums*—Sometimes cities and counties place building moratoriums on an area to control the rate of development. Desert communities have placed them for periods of time due to the inability of the local water company to supply new units with water. Other communities impose such restrictions for economic or traffic  flow reasons. Sometimes communities control growth simply by charging unreasonable development fees or by controlling zoning. A moratorium on new building of rental property obviously will prevent any competing units from coming on the market in the foreseeable future.

*High taxes*—High property taxes and business taxes in an area will work as a disincentive for development. The real estate market will not be strong and the business climate will not fuel an increase in real estate strength. Investors will not be inclined to purchase income properties in such an area, and the prospects for increased incomes and values to such properties are slight.

*Schools*—The quality of local education in large measure determines the desirability of local real estate. In a community where the quality of schools is perceived as substandard, real estate values will be lower. Apartments in these areas will have tenants who are limited in their ability to improve their personal situation. Rental increases will be difficult due to lack of ability to pay.

*Local demographics*—An understanding of local demographics is important to an understanding of the supply and demand for rental units in the local community. Information like types of units currently available, square footage, years built, features, values, and building permits taken out is necessary for understanding the current supply. Information on population, education levels, income levels, types of industries that employ local workers, household composition and percentage of renters as opposed to owners in the local area help the property manager understand the nature of the demand. Information like this can be obtained from the local Chamber of Commerce; the local Planning and Building Department; local apartment, industrial or commercial associations; and various government publications like the *County and City Databook*, 1994, ISBN 0-16-045040-3.

# PULLING IT ALL TOGETHER

As property managers doing our homework on economic research, we've consulted numerous sources to get a picture of the strength and trends in the economy. We've pieced together information that seems to indicate the economy is picking up momentum. Unemployment is the lowest it has been in several years while the gross national product is up and has been increasing for the past three years. Interest rates are favorable and we are beginning to be optimistic about the economy.

Then we pick up the newspaper and a front-page headline says: *"ECONOMIC GROWTH AT 9-YEAR HIGH!"* The sub-headline says: *"Expansion: Financial Markets Ignore Slight Signs Of Inflation, Rallying Again As The Gross Domestic Product Rises At A 5.6% Annual Rate."* Our interest is piqued so we read on.

Clips from the article are particularly interesting to us. *"Washington: The Economy Grew At The Fastest Clip In More Than Nine Years."* (We remember that the real estate cycle always follows the business cycle.) The article continues: *"...The nation's gross domestic product, the total output of goods and services, rose at a 5.6 percent annual rate in the first quarter, Commerce Department figures showed. That's the largest increase since fourth quarter 1987, and it follows a 3.8 percent expansion in fourth quarter 1996...."*

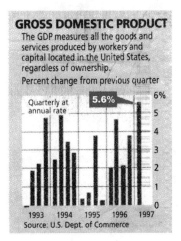

**GROSS DOMESTIC PRODUCT**
The GDP measures all the goods and services produced by workers and capital located in the United States, regardless of ownership.
Percent change from previous quarter

Quarterly at annual rate    5.6%

1993  1994  1995  1996  1997
Source: U.S. Dept. of Commerce

Now there's some solid evidence that the economy is heading toward prosperity. The article continues with **stock market** information: *"...The Dow Jones industrial average, which surged 179 points on Tuesday, rose 46.96 to 7,008.99 Wednesday, its first finish above 7,000 since it began a 700-point slide March 12 (1997)...."*

We may not understand all of the intricacies of the stock market, but we know that people don't invest their money in the stock market unless they have confidence in the economy. Confidence fuels more confidence and it looks like things are really heating up.

The article continues: *"...In the **bond market** the yield on the Treasury's main 30-year bond, a key mortgage-rate interest marker, fell to 6.96 percent, a level unseen since late March...."*

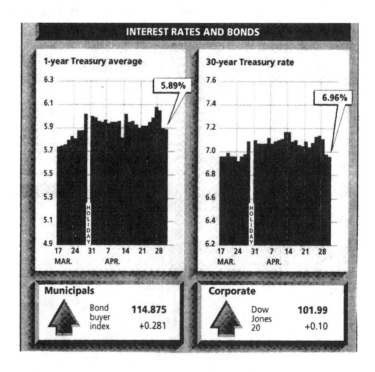

So far, the bond market indicates that interest rates will remain favorable. This will encourage buyers to buy, investors to buy income producing property and builders to build in response to increasing demand.

The article continues: *"...Greenback Starts Climbing Again— The dollar snapped out of a one-day lull to resume climbing Wednesday and flirt with a 4 1/2 year high against the yen on data that showed an unexpectedly strong surge in first-quarter economic growth. The dollar touched an intra day high of 127.13 yen, close to its 4 1/2 year high of 127.14 yen reached April 10 (1997), before settling in New York at 127.06 yen, up from 126.87 yen Tuesday. The dollar settled at 1.7303 marks, up from 1.7243 Tuesday."*

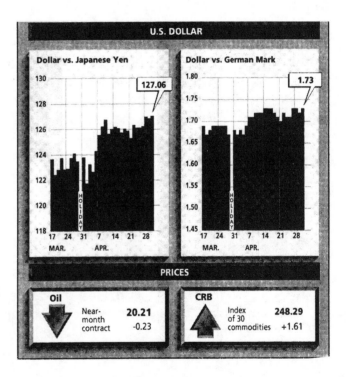

Once again, we may not know everything about the strength of the dollar, but we know that when the dollar is strong, consumers spending it have purchasing power and will spend. Everything bodes well for the business cycle preceding the real estate cycle.

# FURTHER INVESTIGATION

You now look into state information, finding out about unemployment rates for the state you are in. You are also looking for population trends. Is your state increasing or decreasing in population, or staying about the same? How will it fit into the picture of an expanding national economy?

You must get regional and local in your search for economic information. Of course, a burgeoning national economy will take a little while to reflect in local statistics. But call the local Chambers of Commerce and get the latest information on real estate and demographics that they have to offer. Do the same with the Planning and Building Department of your city. Call the local apartment associations, or those dealing with commercial and industrial property if those are your concerns. Compare notes with other property managers in your area. You are looking for any information that will indicate supply and demand, or factors in the economy likely to affect supply and demand in the near future.

Now your economic picture is coming into sharper focus. Combined with the financial analysis of Chapter 3, you will soon be ready to develop a management plan discussed in Chapter 4. Intelligent consideration of economic principles, whether global, national, state, regional or local, is essential for the professional property manager to execute a plan that will maximize the economic potential of the time.

# QUESTIONS

1. Economics is:

   a. a precise science always subject to the same understanding
   b. an inexact science subject to varying interpretation
   c. not a science at all
   d. none of the above

2. The business cycle:

   a. is always in a state of fluctuation
   b. is primarily a flat line of activity
   c. has nothing to do with property management
   d. is irrelevant to real estate

3. The business cycle:

   a. always follows the real estate cycle
   b. is irrelevant to the real estate cycle
   c. always precedes the real estate cycle
   d. occurs simultaneously with the real estate cycle

4. Phases of the business cycle include:

    a. prosperity
    b. recession
    c. recovery
    d. all of the above

5. In times of recession:

    a. supply is trying to catch up with demand
    b. supply has surpassed demand
    c. demand is ahead of supply
    d. supply and demand are about equal

6. An economic depression:

    a. is rare in our economy
    b. is an all-too common event
    c. always follows periods of recession
    d. cannot happen in our economy

7. In times of prosperity:

    a. unemployment is low
    b. consumers have more purchasing power
    c. credit is available
    d. all of the above

8. The real estate cycle:

    a. lags behind the business cycle
    b. is an aberration as people
       always need a place to live
    c. has different phases than the business cycle
    d. precedes the business cycle

9. In a seller's market:

    a. prices decline
    b. there are more sellers than buyers
    c. prices rise
    d. there is an oversupply of houses
       on the market

10. In a buyer's market:

    a. prices decline
    b. there are more buyers than sellers
    c. prices rise
    d. there are not enough houses on
       the market to meet demand

11. When the real estate market is expanding:

    a. the rental market is usually good
    b. multi-family units are being built
    c. commercial and industrial vacancies are reduced
    d. all of the above

12. In any marketplace:

    a. the greater the supply of an item, the higher the price
    b. the greater the demand in relation to supply, the higher the price
    c. the greater the demand in relation to supply, the lower the price
    d. none of the above

13. In real estate, in relation to demand, supply changes:

    a. faster
    b. slower
    c. at about the same rate
    d. there is no correlation

14. Some factors that can change demand are:

    a. favorable interest rates
    b. increased employment opportunities
    c. increased confidence in the economy
    d. all of the above

15. The ability to pay in regards to demand in real estate is:

    a. important
    b. irrelevant
    c. unimportant due to financing
    d. none of the above

16. When a property manager raises the rents because the demand is greater than the supply of rental units and the tenants can afford the increase it is called:

    a. supply side factors
    b. incremental rent increase
    c. economic rent increase
    d. contractual rent increase

17. Local agencies sometimes limit growth in an area by:

   a. prohibitive zoning
   b. exorbitant development fees
   c. moratoriums on building
   d. all of the above

18. High taxes in an area will have the effect of:

   a. decreasing investor interest in the area
   b. flattening out potential income
      for a building
   c. discouraging development
   d. all of the above

19. Economic information:

   a. is not essential to effective
      property management
   b. helps a property manager
      forecast potential income
   c. is more important on the national
      level than the local level
   d. is too complicated to understand

20. International economic considerations:

   a. can have an impact on a local market
   b. are irrelevant to a local market
   c. do not impact a local market
   d. affect the value of the dollar which has
      little to do with the real estate market

# ANSWERS

1. *b*
2. *a*
3. *c*
4. *d*
5. *b*
6. *a*
7. *d*
8. *a*
9. *c*
10. *a*
11. *d*
12. *b*
13. *b*
14. *d*
15. *a*
16. *c*
17. *d*
18. *d*
19. *b*
20. *a*

# Financial Analysis

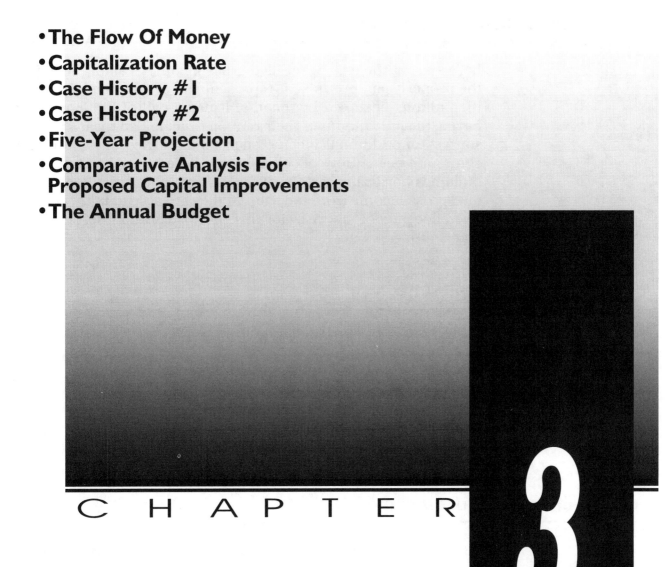

C H A P T E R

**3**

# THE FLOW OF MONEY

Property management is about money, profits. bottom lines and value. It's about the flow of cash through a property. It's about minimizing expenses and waste, and maximizing net operating income. A property manager must have a handle on the numbers and be able to communicate the story the numbers tell to the owner of the property.

## Scheduled Gross Income

Let's start at the top. Scheduled gross income is all of the income the property can produce. It represents all of the units of space in the building occupied by tenants. It means all of the tenants are paying the full amount of their rent on time. It also means that any sources of additional income such as laundries or vending machines are being fully collected. In the United Kingdom apartment buildings bordering certain rivers derive a portion of their scheduled gross income from the salmon they are able to take out of the river. Location on the river for this purpose is an important factor contributing to value.

## Vacancy/Credit Loss

Let's face it. Murphy's Law is alive and well in real estate and you will never collect every penny of what is scheduled. So we must allow for such losses and we usually call this a *vacancy factor*. It's not always due simply to vacancies, but could involve monies we're just not able to collect as we'd like. We try to minimize vacancies and credit losses, but they are facts of life and must be anticipated and accounted for when they occur.

## Effective Gross Income

When we subtract the vacancy factor from the scheduled gross income, we arrive at effective gross income. This is the amount we effectively are able to collect. It is the amount received, also called *adjusted gross income*. It is still called *gross income* because we haven't subtracted any expenses from it yet. It is still *unrefined* in that respect.

So far, the formula looks like this:

| | |
|---|---|
| Scheduled Gross Income | (All possible income) |
| - Vacancy Factor | (Losses due to vacancy and credit losses) |
| Effective Gross Income | (Adjusted Gross Income) |

# Expenses

No income producing property functions without operating expenses. We must be acutely aware of each of them and subtract them from the effective gross income figure. Part of the property manager's job is to anticipate the expenses and keep them in check as much as possible. This must be done without jeopardizing the safety or efficient operation of the facility, thus costing even more money in the long term. For example, while we don't want to allow waste or extravagance, we wouldn't fail to repair a loose or broken hand rail to a staircase and risk injury to a tenant. Appraisers talk about the principle of diminishing returns. The idea is that an owner or manager would invest a certain amount of money for necessary improvements or repairs, but would not go beyond a certain amount of expenditures in that area because any further money spent could not be returned in the operation of the building. A close watch on expenses will enhance the net operating income and therefore the value of the building.

What are the expenses? The Federal National Mortgage Association (FNMA) Form 216 is an operating income statement and is used in the appraisal of income producing properties. It is illustrated later in this chapter and serves as a guide to allowable and important expenses when operating an income property. All listed expenses on the form may not apply to all properties and all areas. Also, the property analysis form of the National Institute of Real Estate Brokers (NIREB), an affiliate of the National Association of Realtors (NAR), offers similar guidelines. That portion dealing with expenses is displayed in the following pages.

### TAXES

Property taxes are an expense on every property. It is usually the largest single expense on a property. It is considered part of the fixed expenses on a property, because along with insurance, it remains about the same regardless of the occupancy level of the building.

### INSURANCE

This could include the basic fire insurance policy as well as various extended coverage policies which would cover losses to machinery and equipment, losses of income, auto liability insurance, commercial general liability insurance, worker's compensation insurance, employer's liability insurance, pollution liability insurance and insurance to cover other special considera-  tions. The property manager should shop for the best insurance at the most reasonable rate that will accomplish the objectives of the owner.

### MANAGEMENT

Management may be a flat fee, but more often it is a reflection of the effectiveness of property management services. Therefore it is a percentage of the effective gross income, the amount of income actually collected. On small residential income producing properties, sometimes owners may claim no management expense as they perform the services themselves. To get an accurate look at the operation of the property, however, we must always include a management expense. Ownership may change, and besides, it's just a part of the financial dynamics of operating the property.

### MAINTENANCE

It is the nature of physical things to deteriorate, so income producing properties will need maintenance. Systems such as heating, air conditioning, electrical, plumbing, fire alarm systems, smoke alarms, sprinklers, structural components, parking and landscaping all must be maintained to a level of safety and attractiveness. With proper maintenance, less turnover within the tenant base will result, new tenants will be attracted more easily, and fewer injuries and malfunctions will occur.

### PAYROLL AND PAYROLL TAXES

Large facilities require a full time staff. Payroll and payroll taxes will have to be handled in a professional manner. If the property manager does not have the time or expertise to handle this function, it should be done by a competent third party or firm.

### LICENSES, PERMITS AND ADVERTISING

The city probably will require a business license. Permits will be required for any improvements or changes made to the property.

Advertising will be a larger and recurring expense. It is unlikely that a large apartment house will ever be at full occupancy, so it may be necessary to advertise continuously. As with other expenses, no more and no less should be spent than is necessary to attain the desired result. The property manager should pay attention to results and continue to utilize the most effective media possible to achieve maximum occupancy.

## UTILITIES

Whatever utilities are paid for by the owner of the building are counted as operating expenses. In most properties, tenants will pay their own electricity. Gas and water may have one meter, requiring the owner to pay. Care should be taken to be sure plumbing is in good working order and is not leaking at any point in the system. Pilot lights and gas lines also

Dials on a gas meter

should be checked to be sure they are functioning properly. This is not only for the purpose of economizing for the owner, but for safety as well.

## SUPPLIES

Every building needs supplies, whether paper products for the restrooms of commercial office buildings, light bulbs for hallways, cleaning and maintenance supplies, or tools to assist with maintenance. Supplies should be purchased at the best available price and stored in such a way as to prevent waste and loss.

## REPLACEMENT RESERVES

Replacement reserves are dollar amounts that are set aside annually to replace certain items in the future that are in the process of wearing out. In a residential apartment building these items may include the roof, the parking lot, carpeting, appliances or other items that need to be replaced periodically. If the roof is going to have to be replaced in five years at an estimated cost of $20,000, how should the owner handle it? Should he or she be caught flat-footed in five years and wonder how to pay for it? Or would it be wiser to set aside a certain amount each year to pay for that large maintenance item? Obviously preparation is always wiser.

How much should be set aside? This can be decided according to two different methods. The first method is called the *straight line* method, where an equal amount for each year is set aside. In the prior example, the owner needs $20,000 in five years to replace the roof. That would require $4,000 per year on the straight line method. It allows for no interest earnings on the amount set aside.

The second method is called the *sinking fund* method. Here the owner recognizes earning a certain interest rate on the amount set aside, compounded each year, with additional deposits made on an annual basis. If we consulted compound interest tables for the sinking fund factor, and if we could earn 8% on our money compounded annually and continue to deposit a fixed amount each year, we would need to set aside only $3,409 per year instead of the full $4,000. In actual practice, few owners elect to physically set aside either sum. They often plan to finance out of the problem or sell or exchange the property by the time the item needs to be replaced. Nevertheless, the item should be accounted for as an annual expense because it is part of the financial dynamics of operating the building. Even though it is not out of pocket in the year claimed, it is a financial force in operation this year and every year leading up to the actual expense. When accounting for the replacement reserve figure, always use the straight line method. It is the more conservative and realistic approach.

## Net Operating Income

When all expenses have been accounted for, they need to be subtracted from the effective gross income. This will yield a very important figure, the annual net income, also called the net operating income. This is what you have in hand after all expenses have been paid. The process has now been extended to look like this.

Scheduled Gross Income
- Vacancy Factor
_____
Effective Gross Income


Effective Gross Income
- Expenses
_____
Annual Net Income          (Net Operating Income)

## Figure 3-1  Section of Property Analysis Form—NIREB

| | | % | | 2 | | 3 | | Comments | |
|---|---|---|---|---|---|---|---|---|---|
| 1 | SCHEDULED GROSS INCOME | | | | | | | | 1 |
| 2 | Less: Vacancy and Credit Losses | | | | | | | | 2 |
| 3 | GROSS OPERATING INCOME | | | | | | | | 3 |
| 4 | Less: Operating Expenses | | | | | | | | 4 |
| 5 | Taxes | | | | | | | | 5 |
| 6 | Insurance | | | | | | | | 6 |
| 7 | Utilities | | | | | | | | 7 |
| 8 | Licenses, Permits, Advertising | | | | | | | | 8 |
| 9 | Management | | | | | | | | 9 |
| 10 | Payroll, Including Payroll Taxes | | | | | | | | 10 |
| 11 | Supplies | | | | | | | | 11 |
| 12 | Services | | | | | | | | 12 |
| 13 | Maintenance | | | | | | | | 13 |
| 14 | Other | | | | | | | | 14 |
| 15 | | | | | | | | | 15 |
| 16 | | | | | | | | | 16 |
| 17 | TOTAL EXPENSES | | | | | | | | 17 |
| 18 | NET OPERATING INCOME Cap Rate List Price     % Cap Rate Market Value     % | | | | | | | | 18 |

# CAPITALIZATION RATE

The capitalization rate, known as the *cap rate*, is the desired rate of return on the investment. It is expressed in terms of a percentage or a decimal. The cap rate expresses the relationship between the value and the income. The cap rate can be determined in a number of ways.

## Summation

The summation method determines the cap rate by strategically including components that are part of the thinking of investors at the time. For example, investors know they can safely earn 3% on money in a bank or savings and loan in an insured account. To be attracted to a real estate investment, the potential buyer must be able to earn at least 3% based on the safe interest rate available in a bank.

But to get involved in a real estate investment, the investor is going to assume some risk. How much more must be earned to be attractive to the real estate investor with the additional risk? The investor wants an additional 3%.

Yet another factor needs to be considered. A real estate investment is non-liquid. If you own a commercial, industrial or residential income property and want your money out, unless you can borrow some of it, you're probably going to have to wait at least six months and maybe up to a year-and-a-half to consummate a sale. Other investment vehicles are not so non-liquid. How much more must the investor earn to be attracted to a non-liquid investment? The investor says add 2%.

One other factor! In purchasing a real property investment, the investor owns a building that will deteriorate over its lifetime. If the investor owns a paper investment, such as a certificate of deposit, that person has an investment that does not deteriorate over time nor require maintenance. One simply goes to the bank at the time of maturity and receives the return *of* the investment and the return *on* the investment. The return *of* the investment is one's original principal amount. The return *on* the investment is the interest earned. To build the return *of* the investment into the overall cap rate on the real estate investment, the investor has to allow for the recapture of the improvement value over the economic life of the improvements.

For example, an investor owns an apartment complex valued at $2,750,000. The overall cap rate is 10% and the net operating income is $275,000. The improvement to value ratio for this property is 70% and the improvements have a 50-year remaining economic life. The overall cap rate of 10% allows for the return *on* and *of* the investment and would be demonstrated like this.

| | | |
|---|---|---|
| Net Operating Income | | $275,000 |
| Minus Building Recapture | | |
| Total Value | $2,750,000 | |
| | × .70 | |
| Improvement Value | $1,925,000 | |
| Divided by 50 Years | ÷ 50 | |
| Value of Building Recapture | | - 38,500 |
| Net Income After Recapture | | $236,500 |
| Divided by Value | | ÷ 2,750,000 |
| Equals Return *on* Investment | | .086 or 8.6% |

This means that with the overall cap rate at 10%, 8.6% of that represents the interest rate or safe rate, the return *on* the investment. An additional 1.4% has been built into the overall cap rate to provide for a return *of* the investment.

Returning to the summation method, how much more must the investor build into the overall cap rate to provide for a return *of* the investment? In keeping with the general approach of this example, the investor says to add another percent and a half for the return *of* the investment. So let's see what we have.

| | |
|---|---|
| 3% | (Interest) |
| 3% | (Risk) |
| 2% | (Non-Liquid) |
| 1.5% | (Return of the Investment) |
| 9.5% | (Overall Cap Rate) |

## Band of Investment

The band of investment method of determining a cap rate is a way of bringing together mortgage and equity rates appropriate to the marketplace. The cap rate that is derived is a weighted average, considering percentages of value occupied by mortgage positions and equity.

Suppose that a first mortgage occupies 50% of the property value and bears an interest rate of 8%. A second mortgage on the property occupies 30% of the property value and bears an interest rate of 10%. The equity position represents 20% of the value and the investor wants a 10% return on the equity. It would work like this.

| | Percent of Value | | Rate | | Product |
|---|---|---|---|---|---|
| First Mortgage | 50 | × | 8% | = | 4% |
| Second Mortgage | 30 | × | 10% | = | 3% |
| Equity | 20 | × | 10% | = | 2% |
| | 100 | | | | 9% |

If the rates represented in the analysis are accurate indicators of what investors demand in the marketplace in return for mortgage money and equity positions, the cap rate should be realistic.

# Comparison

In actual practice, the property manager would want to compare his or her property to other properties that are similar in critical aspects. The manager would want to look at similar type properties that are selling in the approximate price range of this property with similar quality of income. Rating the quality of income would involve taking into consideration some of the following characteristics.

### THE RELIABILITY OF THE INCOME

How certain is the income? The income is more certain if it is leased to financially responsible tenants on a longer term basis than if to less financially secure tenants on a month-to-month basis.

### THE RELIABILITY OF THE ACCURACY OF ANTICIPATED EXPENSES

Is there a good chance that the expenses will increase significantly, stay the same or decrease? A lot of deferred maintenance in a comparable property could lead to an increase in expenses.

### CHANCE OF FUTURE CONSTRUCTION OF COMPETITIVE PROPERTIES

If additional units of similar properties are soon to come on the market, it will create competition for available demand, thus lowering prices and income.

### ACCEPTABILITY AND MARKETABILITY OF THE PROPERTY

The level of this characteristic should be comparable to the property manager's property. Some properties are more desirable and marketable than others. Investors would be more interested in properties that could be marketed at any stage of the business and real estate cycle.

### EXPENSE/INCOME RATIO

These should be similar, meaning that the expenses paid by the owner should be similar to the situation with the subject property. A lower expense/income ratio is generally preferred, but the nature of some properties is that they offer more services, thus creating a higher expense-income ratio.

**BURDEN OF MANAGEMENT**

Some properties require constant attention while others come close to taking care of themselves. A long-term lease with a single tenant who takes care of all repairs and pays taxes and insurance is relatively management free compared to one with continuous turnover of multiple tenants and rent collection problems.

The property manager could rate the importance of each of these characteristics and then look at data involving comparable properties. The manager would look at sales prices of those properties and the net income after recapture of building value, thus determining the interest rate or safe rate. The following example illustrates.

| Property | Sales Price | Net Income After Depreciation | Interest Rate |
|---|---|---|---|
| 1 | $325,000 | $28,500 | 8.8% |
| 2 | $370,000 | $32,000 | 8.6% |
| 3 | $275,000 | $23,400 | 8.5% |
| 4 | $450,000 | $36,900 | 8.2% |
| 5 | $400,000 | $35,000 | 8.75% |

Now that comparable properties have been identified, their data analyzed and their respective interest rates determined, the quality of income factor needs to be applied as follows.

| Property | Actual Interest Rate | Quality of Income | Adjusted Interest Rate |
|---|---|---|---|
| 1 | 8.8% | 80% | 7.04% |
| 2 | 8.6% | 90% | 7.74% |
| 3 | 8.5% | 90% | 7.65% |
| 4 | 8.2% | 70% | 5.74% |
| 5 | 8.75% | 90% | 7.88% |

Based on this data, the average adjusted interest rate is 7.2%. If the subject property were ideal, living up to 100% of its potential in all quality rated areas, this would be the interest rate or safe rate to use. However, if the subject property had a quality rating of 90%, the rate would have to be higher. We would divide the 7.2% rate by 90% to arrive at 8%. That is the safe rate we would use for the subject property.

We would then add in an additional allowance to provide for the return *of* the investment which previously had been deducted, and we would arrive at the overall cap rate. If based on the recapture of the improvement value of the subject property, and 1.5% were the appropriate figure, 8% + 1.5% would yield an overall cap rate of 9.5%.

A responsible property manager should also consult with professionals in the field including other property managers, appraisers and brokers of similar types of properties. Working with an accurate capitalization rate is essential to understanding the value of a given property and getting input from these professionals can be helpful.

## The Importance of the Right Cap Rate

If the cap rate is off by one percentage point, the results can be catastrophic. Consider the following example.

| Property | Net Operating Income | Overall Cap Rate | Value |
|---|---|---|---|
| 1 | $100,000 | 9% | $1,111,111 |
| 2 | $100,000 | 10% | $1,000,000 |
| 3 | $100,000 | 11% | $909,090 |

Notice that if the net operating income stays the same and the only thing that changes is the cap rate, the value varies by about $100,000 each time it changes. The higher the cap rate, the lower the value. The relationship works like this.

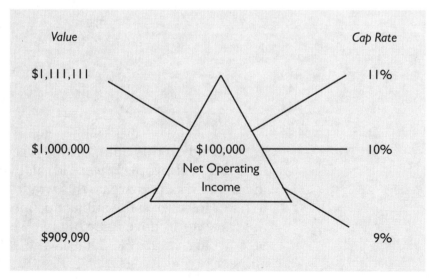

It is therefore crucial that the cap rate be accurate. The following two pages contain the FNMA Form 216, the Operating Income Statement for one to four Family Investment Property and two to four Family Owner-Occupied Property.

## Figure 3-2 Fannie Mae Form 216—Operating Income Statement

### Operating Income Statement
One- to Four-Family Investment Property and Two- to Four-Family Owner-Occupied Property

Property Address

_____ _____ _____ _____
Street                    City                 State      Zip Code

**General Instructions:** This form is to be prepared jointly by the loan applicant, the appraiser, and the lender's underwriter. The applicant must complete the following schedule indicating each unit's rental status, lease expiration date, current rent, market rent, and the responsibility for utility expenses. Rental figures must be based on the rent for an "unfurnished" unit.

| | Currently Rented | Expiration Date | Current Rent Per Month | Market Rent Per Month | Utility Expense | Paid By Owner | Paid By Tenant |
|---|---|---|---|---|---|---|---|
| Unit No. 1 | Yes ___ No ___ | _____ | $_____ | $_____ | Electricity............. | ☐ | ☐ |
| Unit No. 2 | Yes ___ No ___ | _____ | $_____ | $_____ | Gas................... | ☐ | ☐ |
| Unit No. 3 | Yes ___ No ___ | _____ | $_____ | $_____ | Fuel Oil ............. | ☐ | ☐ |
| Unit No. 4 | Yes ___ No ___ | _____ | $_____ | $_____ | Fuel (Other) ....... | ☐ | ☐ |
| **Total** | | | $_____ | $_____ | Water/Sewer ...... | ☐ | ☐ |
| | | | | | Trash Removal ..... | ☐ | ☐ |

The applicant should complete all of the income and expense projections and for existing properties provide actual year-end operating statements for the past two years *(for new properties the applicant's projected income and expenses must be provided)*. This Operating Income Statement and any previous operating statements the applicant provides must then be sent to the appraiser for review, comment, and/or adjustments next to the applicant's figures *(e.g., Applicant/Appraiser 288/300)*. If the appraiser is retained to complete the form instead of the applicant, the lender must provide to the appraiser the aforementioned operating statements, mortgage insurance premium, HOA dues, leasehold payments, subordinate financing, and/or any other relevant information as to the income and expenses of the subject property received from the applicant to substantiate the projections. The underwriter should carefully review the applicant's/appraiser's projections and the appraiser's comments concerning those projections. The underwriter should make any final adjustments that are necessary to more accurately reflect any income or expense items that appear unreasonable for the market. *(Real estate taxes and insurance on these types of properties are included in PITI and not calculated as an annual expense item.)* Income should be based on current rents, but should not exceed market rents. When there are no current rents because the property is proposed, new, or currently vacant, market rents should be used.

**Annual Income and Expense Projection for Next 12 months**

| | By Applicant/Appraiser | Adjustments by Lender's Underwriter |
|---|---|---|
| **Income** *(Do not include income for owner-occupied units)* | | |
| Gross Annual Rental *(from unit(s) to be rented)* ........................ | $_____ | $_____ |
| Other Income *(include sources)* ............................................. | +_____ | +_____ |
| Total ................................................................................. | $_____ | $_____ |
| Less Vacancy/Rent Loss ....................................................... | −_____ ( %) | −_____ ( %) |
| Effective Gross Income ......................................................... | $_____ | $_____ |

| **Expenses** *(Do not include expenses for owner-occupied units)* | | |
|---|---|---|
| Electricity ........................................................................... | _____ | _____ |
| Gas .................................................................................... | _____ | _____ |
| Fuel Oil .............................................................................. | _____ | _____ |
| Fuel ....................................(Type - _____) | _____ | _____ |
| Water/Sewer ....................................................................... | _____ | _____ |
| Trash Removal ..................................................................... | _____ | _____ |
| Pest Control ........................................................................ | _____ | _____ |
| Other Taxes or Licenses ....................................................... | _____ | _____ |
| Casual Labor ....................................................................... | _____ | _____ |
| This includes the costs for public area cleaning, snow removal, etc., even though the applicant may not elect to contract for such services. | | |
| Interior Paint/Decorating ...................................................... | _____ | _____ |
| This includes the costs of contract labor and materials that are required to maintain the interiors of the living units. | | |
| General Repairs/Maintenance ................................................ | _____ | _____ |
| This includes the costs of contract labor and materials that are required to maintain the public corridors, stairways, roofs, mechanical systems, grounds, etc. | | |
| Management Expenses ........................................................... | _____ | _____ |
| These are the customary expenses that a professional management company would charge to manage the property. | | |
| Supplies ............................................................................. | _____ | _____ |
| This includes the costs of items like light bulbs, janitorial supplies, etc. | | |
| Total Replacement Reserves - See Schedule on Pg. 2.................. | _____ | _____ |
| Miscellaneous ..................................................................... | _____ | _____ |
| ......................................................................................... | _____ | _____ |
| ......................................................................................... | _____ | _____ |
| ......................................................................................... | _____ | _____ |
| ......................................................................................... | _____ | _____ |
| ......................................................................................... | _____ | _____ |
| ......................................................................................... | _____ | _____ |
| ......................................................................................... | _____ | _____ |
| **Total Operating Expenses** ................................................. | $_____ | $_____ |

This Form Must Be Reproduced By Seller
Page 1 of 2

## Figure 3-2 (cont'd.) Fannie Mae Form 216—Operating Income Statement

### Replacement Reserve Schedule

Adequate replacement reserves must be calculated regardless of whether actual reserves are provided for on the owner's operating statements or are customary in the local market. This represents the total average yearly reserves. Generally, all equipment and components that have a remaining life of more than one year—such as refrigerators, stoves, clothes washers/dryers, trash compactors, furnaces, roofs, and carpeting, etc.—should be expensed on a replacement cost basis.

| Equipment | Replacement Cost | Remaining Life | | By Applicant/ Appraiser | Lender Adjustments |
|---|---|---|---|---|---|
| Stoves/Ranges .... | @ $ _____ ea. | ÷ ____ Yrs. x | _____ Units = | $ _____ | $ _____ |
| Refrigerators ........ | @ $ _____ ea. | ÷ ____ Yrs. x | _____ Units = | $ _____ | $ _____ |
| Dishwashers ........ | @ $ _____ ea. | ÷ ____ Yrs. x | _____ Units = | $ _____ | $ _____ |
| A/C Units .......... | @ $ _____ ea. | ÷ ____ Yrs. x | _____ Units = | $ _____ | $ _____ |
| C. Washer/Dryers | @ $ _____ ea. | ÷ ____ Yrs. x | _____ Units = | $ _____ | $ _____ |
| HW Heaters ........ | @ $ _____ ea. | ÷ ____ Yrs. x | _____ Units = | $ _____ | $ _____ |
| Furnace(s) .......... | @ $ _____ ea. | ÷ ____ Yrs. x | _____ Units = | $ _____ | $ _____ |
| (Other) .............. | @ $ _____ ea. | ÷ ____ Yrs. x | _____ Units = | $ _____ | $ _____ |
| Roof ................. | @ $ _____ | ÷ ____ Yrs. x One Bldg. = | | $ _____ | $ _____ |

**Carpeting** (Wall to Wall)                                   Remaining Life

| (Units) | ____ Total Sq. Yds. @ $____ Per Sq. Yd. ÷ ____Yrs. = | $ _____ | $ _____ |
|---|---|---|---|
| (Public Areas) | ____ Total Sq. Yds. @ $____ Per Sq. Yd. ÷ ____Yrs. = | $ _____ | $ _____ |

**Total Replacement Reserves.** (Enter on Pg. 1)                              $ _____        $ _____

### Operating Income Reconciliation

$ _____ − $ _____ = $ _____ ÷12 = $ _____
Effective Gross Income    Total Operating Expenses    Operating Income    Monthly Operating Income

$ _____ − $ _____ = $ _____
Monthly Operating Income    Monthly Housing Expense    Net Cash Flow

(Note: Monthly Housing Expense includes principal and interest on the mortgage, hazard insurance premiums, real estate taxes, mortgage insurance premiums, HOA dues, leasehold payments, and subordinate financing payments.)

Underwriter's instructions for 2-4 Family Owner-Occupied Properties

- If Monthly Operating Income is a positive number, enter as "Net Rental Income" in the "Gross Monthly Income" section of Freddie Mac Form 65/Fannie Mae Form 1003. If Monthly Operating Income is a negative number, it must be included as a liability for qualification purposes.

- The borrower's monthly housing expense-to-income ratio must be calculated by comparing the total Monthly Housing Expense for the **subject property** to the borrower's stable monthly income.

Underwriter's instructions for 1-4 Family Investment Properties

- If Net Cash Flow is a positive number, enter as "Net Rental Income" in the "Gross Monthly Income" section of Freddie Mac Form 65/Fannie Mae Form 1003. If Net Cash Flow is a negative number, it must be included as a liability for qualification purposes.

- The borrower's monthly housing expense-to-income ratio must be calculated by comparing the total monthly housing expense for the borrower's **primary residence** to the borrower's stable monthly income.

Appraiser's Comments (Including sources for data and rationale for the projections)

_____        _____        _____
Appraiser Name                   Appraiser Signature              Date

Underwriter's Comments and Rationale for Adjustments

_____        _____        _____
Underwriter Name                 Underwriter Signature            Date

Page 2 of 2

# CASE HISTORY #1

Assuming we now have the correct capitalization rate, let's consider the following case history: Los Altos Manor is a 40-unit apartment complex with 28 of the units renting for $600 per month and 12 of the units renting for $650 per month. There is a 5% vacancy rate. Expenses total $98,400. The overall capitalization rate is 9%. To determine the value of the property, we set it up like this.

$$
\begin{array}{ll}
\text{Scheduled Gross Income} & = 28 \times \$600 = \$16,800 \\
& \phantom{=} 12 \times \$650 = \$\ 7,800 \\
\end{array}
$$

|  |  |
|---|---|
| | 24,600 × 12 = $295,200 |
| Vacancy Factor ($295,200 × .05 = $14,760) | - 14,760 |
| Effective Gross Income (Adjusted Gross Income) | $280,440 |
| Expenses = $98,400 | - 98,400 |
| Net Annual Income (Net Operating Income) | $182,040 |

Value = $182,040 ÷ .09 = $2,022,666.00

We would probably round off this figure and say the property was worth $2,000,000. Now that we see how the bottom line figures line up, let's look at another situation.

# CASE HISTORY #2

Cambridge Manor is a 20-unit complex in a high desert community. The rents are configured like this: 10 units bring in $350 per month, 6 units bring in $400 per month and 4 units bring in $425 per month. There is a 7% vacancy factor. Expenses are distributed like this: taxes are $6,200 per year, insurance is $2,500 per year, management is 5% of adjusted gross income, maintenance is $600 per month, utilities are $400 per month and replacement reserves are $1,300 per year for appliances, $2,000 per year for the roof, and $2,000 per year for carpeting. The cap rate is 10%. To determine the value of the property, we set it up in similar fashion, this time listing out each expense category.

Scheduled Gross Income     $= 10 \times \$350 = \$3,500$

                                     $6 \times \$400 = \$2,400$

                                     $4 \times \$425 = \$1,700$

                                           $\$7,600 \times 12 = \$91,200$

Vacancy Factor ($\$91,200 \times .07 = \$6,384$)              $- 6,384$

Effective Gross Income (Adjusted Gross Income)         $\$84,816$

Annual Expenses

    Taxes                                        $\$6,200$

    Insurance                                2,500

    Management (.05 $\times$ \$84,816)           4,240

    Maintenance ($\$600 \times 12$)             7,200

    Utilities ($\$400 \times 12$)                4,800

    Replacement Reserves               1,300

                                           2,000

                                           2,000

                                  $\$30,240$       $- \$30,240$

Net Annual Income (Net Operating Income)            $\$54,576$

Value $= \$54,576 \div .10 = \$545,760$

In this example, operating expenses including replacement reserves are 35% of the effective gross income. That's not bad, but as a property manager we're going to look for ways to enhance the income and minimize expenses. Maintenance of $600 per month results in the largest single category of expense. This may be excessive and we may want to look into ways to reduce this expense. We understand that these units are probably older units, but perhaps by doing some preventive maintenance we can cut into this high expense. We might also look into the quality of the work that is being done and make sure we're getting what we're paying for. Also, are the rates we're paying competitive or are we paying too much? Some comparison shopping may be in order.

Other considerations might be the vacancy factor (7%) and the rental rate. Is there a way that we can reduce the vacancy rate and at the same time gradually increase the rents? What competition do we have in the marketplace? What is the supply and demand ratio? Are there more units coming on the market? Are there any factors in the community that might be increasing demand in the near future? These factors and others we'll have to look into as we develop a five-year projection.

# FIVE-YEAR PROJECTION

Let's assume we have ascertained the following facts to compile our five-year projection. First, Cambridge Manor is a 20-unit apartment complex with two separate buildings, each 32 years old. Due to the age, maintenance expenses have been high and preventive maintenance has not been routinely performed. It has been decided that preventive maintenance will be performed periodically and at times when a vacancy occurs in an attempt to lower maintenance expenses in the future. For example, new garbage disposals will be installed during the first year of the projection to lower the cost of repairs and save money in the future.

Regarding the occupancy level, it has been determined that there are no permits issued from the building department in the community for the construction of additional apartments. Supply, therefore, is static. Demand stands to increase due to a nearby military base policy that servicemen and women will be able to live off-base at their choosing and the fact that population on the base is set to increase by about 1,500 enlisted men and women over the next 10 months. No other factors contributing to loss of demand or increased demand can be identified in the community. Sources of employment in the community appear to be stable.

Tenancy in the building has been granted on a month-to-month basis. Six of the tenants have been long-term tenants, occupying their units for more than three years. The balance of the tenants have turned over an average of every 11 months. This turnover rate is regarded as too high. To reverse this trend, tenants now will be asked to sign a one-year lease when they move in. In addition, the preventive maintenance and general effort to improve the appearance and quality of the units will be designed to cut down on the turnover rate.

No tax increases are anticipated over the next five years. Insurance increases are provided for in the forecast. We are moving an on-site manager into one of the units, eliminating income from that unit, but creating more efficiency in management and maintenance functions. The general rate of inflation and increasing costs of labor and supplies are difficult to anticipate over a five-year period of time, but a small increase has been provided for that factor. Income is also expected to be enhanced over this period of time by a moderate inflation rate and an increased demand in relation to supply in the local market.

The five-year projection would look something like this.

| Figure 3-3 | Five-Year Projection | | | | | | |
|---|---|---|---|---|---|---|---|
| | Base Year | 1st Year | 2nd Year | 3rd Year | 4th Year | 5th Year | Average Year |
| *Income* | | | | | | | |
| Rental | $87,000 | $89,000 | $93,450 | $98,000 | $103,000 | $108,000 | $98,290 |
| Other | 3,000 | 3,000 | 3,000 | 3,000 | 3,000 | 3,000 | 3,000 |
| Total | $90,000 | $92,000 | $96,450 | $101,000 | $106,000 | $111,000 | $101,290 |
| *Expenses* | | | | | | | |
| Taxes | $6,200 | $6,200 | $6,200 | $6,200 | $6,200 | $6,200 | $6,200 |
| Insurance | 2,500 | 2,500 | 2,600 | 2,600 | 2,700 | 2,700 | 2,600 |
| Management | 4,000 | 4,450 | 4,675 | 4,900 | 5,150 | 5,400 | 4,915 |
| Maintenance | 7,200 | 9,200 | 7,500 | 7,000 | 6,000 | 5,200 | 6,980 |
| Utilities | 4,800 | 5,000 | 5,200 | 5,400 | 5,600 | 5,800 | 5,400 |
| Reserves | 5,300 | 5,300 | 5,300 | 5,300 | 5,300 | 5,300 | 5,300 |
| Total | $30,000 | $32,650 | $31,475 | $31,400 | $30,950 | $30,600 | $31,395 |
| *Net Operating Income* | $60,000 | $59,350 | $64,975 | $69,600 | $75,050 | $80,400 | $69,895 |
| *Debt Service* | $19,296 | $19,296 | $19,296 | $19,296 | $19,296 | $19,296 | $19,296 |
| *Cash Flow* | $40,704 | $40,054 | $45,679 | $50,304 | $55,754 | $61,104 | $50,599 |

This projection is based on the following assumptions: From the base year to the first year of the projection the only increase in income relates to a reduction of the vacancy rate from 7% to 5% and the new vacancy factor (5%) is maintained throughout the projection. The management expense is based on 5% of the adjusted gross income. Income is based on 5% rent increases each year. The increased maintenance expense is due to the preventive maintenance performed to decrease the number of emergency maintenance situations in the future. Debt service is based on a $200,000 first loan at 9%.

# COMPARATIVE ANALYSIS FOR PROPOSED CAPITAL IMPROVEMENTS

Another type of financial oversight performed by a property manager is a comparative analysis showing income and expenses before and after a capital improvement. The property manager must research the costs of labor and materials for any proposed improvement. He or she then must research the market and compare the increased income and resultant cash flow against the capital expenditure to determine the time it will take to return the capital investment. The manager also must consider whether a particular capital improvement is going to result in higher expenses, such as installing a swimming pool increasing liability and thus insurance costs. Any increased expenses would offset increased income proportionately. Based on this analysis the owner will be able to make an informed decision as to whether or not to pursue a particular capital improvement.

The principle of contribution enters into the picture here. How much will the capital improvement contribute to the bottom line net income of the property? When all factors are considered, this is the only basis for making a good decision.

Suppose in the case study of Cambridge Manor the owner is considering remodeling the kitchens in the units. Remember, the units are 32 years old. A modern kitchen is a factor that should increase the rents. To put in new cabinets, counter tops, linoleum, stove and sink, the estimated cost is $2,800 per unit. Market research indicates that units with a remodeled kitchen will command only $25 per month more than units with the original kitchen. The before and after analysis will help the owner decide what to do.

| Figure 3-4 | Comparative Analysis Before and After Capital Expenditure | | |
|---|---|---|---|
| | | *Before* | *After* |
| *Income* | | | |
| Rental | | $87,000 | $92,700 |
| Other | | 2,000 | 2,000 |
| Total | | $89,000 | $94,700 |
| *Expenses* | | | |
| Taxes | | $6,200 | $6,200 |
| Insurance | | 2,500 | 2,500 |
| Management | | 4,000 | 4,635 |
| Maintenance | | 7,200 | 6,000 |
| Utilities | | 4,800 | 5,000 |
| Reserves | | 5,300 | 5,300 |
| Total | | $30,000 | $29,635 |
| *Net Operating Income* | | $59,000 | $65,065 |
| *Debt Service* | | $19,296 | $19,296 |
| *Cash Flow* | | $39,704 | $45,769 |

The capital expenditure to make this improvement is $56,000 ($2,800 x 20 units). The increased cash flow is only $6,065 per year. It would take 9.23 years to return the investment. This is possibly longer than the owner intends to own the units. This marketplace is the high desert, an isolated, locked-in community where supply and demand dictate the rents. The fact that a rental space is clean, safe and available places it near the top of the range for potential income. This analysis will help the owner understand that to make these improvements in this particular community would not enhance the net income and cash flow sufficiently to justify the expenditure of this amount of capital.

# THE ANNUAL BUDGET

A basic tool the property manager must present to the owner of a property is the annual operating budget. With the analyses we've already developed, the annual budget is a fairly simple procedure.

## Figure 3-5   Annual Operating Budget

| Scheduled Gross Income | | |
|---|---|---|
| 9 units @ $350/month | $37,800 | |
| 6 units @ $400/month | $28,800 | |
| 4 units @ $425/month | $20,400 | |
| | $87,000 | |
| Vacancy Factor (5%) | - 4,350 | |
| Gross Collectable Income | $82,650 | |
| Laundry Income | 3,000 | |
| Total Anticipated Income | | $85,650 |
| Expenses | | |
| Taxes | $ 6,200 | |
| Insurance | 2,500 | |
| Management | 4,000 | |
| Maintenance | 7,200 | |
| Utilities | 4,800 | |
| Reserves | 5,300 | |
| Total Expenses | | - 30,000 |
| Net Operating Income | | $55,650 |

*(continued on next page)*

| Figure 3-5 (cont'd.)    Annual Operating Budget | |
|---|---|
| *(continued from previous page)* | |
| *Net Operating Income* | $55,650 |
| *Debt Service* | |
| $200,000 @ 9% | - 19,296 |
| *Cash Flow* | $36,354 |

# QUESTIONS

1. The purpose of financial analysis in property management is to:

   a. track the flow of money

   b. aid in planning

   c. minimize expenses and maximize profits

   d. all of the above

2. Scheduled gross income is:

   a. all of the income a property can possibly produce

   b. the income scheduled after credit losses

   c. a proposed operating budget

   d. a five-year projection

3. Operating expenses:

   a. are unnecessary in the operation of an income producing property

   b. are deducted from scheduled gross income

   c. include debt service

   d. should be minimized

4. Effective gross income is:

    a. income after expenses

    b. what is actually collected

    c. income after debt service

    d. usually greater than scheduled gross income

5. Effective gross income is synonymous with:

    a. adjusted gross income

    b. scheduled gross income

    c. cash flow

    d. monetary return

6. Net operating income:

    a. includes a deduction for debt service

    b. includes a deduction for personal income taxes

    c. does not consider debt service

    d. is the purest expression of effective gross income

7. A higher net operating income:

    a. can be achieved with a higher vacancy rate

    b. is essential to a higher property value

    c. may be detrimental to property value

    d. usually will necessitate a higher capitalization rate

8. Replacement reserves:

    a. are part of the financial dynamics of operating an income producing property

    b. are not necessary for figuring the annual relationship between income and expenses

    c. should not be included in the expenses

    d. are set aside by the sinking fund method

9. The capitalization rate is:

    a. determined by dividing income into value

    b. highest when interest rates are low

    c. the desired rate of return on an investment property

    d. an index expressing the availability of capital

10. The higher the capitalization rate:

    a. the higher the value of the property
    b. the lower the value of the property
    c. the more difficult the property is to buy
    d. capitalization rates are irrelevant to value

11. Capitalization rates:

    a. are accurate within three
       percentage points plus or minus
    b. cannot be precisely determined
    c. need not be precisely determined
    d. must be accurately determined to
       correctly reflect on value

12. The following is one method of determining a capitalization rate for a given property at a given time:

    a. summation
    b. contemplation
    c. reflection
    d. bands of kioli

13. Fannie Mae (FNMA) Form 216 is:

    a. a cost accounting method
    b. an operating income statement
    c. a miscellaneous expenses statement
    d. required for all property managers

14. Maximizing net income of an income producing property would be assisted by:

    a. increasing vacancy
    b. capital improvements
    c. reducing expenses
    d. greater supply than demand

15. A five-year projection on an income producing property:

    a. helps an owner with financial planning
    b. is easy to compile with accuracy
    c. does not require the consideration of economic factors
    d. need not take into account local demographics

16. Debt service affects:

    a. net income
    b. effective gross income
    c. cash flow
    d. net spendable

17. Capital improvements:

    a. are regarded as expenses
    b. always increase cash flow substantially
    c. must be evaluated in relation to the time it takes to recover the investment
    d. always add significantly to the value of a property

18. The bottom line of the annual budget is:

    a. total expenses
    b. cash flow
    c. net income
    d. anticipated income

19. The overall capitalization rate:

    a. is an approximation
    b. includes a return *on* and a return *of* the investment
    c. is the same as the safe rate
    d. is the same as the interest rate

20. Net operating income is the same as:

    a. net annual income
    b. effective gross income
    c. scheduled gross income
    d. net monthly income

# ANSWERS

1. *d*
2. *a*
3. *d*
4. *b*
5. *a*
6. *c*
7. *b*
8. *a*
9. *c*
10. *b*
11. *d*
12. *a*
13. *b*
14. *c*
15. *a*
16. *c*
17. *c*
18. *b*
19. *b*
20. *a*

# Property Analysis

- **Looking At Everything**
- **Market Analysis**
- **Property Analysis**
- **The Objectives Of Ownership**
- **Financial Analysis**
- **The Management Plan**

C H A P T E R

4

# LOOKING AT EVERYTHING

Property analysis refers not only to a physical inspection of the property, but to an integration of the property manager's knowledge of economics, the property's financial analysis and the owner's objectives. This will result in producing a management plan and blending the owner's and manager's efforts toward the accomplishment of agreed objectives.

# MARKET ANALYSIS

The property manager must understand what is happening in the marketplace for this type of property. He or she must consider factors that contribute to demand for the subject property. Regional factors should be considered, all the way down to the local neighborhood. What are employment trends in the area? Is there a predominant industry or company that supplies jobs? Are they growing or cutting back? Are there new industries or companies getting established in the area? Will they have an impact on demand, and what is the likely timing of their influence?

To be attuned to issues like these the property manager needs to read the major newspaper of the area. These newspapers, like the *Los Angeles Times*, usually cover subjects of major economic impact. A recent Sunday edition of the *Times*, in the *Business Section*, reported that the 3,600-acre Irvine Spectrum, a major industrial complex of high-tech companies like Western Digital, AT&T Regional Headquarters, Mazda Motor of America, Toshiba America Information Systems and others, is growing at breakneck speed and shows no signs of slowing down. This area is positioned for growth and is likened to Silicon Valley in Northern California, Boston's Route 128 "Technology Highway," and the Research Triangle, a three-city area in North Carolina.

The development of this kind of complex results in a tremendous increase in jobs in the area. The Irvine Spectrum housed 600 companies in 1989. In 1997 the number had grown to 2,200. While providing 16,000 jobs in 1989, the Spectrum was responsible for 36,000 jobs in 1997. The entire complex was planned to be completed in 40 years, but now expectations are that in 25 years the Spectrum will be built out.

This is important information for a property manager in the area to know. Demand for housing should be steady and values should be increasing. Many employees in the area with good paying jobs should be competing for available housing units. Some will buy, but many will compete for rental space. Since the demand is created by not just one company, but by an entire industrial complex, it can be perceived as broad-based and solid. This information would definitely factor into the management plan developed by the property manager and owner.

Other market factors need to be considered. Is transportation readily available in the vicinity of the rental space? Are there major highways, airports, harbors or shipping lanes and public transportation? Do commercial support facilities exist for the existing housing supply? Are stores and other services located conveniently to the units?

If we are considering an apartment house, what can be said of the neighborhood? Is it crime-ridden or blighted? What other types of properties are found in the neighborhood? Is the complex in an inviting area, or does an abundance of industrial and commercial property cause resistance among would-be tenants? Is the apartment building subject to excessive traffic noise? Are there other factors that appraisers would call *external obsolescence* that would make the neighborhood less desirable? These influences occur outside the property lines and are difficult to do anything about, but can have a devastating effect on desirability and value. Few people want to live next to a foul odor-producing industrial plant, or a dairy farm that attracts flies, or in the flight pattern of the airport.

What about trends of growth in the neighborhood? Is the subject property in the pathway of progress? Is growth or redevelopment taking place? Or is the subject property on the "wrong side of the tracks"? What are the schools like in the area? Neighborhoods with the best schools generally command the highest real estate values for all types of residential property.

What about financing and interest rates in the area? Is financing readily available for single family residences? For apartment buildings? For commercial and industrial properties? When interest rates are favorable and financing is available, we enjoy a time of expansion and prosperity. Capitalization rates can remain relatively low, thereby having a favorable influence on the values of income producing property. This produces an optimistic outlook for owners of these types of properties.

What about factors that might influence the supply of like properties? What is the supply and demand ratio of residential income, commercial and industrial properties in the marketplace at this time? How is it likely to change in the future? Are more units scheduled to compete in the marketplace in the near future? Will there be more supply than demand soon? Or, even with increased supply, will demand continue to be brisk and outpace supply, pushing the values of properties?

These and all factors having an impact on the demand for your property must be taken into consideration, both regionally and locally.

# PROPERTY ANALYSIS

A thorough on-site inspection of the property must be made by the property manager so the entire physical plant is clearly understood. Since capital is never unlimited, the property manager must make a distinction between repairs and maintenance that are necessary to protect the value of the building and those that would be desirable to attract new tenants. The facility's interior and exterior must be examined. Items that could impact the safety of tenants and the public must be addressed immediately. Other conditions that could lead to property damage and impair the value of the property must be given prompt attention. The property manager also should check with local building authorities to ensure that the building is in compliance.

A well-trained property manager can make a big difference to the owner when performing a thorough inspection. Many institutional owners or investment groups have no eyes to see the defects of a property except those of the property manager. They rely on your expertise to protect their investments.

The forms on the following pages from the Institute of Real Estate Management (IREM) will guide the property manager through a thorough inspection of both residential and commercial properties. Separate forms are provided for both the interior and exterior inspections and can be obtained from IREM listed in Chapter 1 of this book.

**Figure 4-1    Apartment Exterior Inspection Report**

**IREM** Institute of Real Estate Management
of the NATIONAL ASSOCIATION OF REALTORS®

**Apartment Exterior Inspection Report**

Property _____    Address _____

Owner _____

Type _____    No. of Stories ____

Reported by _____    Date _____

No. of Apts.:    1's ____    1½'s ____    2's ____
2½'s ____    3's ____    3½'s ____    4's ____
4½'s ____    5's ____    5½'s ____    6's ____
7's ____    8's ____    Other ____    Total ____

### I. Building Exterior

| Items | Character and Condition | Needs | Est. Expense |
|---|---|---|---|
| **Grounds** | | | |
| 1. Soil | | | |
| 2. Grass | | | |
| 3. Shrubs | | | |
| 4. Flowers | | | |
| 5. Trees | | | |
| 6. Fences | | | |
| 7. Urns | | | |
| 8. Walks | | | |
| 9. Cement flashings | | | |
| 10. Parking curbs | | | |
| 11. | | | |
| **Brick and Stone** | | | |
| 12. Front walls | | | |
| A. Base | | | |
| B. Top | | | |
| C. Coping | | | |
| D. Tuck pointing | | | |
| E. Cleanliness | | | |
| 13. Court walls | | | |
| A. Base | | | |
| B. Top | | | |
| C. Coping | | | |
| D. Tuck pointing | | | |
| E. Cleanliness | | | |
| 14. Side walls | | | |
| A. Base | | | |
| B. Top | | | |
| C. Coping | | | |
| D. Tuck pointing | | | |
| E. Cleanliness | | | |
| 15. Rear walls | | | |
| A. Base | | | |
| B. Top | | | |
| C. Coping | | | |
| D. Tuck pointing | | | |
| E. Cleanliness | | | |
| 16. Chimneys | | | |
| 17. | | | |

### II. General Interior

| Vestibules | | | |
|---|---|---|---|
| 1. Steps | | | |
| 2. Risers | | | |
| 3. Floors | | | |
| 4. Marble slabs | | | |

## Figure 4-I (cont'd.)   Apartment Exterior Inspection Report

**II. General Interior** (continued)

| Items | Character and Condition | Needs | Est. Expense |
|---|---|---|---|
| 5. Walls | | | |
| 6. Ceilings | | | |
| 7. Door mats | | | |
| 8. Door glass | | | |
| 9. Transoms | | | |
| 10. Hinges | | | |
| 11. Door knobs | | | |
| 12. Door checks | | | |
| 13. Door finish | | | |
| 14. Kick plates | | | |
| 15. Handrails | | | |
| 16. Mailbox doors | | | |
| 17. Mailbox locks | | | |
| 18. Intercom | | | |
| 19. Signal buttons and connections | | | |
| 20. | | | |
| **Stair Halls** | | | |
| 21. Steps | | | |
| 22. Landings | | | |
| 23. Handrails | | | |
| 24. Woodwork | | | |
| 25. Carpets | | | |
| 26. Walls | | | |
| 27. Ceilings | | | |
| 28. Skylights | | | |
| 29. Windows | | | |
| 30. Window coverings | | | |
| 31. | | | |
| **Rear Halls** | | | |
| 32. Steps | | | |
| 33. Landings | | | |
| 34. Walls | | | |
| 35. Ceilings | | | |
| 36. Handrails | | | |
| 37. Garbage cans | | | |
| 38. Windows | | | |
| 39. Window coverings | | | |
| 40. | | | |
| **Elevators** | | | |
| 41. Signal buttons | | | |
| 42. Doors | | | |
| 43. Cab floors | | | |
| 44. Cab walls | | | |
| 45. Cab ceilings | | | |
| 46. Control mechanism | | | |
| 47. Cables | | | |
| 48. Pulleys | | | |
| 49. Motor | | | |
| 50. Shaft walls | | | |
| 51. Shaft ceiling | | | |
| 52. Shaft floor | | | |
| 53. Floor numbers on doors | | | |
| 54. | | | |
| **Public Light Fixtures** | | | |
| 55. Entrance | | | |
| A. Brackets | | | |
| B. Fixtures | | | |

## Figure 4-1 (cont'd.)   Apartment Exterior Inspection Report

### II. General Interior (continued)

| Items | Character and Condition | Needs | Est. Expense |
|---|---|---|---|
| C. Bulbs | | | |
| D. Switch | | | |
| 56. Vestibule | | | |
| A. Brackets | | | |
| B. Fixtures | | | |
| C. Bulbs | | | |
| D. Switch | | | |
| 57. Halls | | | |
| A. Brackets | | | |
| B. Fixtures | | | |
| C. Bulbs | | | |
| D. Switch | | | |
| 58. | | | |

### III. Basement

| Laundries | | | |
|---|---|---|---|
| 1. Floors | | | |
| 2. Walls | | | |
| 3. Ceilings | | | |
| 4. Washers | | | |
| 5. Driers | | | |
| 6. Vending machines | | | |
| 7. Tubs and faucets | | | |
| 8. Toilet bowls | | | |
| 9. Lavatories | | | |
| 10. Drains | | | |
| 11. Doors | | | |
| 12. Windows | | | |
| 13. Window coverings | | | |
| 14. | | | |
| **Boiler Room** | | | |
| 15. Floor | | | |
| 16. Pipes | | | |
| 17. Fuel bin | | | |
| 18. Fire hazards | | | |
| 19. Ceiling | | | |
| 20. Walls | | | |
| 21. Doors | | | |
| 22. Windows | | | |
| 23. Window coverings | | | |
| 24. Cleanliness | | | |
| 25. Trash containers | | | |
| 26. | | | |
| **Boiler** | | | |
| 27. Flues | | | |
| 28. Tubes | | | |
| 29. Valves | | | |
| 30. Diaphragms | | | |
| 31. Flange unions | | | |
| 32. Grates | | | |
| 33. Ash pits | | | |
| 34. Pointing on brickwork | | | |
| 35. Motors | | | |
| 36. Draft controls | | | |
| 37. Chimney | | | |
| 38. Thermostats | | | |

## Figure 4-1 (cont'd.)   Apartment Exterior Inspection Report

### III.  Basement (continued)

| Items | Character and Condition | Needs | Est. Expense |
|---|---|---|---|
| 39. Hydrostats | | | |
| 40. Stoker | | | |
| 41. Insulation | | | |
| 42. Combustion chambers | | | |
| 43. Water level | | | |
| 44. | | | |
| **Hot-Water Heater** | | | |
| 45. Tank | | | |
| 46. Insulation | | | |
| 47. Ash pit | | | |
| 48. Incinerator | | | |
| 49. Submerged system | | | |
| 50. Hydrolator | | | |
| 51. | | | |
| **Pumps** | | | |
| 52. Motors | | | |
| 53. Sump | | | |
| 54. Pressure | | | |
| 55. Circulating | | | |
| 56. | | | |
| **Lockers** | | | |
| 57. Floors | | | |
| 58. Walls | | | |
| 59. Ceilings | | | |
| 60. Doors | | | |
| 61. Fire hazards | | | |
| 62. Aisles | | | |
| 63. | | | |
| **Central Air Conditioning** | | | |
| 64. Motors | | | |
| 65. Cleanliness | | | |
| 66. Accessibility | | | |
| 67. | | | |
| **General** | | | |
| 68. Plaster | | | |
| 69. Trash and junk | | | |
| 70. Screens | | | |
| 71. | | | |
| 72. | | | |
| 73. | | | |

### Notes and Recommendations

_____

_____

_____

_____

_____

_____

_____

_____

_____

_____

**Figure 4-2   Apartment Interior Inspection Report**

**IREM** Institute of Real Estate Management
of the NATIONAL ASSOCIATION OF REALTORS®

Form 313-983

_____ 20 ___

# APARTMENT INTERIOR INSPECTION REPORT

Name of Property_____ Address _____

Apt. No._____ No. of Rooms _____

Report Submitted by _____

| Items | Character and Condition | Needs | Estimated Expense Involved |
|---|---|---|---|
| **Vestibule** | | | |
| 1. Door | | | |
| 2. Hinges | | | |
| 3. Lock | | | |
| 4. Safety chain | | | |
| 5. Doorplate | | | |
| 6. Transom | | | |
| 7. Floor (carpeting) | | | |
| 8. Walls | | | |
| 9. Ceiling | | | |
| 10. Light fixtures & switches | | | |
| 11. Draperies | | | |
| **Coat Closet** | | | |
| 12. Door | | | |
| 13. Floor | | | |
| 14. Interior walls | | | |
| 15. Ceiling | | | |
| 16. Shelves, rods, hooks | | | |
| **Living Room** | | | |
| 17. Floor (carpeting) | | | |
| 18. Baseboards | | | |
| 19. Walls | | | |
| 20. Ceiling | | | |
| 21. Windows | | | |
| 22. Doors | | | |
| 23. Light fixtures & switches | | | |
| 24. Electric outlets | | | |
| 25. Draperies | | | |
| **Dining Room** | | | |
| 26. Floor (carpeting) | | | |
| 27. Baseboards | | | |
| 28. Walls | | | |
| 29. Ceiling | | | |
| 30. Windows | | | |

## Figure 4-2 (cont'd.)  Apartment Interior Inspection Report

| Items | Character and Condition | Needs | Estimated Expense Involved |
|---|---|---|---|
| **Dining Room (cont'd)** | | | |
| 31.  Doors | | | |
| 32.  Light fixtures & switches | | | |
| 33.  Electric outlets | | | |
| 34.  Draperies | | | |
| 35.  Buffets | | | |
| 36.  Wainscot or chair rail | | | |
| **Kitchen** | | | |
| 37.  Doors | | | |
| 38.  Transoms | | | |
| 39.  Locks | | | |
| 40.  Floor | | | |
| 41.  Baseboards | | | |
| 42.  Walls | | | |
| 43.  Ceiling | | | |
| 44.  Light fixtures & switches | | | |
| 45.  Electric outlets | | | |
| 46.  Dishwashers | | | |
| 47.  Range | | | |
| 48.  Sink | | | |
| 49.  Cabinets | | | |
| 50.  Refrigerator | | | |
| 51.  Pantry | | | |
| 52.  Doorbell | | | |
| 53.  Ventilating hood | | | |
| 54.  Disposal | | | |
| **First Bedroom** | | | |
| 55.  Doors | | | |
| 56.  Floor (carpeting) | | | |
| 57.  Baseboards | | | |
| 58.  Walls | | | |
| 59.  Ceiling | | | |
| 60.  Windows | | | |
| 61.  Light fixtures & switches | | | |
| 62.  Electric outlets | | | |
| 63.  Draperies | | | |
| 64.  Closets | | | |
| **Second Bedroom** | | | |
| 65.  Doors | | | |
| 66.  Floor (carpeting) | | | |
| 67.  Baseboards | | | |
| 68.  Walls | | | |
| 69.  Ceiling | | | |
| 70.  Windows | | | |
| 71.  Light fixtures & switches | | | |
| 72.  Electric outlets | | | |
| 73.  Draperies | | | |
| 74.  Closets | | | |
| **Third Bedroom** | | | |
| 75.  Doors | | | |
| 76.  Floor (carpeting) | | | |

## Figure 4-2 (cont'd.)   Apartment Interior Inspection Report

| Items | Character and Condition | Needs | Estimated Expense Involved |
|---|---|---|---|
| **Third Bedroom (cont'd)** | | | |
| 77.   Baseboards | | | |
| 78.   Walls | | | |
| 79.   Ceiling | | | |
| 80.   Windows | | | |
| 81.   Light fixtures & switches | | | |
| 82.   Electric outlets | | | |
| 83.   Draperies | | | |
| 84.   Closets | | | |
| **Maid's Room** | | | |
| 85.   Doors | | | |
| 86.   Floor (carpeting) | | | |
| 87.   Baseboards | | | |
| 88.   Walls | | | |
| 89.   Ceiling | | | |
| 90.   Windows | | | |
| 91.   Light fixtures & switches | | | |
| 92.   Electric outlets | | | |
| 93.   Draperies | | | |
| 94.   Closets | | | |
| **First Bathroom** | | | |
| 95.   Doors | | | |
| 96.   Floor | | | |
| 97.   Walls | | | |
| 98.   Ceiling | | | |
| 99.   Window | | | |
| 100.  Tub (glass door) | | | |
| 101.  Shower | | | |
| 102.  Shower curtain or door | | | |
| 103.  Lavatory | | | |
| 104.  Toilet bowl | | | |
| 105.  Flush tank | | | |
| 106.  Faucets | | | |
| 107.  Light fixtures & switches | | | |
| 108.  Electric outlets | | | |
| 109.  Exhaust fan | | | |
| 110.  Towel racks, etc. | | | |
| 111.  Cabinets | | | |
| **Second Bathroom** | | | |
| 112.  Doors | | | |
| 113.  Floor | | | |
| 114.  Walls | | | |
| 115.  Ceiling | | | |
| 116.  Window | | | |
| 117.  Tub (glass door) | | | |
| 118.  Shower | | | |
| 119.  Shower curtain or door | | | |
| 120.  Lavatory | | | |
| 121.  Toilet bowl | | | |
| 122.  Flush tank | | | |
| 123.  Faucets | | | |

## Figure 4-2 (cont'd.)   Apartment Interior Inspection Report

| Items | Character and Condition | Needs | Estimated Expense Involved |
|---|---|---|---|
| **Second Bathroom (cont'd)** | | | |
| 124. Light fixtures & switches | | | |
| 125. Electric outlets | | | |
| 126. Exhaust fan | | | |
| 127. Towel racks, etc. | | | |
| 128. Cabinets | | | |
| **Windows and Shades** | | | |
| 129. Frames | | | |
| 130. Sashes | | | |
| 131. Sills | | | |
| 132. Stops | | | |
| 133. Weights | | | |
| 134. Locks | | | |
| 135. Glass | | | |
| 136. Weatherstripping | | | |
| 137. Shades | | | |
| 138. Blinds | | | |
| 139. Drapery fixtures | | | |
| **Linen Closet** | | | |
| 140. Door | | | |
| 141. Floor | | | |
| 142. Ceiling | | | |
| 143. Walls | | | |
| 144. Shelves | | | |
| 145. Drawers | | | |
| 146. Electric Lights | | | |
| **Environmental Controls** | | | |
| 147. Heating equipment | | | |
| 148. Air conditioning unit(s) | | | |

### NOTES

## Figure 4-3 Office Building Exterior Inspection Report

**IREM**

**Office Building Exterior Inspection Report**

Page 1 of 4

Building _____    Address _____

Owner _____

Age of Building _____    Maintenance Priority: ☐ A  ☐ B  ☐ C    No. of Stores _____

Rental Rates:    Office Area _____    Store Area _____    Basement Area _____

Report Submitted by _____    Date _____

| Items | Condition | | | Description | Repairs Needed | Est. Cost |
|---|---|---|---|---|---|---|
| | Good | Fair | Poor | | | |
| **Roofs** | | | | | | |
| 1. Type | | | | | | |
| 2. Flashing | | | | | | |
| 3. Surface (Valleys) | | | | | | |
| 4. Drainage | | | | | | |
| 5. Vents | | | | | | |
| 6. Chimney | | | | | | |
| 7. Misc. Machinery | | | | | | |
| 8. Misc. Machinery | | | | | | |
| 9. Misc. Machinery | | | | | | |
| 10. Other Roof Structures | | | | | | |
| **Walls—North** | | | | | | |
| 11. Type | | | | | | |
| 12. Base | | | | | | |
| 13. Top | | | | | | |
| 14. Tuck Pointing | | | | | | |
| 15. Cracks/Gaps | | | | | | |
| 16. Join of Wall/Frames | | | | | | |
| 17. Buckling | | | | | | |
| 18. Stone Sills | | | | | | |
| 19. Terra Cotta | | | | | | |
| 20. Metal Trim | | | | | | |
| 21. Projections | | | | | | |
| 22. Coping | | | | | | |
| 23. Glass | | | | | | |
| 24. Paint | | | | | | |
| 25. Parapet Walls | | | | | | |
| 26. Other | | | | | | |
| **Walls—East** | | | | | | |
| 27. Type | | | | | | |
| 28. Base | | | | | | |
| 29. Top | | | | | | |
| 30. Tuck Pointing | | | | | | |
| 31. Cracks/Gaps | | | | | | |
| 32. Join of Wall/Frames | | | | | | |
| 33. Buckling | | | | | | |
| 34. Stone Sills | | | | | | |
| 35. Terra Cotta | | | | | | |
| 36. Metal Trim | | | | | | |
| 37. Projections | | | | | | |
| 38. Coping | | | | | | |
| 39. Glass | | | | | | |
| 40. Paint | | | | | | |
| 41. Parapet Walls | | | | | | |
| 42. Other | | | | | | |

313-983

## Figure 4-3 (cont'd.)  Office Building Exterior Inspection Report

### Office Building Exterior Inspection Report
Page 2 of 4

| Items | Condition | | | Description | Repairs Needed | Est. Cost |
|---|---|---|---|---|---|---|
| | Good | Fair | Poor | | | |
| **Walls—South** | | | | | | |
| 43. Type | | | | | | |
| 44. Base | | | | | | |
| 45. Top | | | | | | |
| 46. Tuck Pointing | | | | | | |
| 47. Cracks/Gaps | | | | | | |
| 48. Join of Wall/Frames | | | | | | |
| 49. Buckling | | | | | | |
| 50. Stone Sills | | | | | | |
| 51. Terra Cotta | | | | | | |
| 52. Metal Trim | | | | | | |
| 53. Projections | | | | | | |
| 54. Coping | | | | | | |
| 55. Glass | | | | | | |
| 56. Paint | | | | | | |
| 57. Parapet Walls | | | | | | |
| 58. Other | | | | | | |
| **Walls—West** | | | | | | |
| 59. Type | | | | | | |
| 60. Base | | | | | | |
| 61. Top | | | | | | |
| 62. Tuck Pointing | | | | | | |
| 63. Cracks/Gaps | | | | | | |
| 64. Join of Wall/Frames | | | | | | |
| 65. Buckling | | | | | | |
| 66. Stone Sills | | | | | | |
| 67. Terra Cotta | | | | | | |
| 68. Metal Trim | | | | | | |
| 69. Projections | | | | | | |
| 70. Coping | | | | | | |
| 71. Glass | | | | | | |
| 72. Paint | | | | | | |
| 73. Parapet Walls | | | | | | |
| 74. Other | | | | | | |
| **Light Wells or Court** | | | | | | |
| 75. Skylight | | | | | | |
| 76. Walls | | | | | | |
| 77. | | | | | | |
| 78. | | | | | | |
| **Exterior** | | | | | | |
| 79. Landscaping | | | | | | |
| 80. Curbs | | | | | | |
| 81. Sidewalks/Stairs | | | | | | |
| 82. Railings | | | | | | |
| 83. Handicapped Access | | | | | | |
| 84. Signage | | | | | | |
| 85. Portico/Awning | | | | | | |
| 86. Trash Containers | | | | | | |
| 87. Light Fixtures | | | | | | |
| 88. Light Bulbs | | | | | | |
| 89. Light Switches/Timers | | | | | | |
| 90. Adequacy of Lighting | | | | | | |

**Figure 4-3 (cont'd.)   Office Building Exterior Inspection Report**

## Office Building Exterior Inspection Report
Page 3 of 4

| Items | Condition | | | Description | Repairs Needed | Est. Cost |
|---|---|---|---|---|---|---|
| | Good | Fair | Poor | | | |
| **Entrance** | | | | | | |
| 91. Doors | | | | | | |
| 92. Hinges | | | | | | |
| 93. Locks | | | | | | |
| 94. Checks | | | | | | |
| 95. Transoms | | | | | | |
| 96. Signal Button | | | | | | |
| 97. Building Name | | | | | | |
| 98. Street Numbers | | | | | | |
| **Windows—Office** | | | | | | |
| 99. Type | | | | | | |
| 100. Frames | | | | | | |
| 101. Stops | | | | | | |
| 102. Sash | | | | | | |
| 103. Sills | | | | | | |
| 104. Lintels | | | | | | |
| 105. Anchor Bolts | | | | | | |
| 106. Glass | | | | | | |
| 107. Glazing | | | | | | |
| 108. Caulking | | | | | | |
| 109. Weather Strip | | | | | | |
| 110. Screens | | | | | | |
| 111. Locks | | | | | | |
| **Windows—Store** | | | | | | |
| 112. Frames | | | | | | |
| 113. Transom | | | | | | |
| 114. Sash | | | | | | |
| 115. Glass | | | | | | |
| 116. Caulking | | | | | | |
| 117. Glazing | | | | | | |
| 118. Screens | | | | | | |
| 119. Hinges | | | | | | |
| 120. Sash | | | | | | |
| 121. Locks | | | | | | |
| **Loading Dock** | | | | | | |
| 122. Cleanliness | | | | | | |
| 123. Fire Safety | | | | | | |
| 124. Fire Equip./Alarms | | | | | | |
| 125. Surfaces Clear/Dry | | | | | | |
| 126. Overhead Doors | | | | | | |
| 127. Locks | | | | | | |
| 128. Signal Bell | | | | | | |
| 129. Stairs/Railings | | | | | | |
| 130. Lighting | | | | | | |
| 131. Signage | | | | | | |
| 132. Painted Surfaces | | | | | | |
| 133. Trash Containers | | | | | | |
| 134. Storage Areas | | | | | | |
| 135. City Ords. Compliance | | | | | | |
| 136. Exit Lights/Buzzer | | | | | | |
| 137. Security Alarms | | | | | | |
| 138. Other | | | | | | |

**Figure 4-3 (cont'd.)   Office Building Exterior Inspection Report**

## Office Building Exterior Inspection Report
Page 4 of 4

| Items | Condition | | | Description | Repairs Needed | Est. Cost |
|---|---|---|---|---|---|---|
| | Good | Fair | Poor | | | |
| **Freight Elevator** | | | | | | |
| 139. Appearance | | | | | | |
| 140. Permit Date | | | | | | |
| 141. Mechanical | | | | | | |
| 142. | | | | | | |
| 143. | | | | | | |
| **Exterior Fire Escapes** | | | | | | |
| 144. Signs | | | | | | |
| 145. Access Windows | | | | | | |
| 146. Access Ladders | | | | | | |
| 147. Maintenance | | | | | | |
| 148. Ladder Treads | | | | | | |
| 149. Hand Rails | | | | | | |
| **Misc. Items/Extras** | | | | | | |
| 150. | | | | | | |
| 151. | | | | | | |
| 152. | | | | | | |
| 153. | | | | | | |
| 154. | | | | | | |
| 155. | | | | | | |
| 156. | | | | | | |
| 157. | | | | | | |
| 158. | | | | | | |
| 159. | | | | | | |
| 160. | | | | | | |
| 161. | | | | | | |
| 162. | | | | | | |
| 163. | | | | | | |
| 164. | | | | | | |

**Detailed Notes for Recommendations on Exteriors**

## Figure 4-4  Office Building Interior Inspection Report

**IREM**

## Office Building Interior Inspection Report
Page 1 of 10

Building _____  Address _____

Owner _____

Age of Building _____  Maintenance Priority: ☐ A  ☐ B  ☐ C  No. of Stores _____

Rental Rates:  Office Area _____  Store Area _____  Basement Area _____

Report Submitted by _____  Date _____

| Items | Condition | | | Description | Repairs Needed | Est. Cost |
|---|---|---|---|---|---|---|
| | *Good* | *Fair* | *Poor* | | | |
| **Lobby** | | | | | | |
| 1. Doors | | | | | | |
| 2. Locks | | | | | | |
| 3. Ceiling | | | | | | |
| 4. Walls | | | | | | |
| 5. Floors | | | | | | |
| 6. Floor Mats | | | | | | |
| 7. Lighting Fixtures | | | | | | |
| 8. Glass | | | | | | |
| 9. Directory | | | | | | |
| 10. Signs | | | | | | |
| 11. Mailbox | | | | | | |
| 12. Guard Station | | | | | | |
| **Interior Doors** | | | | | | |
| 13. Type | | | | | | |
| 14. Glass | | | | | | |
| 15. Rails | | | | | | |
| 16. Stiles | | | | | | |
| 17. Handrails | | | | | | |
| 18. Hinges | | | | | | |
| 19. Locks | | | | | | |
| 20. Pulls | | | | | | |
| 21. Push Plates | | | | | | |
| 22. Kick Plates | | | | | | |
| 23. Mail Slot | | | | | | |
| **Stairways** | | | | | | |
| 24. Doors | | | | | | |
| 25. Locks | | | | | | |
| 26. Treads | | | | | | |
| 27. Risers | | | | | | |
| 28. Gates | | | | | | |
| 29. Bannisters | | | | | | |
| 30. Handrails | | | | | | |
| 31. Walls | | | | | | |
| 32. Ceilings | | | | | | |
| 33. Windows | | | | | | |
| 34. Skylights | | | | | | |
| 35. Electric Lights | | | | | | |
| 36. Fire Access | | | | | | |
| 37. Fire Safety | | | | | | |
| 38. Sprinklers | | | | | | |
| 39. Exit Signs/Bulbs | | | | | | |
| 40. Signage | | | | | | |
| 41. Cleanliness | | | | | | |
| 42. | | | | | | |

**Figure 4-4 (cont'd.)    Office Building Interior Inspection Report**

### Office Building Interior Inspection Report
Page 2 of 10

| Items | Condition | | | Description | Repairs Needed | Est. Cost |
|---|---|---|---|---|---|---|
| | Good | Fair | Poor | | | |
| **Corridors** | | | | | | |
| 43. Ceilings | | | | | | |
| 44. Walls | | | | | | |
| 45. Trim | | | | | | |
| 46. Floors | | | | | | |
| 47. Hardware | | | | | | |
| 48. Doors | | | | | | |
| 49. Glass | | | | | | |
| 50. Lighting Fixtures | | | | | | |
| 51. Lighting Switches | | | | | | |
| 52. Convenience Outlets | | | | | | |
| 53. Waste Receptacles | | | | | | |
| 54. Sand Jars | | | | | | |
| 55. Fire Hose | | | | | | |
| 56. Fire Extinguishers | | | | | | |
| 57. Elevator Call Buttons | | | | | | |
| 58. Elevator Call Lights | | | | | | |
| 59. Elev. Doors and Trim | | | | | | |
| 60. Drinking Fountains | | | | | | |
| 61. Required Signs | | | | | | |
| 62. Safety Code Violations | | | | | | |
| 63. Hopper Rooms | | | | | | |
| 64. Maintenance | | | | | | |
| **Office Interiors** | | | | | | |
| 65. Ceilings | | | | | | |
| 66. Walls | | | | | | |
| 67. Floors | | | | | | |
| 68. Lighting | | | | | | |
| 69. Fixtures | | | | | | |
| 70. Switches | | | | | | |
| 71. Elec. Outlets | | | | | | |
| 72. Radiators | | | | | | |
| 73. Air Conditioning | | | | | | |
| 74. Doors | | | | | | |
| 75. Locks | | | | | | |
| 76. Transoms | | | | | | |
| 77. Hardware | | | | | | |
| 78. Baseboards | | | | | | |
| **Windows** | | | | | | |
| 79. Type | | | | | | |
| 80. Frames | | | | | | |
| 81. Sash | | | | | | |
| 82. Sills | | | | | | |
| 83. Stops | | | | | | |
| 84. Weights | | | | | | |
| 85. Glass | | | | | | |
| 86. Glazing | | | | | | |
| 87. Caulking | | | | | | |
| 88. Weatherstripping | | | | | | |
| 89. Locks | | | | | | |
| 90. Screens | | | | | | |
| 91. Window Treatments | | | | | | |

## Figure 4-4 (cont'd.)   Office Building Interior Inspection Report

### Office Building Interior Inspection Report
Page 3 of 10

| Items | Condition | | | Description | Repairs Needed | Est. Cost |
|---|---|---|---|---|---|---|
| | *Good* | *Fair* | *Poor* | | | |
| **Elevators—Passenger** | | | | | | |
| 92. Permit Exp. Date | | | | | | |
| 93. Serviced by | | | | | | |
| 94. Contract | | | | | | |
| 95. Full Maintenance | | | | | | |
| 96. Parts, Oil, Grease | | | | | | |
| 97. Make | | | | | | |
| 98. Type | | | | | | |
| 99. Capacity (Weight) | | | | | | |
| 100. Capacity (Psgrs.) | | | | | | |
| 101. Lobby Door Fronts | | | | | | |
| 102. Corridor Door Fronts | | | | | | |
| 103. Pit | | | | | | |
| 104. Full Automatic | | | | | | |
| 105. Self-leveling | | | | | | |
| 106. Door Operator | | | | | | |
| 107. Electric | | | | | | |
| 108. Air | | | | | | |
| 109. Manual | | | | | | |
| 110. Cab Size | | | | | | |
| 111. Cab Trim | | | | | | |
| 112. Cab Walls | | | | | | |
| 113. Cab Doors | | | | | | |
| 114. Cab Lighting | | | | | | |
| 115. Cab Ceiling | | | | | | |
| 116. Cab Floor | | | | | | |
| 117. Cab Ventilation | | | | | | |
| 118. Position Indicators | | | | | | |
| 119. Floor Indicator | | | | | | |
| 120. Signal Lanterns | | | | | | |
| 121. Signal Buttons | | | | | | |
| 122. Emergency Switches | | | | | | |
| 123. Telephone | | | | | | |
| 124. Elevator Shafts | | | | | | |
| 125. Pits | | | | | | |
| 126. Walls | | | | | | |
| 127. Guide Rails | | | | | | |
| 128. Hoisting Cables | | | | | | |
| 129. Compensating Cables | | | | | | |
| 130. Governor Cables | | | | | | |
| 131. Sheaves | | | | | | |
| 132. Motors | | | | | | |
| 133. Generators | | | | | | |
| 134. Governors | | | | | | |
| 135. Signs in Shaft | | | | | | |
| 136. Floor Nos. on Shaft | | | | | | |
| 137. Floor Nos. on Doors | | | | | | |
| 138. Control Panels | | | | | | |
| 139. Threshold Lights | | | | | | |
| 140. Comments | | | | | | |
| 141. | | | | | | |
| 142. | | | | | | |

**Figure 4-4 (cont'd.)   Office Building Interior Inspection Report**

## Office Building Interior Inspection Report
Page 4 of 10

| Items | Condition | | | Description | Repairs Needed | Est. Cost |
|---|---|---|---|---|---|---|
| | Good | Fair | Poor | | | |
| **Elevators—Freight** | | | | | | |
| 143. Permit Exp. Date | | | | | | |
| 144. Contract | | | | | | |
| 145. Serviced by | | | | | | |
| 146. Full Maintenance | | | | | | |
| 147. Parts, Oil, Grease | | | | | | |
| 148. Make | | | | | | |
| 149. Type | | | | | | |
| 150. Capacity (Pounds) | | | | | | |
| 151. Platform Size | | | | | | |
| 152. Platform Lighting | | | | | | |
| 153. Shaft Doors | | | | | | |
| 154. Cab Gates | | | | | | |
| 155. Hoisting Cables | | | | | | |
| 156. Compensating Cables | | | | | | |
| 157. Governor Cables | | | | | | |
| 158. Pit | | | | | | |
| 159. Motors | | | | | | |
| 160. Generators | | | | | | |
| 161. Signal Buttons | | | | | | |
| 162. Signal Buzzers | | | | | | |
| 163. Shaft Numbers | | | | | | |
| 164. Shaft Safety Signs | | | | | | |
| 165. Guide Rails | | | | | | |
| 166. Comments | | | | | | |
| 167. | | | | | | |
| **Rest Rooms—Men** | | | | | | |
| 168. Floors | | | | | | |
| 169. Floor Drain | | | | | | |
| 170. Walls | | | | | | |
| 171. Wainscot | | | | | | |
| 172. Ceiling | | | | | | |
| 173. Water Closet Type | | | | | | |
| 174. W.C. Enclosure | | | | | | |
| 175. Tank | | | | | | |
| 176. Flushing Valve | | | | | | |
| 177. Vacuum Breaker | | | | | | |
| 178. Seat | | | | | | |
| 179. Bowl | | | | | | |
| 180. Lavatory | | | | | | |
| 181. Trim | | | | | | |
| 182. Soap Dispensers | | | | | | |
| 183. Toilet Tissue Holders | | | | | | |
| 184. Urinal (Wall/Floor) | | | | | | |
| 185. Flushing Valve | | | | | | |
| 186. Stall Panel | | | | | | |
| 187. Hardware on Door | | | | | | |
| 188. Locks | | | | | | |
| 189. Deodorants | | | | | | |
| 190. Ventilation | | | | | | |
| 191. Light Fixtures | | | | | | |
| 192. Switches | | | | | | |

**Figure 4-4 (cont'd.)    Office Building Interior Inspection Report**

## Office Building Interior Inspection Report
Page 5 of 10

| Items | Condition | | | Description | Repairs Needed | Est. Cost |
|---|---|---|---|---|---|---|
| | Good | Fair | Poor | | | |
| **Rest Rms.—Men (cont.)** | | | | | | |
| 193. Windows | | | | | | |
| 194. Waste Receptacles | | | | | | |
| 195. Towel Cabinets | | | | | | |
| 196. Mirrors | | | | | | |
| 197. Signs | | | | | | |
| **Rest Rooms—Women** | | | | | | |
| 198. Floors | | | | | | |
| 199. Floor Drain | | | | | | |
| 200. Walls | | | | | | |
| 201. Wainscot | | | | | | |
| 202. Ceiling | | | | | | |
| 203. Water Closet Type | | | | | | |
| 204. W.C. Enclosure | | | | | | |
| 205. Tank | | | | | | |
| 206. Flushing Valve | | | | | | |
| 207. Vacuum Breaker | | | | | | |
| 208. Seat | | | | | | |
| 209. Bowl | | | | | | |
| 210. Lavatory | | | | | | |
| 211. Trim | | | | | | |
| 212. Soap Dispensers | | | | | | |
| 213. Toilet Tissue Holders | | | | | | |
| 214. Vanity Shelf | | | | | | |
| 215. San. Napkin Vendors | | | | | | |
| 216. Hardware on Door | | | | | | |
| 217. Locks | | | | | | |
| 218. Deodorants | | | | | | |
| 219. Ventilation | | | | | | |
| 220. Light Fixtures | | | | | | |
| 221. Switches | | | | | | |
| 222. Windows | | | | | | |
| 223. Waste Receptacles | | | | | | |
| 224. Towel Cabinets | | | | | | |
| 225. Mirrors | | | | | | |
| 226. Signs | | | | | | |
| **Emp. Rest Rms.—Men** | | | | | | |
| 227. Showers | | | | | | |
| 228. Water Closet | | | | | | |
| 229. Type | | | | | | |
| 230. Lavatory | | | | | | |
| 231. Urinal | | | | | | |
| 232. Lavatory Trim | | | | | | |
| 233. Floors | | | | | | |
| 234. Walls | | | | | | |
| 235. Ceiling | | | | | | |
| 236. Doors | | | | | | |
| 237. Lighting | | | | | | |
| 238. Heating | | | | | | |
| 239. Ventilation | | | | | | |
| 240. Switches | | | | | | |
| 241. | | | | | | |

## Figure 4-4 (cont'd.)   Office Building Interior Inspection Report

### Office Building Interior Inspection Report
Page 6 of 10

| Items | Condition | | | Description | Repairs Needed | Est. Cost |
|---|---|---|---|---|---|---|
| | Good | Fair | Poor | | | |
| **Emp. Rest Rms.—Women** | | | | | | |
| 242. Showers | | | | | | |
| 243. Water Closet | | | | | | |
| 244. Type | | | | | | |
| 245. Lavatory | | | | | | |
| 246. Trim | | | | | | |
| 247. Floors | | | | | | |
| 248. Walls | | | | | | |
| 249. Ceiling | | | | | | |
| 250. Doors | | | | | | |
| 251. Lighting | | | | | | |
| 252. Heating | | | | | | |
| 253. Ventilation | | | | | | |
| 254. Switches | | | | | | |
| 255. | | | | | | |
| **Locker Rooms—Men** | | | | | | |
| 256. Floors | | | | | | |
| 257. Walls | | | | | | |
| 258. Ceiling | | | | | | |
| 259. Lighting | | | | | | |
| 260. Switches | | | | | | |
| 261. Heating | | | | | | |
| 262. Ventilation | | | | | | |
| 263. Doors | | | | | | |
| 264. Fire Hazards | | | | | | |
| **Locker Rooms—Women** | | | | | | |
| 265. Floors | | | | | | |
| 266. Walls | | | | | | |
| 267. Ceiling | | | | | | |
| 268. Lighting | | | | | | |
| 269. Switches | | | | | | |
| 270. Heating | | | | | | |
| 271. Ventilation | | | | | | |
| 272. Doors | | | | | | |
| 273. Fire Hazards | | | | | | |
| **Basement Stairway** | | | | | | |
| 274. Entrance Door | | | | | | |
| 275. Treads | | | | | | |
| 276. Risers | | | | | | |
| 277. Handrails | | | | | | |
| 278. Walls | | | | | | |
| 279. Landings | | | | | | |
| 280. Ceilings | | | | | | |
| 281. Lighting | | | | | | |
| **Basement Area** | | | | | | |
| 282. Floors | | | | | | |
| 283. Sump Pumps | | | | | | |
| 284. Walls | | | | | | |
| 285. Ceilings | | | | | | |
| 286. Fire Doors | | | | | | |
| 287. No. of Exits | | | | | | |
| 288. Sprinkler System | | | | | | |

**Figure 4-4 (cont'd.)   Office Building Interior Inspection Report**

## Office Building Interior Inspection Report
Page 7 of 10

| Items | Condition | | | Description | Repairs Needed | Est. Cost |
|---|---|---|---|---|---|---|
| | Good | Fair | Poor | | | |
| **Basement Area (cont.)** | | | | | | |
| 289. Lighting | | | | | | |
| 290. Convenience Outlets | | | | | | |
| 291. Ventilation | | | | | | |
| 292. Elevator Service | | | | | | |
| 293. Storage Space | | | | | | |
| 294. Heating | | | | | | |
| 295. Utility Space | | | | | | |
| 296. Carpenter Shop | | | | | | |
| 297. Plumber | | | | | | |
| 298. Paint Shop | | | | | | |
| 299. Superintendent's Ofc. | | | | | | |
| 300. | | | | | | |
| **Boiler Room** | | | | | | |
| 301. Floor | | | | | | |
| 302. Walls | | | | | | |
| 303. Ceiling | | | | | | |
| 304. Fire Doors | | | | | | |
| 305. Fire Hazards | | | | | | |
| 306. Ventilation | | | | | | |
| 307. Lighting | | | | | | |
| 308. Switches | | | | | | |
| **Boilers** | | | | | | |
| 309. Type | | | | | | |
| 310. Pressure, High | | | | | | |
| 311. Pressure, Low | | | | | | |
| 312. Flues | | | | | | |
| 313. Tubes | | | | | | |
| 314. Draft Control | | | | | | |
| 315. Valves | | | | | | |
| 316. Blow-off Pit | | | | | | |
| 317. Vents | | | | | | |
| 318. Grates | | | | | | |
| 319. Firebox | | | | | | |
| 320. Pointing Fire Brick | | | | | | |
| 321. Steam Line Insulation | | | | | | |
| 322. Fuel | | | | | | |
| 323. Storage Tanks | | | | | | |
| 324. Coal Chutes | | | | | | |
| 325. Coal Bins | | | | | | |
| 326. Stokers | | | | | | |
| 327. Oil Burners | | | | | | |
| 328. Gas Burners | | | | | | |
| 329. Injectors | | | | | | |
| 330. Low Water Cutout | | | | | | |
| 331. Pop-off Valves | | | | | | |
| 332. Gauges, Pressure | | | | | | |
| 333. Gauges, Water Level | | | | | | |
| 334. Automatic Controls | | | | | | |
| 335. Diaphragms | | | | | | |
| 336. Flanges | | | | | | |
| 337. Gaskets | | | | | | |

## Figure 4-4 (cont'd.)  Office Building Interior Inspection Report

### Office Building Interior Inspection Report
Page 8 of 10

| Items | Condition | | | Description | Repairs Needed | Est. Cost |
|---|---|---|---|---|---|---|
| | Good | Fair | Poor | | | |
| **Boilers (cont.)** | | | | | | |
| 338. Packing Glands | | | | | | |
| 339. Draft Regulators | | | | | | |
| 340. Smoke Detectors | | | | | | |
| 341. Condensate Return | | | | | | |
| **Water Softeners** | | | | | | |
| 342. Type | | | | | | |
| 343. Sand Filters | | | | | | |
| 344. Valves | | | | | | |
| 345. Differential Gauges | | | | | | |
| 346. Filter Tank | | | | | | |
| 347. Softener | | | | | | |
| **Salt Tank** | | | | | | |
| 348. Coating | | | | | | |
| 349. Float Valve | | | | | | |
| 350. Overflow | | | | | | |
| 351. Tank | | | | | | |
| **Vacuum Pump Make** | | | | | | |
| 352. Storage Tank | | | | | | |
| 353. Ctrl. (Elec.) Make | | | | | | |
| 354. Ctrl. (Elec.) Voltage | | | | | | |
| 355. Float Switch Voltage | | | | | | |
| 356. Neg./Pressure Gauge | | | | | | |
| 357. Strainer | | | | | | |
| 358. Motor | | | | | | |
| 359. Type | | | | | | |
| 360. Horsepower Load | | | | | | |
| **Hot Water Heaters** | | | | | | |
| 361. Inside Lining | | | | | | |
| 362. Steam Coils | | | | | | |
| 363. Insulation | | | | | | |
| 364. Gaskets | | | | | | |
| 365. Thermostat | | | | | | |
| 366. Steam Trap | | | | | | |
| 367. Safety Valve | | | | | | |
| 368. Firebox | | | | | | |
| 369. Fuel | | | | | | |
| 370. Burner | | | | | | |
| **Pumps** | | | | | | |
| 371. Sump | | | | | | |
| 372. Pressure | | | | | | |
| 373. Feed Water | | | | | | |
| 374. Circulating | | | | | | |
| 375. Vacuum | | | | | | |
| **Compressors** | | | | | | |
| 376. Filters | | | | | | |
| 377. Automatic Switch | | | | | | |
| 378. Safety Valve | | | | | | |
| 379. Drive | | | | | | |
| 380. Motor Horsepower | | | | | | |
| 381. Tank Capacity | | | | | | |
| 382. Purpose of Comp. Air | | | | | | |

**Figure 4-4 (cont'd.)   Office Building Interior Inspection Report**

## Office Building Interior Inspection Report
Page 9 of 10

| Items | Condition | | | Description | Repairs Needed | Est. Cost |
|---|---|---|---|---|---|---|
| | Good | Fair | Poor | | | |
| **Vac. Pump—Cleaning Sys.** | | | | | | |
| 383. Auto. Switch Controls | | | | | | |
| **Air Conditioning** | | | | | | |
| 384. Window Units—Misc. | | | | | | |
| 385. | | | | | | |
| 386. | | | | | | |
| 387. | | | | | | |
| 388. | | | | | | |
| 389. Central System | | | | | | |
| 390. | | | | | | |
| 391. | | | | | | |
| 392. | | | | | | |
| 393. Orig. Installation Age | | | | | | |
| 394. Refrigeration | | | | | | |
| 395. Unit | | | | | | |
| 396. Refrigerant | | | | | | |
| 397. Compressor | | | | | | |
| 398. Capacity | | | | | | |
| 399. H.P. Connec. Load | | | | | | |
| 400. Performance | | | | | | |
| 401. Cooling Tower | | | | | | |
| 402. Air Distribution | | | | | | |
| 403. Ducts | | | | | | |
| 404. Insulation | | | | | | |
| 405. Grills | | | | | | |
| 406. Thermostats | | | | | | |
| 407. Zones | | | | | | |
| 408. Fans | | | | | | |
| 409. Performance | | | | | | |
| 410. | | | | | | |
| **Electric Panel Room** | | | | | | |
| 411. Transformer Capacity | | | | | | |
| 412. Voltage | | | | | | |
| 413. Cycle | | | | | | |
| 414. Power | | | | | | |
| 415. Lighting | | | | | | |
| 416. Phase Single | | | | | | |
| 417. Phase Three | | | | | | |
| 418. Panel Board Maker | | | | | | |
| 419. Amperage Capacity | | | | | | |
| 420. Power Circuits | | | | | | |
| 421. Lighting Circuits | | | | | | |
| 422. Emergency Circuits | | | | | | |
| 423. Standby Circuits | | | | | | |
| 424. Spare Circuits | | | | | | |
| 425. Fuses | | | | | | |
| 426. Circuit Breakers | | | | | | |
| 427. Meters | | | | | | |
| 428. Lighting Meter | | | | | | |
| 429. Power Meter | | | | | | |
| 430. Tenants' Meters | | | | | | |
| 431. | | | | | | |

## Figure 4-4 (cont'd.)   Office Building Interior Inspection Report

### Office Building Interior Inspection Report
Page 10 of 10

| Items | Condition | | | Description | Repairs Needed | Est. Cost |
|---|---|---|---|---|---|---|
| | Good | Fair | Poor | | | |
| **Misc. Items/Extras** | | | | | | |
| 432. | | | | | | |
| 433. | | | | | | |
| 434. | | | | | | |
| 435. | | | | | | |
| 436. | | | | | | |
| 437. | | | | | | |
| 438. | | | | | | |
| 439. | | | | | | |
| 440. | | | | | | |
| 441. | | | | | | |
| 442. | | | | | | |
| 443. | | | | | | |
| 444. | | | | | | |
| 445. | | | | | | |
| 446. | | | | | | |
| 447. | | | | | | |
| 448. | | | | | | |
| 449. | | | | | | |
| 450. | | | | | | |

**Detailed Notes for Recommendations on Interiors**

# THE OBJECTIVES OF OWNERSHIP

Owners in different situations will have different objectives. These objectives will determine how the management plan is written and what you will do with the information you have gathered.

Private individual owners may not have given any consideration to goals and objectives in the ownership of income property. As a property manager you will be able to show them different options. If they are willing to expend additional capital to make improvements, they will be able to increase the income and the value of the building. This, no doubt, will take several years to accomplish and would be reflected in your five-year forecast.

Some owners are interested primarily in the tax shelter benefits of ownership. They may not be willing to expend any capital for improvements. They are in a holding pattern and are happy with the money they save in taxes through depreciation. It's their property and the management plan will reflect their purpose for owning the property.

Some corporate owners and investment groups such as Real Estate Investment Trusts (REITs) are highly motivated for profit and will expend the necessary capital to increase the value of their facilities. Other institutions, such as trust departments of banks administering a trust for a beneficiary, are going to be very conservative. Their main objective is to lose nothing, so the investment income can continue for their client. They will spend money to protect the value of the facility, but not to try to increase its income.

# FINANCIAL ANALYSIS

With an understanding of the regional and local marketplace, comparable competing properties in the marketplace and the relative strengths of the subject property, the property's physical characteristics and owner's objectives, a financial analysis of the property needs to be prepared as demonstrated in Chapter 3. The property manager should know approxi-  mately the capital resources of the owner and the income requirements. He or she should know the leases in place on the property and have access to previous income statements. The manager should understand all expenses including property taxes, insurance premiums, management, maintenance, utilities, replacement reserves and any special assessments on the property.

Integrating all of this information, the manager will want to prepare an operating budget as a guide to keep expenses in line and income up, a five-year forecast to assist in planning, and a comparative analysis for capital expenditures, should there be a need to increase income. All of these reports can be found in Chapter 3.

# THE MANAGEMENT PLAN

The management plan will consist of those financial reports and projections that are accepted by ownership. If a comparative analysis for capital expenditures makes sense to the owner, it will be adopted as part of the management plan. This will reflect his or her goals and objectives and will indicate what the owner is willing and able to do. The five-year forecast will be adjusted according to the owner's wants and desires. It is the long term road map to the overall objective, while the operating budget is the short term compass to keep management on course.

The management plan also must reflect the respective duties of management and ownership. How much latitude will management have in spending money for advertising or for completing needed repairs? Who will hire employees and contract with workers? Whose employees are they, the management company's or the owner's? Tax and legal responsibility should be clearly established in a contract so no misunderstandings occur.

The owner of the property obviously has to stand as a backup for all financial shortfalls. If the income of the building is not sufficient to pay all necessary expenses, the owner must write checks. Anticipation of this, when and for what items and how much should be set forth in advance for ownership. The management fee must be agreed upon, as well as the method and timing of payment. Required reports and when they should be provided by management should be set forth clearly in writing.

Authority and responsibility should go hand in hand. All property managers should have authority commensurate with their responsibility. And whatever that is, it should be laid out in a contract in plain English. Rights of reimbursement for the manager also should be well established, as well as distribution of income and duties and responsibilities of the owner.

A management plan needs a comprehensive financial plan with enough flexibility to adjust to a changing marketplace, and a contract that allows management and ownership to work together toward the accomplishment of the owner's objectives.

When a well thought-out plan comes together with all the essential ingredients, property incomes and values can be maximized and their true highest and best use can be attained.

# QUESTIONS

1. A management plan takes into consideration:

   a. supply and demand in the area
   b. a financial analysis of the subject property
   c. the owner's objectives
   d. all of the above

2. The Irvine Spectrum in Southern California is:

   a. responsible for causing vacancies in the housing market
   b. a demand source for housing
   c. a large employer
   d. likely to decline within the next five years

3. External obsolescence refers to:

   a. a factor external to property lines that diminishes appeal
   b. an obsolete item attached to the exterior of the building
   c. a factor within the property lines that diminishes value
   d. an accounting procedure

4. All owners should spend money on their facilities to:

    a. offer an increased appeal to tenants

    b. ensure the safety of the
       occupants of the building

    c. increase the net operating
       income within five years

    d. none of the above

5. The Apartment Exterior Inspection Report considers all of the following items except:

    a. soil

    b. vestibules

    c. basement

    d. attic

6. The Apartment Exterior Inspection Report allows for the following:

    a. character and condition of the item

    b. estimated expense to correct the item

    c. notes and recommendations

    d. all of the above

7. The Apartment Exterior Inspection Report considers all of the following items pertaining to brick and stone except:

    a. chimneys

    b. court walls

    c. mortar

    d. cleanliness

8. The Apartment Exterior Inspection Report considers some "general interior" areas including:

    a. the living room

    b. the kitchen

    c. the vestibules

    d. all of the above

9. The Apartment Interior Inspection Report allows a manager to:

    a. prioritize repairs

    b. determine what items don't need to be fixed

    c. estimate the total cost of repairs

    d. all of the above

10. On the Apartment Interior Inspection Report, the inspection of the bedroom is:

    a. cursory at best
    b. thorough from ceiling to floor
    c. not systematic
    d. none of the above

11. On the Apartment Interior Inspection Report, the inspection of the kitchen is:

    a. for structural items only
    b. for fixtures only
    c. inclusive of structural items and functioning appliances
    d. for electrical items only

12. The Office Building Exterior Inspection Report allows for:

    a. assessment of condition of the item
    b. item manufacturer's name
    c. list cost of the item
    d. none of the above

13. On the Office Building Exterior Inspection Report, the freight elevator section considers all of the following items except:

    a. appearance
    b. electrical
    c. permit date
    d. mechanical

14. The Office Building External Inspection Report deals with all of the following items except:

    a. walls
    b. external drainage
    c. windows
    d. loading dock

15. All of the following would be considered "lobby" items on the Office Building Interior Inspection Report except:

    a. restrooms
    b. directory
    c. guard station
    d. glass

16. Corridor items on the Office Building Interior Inspection Report should be functional. These would include:

    a. fire extinguishers
    b. elevator call buttons
    c. drinking fountains
    d. all of the above

17. Passenger elevators would be one of the most crucial safety items in an office building. A property manager would inspect all of the following items except:

    a. permit expiration date
    b. cab door operation
    c. oil and grease
    d. none of the above

18. A basement area in an office building is likely to include:

    a. sump pumps
    b. security office
    c. no storage space
    d. a cafeteria

19. Objectives of ownership always include:

    a. increasing the net operating income
    b. improving the property
    c. selling today for a profit
    d. none of the above

20. A management plan must set forth:

    a. the authority of management
    b. the responsibilities of ownership
    c. a comprehensive financial plan
    d. all of the above

# ANSWERS

1. *d*
2. *b*
3. *a*
4. *b*
5. *d*
6. *d*
7. *c*
8. *c*
9. *d*
10. *b*
11. *c*
12. *a*
13. *b*
14. *b*
15. *a*
16. *d*
17. *d*
18. *a*
19. *d*
20. *d*

# Marketing

- **Keeping A Full House**
- **Determining The Rental Rate**
- **Marketing Factors**
- **Attracting Tenants**
- **Screening Tenants**
- **Demonstrating The Property**
- **Handling Objections**
- **Close**
- **The Application**
- **Signing Up The Applicant**

C H A P T E R

5

## KEEPING A FULL HOUSE

Marketing space that has become available is an essential part of the property manager's job. The effort that has to be put forth will vary according to many factors. There are times when it may be relatively easy to rent available space and not much money or effort is required. There will be other times when vacancies are widespread in the area and renting will take a great effort. At these times it must be remembered that a certain amount of money per month is being lost due to the vacancy. If a unit of space rents for $1,000 per month, that's $1,000 every month that is lost while the unit sits vacant. There is no benefit to that situation and the property manager must do whatever it takes to rent the unit.

## DETERMINING THE RENTAL RATE

How much do you ask for the rental space? You could go through the exercise of adding up all of the expenses and debt service payments over a 12-month period, then divide by 12 to get a monthly figure, then divide that by the number of units in your building to see how much money on average each unit has to bring in to break even. Then add in a factor so the owner has some return on his or her investment as expressed in the management plan. Frankly, such an exercise would be futile except as a reference point.

Rents are not what we would like them to be in order to break even or to make a certain percentage of profit. Rents are what they are as referenced to the marketplace, so we must reference our available space to the marketplace. We must survey the marketplace and know what the competition is getting for similar space with similar amenities. This is called the *market* rent and it is all we can count on. We can check the newspapers, property management companies in the area or knock on doors of similar units nearby and ask what tenants are paying. As no two buildings are identical in the characteristics and amenities offered, we must make adjustments as an appraiser would to determine the correct amount of rent we should charge.

If an apartment building in the area has a pool and yours doesn't, how much more rent do they receive because of the pool than a similar building without a pool? This could be determined by what an appraiser calls a *paired sales analysis*. You

pair up two properties that are as identical as possible in all respects except for one variable. In this case they would be similar types of apartment buildings in a similar part of town with similar square footage, bathrooms, laundry facilities, parking and other amenities. The only perceivable difference is the pool. So how much more per month does the building with the pool demand in rental income than the building without the pool? That's how much the pool is worth per unit.

When reviewing the comparable rents of the pool property with yours, you subtract the added value attributed to the pool from what the competing management actually receives. This represents what the competitors would get if they didn't have the pool and it more accurately reflects on what you can expect to receive for your rental unit because you don't have a pool. There may be other differences between your property and the pool property. If so, you must subtract the value of those features from the pool property if it has something else of value that your property does not have. If, however, your property has a feature that the pool property doesn't have, you must add the value of that feature to the rents of the pool property. That answers how much the pool property would rent for if it had that feature as your property does. The value of each feature is determined by a paired sales analysis. In that fashion, the pluses and minuses of all of the differences are reconciled, and the adjusted values of the comparable properties will reflect on the indicated value of your property in the marketplace.

This process is not as complicated as it sounds. Remember, however, that if the comparable properties you choose have too many differences that have to be accounted for with adjustments, they may not be the right comparables for your property. The more differences between the properties, the more adjustments that are required. The more adjustments, the more room for error. Choosing properties that are the most similar to yours will keep adjustments to a minimum.

# MARKETING FACTORS

Characteristics inherent in the property and factors relating to your property's particular marketplace will dictate the kind of effort necessary to fill the property with tenants.

## New or Established Property

Is the property you're renting new or is it established in the marketplace? If it is established, the effort to rent available space will be less than if the property is new. A new property may require a campaign to create an awareness in the community. This could mean banners and flags, open houses, grand openings with balloons as well as substantial advertising.

## Type of Property

Is the property residential, commercial or industrial? These different property types will require different approaches. A family looking for an apartment probably will buy the local newspaper. A company looking for an industrial plant probably would make discreet inquiries with a broker of industrial properties. A billboard near the property also might attract the tenant. A prominent sign on a commercial property or a display ad in the business section of the newspaper might get the job done. Potential tenants for each of these property types will go about looking for the property they need in different ways. We must determine how we can meet them in the marketplace.

## Vacancy Rate

What is the area-wide vacancy rate for this type of property at this time? In other words, what is the current supply and demand ratio of your type of property in your area? If demand is high and supply is short, you may not have to spend a lot of money or time marketing the property. However, if there is an oversupply of similar rental space available and low demand, a greater effort along with some creativity may have to be utilized to get the results. A property manager should always have his or her fingers on the pulse of supply and demand in the local area.

## Seasons

Some properties obviously are more affected by seasons than other properties. Residential rental units in recreational areas like the mountains or the ocean have peak seasons when demand is high and there is a scarcity of available units. Premium rents can be charged during these times. Tenancy usually is for shorter periods of time and is often arranged far in advance of the dates. Even properties not so obviously affected by seasons are impacted by the flow of time. Memorial Day marks the beginning of summer and Labor Day the end. People looking for residential space often

want to be settled before these holidays. That means demand is greatest just prior to these dates. The wise property manager meets demand in the marketplace, making sure people looking for rental space are aware of what that property offers.

## Property Particulars

How many units do you have available? Just one or quite a few? Is the unit a high or low ticket item? Is the market rent $250 per month or $2,500 per month? Are the units available now or later? Questions like these will determine the urgency of your need to rent the space. The greater the urgency, the more time, effort and money you expend to get the job done. What is the traffic location of the property? If the property is in a high traffic location, a sign could be the most important part of your marketing effort. If the property is in a more remote area with only a trickle of traffic, a sign might be only a small part of the effort.

## From Whence the Demand?

What type of clients are suitable for your rental property? We recognize that you cannot discriminate due to reasons of race, creed, color, sex, marital status and the like. Nevertheless, what kind of people would fit with your property best? Retired people? Young couples with children? Singles? Young or old? If your property has a spa, tennis courts, a pool and a gym, youthful and single might be your target market. If it has a nearby golf course and you can offer lawn bowling, the retired market might be more appropriate. The question you must ask is, "Where can I find these types of people?" What do they read? Where do they go? They must be reached where they are or where they might be found looking for a place to live.

# ATTRACTING TENANTS

Once property and marketplace characteristics are identified, the best methods for attracting tenants can be implemented. Consider the following strategies.

## Preparing the Property

Despite all of the creative methods of reaching prospective tenants, if the property does not look inviting, they will not come! In commercial and industrial property, businesses have an image to project and clients to attract. If the space they are considering will not help them accomplish that, there is no reason to rent the space.

Individuals and families also have images of themselves and images that they want others to perceive of them. Where you live and what you drive are important contributors to your image. You may not be able to help them with what they drive, but you are providing the place where they will live. If your apartment building is shabby on the outside, whether it's a four-plex or a 60-unit complex, it will not present the kind of image acceptable to the kind of client you want. This is to be their home! Images they most likely want to project are: they are in control; and they live in an apartment that is nice, safe, stylish and attractive. They also may have concerns about who the other tenants are. If the building presents a shabby, unkempt appearance, what kind of people find that acceptable? Do they want to be neighbors with them? Who will their children be playing with? Will they be safe? What does the appearance of the building say about the likelihood of crime? Crime, of course, occurs everywhere in isolated instances, but some buildings look like crime is an everyday occurrence. People feel that in their gut and keep on going.

Another thing people understand instinctively is that the interior of a building is usually about the same quality as the exterior. If a building is sharp on the outside, it's probably sharp on the inside. If it's shabby on the outside, the same is probably true on the inside. This is the assumption appraisers make while looking at comparable properties when they do not have access to the interior. Only rarely is this not the case. If you have units that you have fixed up and decorated nicely on the interior but you've neglected the exterior, yours will be one of those exceptions. Nobody will ever know it, however, because the majority of prospective tenants will never get out of their cars if the exterior of the building is not inviting.

So the property manager must prepare the property. It is an important part of the marketing process. The exterior must be appealing from the curb. Paint should be neat and attractive. Doors, windows, screens and trim should be in good repair. Landscaping need not be lavish, but should be neat and inviting, and have a positive effect on the appearance of the property.

The interior of the unit should be clean and ready to show. First impressions count. Even though the carpet is about to be cleaned, the first sight of it showing filthy stains conjures up unpleasant images of the activities and lifestyle that was carried on here previously. Painting should be finished. Towel racks and window coverings should be in place. Kitchen and bathroom fixtures should be functioning properly, with any leaks already repaired.

We are concerned here with things the prospective tenant sees and smells. The source of unpleasant odors should be eradicated. Then pleasant odors should be introduced with air fresheners or pine-scented cleaners. A couple of drops of vanilla extract on a hot stove or oven does wonders for the olfactory senses in the kitchen. The bathroom should smell clean and fresh. With these simple efforts we are conjuring up pleasant and desirable images of the apartment as a place to call home.

It may not always be possible to have a unit available to show that is in *move-in* condition. There are several alternatives when this is the case. If it is a large apartment complex, vacancy will never be at zero. Someone will always be moving in or out. So take advantage of the vacancy factor and use one of the units as a model. Furnish it attractively but simply, not being extravagant but commensurate with the economic means of the tenants. Keep the walls and flooring the same as in all of the units. Don't wallpaper the model or have special window coverings to make it more attractive. This will backfire when the tenant moves into his or her unit. They may ask for changes or be disgruntled when those changes are not forthcoming.

Another possibility is to have a stipulation in the rental contract that current tenants agree to allow their units to be shown by the manager to prospective tenants. If there is resistance to this request, it may not be a good idea to insist on this clause. It may be possible, however, to obtain this agreement for a small rent concession with one or two tenants. The concession could well be worth it if it prevents you from losing a qualified tenant. You would want to have an understanding that the unit should be presentable during the hours that you need to show it. The alternative of last resort would be to show a unit dirty and in disrepair. It's just too hard to appeal to the prospect when so many of the images are negative. If the first two alternatives are not available, it's probably better to get the prospect's name, phone number and as much other information as you can and call him or her as soon as possible to show a unit.

## Newspapers and Other Papers

In most areas there are newspapers of various sizes and levels of effectiveness. Sometimes it is possible to use a more local paper, save money and still find a tenant. In many areas, there are throw-aways and free shopping papers that are widely read. In other times and locations, the larger, more expensive newspaper is required to get the job done. You must learn your area and which papers are effective.

### CLASSIFIED ADS

Classified ads are the smaller ads most people looking for an apartment would investigate. A column is about an inch wide and most ads are sold by the number of words or by the column inch. You must get the most for your advertising dollar in a very small space. While this is true, some advertisers abbreviate so much that the reader tires of the effort to interpret all of the initials and moves on to the next ad. Consider the difficulty of understanding the following ad.

> 2bd 1ba w/w cpt. a/c, 1/r
> sec. sm. dep. o.a.c.

When it starts to look like an e-mail address, a lot of people are going to tune out. Also, ads should avoid a lot of unnecessary words. Consider the following.

> 3 bd 2 ba. Clean and nice. Available
> now. Security deposit required.

Most readers would assume the unit was available now, otherwise it wouldn't be advertised. Or if it weren't available for several weeks the ad would state that. Clean and nice? It has to be clean or most tenants wouldn't even consider it. Nice? What does that mean? Security deposit required? Almost all units require a security deposit so it's not news and is not going to make the phone ring. That's the purpose of the ad you know, to make the phone ring. To put you in conversation with someone who could actually move in and pay the rent. So don't waste your advertising dollar on words that don't help the phone to ring.

By the same token, don't make the phone ring so much by not having any qualifying information in the ad that it wastes a lot of your time. If you won't have a unit available for two weeks, say so! Why waste time talking to lots of people who have to be in in four days? If you won't accept pets, tell them in the ad! Why waste time talking to pet owners who are hoping to find a place for their six cats? Eliminate them from the outset.

There is a formula in classified advertising that is well known in marketing circles as the *AIDA* formula. It goes like this.

**A**–Attention

**I**–Interest

**D**–Desire

**A**–Action

A classified ad is small and there's not a lot of space to accomplish each of these steps, but let's see how it might work. First, you must grab a reader's attention. Look at this string of ads that appeared recently in the classified section of a newspaper.

| |
|---|
| ● Large 2BR, a/c, ciel fan, clean. Near Ball/Knott. $640/mo. 714-555-7296. |
| Lge 2Br, 1Ba, $675/mo + $675 dep. 301 N. Blaisy. Don't contact tenants. 714-555-9107 |
| ● LRG 2BR 2BA 4-PLEX ● Encl gar, w/d hkups, a/c, d/w. Sml pet ok. $725. 555-2087 |
| Lrg 3br, 2ba. New crpt, tile, pnt. AC, dw, gar, fnced yrd, $875. wtr pd. 714-555-2899 |
| Luxury spac 2br 2ba, lg prv patio. Pool, a/c, rec rm, walk to schls. From $745, 555-8774 |
| Private 2Br 1Ba, new crpt/pnt, 2-car gar, coin op lndry, 807 Cogdonia, $710. Agt 555-3133 |
| Quiet, clean 1BR, downstairs, patio, walk-in closet, $150 sec. $520 mo. 714-555-2430 |
| Spacious 2BR upper, gar, pool, lndry, sm quiet cmplx, no pets nr Disnylnd $650. 555-6246 |

| |
|---|
| SPECIAL ON MOVE IN One bedroom apartments available now. From $500 to $600. If you are interested please call 714- 555-8098 or 714-555-3450 Open Monday thru Saturday |
| ■ **$495 MOVES YOU IN** ■ Large 1 & 2Br, $585 & up. Pool, all utilities paid. Cats OK. Near 22 frwy & Beach Blvd. (714) 555-3687. |
| 2BR 1½BA TOWNHOME Available now in Garden Grove Move-in Special, NO DEPOSIT Call Rafaela 714-555-3751 |
| **$450 MOVES YOU IN** 1Bd, 1Ba, apartment. Call Mngr -Christina (714) 555-7252. Rent: $515 Deposit: Euclid/ Palma Vista. SPM 555-8788 |

Some pretty ordinary looking ads and then all of a sudden one with a bold heading that calls attention to the low move-in costs. That should get the attention of people who need to find a place to live but don't have a lot of up-front cash. Here are some other ads that show various attempts at fulfilling the *attention* step of the AIDA formula.

The next step is to generate interest. In this type of ad, interest is accomplished by simply expressing the basic features of the property. *"...3 bedroom, 2 bath, enclosed garage..."* When it matches what the prospect is looking for, interest generates for that person. Your property will not be of interest to everyone. But how many tenants do you need for one unit? Just the right one!

The next step is to create desire. This is done through an appeal to the emotions, mentioning an additional feature in such a way as to conjure up an appealing image that makes the prospect desire the property. *"...Lovely floral gardens...Quiet setting...Underground parking garage..."* Whatever the feature is, the prospect begins to think, "Boy, that would be nice. I never thought of that!" And desire is born.

Action is the next step. All of this attention, interest and desire is without merit if the prospect never calls. If we just say, *"Call now!"* that's not likely to have much effect on our readers. That's what *we* want them to do, but people do what *they* want to do, not what *we* want them to do. They act in their own best interests. So it would be better if we could stimulate them to action by appealing to what will benefit them. If we said, *"One unit left,"* the prospect might reason that since the features sound very appealing and he or she would like to live in such a place, it's better to call right away so as not to miss out. If we said, *"Move in special with this ad!"*, prospects again figure that since the rental unit sounds so appealing and matches what they want anyway, why not take advantage of some special concessions on move-in costs? Bait the hook to suit the fish.

Here are some classified ads that bring it all together.

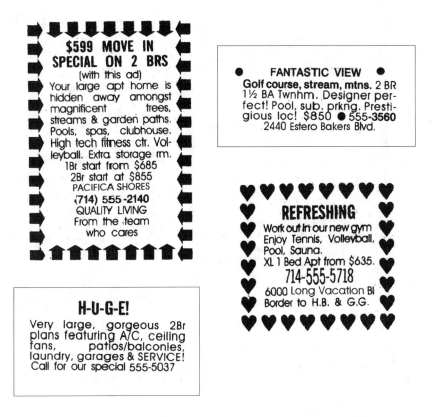

## DISPLAY ADS

Display ads are larger, more expensive ads that are meant to draw more attention. They are obviously for larger residential complexes, usually with some ongoing vacancies at all times. They are usually wider than one column and may on occasion take up a whole page. They can use graphics and pictures, and can tell a more complete story. However, they still should include the means of gaining a prospect's attention, interest, desire and action. Following are some display ads for an apartment building in a local newspaper.

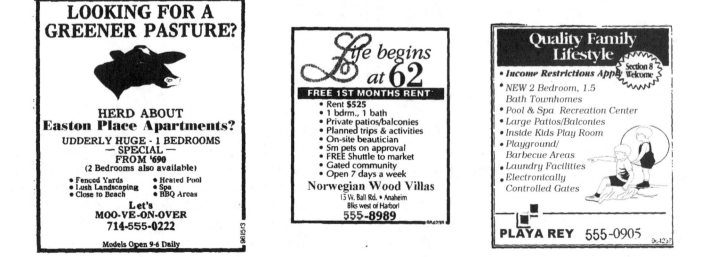

## Signs On or Near the Property

Signs can be a very effective means of finding the right tenant. Many people simply drive around looking in general areas where they think they might be interested in living. If they see a sign and like what they see of the property, they'll call and want more information or want to see the inside. Some signs have been expanded to banners and have been hung on apartment complexes with very creative messages. One favorite, brightly colored banner, positioned next to a crowded freeway at rush hour says, *"If you lived here, you'd be home now!"*

When a property is soon to be available, a sign should go up right away. This may save additional expense of advertising. In rare instances a sign should not be used, or should be used with caution. If the property is a single unit, vacant and in a remote area or far from the property manager, the sign may invite break-ins and vandalism. These circumstances should be weighed carefully.

When using signs continuously in an area, a property manager should design a distinctive sign so as to benefit from name recognition over time. A manager can build a reputation with his or her name and make it easier in the future to rent the properties.

## Fliers

Fliers allow a property manager to say much more than in a newspaper ad. You can include photos and graphics and tell the whole story of a property, listing all the advantages, facts and emotional appeals. Fliers are also less expensive than newspaper advertising. The problem with fliers is where to put them. If you put them on the windshields of cars in a parking lot you're wasting the effort because the vast majority of those people will not be candidates for tenancy. Fliers also have a *low ticket item* connotation and tend to cheapen a quality property. They should be used sparingly and in the right place. One good spot is in the hands of quality tenants who might pass it on to someone they know who also would like to live in your units. Another place might be in the window of a nearby store where the general public sees it. Don't post it on telephone poles where typically garage sales are posted. It will not have much appeal as a quality property. And remember to date fliers and take them down when they're obsolete. If your fliers remain in place forever, it'll be like the boy who cried wolf. No one will believe you anymore.

## Rental Guides

In some areas there are rental guides that are comprised of listing upon listing of residential rental properties available. Placement in the publication is usually free for the landlord or property manager and the prospective tenant pays a nominal fee for so many weeks of receiving the listings. The lists are updated every week to stay current. Prospects are not prequalified in any way but they will find out about your property as they read the list. The price is right and it can generate a lot of activity.

## Agencies

Apartment agencies locate tenants and qualify them as part of their service at no charge to the tenant. You would provide all of the facts about your units to the agency. They would advertise to attract tenants, run credit checks and send them out to look at properties that sound of interest to them. The agency then either takes applications and deposits and send them to you prequalified, ready to sign your lease, or signs them to your lease in advance. They charge a fee based on the first month's rent—sometimes 50%, sometimes 100%. It can be a cost-effective way to find a quality tenant. And if the tenant doesn't work out, the agency can be made to stand behind their recommendation and provide another tenant at no additional charge.

Some individual real estate agents working in real estate offices also may provide this service to you and prospective tenants. Your relationship should be set out clearly in a written contract and they should be made to stand behind their recommendations.

## Organizations

Colleges, military bases and some large employers have housing offices where they provide assistance to their students and members to find housing. It is to the advantage of the organizations to do so. They will be happy to have all of the information about your apartment units available to their people so they can contact you for an appointment. This is a good place for your fliers or whatever information they will allow you to post. Develop a good relationship with the person who works in that office and you will probably never have any trouble with referrals and recommendations for your units.

The Housing Authority of the various counties under the auspices of the Department of Housing and Urban Development (HUD) and Section 8 also offers a list of tenants who are looking for a house or apartment. These tenants are on some type of government assistance, but Section 8 will pay the majority of their rent. The tenant pays the remaining portion (usually about 20%) and if he or she fails to pay, the person will lose all benefits. The Housing Authority requires that the property be clean and safe and it does an inspection before the tenant moves in and after the tenant moves out. Any damages are paid for by the Housing Authority; then you can rent it to another tenant. The Housing Authority has already conducted a rent survey and will tell you what it will pay for what size unit in what areas, so much of the work is done for you. The rents are virtually guaranteed and the condition of the property is guaranteed, so it's not a bad way to go in some situations.

## Bulletin Boards

Certain organizations have bulletin boards which they won't mind your using to post useful information like available housing. Churches, union halls, senior centers, school offices, businesses and the like have nothing to lose and everything to gain by allowing such information to be made known. Use a bright colored 3 x 5 card, date it, and put in large bold letters, "RENTAL AVAILABLE." Put pertinent information on the card as you would with a classified ad. Some bulletin boards will be read and get more response than others. Take the cards down when they are obsolete, the same as with fliers. Do not put cards or fliers in mailboxes without a postage stamp on them.

## Bus Stops and Busses

A highly visible form of advertising is bus stop benches and enclosures, and the sides of busses themselves. This medium probably would be used by a manager with a large complex that continuously has vacancies. Many real estate companies use this medium. The cost to benefit relationship would have to be investigated to decide if this type of advertising is for you.

## Billboards

Billboard advertising is expensive and would have to be reserved for properties that have the budget to accommodate it. Location also would be critical to the success of this method. Proper research will reveal the answer.

## TV and Radio

TV and radio are also possibilities, but obviously would have to be reserved for large complexes with continuous vacancies and a substantial budget. TV and radio time can be negotiated and deals can be worked out in certain markets. For example, if a radio station has air time that is not committed, it might make a deal based on a certain fee percentage of each tenant you acquire. With this type of arrangement, you don't pay unless  and until you benefit, the same as with an apartment agency. You will never know until you ask. If such an arrangement cannot be made at the present time, leave your name and phone number with the sales manager and perhaps sometime in the future this can be worked out.

## Word-Of-Mouth

One of the least expensive and best ways to find a new tenant is through word of mouth. That's the recommendation of some of your best tenants to friends and acquaintances—people they would enjoy as neighbors in your building. You probably want to reserve soliciting word of mouth recommendations to your best tenants. They are likely to make the best referrals. After all, you wouldn't want to publish a notice to all of your tenants that you're looking for referrals from them and then receive a lot of referrals from the kind of tenant you'd like to replace. Their referrals may be just like them!

Even if your referrals come from your best tenants, there can be difficulties with this method. If a close friend or relative of a tenant is referred, that good tenant who made the referral is hoping and expecting that the referral will be accepted and the person will soon be moving in. But it's important that each applicant stand on his or her own merits. The referral may have some serious income or credit questions that would prevent you from accepting any other applicant with those conditions. You have to turn down this applicant also. This can create hard feelings and put a strain on a relationship that previously had no problems. You should tell your tenants that you will have to qualify all applicants on their own and that you can't make any favors to get someone in. This still will not avoid all hard feelings, but it's better to be on record.

What if you accept the referred applicant and he or she develops problems later? Any action you may have to take could jeopardize the relationship with the tenant who is a relative or friend. Still, it's difficult to turn down a word-of-mouth referral. Quite often they work out well.

## Waiting List

All property managers should maintain a waiting list. Applicants who inquire about a three-bedroom unit when only twos are available should be reachable in the near future should conditions change. This can be the quickest, most cost efficient way to find a tenant. The dollars have already been spent that resulted in the initial contact. Why not ride piggy back on those dollars and turn one of those qualified applicants into a tenant?

## Direct Mail

This is an aggressive technique that can be very effective in times of oversupply and lagging demand. Send an appealing invitation to tenants of nearby rental units. Include a cover letter explaining your offer and a brochure detailing the amenities and benefits of living in your complex. You might decide to schedule an open house so that prospects can come by and inspect the property.

Greet them with refreshments and offer a tour of the premises, showing them a model or specific units that are available. Structure a special incentive for such prospects, including paying moving costs or half off the first month's rent. The amenities of your building may meet the needs of certain tenants better than their existing place of residence. You probably should avoid this technique in situations where you know the other manager or company personally or have cooperated with them professionally. It is important to maintain relationships in business and in life.

# SCREENING TENANTS

Now that you've attracted lots of prospects by the marketing techniques mentioned above, let's make sure they're desirable. You don't have to accept everyone who applies. In fact, you owe it to your owner to be as discriminating as possible to protect the investment in the property. Did you hear the word *discriminating*? You thought it was illegal to discriminate? It is, on the basis of religion, race, sex, creed, color, national origin or marital status. But it is not illegal to discriminate on the basis of ability to pay, willingness to pay or the likelihood that the prospects will do damage to the property. It just makes good sense to give consideration to these issues. Work hard at this early stage to get good tenants. It will reduce the number of problems you have later.

## Ask a Lot of Questions

 How many rooms are they looking for? How many are in their family? How many occupants will be in the unit? Where do they live now? Why are they leaving? How many children do they have? Do they have any pets? Do they have a waterbed? When do they need to take occupancy? If any of these answers don't match up with your requirements you can tell them so and eliminate them early in the process, saving a lot of time. If—based on preliminary questioning—they look like a prospect for your units, set a time for them to see the property.

## Ability to Pay

Different ratios of income to debt may be used in different areas. In some areas, it is felt that a tenant needs to pay no more than 25% of his or her gross income for housing or rent. This would be called the *front end* ratio. In other areas a higher percentage may be allowed for the front end ratio out of necessity. Another rule of thumb is sometimes called the *back end* ratio. This would include all fixed debt an individual had, including housing costs, car payments, credit cards and other consumer debt. The generally accepted maximum ratio would be 40% of their gross income. This, as all figures, should be referenced to your local area.

The best way to verify income is to ask to see pay stubs. That prevents any type of deception on the phone.

## Willingness to Pay

This has to do with a person's character. The best way to make a guess about his or her willingness to pay is to check credit history. You could call random references on the application and request payment information, or you could just have the local apartment association run a full credit check for a nominal fee charged to the tenant. A good payment record in the past is probably the best indicator of what the tenant intends for the future.

Peripheral issues that would contribute to your opinion of a tenant's willingness to pay are history of employment stability, amount of reserves and references. You should check especially with current and previous landlords. Beware, however, that various sources of reference may have a vested interest in seeing to it that the tenants move on and might be favorable just to get rid of them. Each piece of information is only part of the puzzle and you should look for consistency in all of the stories and all of the information.

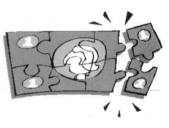

## Likelihood to Damage the Property

There are a number of clues that would reveal tenants' likelihood to damage property. Do they have pets? How many and what kind? One kitten can shred carpets and drapes and create an odor from the litter box. Multiple cats could be disastrous. Any animal allowed in the unit that is not contained in a cage or an enclosed tank has potential for damage. Set your own rules about that.

Do the tenants have a waterbed? A waterbed that leaks or bursts can do significant damage to carpeting and flooring. Check the laws for your state or local area. You may have to make reasonable accommodations for a water bed if the tenant will provide an insurance policy to pay any damage.

Another indicator could be ascertained by paying a visit to the tenant's current residence. You can be in the area and call them with application in hand ostensibly to gather a bit more information. The main benefit of this kind of visit is to see how they live. Have they destroyed the unit they currently live in? Are there animals around that are not listed on your application? Is there an automobile engine sitting on the carpet in the living room? Is the carpet filthy and are there holes in the walls? Habits die hard and what their current residence looks like will be what yours will look like in a short time. This is the best indicator of whether you can trust them with the assets of your property.

# DEMONSTRATING THE PROPERTY

When showing the property you do not just walk through empty rooms stating, "This is the kitchen," "This is the living room," and so forth. Might sharp tenants not be able to figure out the identity of the rooms themselves? You must create an image as you demonstrate the property and you must sell the benefits. It has been said that nobody wants to buy a *drill*; it's *holes* that they want!

When showing a small kitchen, enthusiastically emphasize the benefits. Say something like this. "This is what's called an efficiency kitchen. Everything you need is within a few steps from the counterspace and cutting board. Just turn around and within a step or two is the stove, the sink and dishwasher. Everything is handy for presenting the food to the lovely dining room. And cleanup is a breeze, just a few minutes and you're done."

When showing a large kitchen, again emphasize the benefits. "Isn't this kitchen beautiful? Plenty of cabinet space for storage, counter space galore to prepare the food, beautiful stove and dishwasher."

All spacious, lovely and inviting! "The living room isn't just a living room. It has the small balcony outside with the sliding glass door and screen, and the lovely trees offering privacy and the refreshing breeze that wafts through at the end of the day. What a wonderful, peaceful, comfortable place to relax!"

People don't want square and rectangular rooms. They want a place where they can *feel* a certain way—comfortable, secure, relaxed, restful and happy. This is the image you must work to create. Show the *lighting.* Show the *privacy.* Show the *safety* and *security.* Let the prospect feel the breeze if it's available. Sell the benefits and sign up many more tenants.

# HANDLING OBJECTIONS

Yes, handling objections! You're doing a bit of selling here, you know. If the prospect objects saying, "The bedroom is too small," you owe your employer your best effort to overcome the objection. Feed it back to them.

> Prospective Tenant (PT): *The bedroom's too small!*
>
> Property Manager (PM): *The bedroom's too small?*
>
> PT: *Well yeah, it just doesn't seem to be very big.*
>
> PM: *Do you have a lot of furniture?*
>
> PT: *Just a dresser, bed and night stand.*
>
> PM: *Would you put the head of the bed up against the window, and maybe the dresser over there?*
>
> PT: *Yeah, it might fit.*
>
> PM: *The rooms are about average size for the area, but we've priced them competitively. Let's take a look at the kitchen.*

Many objections are expressed just to slow down the pace a bit, a kind of thinking out loud process. Some don't have very much validity even to the person expressing them. When you can help them rationalize how to deal with the various characteristics they find, you are helping them move in. Sometimes there are advantages to the features found in the apartment that the tenant has never considered. Maybe the features have been built in for the purpose of energy efficiency to keep the bills down.

> Prospective Tenant: *Oh, the stove is electric! I much prefer gas.*
>
> Property Manager: *A lot of our tenants were used to gas, but when they moved here, they got used to the electric right away. What they found was it saved them on the monthly utility bills and it actually makes the kitchen easier to clean. Gas tends to send up a lot more oil and vaporizing debris that settles on the stove top and all surfaces. So most of them end up preferring the electric.*

Now you're not going to be able to answer all objections and you're not going to be able to make everyone happy. You can't color coordinate to suit every tenant and you can't change the carpet every time someone doesn't like the way it looks. You have to operate within certain economic constraints and you have to appeal to the *general* public. That means go with what *most* people will like. But know the drawbacks and the benefits. Be honest with people and give them a vision of the agreeable lifestyle they would have by living in your building.

# CLOSE

There is an old saying, "A man convinced against his will, is of the same opinion still." When it comes to sales, truer words were never spoken. You cannot get someone to do what they don't want to do. But if the benefits you pointed out are advantageous to them, they may be in agreement with you. Invite them to fill out an application and ask for a deposit. It's up to you to make the first move.

# THE APPLICATION

Have the prospect fill out the application completely. Leaving out any information may be interpreted as having something to hide. Current address should be obtained. Names and ages of all occupants should be provided. Current and previous residences, landlords, phone numbers, length of time and reason for leaving should all be clearly stated. Drivers' license numbers and social security numbers can provide valuable information. Employment history and income will tell whether or not the prospects can afford to live in your building and the likelihood of them paying. Get credit card numbers, name of bank, current license number of car and persons to notify in case of emergency. Then scrutinize the application very carefully. If there are any inconsistencies seek clarification. Call the references and ask questions. Ask references

to give you information without revealing everything the applicant wrote on the application. See if the applicant's story matches up with the referral's story. If the applicant has misrepresented something up front, chances are there will be some problems down the line.

## Figure 5-1   Standard Application

### APPLICATION TO RENT AND RENTAL DEPOSIT

Application to rent property at _____

**Full name of applicant** _____    **Co-applicant/spouse** _____

Phone (____) _____ Date of birth ___/___/___    Phone (____) _____ Date of birth ___/___/___

Present address _____    Present address _____

City/State/Zip _____    City/State/Zip _____

Name of current landlord/manager _____    Name of current landlord/manager _____

Landlord/manager's phone (____) _____    Landlord/manager's phone (____) _____

How long at present address _____    How long at present address _____

Reason for leaving _____    Reason for leaving _____

If present address is less than one year, list prior address and indicate landlord/managers name and phone number: _____

Name(s) of all other occupant(s) and relationship to applicant: _____

An application to rent is required for any occupant 18 years of age or over.

Pet(s) (number and type) _____

**Applicant:** Soc. Sec. No. _____ Driver's license no. _____ State _____ Expires _____

Present employer _____ How long with this employer _____

Employer's address _____ City _____ Zip _____ Phone (____)

Position or title _____ Gross income $_____ per _____

Other income $_____ per _____ Source _____

Auto make _____ Model _____ Year _____ License no. _____ State _____ Color _____

If present employment is less than one year, list immediate prior employment information: _____

**Co-applicant:** Soc. Sec. No. _____ Driver's license no. _____ State _____ Expires _____

Present employer _____ How long with this employer _____

Employer's address _____ City _____ Zip _____ Phone (____)

Position or title _____ Gross income $_____ per _____

Other income $_____ per _____ Source _____

Auto make _____ Model _____ License no. _____ State of registry _____ Color _____

If present employment is less than one year, list immediate prior employment information: _____

Do you plan to use liquid filled furniture? ☐ No ☐ Yes Type _____

Has either applicant been a party to an unlawful detainer action or filed bankruptcy within the last seven years? ☐ No ☐ Yes

If yes, explain _____

In case of emergency, person to notify _____ Relationship _____

Address _____ City _____ Zip _____ Phone (____)

**Credit Information**

| Appl./Co-appl. | Name of creditor | Account number | Monthly payment | Balance Due |
|---|---|---|---|---|
| | | | | |
| | | | | |

**Bank Account Information**

| Appl./Co-appl. | Name of bank | Address/branch | Account number | Type of account |
|---|---|---|---|---|
| | | | | |

Applicant(s) represent(s) the above information to be true, correct and complete and hereby authorize(s) verification of the information provided, including obtaining credit report(s) at the actual cost of $_____ to be paid by applicant(s). The cost of the credit report is not a deposit or rent, and will not be applied to future rent or refunded, even if the application to rent is declined. Applicant(s) understand(s) that the landlord may terminate any rental agreement entered into for any misrepresentation made above.

Date _____ Time _____    Date _____ Time _____

Applicant _____ Phone (day) _____ Phone (eve.) _____    Co-applicant _____ Phone (day) _____ Phone (eve.) _____

Applicant(s) has/have deposited the Sum of _____ Dollars $_____

evidenced by: ☐ Cash ☐ Cashier's Check ☐ Personal Check ☐ or _____ payable

to _____ , to be held uncashed until approval of the application to rent, as deposit

on the property located at _____ at a monthly rent of $_____.

The property to be occupied only by the person(s) named in the application. In the event the application to rent is not approved within _____ days, this deposit shall be returned to applicant(s). If approved, the ☐ month-to-month rental, ☐ lease, or ☐ other _____

shall commence on _____ , 20___. Additional Terms: _____

### TOTAL SUMS DUE PRIOR TO OCCUPANCY:

Rent for the period _____ to _____ $_____

Security deposit (not applicable toward last months rent) .................. $_____

Other _____ $_____

Other _____ $_____

Total . . . . . . . . . . . . . . . . . . . . . . . . . . . . . . . . . . . . . . . . . . . . . . $_____

Less amount received above . . . . . . . . . . . . . . . . . . . . . . . . . . . . . . $_____

Balance due, on or before _____ , 20___ $_____

In addition to the above, applicant(s) has/have paid $_____ for the credit report(s) and agree(s) to execute the lease or rental agreement on the reverse. The undersigned has/have read the foregoing and acknowledges receipt of a copy.

Applicant _____ Date _____    Co-applicant _____ Date _____

OFFICE USE ONLY

Reviewed by Broker or Designee _____

Date _____

# SIGNING UP THE APPLICANT

If the applicant has been thoroughly investigated and found desirable to have as a tenant, have him or her come in to sign the rental agreement. Before signing the rental agreement, however, go over the rules of the building with the prospect. New tenants should have a clear understanding of what is expected of them and what will not be tolerated. Let them know in a friendly but firm way that if they anticipate difficulty with any of these rules, it would be better to state it now and reconsider the decision to move in because the rules are for the benefit of all and will be enforced.

## Figure 5-2    The Rules

**JTA PROPERTY MANAGEMENT
RESIDENTIAL LEASE AGREEMENT
AND DEPOSIT RECEIPT
ADDENDUM**

**Tenant:**_____

**Address:**_____

1. **Rent** - All rent must be paid in full each month. Tenant may <u>not</u> discount or deduct their rent at any time for any reason

2. **Security Deposit** - It is clearly understood that the Security Deposit is <u>not</u> to be used toward the last months rent. It is a Deposit for the performance of the terms of the Residential Lease Agreement. Said Security Deposit will be returned to the Tenant within 3 (three) weeks <u>after</u> the Tenant has vacated the property and has returned <u>all</u> keys.

3. **Deductions from Security Deposit** - Could be the following costs:
   - Any necessary cleaning, beyond normal wear and tear i.e. carpets, appliances, bathrooms, floors, walls windows, window coverings, etc.
   - Any damage repairs caused by neglect or abuse of Tenant.
   - Removal of Tenants personal effects, property or unwanted items.
   - Touch-up, prep., repair, to walls from picture hook holes.
   - Pest control spraying (if Tenant had a pet).

4. **Notice to Vacate** - A <u>minimum</u> of a 30 (thirty) Day <u>Written</u> Notice to Vacate is required from all Tenants, whether in the last 30 (thirty) Days of a multiple month Lease Agreement, or on a month to month basis. The 30 (thirty) Day Notice is effective 30 (thirty) days from the date received in our office. All rent will continue to be due ad payable in full. Tenant will allow the showing of the property during this 30 (thirty) Day Notice period with the maximum of a 24 (twenty-four) hour notice.

5. **Smoke Detector** - Tenant is aware of a working smoke detector in the premises and is solely responsible for and it's maintenance, replacing the battery and keeping it in proper working condition. Tenant is responsible for checking the battery on a monthly basis.

6. **Renter's Insurance** - Tenant is responsible to insure their own personal property and to cover themselves with liability coverage. A Tenant's personal property is <u>not</u> insured by the property Owner, not Agent.

7. **Heater Filters** - Tenant shall vacuum and or replace the heater filters twice each year, where applicable.

## Figure 5-2 (cont'd.)    The Rules

8.   **Breaking a Lease** - In the event a Tenant breaches (breaks) this lease before the lease period is over, Tenant shall be responsible and liable for <u>all</u> expenses incurred to re-lease the report.  Expenses will include, but are not limited to:
     - Rent amount for any remaining unpaid days, months before the expiration of the Lease.
     - Real Estate commissions for a new similar lease.
     - All advertising costs.
     - Any other costs directly relating to the re-leasing of the property.

9.   **Alterations** - Tenant is <u>not</u> allowed to make any alterations, re-keying of locks, replacements, or additions of locks, knockers, or other attachments on any door without the <u>written</u> consent of the Owner or Agent

14.  **Carpet Care** - Tenant agrees to pay for carpet cleaning if Owner or Agent determines that it is needed to restore carpet to same condition as upon move-in.

15.  **Washer, Dryer, and Refergator Care** - If a washer and dryer are in the premises that is provided by the Owner, the Tenant is responsible for the care and maintenance of them.  If either machine stops working while the Tenant is occupying the premises, the Tenant is liable and responsible for the repair coordination and costs.  Replacing either machine is completely at the discretion of the Owner.

16.  **Peace and Quiet** - If you are moving into a multiple residence, consideration must be given to the comfort of others.  Each Tenant is asked to notify JTA Property Management if any other Tenant is creating a problem, i.e., excessive noise, parking, trash accumulation, etc.  If this persists from any Tenant, and it is confirmed by Owner or Agent, this will be sufficient grounds to ask the offending Tenant to <u>vacate</u> the premises.

17.  **Defects, Damage, Responsibility** - Tenant understands and agrees that the Owner intends to remedy any defects or damage that make the occupancy of the premises uncomfortable, i.e., plumbing leaks, electrical or structural items, etc.
     - Tenant agrees to assume financial responsibility for all expenses incurred as a result of Tenant's neglect or abuse to appliances, premises, or property.
     - Tenant agrees to communicate to Owner or Agent, any malfunctions or damage to appliances etc., due to either normal wear and tear or neglect or abuse, so that the appliances, etc., can be maintained at the level of performance in which they were in when the Tenant moved in.

18.  **Assigned Keys** - Upon vacating the property, Tenant <u>must</u> return all keys to Owner or Agent. Tenant will continue to be financially liable for rent until all keys are returned.

| | | |
|---|---|---|
| Tenant 1 - Signature                    Date | JTA Property Management                   Date |
| Tenant 1 - PRINT | JTA - Agent |
| Tenant 2 - Signature                    Date | Tenant 2 - PRINT |

**JTA PROPERTY MANAGEMENT**

When the rules have been understood and agreed upon by the tenants, have them sign or initial in the appropriate place so there can be no misunderstanding at a later time. Then ask them to read and sign the rental agreement. Let them know that the rental agreement is the only binding agreement you will have and the terms of the agreement will be enforced. The required certified funds to take possession of the rental unit should be provided at the time of signing.

## Figure 5-3 Standard Rental Agreement Form

# RESIDENTIAL LEASE
THIS IS INTENDED TO BE A LEGALLY BINDING AGREEMENT--READ IT CAREFULLY

_____ , California _____ 20 ____
_____ , Landlord, and
_____ , Tenant, agree as follows:

1. **PROPERTY:** Landlord leases to Tenant and Tenant hires from Landlord the "premises" described as: _____
_____ . Inventory of personal property, if any, to be attached.

2. **TERM:** The term of this lease shall be for a period of _____
commencing_____ 20 _____ and terminating_____ 20 _____ .

3. **RENT:** Tenant agrees to pay a total rent of $_____ , payable as follows: _____
_____ . Rent installments are payable in advance.

4. **LATE CHARGE:** Tenant acknowledges that late payment of rent may cause Landlord to incur costs and expenses, the exact amount of such costs being extremely difficult and impractical to fix. Such costs may include, but are not limited to, processing and accounting expenses, late charges that may be imposed on Landlord by terms of any loan secured by the property, costs for additional attempts to collect rent, and preparation of notices. Therefore, if any installment of rent due from Tenant is not received by Landlord within _____ calendar days after date due, Tenant shall pay to Landlord an additional sum of $ _____ as a late charge which shall be deemed additional rent. The Parties agree that this late charge represents a fair and reasonable estimate of the costs that Landlord may incur by reason of Tenant's late payments. Acceptance of any late charge shall not constitute a waiver of Tenant's default with respect to the past due amount, or prevent Landlord from exercising any other rights and remedies under this agreement, and as provided by law.

5. **PAYMENT:** The rent shall be paid at _____ .

6. **SECURITY DEPOSIT:** $ _____ as a security deposit has been received. Landlord may use therefrom such amounts as are reasonably necessary to remedy Tenant's default in the payment of rent, to repair damages caused by Tenant, or by a guest or a licensee of the Tenant, to clean the premises, if necessary, upon termination of tenancy, and to replace or return personal property or appurtenances exclusive of ordinary wear and tear. If used toward rent or damages during the term of tenancy, Tenant agrees to reinstate said total security deposit upon five days written notice delivered to Tenant in person or by mail. No later than two weeks after the Tenant has vacated the premises, the landlord shall furnish the Tenant with an itemized written statement of the basis for, and the amount of, any security received and the disposition of the security and shall return any remaining portion of the security to the Tenant.

7. **UTILITIES:** Tenant agrees to pay for all utilities and services based upon occupancy of the premises and the following charges: _____
_____
except_____ which shall be paid for by Landlord.

8. **CONDITION:** Tenant has examined the premises and all furniture, furnishings and appliances if any, and fixtures including smoke detector(s) contained therein, and accepts the same as being clean, and in operative condition, with the following exceptions: _____
_____

9. **OCCUPANTS:** The premises are for the sole use as a residence by the following named persons **only:** _____
_____

10. **PETS:** No animal, bird or pet shall be kept on or about the premises without Landlord's prior written consent, except _____

11. **USE:** Tenant shall not disturb, annoy, endanger or interfere with other Tenants of the building or neighbors, nor use the premises for any unlawful purposes, nor violate any law or ordinance, nor commit waste or nuisance upon or about the premises.

12. **RULES & REGULATIONS:** Tenant agrees to comply with all CC&R's, Bylaws, reasonable rules or regulations, decisions of owners' association which are at any time posted on the premises or delivered to Tenant, or adopted by owners' association, and to be liable for any fines or charges levied due to violation(s).

13. **MAINTENANCE:** Tenant shall properly use and operate all furniture, furnishings and appliances, electrical, gas and plumbing fixtures and keep them as clean and sanitary as their condition permits. Excluding ordinary wear and tear, Tenant shall notify landlord and pay for all repairs or replacements caused by Tenant(s) or Tenants invitees' negligence or misuse. Tenant's personal property is not insured by Landlord.

14. **ALTERATIONS:** Tenant shall not paint, wallpaper, add or change locks or make alterations to the property without Landlord's prior written consent.

15. **KEYS:** Tenant acknowledges receipt of_____ keys to premises and_____ .
At Tenant's expense, Tenant may re-key existing locks and shall deliver duplicate keys to landlord upon installation.

16. **ENTRY:** Upon not less than 24 hours notice, Tenant shall make the premises available during normal business hours to Landlord, authorized agent or representative, for the purpose of entering to (a) make necessary or agreed repairs, decorations, alterations or improvements or supply necessary or agreed services, or (b) show the premises to prospective or actual purchasers, mortgagees, tenants, or contractors. In an emergency, Landlord, authorized agent or representative may enter the premises, at any time, without prior permission from Tenant.

17. **ASSIGNMENT & SUBLETTINGS:** Tenant shall not let or sublet all or any part of the premises nor assign this agreement or any interest in it.

18. **POSSESSION:** If Tenant abandons or vacates the premises, Landlord may terminate this agreement and regain lawful possession.

19. **HOLD OVER:** Any holding over at the expiration of this lease shall create a month to month tenancy at a monthly rent of $ _____ payable in advance. All other terms and conditions herein shall remain in full force and effect.

20. **ATTORNEY'S FEES:** In any action or proceeding arising out of this agreement, the prevailing party shall be entitled to reasonable attorney's fees and costs.

21. **WAIVER:** The waiver of any breach shall not be construed to be a continuing waiver of any subsequent breach.

22. **NOTICE:** Notice to Landlord may be served upon Landlord or Manager at_____ .

23. **ESTOPPEL CERTIFICATE:** Within 10 days after written notice, Tenant agrees to execute and deliver an estoppel certificate as submitted by Landlord acknowledging that this agreement is unmodified and in full force and effect or in full force and effect as modified and stating the modifications. Failure to comply shall be deemed Tenants acknowledgement that the certificate as submitted by Landlord is true and correct and may be relied upon by a lender or purchaser.

24. **ADDITIONAL TERMS AND CONDITIONS:** _____

25. **ENTIRE CONTRACT:** Time is of the essence. All prior agreements between the parties are incorporated in this agreement which constitutes the entire contract. Its terms are intended by the parties as a final expression of their agreement with respect to such terms as are included herein and may not be contradicted by evidence of any prior agreement or contemporaneous oral agreement. The parties further intend that this agreement constitutes the complete and exclusive statement of its terms and that no extrinsic evidence whatsoever may be introduced in any judicial or other proceeding, if any, involving this agreement.

26. **ACKNOWLEDGEMENT:** The undersigned have read the foregoing prior to execution and acknowledge receipt of a copy.

Landlord _____         Tenant _____
(or authorized agent)
Landlord _____         Tenant _____

Walk through the rental unit with the new tenant and go over a Condition and Inventory Checklist. This will prevent any discrepancy later when the tenant moves out. Have the tenant sign the form, giving him or her a copy with a welcome to the building!

## Figure 5-4    Condition and Inventory Checklist

### STATEMENT OF CONDITION

PROPERTY _____ UNIT _____

Type of Unit _____ Occupant _____ Move in Date _____

This move-in, move-out form is for your protection. When completing this form, be specific and check carefully. Among things you should look for are dust, dirt, grease, stains, burns, damages and wear. Use additional paper if necessary. California Civil Code 1950.5 stipulates that your security deposit is refundable to the extent not used for unpaid rent, damage and reasonable cleaning charges, normal wear and tear excepted.

| | CONDITION | |
|---|---|---|
| ITEMS | MOVE-IN | MOVE-OUT |
| **Living Room & Dining Room** | | |
| Doors and Locks | | |
| Carpeting | | |
| Floors and Baseboards | | |
| Walls and Ceiling | | |
| Draperies | | |
| Electrical Fixtures | | |
| Electrical Switches, Outlets | | |
| Windows, Screens | | |
| Misc._____ | | |
| | | |
| | | |
| | | |
| | | |
| **Kitchen** | | |
| Floors and Baseboards | | |
| Walls and Ceiling | | |
| Electrical Fixtures | | |
| Electrical Switches, Outlets | | |
| Range, Fan, Hood | | |
| Oven | | |
| Refrigerator | | |
| Plumbing | | |
| Sink & Disposer | | |
| Cabinets, Counter Surfaces | | |
| Windows, Screens | | |
| Draperies / Curtains | | |
| Misc._____ | | |
| | | |
| | | |
| | | |

## Figure 5-4 (cont'd.)   Condition and Inventory Checklist

CONDITION

| | MOVE-IN | | MOVE-OUT | |
|---|---|---|---|---|
| **Bedrooms** | #1 | #2 | #1 | #2 |
| Doors and Locks | | | | |
| Carpeting | | | | |
| Floors & Baseboards | | | | |
| Walls and Ceiling | | | | |
| Windows and Screens | | | | |
| Draperies | | | | |
| Electrical Fixtures | | | | |
| Electrical Switches, Outlets | | | | |
| Closets, Doors, Tracks | | | | |
| Misc._____ | | | | |

| | MOVE-IN | | MOVE-OUT | |
|---|---|---|---|---|
| **Bedrooms** | #3 | #4 or ____ | #3 | #4 or ____ |
| Doors and Locks | | | | |
| Carpeting | | | | |
| Floors & Baseboards | | | | |
| Walls and Ceiling | | | | |
| Windows and Screens | | | | |
| Draperies | | | | |
| Electrical Fixtures | | | | |
| Electrical Switches, Outlets | | | | |
| Closets, Doors, Tracks | | | | |
| Misc._____ | | | | |

| | MOVE-IN | | MOVE-OUT | |
|---|---|---|---|---|
| **Bathrooms** | #1 | #2 | #1 | #2 |
| Doors and Locks | | | | |
| Floors & Baseboards | | | | |
| Walls and Ceiling | | | | |
| Windows and Screens | | | | |
| Window Covering | | | | |
| Shower, Tub | | | | |
| Shower Door, Curtain | | | | |
| Toilet | | | | |
| Sink, Medicine Cabinet | | | | |
| Plumbing Fixtures | | | | |
| Electrical Fixtures, Fan | | | | |
| Electrical Switches, Outlets | | | | |
| Towel Racks | | | | |
| Misc._____ | | | | |

| | MOVE-IN | | MOVE-OUT | |
|---|---|---|---|---|
| **Other Items** | | | | |
| Heating | | | | |
| Air Conditioning | | | | |
| Patio, Balcony | | | | |
| Yard Areas | | | | |
| Fencing | | | | |
| Garage or Carport | | | | |
| Misc._____ | | | | |

UNIT INSPECTED AND ACCEPTED AS NOTED

Date _____

Signature of Tenant

Signature of Landlord/Agent

UNIT INSPECTED AND VACATED AS NOTED

Date _____

Signature of Tenant

Signature of Landlord/Agent

# QUESTIONS

1. Marketing rental space:

    a. varies in effort depending on supply and demand

    b. is easy or difficult commensurate with local vacancy levels

    c. is necessary to protect the value of the property

    d. all of the above

2. The techniques of renting space in commercial, industrial and residential property:

    a. are the same based on supply and demand

    b. are not significantly different because all space needs to be rented

    c. differ because potential tenants for each type of property go about their search differently

    d. none of the above

3. Determining the rental rate:

    a. is best done by finding out what similar properties rent for

    b. is primarily attributed to the rate of return desired by the investor

    c. is best done by the break-even approach

    d. is of minor importance in the marketing process

4. Market rent is:

    a. the rent stated in the contract

    b. the rent actually collected

    c. the rent similar properties are receiving in the marketplace

    d. the rent paid by grocery stores

5. A paired sales analysis:

    a. is only used on properties worth half a million dollars or more

    b. determines the contributory value of an isolated feature of a property

    c. groups all the comparable sales of a particular type of property in an area by twos

    d. is used only by accountants

6. A rent survey:

    a. helps a property manager decide how much rent to charge

    b. determines the number of tenants currently in occupancy

    c. can be obtained from the local apartment association

    d. identifies the square footage of a multi-unit residential property

7. In using the comparative market approach:

    a. give the comparable property a plus adjustment if it has a feature that the subject does not

    b. give the comparable property a minus adjustment if it has a feature that the subject does not

    c. give the subject property a plus adjustment if it has a feature that the comparable does not

    d. give the subject property a minus adjustment if it has a feature that the comparable does not

8. Renting an established property:

    a. may require less effort than renting a new one

    b. requires more effort because no one knows there is a vacancy

    c. requires more effort because the expectancy level is higher

    d. is accomplished by using the same methods as for a new property

9. Seasonal factors affect the renting of property:

   a. always

   b. because they impact supply and demand

   c. because different people like different kinds of weather

   d. by stabilizing annual leases

10. Targeting certain types of people as prospective tenants:

    a. is illegal

    b. is unethical

    c. makes sense when matching them to the amenities your property has to offer

    d. none of the above

11. Preparing a property for showing involves making a property appear:

    a. inviting

    b. neutral

    c. safe

    d. clean

12. If a property is not available to show that is in move-in condition, another alternative would be:

    a. have a model available

    b. secure the right to show a current tenant's unit

    c. show a unit that is dirty and in disrepair

    d. both a and b

13. The best source of advertising to rent space is:

    a. newspapers

    b. rental agencies

    c. signs on property

    d. it depends on property types and local economic conditions

14. In print advertising a generally accepted formula is:

   a. ARRC—advertise, receive calls, rent and collect
   b. AIDA—attention, interest, desire and action
   c. RRR—Reading, rentals and reaction
   d. ARM—always ready to market

15. Frequent problems with classified ads include:

   a. too many abbreviations
   b. wasting words on obvious or understood concepts
   c. inability to gain attention
   d. all of the above

16. Signs on properties are good in all of the following situations except:

   a. a multi-unit housing project
   b. a commercial store-front location
   c. a vacant single-unit property in a remote area
   d. a four-plex with three units occupied

17. The advantages of a rental agency to the owner and property manager would be all of the following except:

   a. no charge to owner
   b. tenant is prequalified
   c. the agency will stand behind its selection
   d. charges are incurred only when results are obtained

18. A disadvantage of word of mouth advertising would be:

   a. the expense
   b. lack of qualifying the tenant
   c. potential hurt feelings and relationships
   d. relying on only certain tenants to provide a recommendation

19. A property manager should be concerned with a potential tenant's:

    a. ability to pay
    b. willingness to pay
    c. likelihood to damage the property
    d. all of the above

20. All of the following items should be on a tenant application to rent an apartment except:

    a. social security number
    b. number of occupants
    c. place of employment
    d. race of prospect

# ANSWERS

1. *d*
2. *c*
3. *a*
4. *c*
5. *b*
6. *a*
7. *b*
8. *a*
9. *b*
10. *c*
11. *a*
12. *d*
13. *d*
14. *b*
15. *d*
16. *c*
17. *a*
18. *c*
19. *d*
20. *d*

# Leases

- **Basics On Leases**
- **Leasehold Estates**
- **Types Of Leases**
- **Essential Elements Of A Valid Contract**
- **Rights And Responsibilities Of Lessees And Lessors**
- **Special Clauses**
- **Other Issues**

C H A P T E R 6

# BASICS ON LEASES

Leases are the written agreements by which possession of the property is transferred and the stream of income is secured. The agreement may include a series of additional documents, riders and exhibits setting forth special areas of concurrence not mentioned in the body of a standard lease.

# LEASEHOLD ESTATES

An estate tells us the types and duration of interests that an individual has in real property. In their broadest sense, estates come in two types—freehold estates and less than freehold estates. Leases are less than freehold estates and will terminate at some predetermined date or by mutual or unilateral decision. Freehold estates may continue until the death of the owner and even then pass on to his or her heirs. There are four distinct types of less than freehold, or leasehold estates.

## Estate for Years

The estate for years is an arrangement by which the tenant takes possession on a particular date and will remain in possession until a particular date. In other words, it is an agreement that has a designated beginning and end. It does not have to endure for a plurality of years as its title seems to indicate, but can be for any period of days, weeks, months or years. Since the ending date has already been agreed upon, notice to terminate is not required. This is typically called a *lease*.

## Periodic Tenancy

A periodic tenancy goes from period to period. It may be month-to-month or week-to-week. Notice equal to the length of the period of tenancy must be given to terminate the tenancy. If an estate for years has been fulfilled, sometimes the parties to the agreement allow the tenancy to move to a periodic tenancy, such as month-to-month.

## Estate at Will

An estate at will is a tenancy agreement that endures as long as both parties are willing. The owner of a property may be planning to sell it and may say to the prospective tenant, "Go ahead and move in for now. I'll be showing the property in an effort to sell it. I'll give you notice when it's time to move out." The tenant moves in on that basis. Either party may say to the other, "I'm giving you notice. I'm no longer willing to remain in this tenancy." Since both are no longer willing and one has given notice, the tenancy can come to an end. This is not the kind of agreement you want to have in a building where you want stability and a steady stream of income.

## Estate at Sufferance

This is a situation where the tenant has come into possession of the property in a lawful manner. He or she has signed some type of lease or rental agreement, and is not a trespasser. But the tenant has stayed beyond the prescribed duration of the agreement and occupies the property hostile to the landlord's wishes. This is what is called "suffering with a tenant." The landlord cannot accept rent money from the tenant under these circumstances or it will be interpreted as the landlord consenting to the tenant's continued possession of the property. The property manager must proceed with eviction at this time.

# TYPES OF LEASES

Leases come in different types and styles and with different provisions. Leases also can be custom designed to combine features and clauses of different kinds of lease agreements. The owner's objectives and legal counsel should combine to determine the best type of lease to use for the various types of properties.

## Gross Lease

A gross lease means that the tenants pay the rental payments only and the landlord pays all of the fixed and variable expenses. Fixed expenses would be property taxes and insurance because they remain about the same regardless of the occupancy level of the building. Variable expenses would be items such as maintenance, advertising and utilities. In this type of lease the owner never knows exactly how much money he or she is going to net because certain expenses are going to vary from month to month. Residential apartment buildings are usually this type of lease, with the singular exception of electricity often being on separate meters and paid by the tenant.

## Net Lease

In a net lease the tenant makes the rental payment plus pays certain agreed upon expenses. This gives the landlord more of an idea of what he or she is going to net each month because the burden of the variable expenses is not theirs. Technically, net leases can be of these varying types.

### NET LEASE (SINGLE NET LEASE)

In this type of net lease, the tenant pays the rent plus utilities, property tax and any special assessments on the property.

### NET NET LEASE (DOUBLE NET LEASE)

In this arrangement, the tenant pays rent, utilities, property tax, special assessments and insurance premiums.

### NET NET NET LEASE (TRIPLE NET LEASE)

In a triple net lease, the tenant pays all of the above items plus takes on responsibility for repairs and maintenance, leaving the landlord to pay only the debt service and truly receiving a *net* amount of income each month.

This breakdown on net leases may not be understood by all tenants in this manner, so no matter what nomenclature is used on a particular lease the terms should be spelled out so all parties have the same understanding. Various forms of net leases are used frequently for commercial properties, and triple net leases are often used on industrial properties and nationwide franchise businesses.

## Figure 6-1  Standard Office Lease—Gross

# STANDARD OFFICE LEASE—GROSS
### AMERICAN INDUSTRIAL REAL ESTATE ASSOCIATION

**1. Basic Lease Provisions** ("Basic Lease Provisions")

 1.1 **Parties:** This Lease, dated, for reference purposes only, _____, 20_____,
is made by and between _____
(herein called "Lessor") and _____
doing business under the name of _____, (herein called "Lessee").

 1.2 **Premises:** Suite Number(s) _____, _____ floors, consisting of approximately _____ feet, more or less, as defined in paragraph 2 and as shown on Exhibit "A" hereto (the "Premises").

 1.3 **Building:** Commonly described as being located at _____
in the City of _____
County of _____
State of _____, as more particularly described in Exhibit _____ hereto, and as defined in paragraph 2.

 1.4: **Use:** _____
_____, subject to paragraph 6.

 1.5 **Term:** _____ commencing_____ ("Commencement Date")
and ending _____, as defined in paragraph 3.

 1.6 **Base Rent:** _____ per month, payable on the _____ day of each month,
per paragraph 4.1 _____
_____

 1.7 **Base Rent Increase:** On _____ the monthly Base Rent payable under paragraph 1.6 above shall be adjusted as provided in paragraph 4.3 below.

 1.8 **Rent Paid Upon Execution:** _____
for _____

 1.9 **Security Deposit:** _____

 1.10 **Lessee's Share of Operating Expense Increase:** _____% as defined in paragraph 4.2.

**2. Premises, Parking and Common Areas.**

 2.1 **Premises:** The Premises are a portion of a building, herein sometimes referred to as the "Building" identified in paragraph 1.3 of the Basic Lease Provisions. "Building" shall include adjacent parking structures used in connection therewith. The Premises, the Building, the Common Areas, the land upon which the same are located, along with all other buildings and improvements thereon or thereunder, are herein collectively referred to as the "Office Building Project." Lessor hereby leases to Lessee and Lessee leases from Lessor for the term, at the rental, and upon all of the conditions set forth herein, the real property referred to in the Basic Lease Provisions, paragraph 1.2, as the "Premises," including rights to the Common Areas as hereinafter specified.

 2.2 **Vehicle Parking:** So long as Lessee is not in default, and subject to the rules and regulations attached hereto, and as established by Lessor from time to time, Lessee shall be entitled to rent and use _____ parking spaces in the Office Building Project at the monthly rate applicable from time to time for monthly parking as set by Lessor and/or its licensee.

  2.2.1 If Lessee commits, permits or allows any of the prohibited activities described in the Lease or the rules then in effect, then Lessor shall have the right, without notice, in addition to such other rights and remedies that it may have, to remove or tow away the vehicle involved and charge the cost to Lessee, which cost shall be immediately payable upon demand by Lessor.

  2.2.2 The monthly parking rate per parking space will be $_____ per month at the commencement of the term of this Lease, and is subject to change upon five (5) days prior written notice to Lessee. Monthly parking fees shall be payable one month in advance prior to the first day of each calendar month.

 2.3 **Common Areas—Definition.** The term "Common Areas" is defined as all areas and facilities outside the Premises and within the exterior boundary line of the Office Building Project that are provided and designated by the Lessor from time to time for the general non-exclusive use of Lessor, Lessee and of other lessees of the Office Building Project and their respective employees, suppliers, shippers, customers and invitees, including but not limited to common entrances, lobbies, corridors, stairways and stairwells, public restrooms, elevators, escalators, parking areas to the extent not otherwise prohibited by this Lease, loading and unloading areas, trash areas, roadways, sidewalks, walkways, parkways, ramps, driveways, landscaped areas and decorative walls.

 2.4 **Common Areas—Rules and Regulations.** Lessee agrees to abide by and conform to the rules and regulations attached hereto as Exhibit B with respect to the Office Building Project and Common Areas, and to cause its employees, suppliers, shippers, customers, and invitees to so abide and conform. Lessor or such other person(s) as Lessor may appoint shall have the exclusive control and management of the Common Areas and shall have the right, from time to time, to modify, amend and enforce said rules and regulations. Lessor shall not be responsible to Lessee for the non-compliance with said rules and regulations by other lessees, their agents, employees and invitees of the Office Building Project,

 2.5 **Common Areas—Changes.** Lessor shall have the right, in Lessor's sole discretion, from time to time:

  (a) To make changes to the Building interior and exterior and Common Areas, including, without limitation, changes in the location, size, shape, number, and appearance thereof, including but not limited to the lobbies, windows, stairways, air shafts, elevators, escalators, restrooms, driveways, entrances, parking spaces, parking areas, loading and unloading areas, ingress, egress, direction of traffic, decorative walls, landscaped areas and walkways; provided, however, Lessor shall at all times provide the parking facilities required by applicable law;

  (b) To close temporarily any of the Common Areas for maintenance purposes so long as reasonable access to the Premises remains available;

  (c) To designate other land and improvements outside the boundaries of the Office Building Project to be a part of the Common Areas, provided that such other land and improvements have a reasonable and functional relationship to the Office Building Project;

  (d) To add additional buildings and improvements to the Common Areas;

  (e) To use the Common Areas while engaged in making additional improvements, repairs or alterations to the Office Building Project, or any portion thereof;

  (f) To do and perform such other acts and make such other changes in, to or with respect to the Common Areas and Office Building Project as Lessor may, in the exercise of sound business judgment deem to be appropriate.

**3. Term.**

 3.1 **Term.** The term and Commencement Date of this Lease shall be as specified in paragraph 1.5 of the Basic Lease Provisions.

 3.2 **Delay in Possession.** Notwithstanding said Commencement Date, if for any reason Lessor cannot deliver possession of the Premises to Lessee on said date and subject to paragraph 3.2.2, Lessor shall not be subject to any liability therefor, nor shall such failure affect the validity of this Lease or the obligations of Lessee hereunder or extend the term hereof; but, in such case, Lessee shall not be obligated to pay rent or perform any other obligation of Lessee under the terms of this Lease, except as may be otherwise provided in this Lease, until possession of the Premises is tendered to Lessee, as hereinafter defined; provided, however, that if Lessor shall not have delivered possession of the Premises within sixty (60) days following said Commencement Date, as the same may be extended under the terms of a Work Letter executed by Lessor and Lessee, Lessee may, at Lessee's

Initials:_____

_____

**FULL SERVICE—GROSS**

PAGE 1 of 10 PAGES

## Figure 6-2 Standard Office Lease—Net

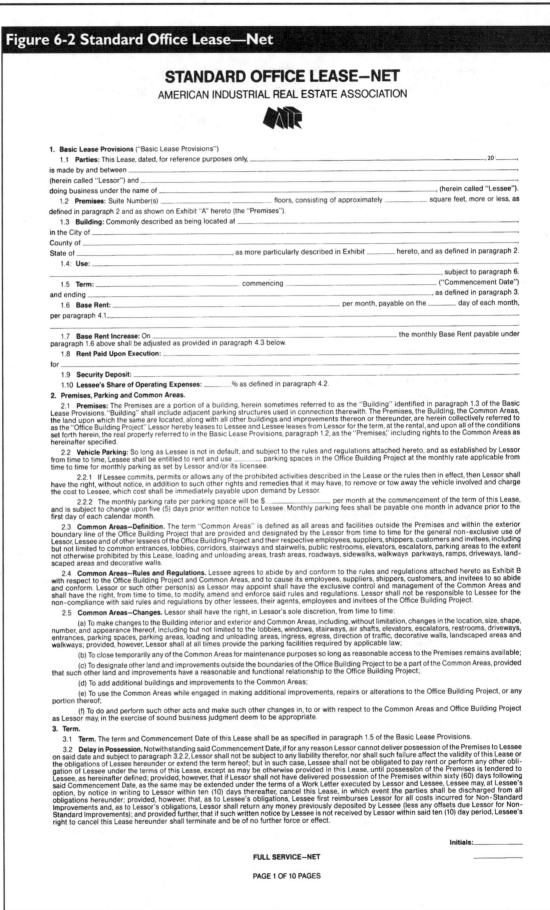

# STANDARD OFFICE LEASE—NET
### AMERICAN INDUSTRIAL REAL ESTATE ASSOCIATION

**1. Basic Lease Provisions** ("Basic Lease Provisions")

1.1 **Parties:** This Lease, dated, for reference purposes only, _____, 20'_____,
is made by and between _____,
(herein called "Lessor") and _____
doing business under the name of _____, (herein called "Lessee").

1.2 **Premises:** Suite Number(s) _____, _____ floors, consisting of approximately _____ square feet, more or less, as defined in paragraph 2 and as shown on Exhibit "A" hereto (the "Premises").

1.3 **Building:** Commonly described as being located at _____
in the City of _____
County of _____
State of _____, as more particularly described in Exhibit _____ hereto, and as defined in paragraph 2.

1.4: **Use:** _____
_____, subject to paragraph 6.

1.5 **Term:** _____ commencing _____ ("Commencement Date")
and ending _____, as defined in paragraph 3.

1.6 **Base Rent:** _____ per month, payable on the _____ day of each month,
per paragraph 4.1_____

1.7 **Base Rent Increase:** On _____ the monthly Base Rent payable under
paragraph 1.6 above shall be adjusted as provided in paragraph 4.3 below.

1.8 **Rent Paid Upon Execution:** _____
for _____.

1.9 **Security Deposit:** _____

1.10 **Lessee's Share of Operating Expenses:** _____% as defined in paragraph 4.2.

**2. Premises, Parking and Common Areas.**

2.1 **Premises:** The Premises are a portion of a building, herein sometimes referred to as the "Building" identified in paragraph 1.3 of the Basic Lease Provisions. "Building" shall include adjacent parking structures used in connection therewith. The Premises, the Building, the Common Areas, the land upon which the same are located, along with all other buildings and improvements thereon or thereunder, are herein collectively referred to as the "Office Building Project." Lessor hereby leases to Lessee and Lessee leases from Lessor for the term, at the rental, and upon all of the conditions set forth herein, the real property referred to in the Basic Lease Provisions, paragraph 1.2, as the "Premises," including rights to the Common Areas as hereinafter specified.

2.2 **Vehicle Parking:** So long as Lessee is not in default, and subject to the rules and regulations attached hereto, and as established by Lessor from time to time, Lessee shall be entitled to rent and use _____ parking spaces in the Office Building Project at the monthly rate applicable from time to time for monthly parking as set by Lessor and/or its licensee.

2.2.1 If Lessee commits, permits or allows any of the prohibited activities described in the Lease or the rules then in effect, then Lessor shall have the right, without notice, in addition to such other rights and remedies that it may have, to remove or tow away the vehicle involved and charge the cost to Lessee, which cost shall be immediately payable upon demand by Lessor.

2.2.2 The monthly parking rate per parking space will be $ _____ per month at the commencement of the term of this Lease, and is subject to change upon five (5) days prior written notice to Lessee. Monthly parking fees shall be payable one month in advance prior to the first day of each calendar month.

2.3 **Common Areas—Definition.** The term "Common Areas" is defined as all areas and facilities outside the Premises and within the exterior boundary line of the Office Building Project that are provided and designated by the Lessor from time to time for the general non-exclusive use of Lessor, Lessee and of other lessees of the Office Building Project and their respective employees, suppliers, shippers, customers and invitees, including but not limited to common entrances, lobbies, corridors, stairways and stairwells, public restrooms, elevators, escalators, parking areas to the extent not otherwise prohibited by this Lease, loading and unloading areas, trash areas, roadways, sidewalks, walkways, parkways, ramps, driveways, land-scaped areas and decorative walls.

2.4 **Common Areas—Rules and Regulations.** Lessee agrees to abide by and conform to the rules and regulations attached hereto as Exhibit B with respect to the Office Building Project and Common Areas, and to cause its employees, suppliers, shippers, customers, and invitees to so abide and conform. Lessor or such other person(s) as Lessor may appoint shall have the exclusive control and management of the Common Areas and shall have the right, from time to time, to modify, amend and enforce said rules and regulations. Lessor shall not be responsible to Lessee for the non-compliance with said rules and regulations by other lessees, their agents, employees and invitees of the Office Building Project.

2.5 **Common Areas—Changes.** Lessor shall have the right, in Lessor's sole discretion, from time to time:

(a) To make changes to the Building interior and exterior and Common Areas, including, without limitation, changes in the location, size, shape, number, and appearance thereof, including but not limited to the lobbies, windows, stairways, air shafts, elevators, escalators, restrooms, driveways, entrances, parking spaces, parking areas, loading and unloading areas, ingress, egress, direction of traffic, decorative walls, landscaped areas and walkways; provided, however, Lessor shall at all times provide the parking facilities required by applicable law;

(b) To close temporarily any of the Common Areas for maintenance purposes so long as reasonable access to the Premises remains available;

(c) To designate other land and improvements outside the boundaries of the Office Building Project to be a part of the Common Areas, provided that such other land and improvements have a reasonable and functional relationship to the Office Building Project;

(d) To add additional buildings and improvements to the Common Areas;

(e) To use the Common Areas while engaged in making additional improvements, repairs or alterations to the Office Building Project, or any portion thereof;

(f) To do and perform such other acts and make such other changes in, to or with respect to the Common Areas and Office Building Project as Lessor may, in the exercise of sound business judgment deem to be appropriate.

**3. Term.**

3.1 **Term.** The term and Commencement Date of this Lease shall be as specified in paragraph 1.5 of the Basic Lease Provisions.

3.2 **Delay in Possession.** Notwithstanding said Commencement Date, if for any reason Lessor cannot deliver possession of the Premises to Lessee on said date and subject to paragraph 3.2.2, Lessor shall not be subject to any liability therefor, nor shall such failure affect the validity of this Lease or the obligations of Lessee hereunder or extend the term hereof; but in such case, Lessee shall not be obligated to pay rent or perform any other obligation of Lessee under the terms of this Lease, except as may be otherwise provided in this Lease, until possession of the Premises is tendered to Lessee, as hereinafter defined; provided, however, that if Lessor shall not have delivered possession of the Premises within sixty (60) days following said Commencement Date, as the same may be extended under the terms of a Work Letter executed by Lessor and Lessee, Lessee may, at Lessee's option, by notice in writing to Lessor within ten (10) days thereafter, cancel this Lease, in which event the parties shall be discharged from all obligations hereunder; provided, however, that, as to Lessee's obligations, Lessee first reimburses Lessor for all costs incurred for Non-Standard Improvements and, as to Lessor's obligations, Lessor shall return any money previously deposited by Lessee (less any offsets due Lessor for Non-Standard Improvements); and provided further, that if such written notice by Lessee is not received by Lessor within said ten (10) day period, Lessee's right to cancel this Lease hereunder shall terminate and be of no further force or effect.

Initials:_____

FULL SERVICE—NET                    _____

PAGE 1 OF 10 PAGES

## Percentage Lease

A percentage lease is often used for retail stores. The *percentage* part of this lease refers to the gross sales and reflects on the tenant's ability to pay. Any combination of base and/or percentage of the gross receipts can be arranged. When business is good, the tenant pays more and the landlord benefits from the good times as well. When business is slow, the landlord accepts less rent and the burden is not so hard on the tenant at a time when ability to pay is diminished. The following types of percentage leases can be arranged.

### BASE OR PERCENTAGE METHOD

In this method the tenant pays either a flat amount as base rent *or* a percentage of the gross receipts if they exceed a certain amount. Let's suppose a hardware store is renting a facility on the following terms. The base rent will be $1,200 per month. However, if the store grosses a minimum of $65,000 for the month, the tenant pays 2% of the gross instead of the base rent. Two percent of $65,000 is $1,300 and the rent would go up from there as the gross receipts increase.

### BASE AND PERCENTAGE METHOD

Here, the tenant pays the base rent *plus* a percentage of the store's gross receipts. Let's suppose the base rent is $600 per month. Even if sales are zero, $600 per month must be paid. In addition, the tenant must pay 1% of gross receipts. So in the above example, if gross sales are $65,000, 1% equals $650. The monthly rent would be $600 (base) plus $650 (percentage of gross) to equal $1,250.

### BASE AND PERCENTAGE ON GROSS OVER MINIMUM

In this method, the tenant pays the agreed upon base rent *plus* a percentage of the gross only if it exceeds a certain amount. Let's suppose the hardware store pays the base of $600 per month and if sales reach a minimum of $30,000, an additional 1.5% on the gross sales amount. In this example 1.5% x $30,000 = $450 + $600 (base) would equal a monthly rent of $1,050.

## PERCENTAGE OF BASE AND PERCENTAGE ON GROSS OVER MINIMUM

Here, the tenant pays a percentage of gross receipts up to a certain amount. Once the gross receipts exceed that amount, a different percentage kicks in. Let's suppose the agreement is that the tenant will pay 3% of the gross receipts per month up to $50,000 and 1.5% on gross receipts in excess of $50,000. If receipts for the month were $75,000, the calculations would look like this.

$$3\% \times \$50,000 = \$1,500$$
$$1.5\% \times \$25,000 = \underline{\quad 375}$$
$$\$1,875 \quad \text{(Monthly Rent)}$$

# Graduated Lease

A graduated lease (sometimes called a step-up lease) is usually a long-term lease with an escalation clause which allows for a rent increase based upon the occurrence of a certain event. Sometimes that event has to do with completing improvements and providing certain amenities that benefit the subject property. Sometimes it is tied to a measure of inflation such as the Consumer Price Index (CPI).

Section 4.3 (Rent Increase), subparagraph one of the Standard Office Lease (Gross) of the American Industrial Real Estate Association (AIREA) addresses this issue.

> "At the times set forth in Paragraph 1.7 of the Basic Lease Provisions, the monthly Base Rent payable under Paragraph 4.1 of this Lease shall be adjusted by the increase, if any, in the Consumer Price Index of the Bureau of Labor Statistics of the Department of Labor for All Urban Consumers. 'All items' for the city nearest the location of the Building, herein referred to as CPI since the date of this Lease."

Subsequent sections go on to describe the method and time of such adjustment. This type of escalation clause addresses the tenant's ability to pay and spreads some of the wealth to the landlord at an affordable time for the tenant. Any type of gross or net lease could contain an escalation clause and thereby also be a graduated or step-up lease.

# ESSENTIAL ELEMENTS OF A VALID CONTRACT

A lease is a contract and must comply with the legal requirements of a contract to be valid. The following are the legal requirements of a valid contract.

## Mutual Consent

Both parties must consent to all of the terms of the contract. This means there must be a meeting of the minds. Both parties must willingly agree to enter into the contract. There can be no duress, menace or coercion. And both parties must understand the terms of the contract. When having a tenant sign the lease to an apartment, the property manager should go over each clause and stipulation to make sure the tenant understands. If a late charge is effective five days after the due date of the rent and if the late charge is a certain percentage or flat amount, make sure the tenant understands that and knows it will be enforced. There will be no exceptions. This way the tenant enters into the contract willingly and with full knowledge. Having a place for the tenant's initials by each clause is not a bad idea so he or she cannot say at a later time, "I didn't understand."

## Consideration

In legal terms, consideration can be anything of value. It doesn't necessarily have to be money. It can be a promise, services in labor or an agreement *not* to do a certain act. It cannot be an illegal act or services which have already been provided. The idea is that there must be some value given for value received. While all of this is true, in most cases there can be no more valuable consideration for taking up space in an income producing property than cold, hard cash. It contributes in the most direct fashion to the gross income, which pays the expenses, which trickles down to the bottom line. Get certified funds when signing the tenant to the lease, or submit personal checks far enough in advance that they have time to clear the bank before the tenant takes possession of the property.

## Capacity

Know the laws in your state regarding capacity. The local associations for the types of property you're managing ought to be able to help you here. Individuals who sign a lease without having legal capacity do not have the ability to create a binding agreement. The contract is void at the outset. With some possible variations state by state, individuals who do not have legal capacity are *minors* and *mental incompetents*. A minor is any person who is under the age of 18. In most states the exception to this is a minor who has been emancipated either by court order or by marriage. Such a person would have legal capacity. In that situation, a copy of the court order or marriage certificate should be obtained and independently verified with the court to establish legitimacy.

A person who is mentally incompetent must be declared so by a court of law. The court of popular opinion is not sufficient to attain that status in a legal sense. The challenge for the property manager is detecting when an applicant may be mentally incompetent. There are some forms of mental illness that have extended periods of lucidness, making it difficult for a layperson to detect a problem. Other forms of mental illness are, of course, more obvious. A mental incompetent trying to rent an apartment is not going to volunteer such status, so this is where scrutinizing the application is extremely important. If a person is truly mentally incompetent and this has been determined by a court, he or she is unlikely to have a cohesive employment record. Check it out thoroughly. Find out the reasons for their leaving any employment they may have had. There may be income sufficient to pay the rent, from family or the state, but the disruption that could be caused by an unstable tenant would not be worth it. Besides, the bottom line is that such a person does not have legal capacity.

## Lawful Object

The object of the contract must be lawful. It cannot be an illegal act or an illegal substance or item. The purpose of the contract must be legal. Renting an apartment seems like a simple item and in most cases the object of and the operation of the contract is legal. However, if a residential tenant is engaged in illegal activity in the unit (i.e., drugs, prostitution), the violation of law can be considered a breach of contract. Similarly, if an industrial or commercial tenant violates the law in conducting business (i.e., exceeding pollution restrictions) this too can be considered a breach of contract.

## In Writing

The statute of frauds holds that any agreement that is not to be performed within a year must be in writing. It is unenforceable otherwise. A lease for more than a year must be in writing under the statute of frauds. However, there are some interesting qualifications.

First, let us recommend that all agreements pertaining to the letting of real property be in writing. It is always helpful to clarify the details of an agreement by succinctly stating them in written form and having each party to the agreement sign consent and understanding. Too much is at stake to leave the outcome to chance. The statute of frauds *requires* an agreement to be in writing if it is not to be completely performed within a year. This is obviously due to the passage of time. As time passes, it is easier and easier to forget the commitments that have been made. So it *must* be in writing to be enforced. Why not be just as careful on all agreements, even of shorter duration?

Second, it may be assumed that if an agreement must be in writing, it must also be signed by all parties to the transaction. This is not necessarily the case with leases, although signatures are certainly recommended. The courts have held that the lessor and lessee need not both always sign the lease. The lease becomes an implied contract, what some call the *duck theory of law*. If it quacks like a duck, waddles like a duck and swims like a duck, it's not unreasonable to assume it's a duck.

Let's suppose the lessor has signed the lease agreement. The tenant moves in without signing. After four months, the tenant decides not to continue to pay. In court he or she protests to the judge, "Your honor, I never signed the lease!" The judge would ask, "Are you the person who took possession of the described property?" "Yes." Are you the person who made the prescribed rental payments for four months?" "Yes." The tenant has just quacked like a duck and the court's decision probably would be that the person is liable for the rent. But never leave this to even the slightest chance. It's not worth the time, risk or uncertainty. If you have a written agreement (and why wouldn't you?) always get signatures!

## EVERY LEASE SHOULD INCLUDE

- Names of lessor and lessee

- Names and number of occupants

- Property description

- Amount of payment

- Term of the lease (Time duration)

- Terms of the lease (Month-to-month? Annual?)

- Get it in writing!

- Get signatures!

## Figure 6-3   Residential Lease Agreement

### RESIDENTIAL RENTAL AGREEMENT

This Agreement is between _____ owner of_____

_____ acting through its Manager of these Apartments,  Humphrey Management Company, INC.
(hereinafter called "Management") and

Resident _____Resident_____

Resident _____Resident_____

Resident _____Resident_____
(hereinafter called "Resident(s)").

Management agrees to rent to Resident, and Resident agrees to rent from Management, Apartment Number _____

located at _____ .

1. **TERMS AND RENT:** Resident agrees to rent from Management on the terms set forth, the above-described Premises for a

term of _____ , beginning on _____ , 20_____,

and ending on _____ , 20 _____, and thereafter on a month to month basis,

for monthly rental in the amount of $ _____ . If the term provided above be for other than month-to-month, the amount of rent will remain unchanged to the expiration of such term.

2. **SECURITY DEPOSITS:** Resident agrees to pay Management, upon execution hereof, the sum of $ _____ , to be held by Management to secure Resident's performance of this Agreement, and Resident's covenants herein. Management may apply such portion(s) of the deposit as are reasonably necessary to remedy any default(s) by Resident in the payment of rent or to repair damage to the Premises caused by Residents or their invitees or licensees, including reasonable repair or replacement of, without limitations, furniture, fixtures, appliances, floors and/or floor coverings, windows, ceilings or walls in or about the Premises. Resident remains liable for and shall promptly pay Management all sums in excess of any deposit required for said repair or replacement purposes. If Management applies any portion(s) of such deposit to any such purpose prior to termination of this tenancy, Resident shall promptly pay Management the amount necessary to restore the deposit to the original amount. Resident agrees that no portion of such deposit shall be a reduction of or offset against rent or any other payment due Management from Resident hereunder. Management's right to possession of the Premises for Resident's default of any covenant or term herein shall not be in any manner limited because Management holds such deposit, or any portion thereof. Upon termination of the tenancy for any reason, if Resident does not leave the Premises in as good condition as when received by Resident from Management, reasonable use and wear excepted, Management may apply such portion of the security deposits as may be reasonably necessary to restore the Premises to such condition including, without limitation, for final cleaning of floors, carpets, window coverings, windows, walls, fixtures and appliances.

3. **USE OF PROPERTY:** The premises shall be used only as a private residence for the persons previously named in application for residence. Resident agrees that no occupants in excess of those stated herein and named on the application shall occupy the Premises for over two weeks, except upon prior written consent of Management. Resident shall not violate any federal, state, county or local law within the Premises or apartment complex. No business or commercial activities are allowed on the Premises.

4. **UTILITIES:** Resident agrees to pay for all utilities, including utility deposits, except _____ .

5. **RENT PAYMENT:** Resident understands the entire rent for each month is due on or before the first (1st) day of the month and agrees to pay the same on that date, to Resident Manager at the Rental Office in the Apartment Community. Furthermore, Resident(s) understands that rent is due in full on the first (1st) day of each month and that rent paid after the first day of each month is considered late and subject to legal action at that time. No cash accepted. Payment must be made in form of a personal check, cashier's check, certified check or money order.

6. **LATE PAYMENTS AND RETURNED CHECKS:** Time is of the essence, and if the rent is paid after the third (3rd) day of the month, a late charge of $25.00 will be due as additional rent. If Management elects to accept rent after the SEVENTH day of the month, payments will only be accepted in the form of cashier's check or money order. In the event Resident's check is dishonored by the bank, Resident agrees to pay Management additional rent in the amount of $25.00 along with the appropriate additional rent for late payment in the form of a cashier's check, certified check or money order and furthermore Resident agrees that after the second such dishonored check, all future payments will be in the form of a cashier's check, certified check or money order. If Management agrees to accept rent paid late, this does not waive Management's right to not accept future late payments.

7. **CONDITION-REPAIRS:** Resident has inspected and accepts the premises, and all improvements, furnishings and fixtures therein as being in good condition, except as noted on the Move-In Inventory and Condition Form, and agrees to maintain the same in said condition. Resident agrees not to alter, install improvements in, paint, or redecorate the premises or any part of the apartment property without the prior expressed written consent of the Management. The cost of restoring the Premises or apartment property to its prior condition resulting from Resident's violation of this term shall be promptly paid by the Resident upon demand by the Management.

8. **PETS:** No animal(s) or pets of any kind shall be permitted in or about the apartment.

9. **INSPECTION:** Resident agrees that Management may enter the Premises to make repairs in the event of an emergency. If notice of termination of this Agreement has been given by either party, Resident agrees that Management may show the Premises between the hours of 9:00 A.M. and 5:00 P.M. Management shall make reasonable efforts to provide 24-hour prior posted notice of the intent to enter the Premises.

10. **TERMINATION BY RESIDENT:** If the term provided in Paragraph 1 above be for other than month to month, this Agreement shall be deemed a lease for said term; any holdover thereafter shall be from month to month on the terms and conditions of this Agreement. If the term provided in Paragraph 1 above or by expiration of a lease for a term as provided herein be for month to month, Resident may terminate this tenant by giving 30 days prior written notice to Management at the Rental Office, and Resident shall remain liable for the entire rent for said 30-day period. Any holding over by the Resident beyond said 30-day period without the prior written consent of the Management shall be deemed a Tenancy at Sufferance without the consent of the Management, and Resident shall be liable to the Management for treble rent as damages. Management may elect to treat the tenancy as not terminated until all personal property of Resident has been removed therefrom and/or all keys returned to the Management.

11. **SUBLEASE:** Resident shall not let, sublet, assign, or transfer all or any part of the Premises without the prior written consent of the Management. Any such attempted lease, sublease, assignment or transfer shall be void.

12. **ABANDONMENT:** Resident shall not vacate or abandon the Premises at any time during the term of this Agreement. Abandonment shall be conclusively presumed if the rent has been due and unpaid for 14 consecutive days and, upon the failure of Resident to respond to a notice directed to Resident at the Premises within 18 days after delivery or mailing thereof by Management. If Resident shall abandon, vacate or surrender said premises, or be dispossessed by process of law, or otherwise, then Management shall have the right to take immediate possession of and re-enter said Premises, and remove any and all personal property therein, and Resident hereby waives any and all claims for damages arising out of such entry or removal of property.

## Figure 6-3 (cont'd.)   Residential Lease Agreement

**13. BREACH:** In the event of any breach of this Agreement by Resident, then Management, in addition to any other rights or remedies, shall have the immediate right of re-entry and may remove any and all personal property and effects of the Resident, and the Management may retain possession of such personal property until all charges of every kind including rent, cleaning, shortages, or damage to the Premises shall be paid in full. Management shall have the lien granted by law upon all baggage and other property of Resident, and may enforce said lien as provided by law. Said lien may be enforced whenever rent or other charges are due and unpaid and regardless of whether a 30-day notice to quit or a 3-day notice to pay rent or quit shall have been served. Enforcement of the lien shall not operate to waive any other rights of Management in unlawful detainer or otherwise.

**14. LIABILITY:** Resident agrees to hold Management harmless from all claims of loss or damage to property, and of injury or death to persons caused by the intentional acts or negligence of the Resident, his guests or invitees, or occurring on the premises rented for Resident's exclusive use. Resident expressly absolves Management from any and all liability for any loss or damage to Resident's property or effects arising out of water leakage, or breaking pipes, or theft, or other causes beyond the reasonable control of Management. All Resident's possessions placed in public or private storerooms within the building are so placed at the Resident's sole risk, and the Management shall have no liability for any loss or damage caused to said possessions whatsoever.

**15. SUBORDINATION:** This Agreement shall be subordinate and junior to any and all liens and encumbrances, whether existing or to be existing, placed by Management on the property of which the Premises are a part.

**16. BENEFIT:** All rights given herein to Resident shall also extend and inure to the benefit of the Management or to any other person designated by Resident or Management as the recipient of said rights, and their respective assigns and successors in interest.

**17. ATTORNEY'S FEES:** If legal action be necessary to enforce compliance with this Agreement, reasonable attorney's fees may be awarded by the court to the prevailing party. If attorney's fees are awarded to the Management, then the award shall be regarded as additional accrued rent.

**18. NOTICES:** Resident agrees to accept all Notices to Resident, which may be delivered personally or by depositing the same in the United States mail, postage prepaid, and addressed to Resident at the Premises, whether or not the Resident has departed from, abandoned, or vacated the Premises.

**19. TIME:** Time is of the essence of this Agreement, and each provision herein. All rights, remedies, elections, and powers granted Management by this Agreement or by law are cumulative and no one remedy is exclusive of any other. This Agreement shall be binding upon the heirs, administrators, and assigns of all of the parties hereto, and all of the parties hereto shall be jointly and severally liable hereunder.

**20. ENFORCEABILITY:** Humphrey Management Company, Inc. is designated by Owner as its general agent with authority to manage and administer the Premises and apartment complex and to enter into, administer and enforce this Agreement. In the event of any actual or alleged failure, breach or default hereunder by Owner; 1) The sole and exclusive remedy shall be against the Owner partnership and its partnership assets; 2) No partner of Owner shall be sued or named as a party to any suit or action; 3) No service of process shall be made against any partner of Owner; 4) No partner of Owner shall be required to answer or otherwise plead to any service of process; 5) No judgment will be taken against any partner of Owner; 6) Any judgment taken against any partner of Owner may be vacated and set aside as to any such partner; 7) No writ of execution will ever be leveled against any assets of any partner of Owner; 8) These covenants and agreements are enforceable both by Owner and also by any partner of Owner.

**21. SERVICE OF PROCESS:** Resident is hereby notified that M. T. Corporation, 000 South St., #1000, Los Angeles, CA 90017, is the agent of Management designated to receive service of process in any legal action against Owner, the Resident agrees no such service will be made except upon said agent.

**22. JOINT OBLIGATION:** When this Agreement is signed by more than one person as Resident, all such persons shall be jointly and severally liable for the payment of the agreed rental and for the performance of all covenants to be kept by Resident hereunder. Without limiting the obligations imposed by the foregoing, where more than one person is Resident, rent and other charges shall, when paid by check, be paid in totem by a single instrument.

**23. RENT CONCESSIONS.** Lessee acknowledges that he is receiving a rent concession of _____

_____

as an incentive to sign and fulfill this Lease Agreement. If the lease term if not fulfilled, the lessee will pay Humphrey Mgmt. Company,      Inc. for the concession, in addition to any other charges that are due under the term of this Agreement.

**24. RESIDENT INFORMATION GUIDELINES — QUIET CONDUCT:** Resident has read and agrees to comply with and ackowledges receipt of a copy of the Community Policies now in effect, the same being expressly incorporated herein by this reference, and further agrees to comply with such amendments thereto as may from time to time be made by owner without prior notice. Resident agrees not to harass, annoy or endanger any other Resident or person, or create or maintain a nuisance, or disturb the peace or solitude of any other Resident or commit waste in or about the Premises.

**25. ATTACHMENTS TO THE AGREEMENT:** The Resident certifies that he/she has received a copy of this Agreement and the following Attachments to this Agreement and understands that these Attachments are part of the Agreement.

        1. Attachment #1 Community Policies

        2. Attachment #2 Move-In Inventory & Condition Form

26. The following additions are hereby incorporated into this Agreement _____

_____

_____

**27. ENTIRE AGREEMENT:** Concerning this Agreement and leasing of any apartment, it is not the policy of Management or its agents to enter into any oral agreements or to rely upon any oral representation(s). This Agreement contains the entire agreement between the parties hereto; all representations of Management and/or to Resident are hereby merged herein. No representation or agreement made before or after this Agreement shall be valid or enforceable unless in writing and signed by the Resident Manager.

IN WITNESS WHEREOF MANAGEMENT AND RESIDENT HAVE EXECUTED THIS AGREEMENT IN TRIPLICATE ON THE DATE FIRST WRITTEN BELOW.

_____        _____

Resident                                 Date

_____        _____

Resident                                 Date

_____        _____        _____

Agent                                  Title                             Date

# RIGHTS AND RESPONSIBILITIES OF LESSEES AND LESSORS

The rights of each party dovetail with the responsibilities of the other party. The tenant has the right to expect the landlord to fulfill all legal responsibilities and vice-versa.

## Rights of Lessees

Lessees hold an estate in real property and have acquired certain rights and interests by virtue of paying consideration. These rights are protected in the law.

### TO BE LEFT ALONE

This is called *quiet enjoyment* in the law. So the landlord cannot excessively visit the property. He or she cannot enter the property without permission or giving proper notice (usually 24 hours) for inspection, except in case of emergency.

### TO ASSIGN THE LEASE

Unless prohibited in the lease, the tenant shall have the right to assign the lease. This means to have a new tenant take possession of the property and take responsibility for the lease agreement, making payments directly to the lessor. Needless to say, most residential lease agreements do prohibit the assignment of a lease. Imagine the unqualified, undesirable tenants that would be in possession if assignment of residential leases were allowed. However, if the landlord reserved the right to qualify the new tenant in the event the existing tenant had to leave the property prior to the expiration of a lease, the tenant's cooperation could help avoid a vacancy in the unit.

Industrial and commercial lessors also typically protect their interests in the area of assignment. The following clause appears in Paragraph 12.1 of the Standard Office Lease (Gross) of the American Industrial Real Estate Association (AIREA).

"Lessor's Consent Required: Lessee shall not voluntarily or by operation of law assign, transfer, mortgage, sublet, or otherwise transfer or encumber all or any part of Lessee's interest in the Lease or in the Premises, without Lessor's prior written consent, which Lessor shall not unreasonably withhold. Lessor shall respond to Lessee's request for consent hereunder in a timely manner and any attempted assignment, transfer, mortgage, encumbrance or subletting without such consent shall be void, and shall constitute a material default and breach of this Lease without the need for notice to Lessee under Paragraph 13.1. 'Transfer' within the meaning of this Paragraph 12 shall include the transfer or transfers aggregating: (a) if Lessee is a corporation, more than twenty-five percent (25%) of the voting stock of such corporation, or (b) if Lessee is a partnership, more than twenty-five percent (25%) of the profit and loss participation in such partnership."

It should be pointed out that assignment and subletting are two different processes. Assignment causes the tenant to give up use and possession of the entire property and makes the assignee responsible for making the payment to the lessor. If the lessor has allowed the assignment he or she relieves the original tenant (the assignor) of all liability and accepts the assignee as the debtor.

In subletting, the original tenant gives up use and possession of all or part of the property and receives payment from the sub-lessee. However, the original tenant is still fully responsible for the entire lease payment to the landlord.

### TO TERMINATE THE LEASE UNDER CERTAIN CONDITIONS

Those conditions would include the landlord failing to keep the property in habitable condition, failing to repair necessary items, making outrageous alterations to the property that made quiet enjoyment difficult, or rendering the property unusable for the purpose for which it was originally leased. Also, if the government has intervened and has condemned the property to acquire it by the power of eminent domain, the tenant may terminate the lease.

## Responsibilities of Lessees

Being in possession of someone else's real property and making a financial committment to pay consideration for the use of it obligates the lessee to certain requirements. The following are minimal responsibilities.

### PAY RENT WHEN DUE

This is a primary requirement. If a tenant does this, other requirements are usually followed as well, and the tenant is on the way to a triple-A rating.

**FOLLOW THE RULES**

This would include not interfering with the rights of other tenants, not disturbing other tenants and not doing anything that would damage or destroy the premises. All laws should be obeyed, all property rules should be followed and all provisions of the lease agreement should be honored. This includes giving proper notice when moving out.

**REPAIR CONCESSIONS**

Subject to local laws, a tenant *may* make necessary repairs if he or she has been unable to get the landlord to do it. The repairs should be evidenced by a receipt showing the amount charged and the work done. It can be deducted from the monthly rent. In some areas there are restrictions on how many times this can be done per year.

# Rights of Lessors

Primary financial responsibility for the property lies with the lessor. Consequently, the lessor has the right to certain expectations within the law.

**RECEIVE THE RENT ON TIME**

This is usually the landlord's primary concern. If the rent is not received, the landlord could sue for each installment as it is past due. This is obviously not a practical remedy. If the tenant has vacated the property on one's own, the landlord could take possession and re-let the premises. In most cases, however, when rent is not received, eviction may be the only recourse.

The process of **eviction** takes place in three steps.

**(1) Three-day notice to pay or quit:** This notice is given to the tenant or posted on the property. If the tenant doesn't respond, proceed to the next step.

**(2) File unlawful detainer action:** This is filed in court and when the tenant receives notice of it, he or she has five days to respond. If there is none, a default hearing is set.

**(3) Writ of possession:** At the default hearing, a writ of possession is executed and the sheriff's office serves an eviction notice. Tenants have five days to move out or the sheriff can physically remove them.

**THE THREE STEPS TO EVICTION**

(1) Three-Day Notice to Pay or Quit

(2) File Unlawful Detainer Action

(3) Execute Writ of Possession

When eviction is performed correctly it is quite efficient and should take no more than two weeks. In actuality, however, eviction is often delayed due to court scheduling problems, contrived complaints by the tenants and failure to serve all occupants of the building, whether they are on the lease or not. While the eviction may be valid for the lessees listed on the lease, other parties in possession may be able to stay, and the process has to start all over again.

This is a strong reason to insist that the tenants honor the use clause in the lease. When people occupy a rental unit and are not on the lease, they are not accountable and have no vested interest in caring for the property or being courteous to other tenants. They also have no financial obligation. The number of occupants permitted in a unit has been agreed upon and is one of the factors determining the amount of rent. Additional occupants increase wear and tear on a property and usually result in higher repair bills. All utilities paid by the landlord will be higher. Items like doors, paint, carpet and appliances will wear out faster. For all reasons considered, unplanned and unnamed occupants should not be allowed to live indefinitely in the unit. Add to this the problem of eviction and the property manager's policy should be clear.

Another factor that can delay the eviction process is bankruptcy. If a tenant in the midst of eviction files for bankruptcy, the eviction process stops until the bankruptcy is resolved. The property manager must comply with all laws regarding bankruptcy. A small percentage of tenants will go through this process. The only remedy is preventative—a careful screening of the application trying to select the strongest candidate for tenancy.

**Figure 6-4   Three-Day Notice to Pay or Quit**

## NOTICE TO PAY RENT OR QUIT
### (C.C.P., Sec. 1161)

TO _____

AND DOES I-XII TENANTS IN POSSESION. Within **THREE DAYS** after the service on you of this notice, you are hereby required to **PAY THE RENT** of the premises hereinafter described, of which you now hold possession, amounting to the sum of _____

_____

(**$**        ) at the rental rate of _____

_____

(**$**        ) per month, being the _____

rent due from the _____ or you are hereby required to **DELIVER UP POSSESSION** of the hereinafter described premises, within **THREE DAYS** after service on you of this notice, to the undersigned, or Jay Tennen, who is authorized to receive the same or the undersigned will institute legal proceedings against you to recover possession of said premises with **ALL RENTS DUE AND DAMAGES.**

The premises herein referred to are situated in the City of Los Angeles, County of Los Angeles, State of California, designated by the number and street as _____

_____.

Dated this _____.

_____

Penal code Section No. 594 reads: "Any person or persons who willfully or maliciously destroys or damages any Real or Personal Property not their own will be punished by Fine or Imprisonment or both."

NEW STATE REGULATIONS REGARDING CREDIT REPORTING WILL BECOME EFFECTIVE ON JULY 1, 1993

THE LAW -- SECTION 1785.26 OF THE CALIFORNIA CIVIL CODE -- STATES THAT ACTUAL AND POTENTIAL DEBTORS MUST BE TOLD IF A NEGATIVE CREDIT REPORT MIGHT BE SUBMITTED AGAINST THEM.  THE NOTICE MUST BE SERVED IS SUFFICIENT IN THE FOLLOWING FORM SUGGESTED BY THE CODE:

AS REQUIRED BY LAW, YOU ARE HEREBY NOTIFIED THAT A NEGATIVE CREDIT REPORT REFLECTING ON YOUR CREDIT RECORD MAY BE SUBMITTED TO A CREDIT REPORTING AGENCY IF YOU FAIL TO FULFILL THE TERMS OF YOUR CREDIT OBLIGATION.

## EXPECT TENANT TO COMPLY WITH ALL LAWS, RULES AND CLAUSES OF THE CONTRACT

Enforcement of the rules is essential to the smooth running of the property. When the tenant is out of compliance and refuses to get in compliance, the violation probably constitutes a breach of contract, and eviction should be started. If a tenant is permitted to violate law, property rules or clauses of the contract, other tenants will follow suit and chaos will result. The chaos will be evident to all and quality tenants will not desire to live there. The inevitable result will be loss of income and a difficult process to reestablish order.

## Responsibilities of Lessors

Since the lessor holds paramount title to the property, it is incumbent upon the lessor to comply with all laws related to the ownership of real property. Doing this will ensure tenants' rights and protect the property.

### OBSERVE HEALTH AND SAFETY CODES

The landlord must provide an environment that is safe for the tenants. Any condition that would impair the health or safety of tenants (sewage problem, mold, rats, bees, an attractive nuisance like an uncovered hole, traffic and parking situation or whatever it may be) must be corrected immediately.

### OBEY FAIR HOUSING LAWS

It is illegal to discriminate against anyone for reasons of race, religion, sex, marital status, age or physical disability. The property manager, representing the property owner, must focus on material facts, and be fair to all tenants.

### FOLLOW ALL LAWS

The property manager should be aware of all laws regarding treatment of the tenant, including proper notice before entering except in an emergency, returning the deposit within 21 days and demanding a deposit no larger than the maximum allowable and giving proper notice to terminate the lease.

## What the Lessor Must Not Do

The lessor and those representing the lessor must not violate any laws in trying to remove the tenant. It may be tempting to turn off utilities, change the locks, make the property uninhabitable by removing doors or windows, violating the tenant's right to quiet enjoyment or any other means available when dealing with an undesirable tenant. These measures usually cost more money in the long run and must be avoided.

# SPECIAL CLAUSES

Special clauses deal with certain specific issues regarding the leasing of real property and attempt to set out in advance the obligations of lessor and lessee pertaining to these issues. They also set out in advance procedures that must be followed and the remedies of the parties in the event there is a violation.

## Compliance Clause

In commercial and industrial properties, the compliance clause designates which party is responsible for compliance with new laws on any level of government from local to national. It would include modifications to the building due to the requirements of the Americans with Disabilities Act.

Paragraph 6.2 (b) of the Standard Office Lease (Gross) of the American Industrial Real Estate Association (AIREA) contains a compliance clause.

> "Except as provided in paragraph 6.2 (a) Lessee shall, at Lessee's expense, promptly comply with all applicable statutes, ordinances, rules, regulations, orders, covenants and restrictions of record, and requirements of any fire insurance underwriters or rating bureaus, now in effect or which may hereafter come into effect, whether or not they reflect a change in policy from that now existing, during the term or any part of the term hereof, relating in any manner to the Premises and the occupation and use by Lessee of the Premises. Lessee shall conduct its business in a lawful manner and shall not use or permit the use of the Premises or the Common Areas in any manner that will tend to create waste or a nuisance or shall tend to disturb other occupants of the Office Building Project."

## Use Clause

All owners want to protect their properties from devaluation due to inappropriate uses. A typical *use* clause in a residential lease agreement reads as follows.

"The premises shall be used only as a private residence for the persons previously named in application for residence. Resident agrees that no occupants in excess of those stated herein and named on the application shall occupy the Premises for over two weeks, except upon prior written consent of Management. Resident shall not violate any federal, state, county or local law within the Premises or apartment complex. No business or commercial activities are allowed on the Premises."

For industrial and commercial property, the intended use by the tenant is filled in on the first page under Basic Lease Provisions, and a *use* clause binds that use upon the tenant exclusively. Quoting the Standard Office Lease (Gross) of American Industrial Real Estate Association (AIREA), the use clause says:

"The Premises shall be used and occupied only for the purpose set forth in paragraph 1.4 of the Basic Lease Provisions or any other use which is reasonably comparable to that use and for no other purpose."

## Maintenance Clause

In residential properties, this clause usually states that the lessor will make any necessary repairs due to normal wear and tear, but that the lessee will be responsible for repairs due to his or her negligence or over-use of the premises.

In commercial and industrial properties, the clause in the AIREA lease form is extensive and quite explicit. Here are some excerpts.

"Paragraph 7.1 Lessor's Obligations: Lessor shall keep the Office Building Project, including the Premises, interior and exterior walls, roof, and common areas, and the equipment whether used exclusively for the Premises or in common with other premises, in good condition and repair..."

"Paragraph 7.2 Lessee's Obligations: Notwithstanding Lessor's obligation to keep the Premises in good condition and repair, Lessee shall be responsible for payment of the cost thereof to Lessor as additonal rent for that portion of the cost of any maintenance and repair of the Premises, or any equipment (wherever located) that serves only Lessee or the Premises, to the extent such cost is attributable to causes beyond normal wear and tear. Lessee shall be responsible for the cost of painting, repairing or replacing wall coverings, and to repair or replace any Premises improvements that are not ordinarily a part of the Building or that are above the Building standards."

"Paragraph 7.3 Alterations and Additions: Lessee shall not, without Lessor's prior written consent make any alterations, improvements, additions, Utility Installations or repairs in, on or about the Premises, or the Office Building Project... 'Utility Installation' shall mean carpeting, window and wall coverings, power panels, electrical distribution systems, lighting fixtures, air conditioning, plumbing, and telephone and telecommunications wiring and equipment. At the expiration of the term, Lessor may require the removal of any or all of said alterations, improvements, additions or Utility Installations, and the restoration of the Premises and the Office Building Project to their prior condition, at Lessee's expense. Should Lessor permit Lessee to make its own alterations, improvements, additions or Utility Installations, Lessee shall use only such contractor as has been expressly approved by Lessor, and Lessor may require Lessee to provide Lessor, at Lessee's sole cost and expense, a lien and completion bond in an amount equal to one and one-half times the estimated cost of such improvements, to insure Lessor against any liability for mechanic's and materialman's liens and to insure completion of the work..."

## Liability Indemnity Clause

Owners want to be indemnified against liability caused by actions of their tenants. A liability indemnity clause in a standard residential lease agreement reads like this.

"Resident agrees to hold Management harmless from all claims of loss or damage to property, and of injury or death to persons caused by the intentional acts or negligence of the Resident, his guests or invitees, or occurring on the premises rented for Resident's exclusive use. Resident expressly absolves Management from any and all liability for any loss or damage to Resident's property or effects arising out of water leakage, or breaking pipes, or theft, or other causes beyond the reasonable control of Management. All Resident's possessions placed in public or private storerooms within the building are so placed at the Resident's sole risk, and the Management shall have no liability for any loss or damage caused to said possessions whatsoever."

AIREA's standard office lease form requires both lessor and lessee to maintain liability insurance and property insurance. The lessor's property insurance covers the building and premises owned by the lessor. The lessee's property insurance covers the personal property, fixtures, equipment and improvements made by the lessee. Coverage is to be not less than 100% replacement cost for loss due to fire, vandalism, malicious mischief, sprinkler leakage and earthquake sprinkler leakage. Lessee must deliver to Lessor a copy of the required insurance policy.

## Damage or Destruction Clause

AIREA's standard office lease form contains an extensive clause in the event of damage to or destruction of the property. Obviously such an occurrence could interfere with the carrying on of the lessee's business. How would such an occurrence be handled? Definitions are first offered for terms ranging from *partial damage* to *total destruction*. Consideration is given to whether the damage is the fault of the lessee or not. Then consideration is given as to whether the loss is insured or uninsured. Does the loss take place within 12 months of the expiration of the lease? If so, the lessor may, at his or her discretion, terminate the lease. If the damages were not due to negligence on the part of the lessee, and the damages interfere with the lessee's business, the lessee may be entitled to abatement of rent to the extent that the operation and profitability of the lessee's business is adversely affected.

In residential property leases, a similar policy of fairness to the tenant is set forth. However, if the tenant is the cause of the damages, prompt restitution will be required.

## Default Clause

The lessor will want to set forth his or her remedies in the event of a default. In a standard residential lease agreement, the clause reads like this.

"In the event of any breach of this Agreement by Resident, then Management, in addition to any other rights or remedies, shall have the immediate right of re-entry and may remove any and all personal property and effects of the Resident, and the Management may retain possession of such personal property until all charges of every kind including rent, cleaning, shortages or damage to the Premises shall be

paid in full. Management shall have the lien granted by law upon all baggage and other property of Resident, and may enforce said lien as provided by law. Said lien may be enforced whenever rent or other charges are due and unpaid and regardless of whether a 30-day notice to quit or a 3-day notice to pay rent or quit shall have been served. Enforcement of the lien shall not operate to waive any other rights of Management in unlawful detainer or otherwise."

AIREA's Standard Office Lease form has specific definitions and procedures for default. Some excerpts from Paragraph 13 follow.

"13.1 Default: The occurrence of any one or more of the following events shall constitute default of this Lease by Lessee:

a. The vacation or abandonment of the Premises by the Lessee. Vacation of the Premises shall include the failure to occupy the Premises for a continuous period of sixty (60) days or more, whether or not the rent is paid.

b. The breach by lessee of any of the covenants, conditions or provisions of the following paragraphs: alterations, assignment or subletting, vacation or abandonment, insolvency, false statement, estoppel certificate, subordination, auctions or easements, all of which are hereby deemed to be material, non-curable defaults without the necessity of any notice by Lessor to Lessee thereof.

c. The failure by Lessee to make any payment of rent or any other payment required to be made by Lessee hereunder, as and when due, where such failure shall continue for a period of three (3) days after written notice thereof from Lessor to Lessee.

d. The discovery by Lessor that any financial statement given to Lessor, or its successor in interest or by any guarantor of Lessee's obligation hereunder, was materially false."

# OTHER ISSUES

The AIREA standard office lease form continues for ten long pages with various clauses and provisions including options, security measures, easements, performance under protest, parties with authority to represent lessee, conflict, lender modification, multiple parties, work letter, and attachments including floor plan, general rules and parking rules.

Residential property managers will want to cover issues such as the following either in the standard lease agreement or in a cover letter or addendum.

## Pets

If the owner of an apartment building agrees to allow tenants to keep pets, certain understandings must exist between lessor and lessee. The allowance of pets is a balance between achieving a higher level of occupancy by opening the doors to a greater number of potential tenants and maintaining the premises in good condition without incurring excessive repair and maintenance bills.

## Lead-Based Paint

Properties constructed prior to 1978 may have lead based paint. This can be hazardous to the health of tenants, especially toddlers. The paint crystallizes and is inhaled. It can impact the development of a small child by creating unsafe lead levels in the bloodstream. If a property has been constructed prior to 1978 the tenant needs to be notified of the danger of lead paint. A disclosure statement should be signed by the tenants and the booklet *Protect Your Family From Lead In Your Home* should be given to them.

## Keys and Locks

 Keys should be turned in to management and possession given up before security deposits are returned. The tenant should understand that he or she does not have the right to change the locks or add any additional locks to which management does not have access. In case of fire or other emergency the safety of all residents could depend on the manager's ability to access a unit.

**Figure 6-5   Pet Rider**

## Pet Permit

Apartments #_____

Dated:_____

Between_____and_____

1.   Resident agrees that only the pet described and named below will occupy the premises.  No additional or different pet is authorized under this agreement.

2.   Resident agrees that pet will be kept inside the apartment at all times except when on a leash and accompanied by and under control of the resident or other responsible person.

3.   If, in the opinion of management, the pet becomes annoying, bothersome, or in any way a nuisance to other residents or to the apartment operation, management may revoke this permit, and, upon notice, resident will immediately remove the pet from the premises.

4.   Resident agrees to deposit with management upon execution of this permit, the additional sum of $_____ __ _$_____ of this sum is regarded as additional security deposit subject to the provisions under paragraph 6 of the primary rental agreement for the apartment.  $_____ of this sum is non-refundable.  If the pet is permanently removed from the premises, and the management's inspection finds your apartment clean, odor-free and undamaged, the refundable portion of the pet deposit will be refunded.

5.   Resident agrees and warrants that the pet will not exceed 12 inches in height and 15 pounds in weight (full grown).

6.   Resident agrees to walk his/her pet only in areas specified by the management.

7.   Management reserves the right to impose additional rules and regulations governing pets on the premises and resident agrees to abide by all such additional rules and regulations.

8.   Resident indemnifies management and the owner of these apartments from all liability whatsoever concerning or related to the pet, including pound costs, injuries, damage, attorney's fees and costs.

9.   In the event the resident leaves his/her pet unattended for more than 24 hours, management is thereby authorized to enter the resident's apartment, remove the animal, and place it with a responsible person, or other person designated by resident, or with a kennel at resident's expense, or turn the pet over to the Pound or other authorities, all at the resident's expense.

10.   Any noncompliance by resident or the pet with the terms of this permit, or with the rules and regulations governing pets on the premises, shall entitle management to revoke this permit, in which case the resident will immediately remove the pet from the premises at the management's request, or, at the management's election, management may terminate the rental agreement on seven (7) days notice.  If management accepts rent while resident is in noncompliance with the terms of this permit, such will not constitute a waiver of management's rights to terminate this permit, or terminate the rental agreement, for such noncompliance.

11.   Description of Pet:                                     Management:

     Type of Pet_____          _____

     Breed_____          _____

     Age_____Color_____

## Figure 6-6   Lead-Based Paint Disclosure

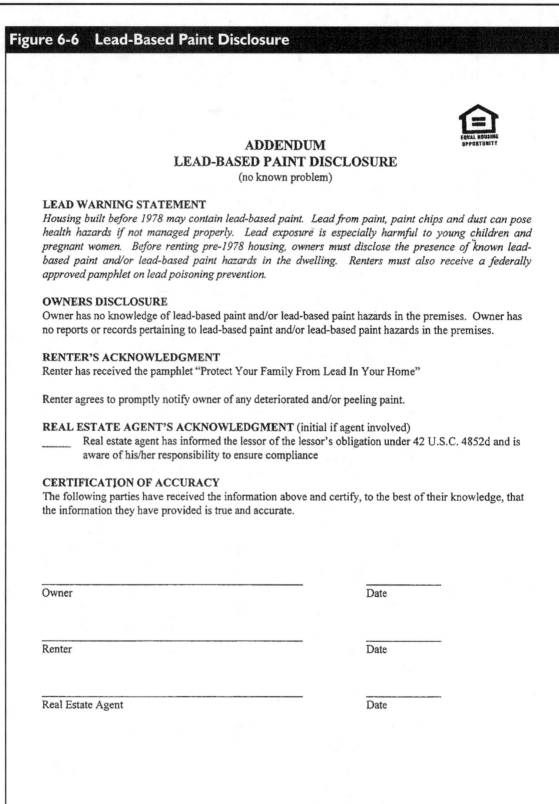

**ADDENDUM**
**LEAD-BASED PAINT DISCLOSURE**
(no known problem)

**LEAD WARNING STATEMENT**
*Housing built before 1978 may contain lead-based paint. Lead from paint, paint chips and dust can pose health hazards if not managed properly. Lead exposure is especially harmful to young children and pregnant women. Before renting pre-1978 housing, owners must disclose the presence of known lead-based paint and/or lead-based paint hazards in the dwelling. Renters must also receive a federally approved pamphlet on lead poisoning prevention.*

**OWNERS DISCLOSURE**
Owner has no knowledge of lead-based paint and/or lead-based paint hazards in the premises. Owner has no reports or records pertaining to lead-based paint and/or lead-based paint hazards in the premises.

**RENTER'S ACKNOWLEDGMENT**
Renter has received the pamphlet "Protect Your Family From Lead In Your Home"

Renter agrees to promptly notify owner of any deteriorated and/or peeling paint.

**REAL ESTATE AGENT'S ACKNOWLEDGMENT** (initial if agent involved)
_____   Real estate agent has informed the lessor of the lessor's obligation under 42 U.S.C. 4852d and is aware of his/her responsibility to ensure compliance

**CERTIFICATION OF ACCURACY**
The following parties have received the information above and certify, to the best of their knowledge, that the information they have provided is true and accurate.

_____          _____
Owner                                                                Date

_____          _____
Renter                                                               Date

_____          _____
Real Estate Agent                                           Date

## Parking

Each tenant will have certain parking spaces assigned to him or her. They should understand that they are restricted to parking only in these designated spaces. Guest parking will be limited to certain designated parking spaces. Invitees of the tenant need to be courteous of all residents' parking spaces and observe the rules for guest parking. The tenants are responsible for their guests abiding by these and all rules.

## Waterbeds

Management policy on waterbeds needs to be clearly stated. Waterbeds obviously can cause property damage and, on occasion, have resulted in bodily harm. If waterbeds are to be allowed, special covenants and conditions need to be established and communicated to the tenants to minimize the owner's risk of liability and loss.

## Common Areas

Common areas of an apartment complex may include a swimming pool, tennis courts, greenbelts and walkways, barbecue areas and parking lots. Recreational facilities are provided for the enjoyment of all and must be used with care. Notify tenants of the rules governing the use of such facilities. Have them initial a rider saying they understand the rules and agree to abide by them. Post the rules also. Measures like this can prevent accidents and injury and possibly reduce liability in the event of carelessness or negligence on the part of tenants.

## Violation of Covenants

Covenants are promises, and basically to violate a covenant is to break the rules that have been made part of the lease agreement—rules the tenant has agreed to follow. The tenant should understand that management may terminate the lease based on violation of covenants by giving the tenant written notice. The tenant should be asked to vacate and if they do not, the laws of your particular state should be followed to evict.

## Change of Terms

Sometimes it is necessary for management to change rules or increase the rent. Tenants should understand that such things happen from time to time and should receive proper written notice of any changes.

**Figure 6-7    Notice of Change of Terms of Tenancy**

# NOTICE OF CHANGE OF TERMS OF TENANCY
## CC 827

TO: _____
(LIST ALL AUTHORIZED ADULT TENANTS IN POSSESSION)

AND TO ALL OTHERS IN POSSESSION OF THE PREMISES COMMONLY KNOWN AS:

_____ , APARTMENT NO. _____
(STREET ADDRESS)

_____ , CALIFORNIA_____ ,
(CITY)                                                           (ZIP CODE)

YOU ARE HEREBY NOTIFIED THAT 30 DAYS AFTER SERVICE UPON YOU OF THIS NOTICE, OR

_____, WHICHEVER IS LATER, YOUR TENANCY OF THE ABOVE DESIGNATED

PREMISES WILL BE CHANGED AS FOLLOWS:

1. THE MONTHLY RENT, WHICH IS PAYABLE IN ADVANCE ON OR BEFORE THE    _____

   DAY OF EACH MONTH, WILL BE THE SUM OF $ _____

2. OTHER CHANGES: _____

   _____

   _____

EXCEPT AS HEREIN PROVIDED, ALL OTHER TERMS OF YOUR TENANCY SHALL REMAIN IN FULL FORCE AND EFFECT.

   *"AS REQUIRED BY LAW, YOU ARE HEREBY NOTIFIED THAT A NEGATIVE CREDIT REPORT*
   *RELECTING ON YOUR CREDIT RECORD MAY BE SUBMITTED TO A CREDIT REPORTING AGENCY*
   *IF YOU FAIL TO FULFILL THE TERMS OF YOUR CREDIT OBLIGATIONS."* CC 1785.26 (c) (2)

DATE:_____   _____  20 _____

UNAUTHORIZED USE PROHIBITED

                                              _____
                                              (OWNER OR AGENT)

EQUAL HOUSING
OPPORTUNITY

# QUESTIONS

1. The purpose of a lease is to:

    a. transfer possession of a property

    b. identify the parties involved in the lease

    c. obligate the tenant to the rent payments

    d. all of the above

2. An estate for years is:

    a. the long-term ownership of real property

    b. a type of freehold estate

    c. a lease with a beginning and ending date

    d. a lease longer than one year

3. A periodic tenancy is:

    a. a month-to-month tenancy

    b. a period to period tenancy

    c. the type of tenancy that requires notice to terminate

    d. all of the above

4. In a gross lease:

    a. the landlord knows exactly what the periodic net will be

    b. the tenant pays the lease amount plus fixed expenses

    c. the tenant pays only the rent

    d. the tenant pays rent and all expenses

5. In a triple net lease:

    a. the tenant pays the rent only

    b. the landlord receives a predictable net amount per period

    c. the landlord pays for maintenance and repairs

    d. the tenant pays rent plus variable expenses only

6. A percentage lease works in the following manner:

    a. the tenant pays a base rent and a percentage of gross receipts

    b. the tenant pays a base rent or a percentage of gross receipts

    c. the tenant pays a percentage of gross receipts only if they exceed a specified minimum

    d. this type of lease can have any combination of base rent and percentage of gross receipts

7. The term that goes with graduated lease is:

    a. step-up lease

    b. enforced provision lease

    c. elevated lease

    d. variable lease

8. The essential elements of a valid contract include:

    a. mutual consent, performance, lawful object and consideration

    b. meeting of the minds, payment of money, capable parties and lawful object

    c. mutual consent, consideration, capacity, lawful object

    d. mutual consent, capacity, lawful object, money

9. Leases should be in writing:

    a. only if not to be performed within a year

    b. only if the parties are legal aliens

    c. only for commercial properties

    d. it is always recommended that agreements to let real property be in writing

10. The *duck theory of law* means that:

    a. wildlife in parks near rental property is always protected

    b. one's actions speak louder about commitment than the absence of one's signature

    c. contracts entered into because of fraud are valid until rescinded

    d. if one rule is allowed to be broken, others will follow

11. Quiet enjoyment means:

    a. enjoying the use and possession
       of property without noise
    b. the absence of disturbance
       from neighbors
    c. not being disturbed by the
       owner or the owner's agent
    d. none of the above

12. Assignment of a lease:

    a. means a new tenant takes the former
       tenant's place in the lease, making
       payments directly to the lessor
    b. means a new tenant takes some
       of the space and makes payment
       to the original lessee
    c. is forbidden by law
    d. is always permitted in every lease

13. Lessees must:

    a. pay the rent on time
    b. take care of the premises
    c. respect the rights of other tenants
    d. all of the above

14. Lessors should do all of the following except:

    a. obey fair housing laws
    b. change the locks on a tenant's
       door to encourage moving
    c. observe health and safety codes
    d. enter an apartment with no advance
       notice if smoke is coming from the unit

15. The compliance clause in a lease deals with:

    a. the lessor complying with
       health and safety codes
    b. the lessee complying with
       occupancy restrictions
    c. which party to the lease is responsible
       for complying with new laws
    d. the building being in compliance
       with local building codes

16. The use clause in a lease deals with:

    a. who may use the premises
    b. what the premises may be used for
    c. whether or not the property
       conforms to local zoning
    d. a and b above

17. The documents used to bind parties to a lease:

    a. should be the result of legal counsel
       and the owner's objectives
    b. are always standard forms
    c. are always standard forms
       customized by the property manager
    d. need not address all material issues

18. For a lease to be effective it must:

    a. protect the interests of the lessor
       and meet the needs of the lessee
    b. prohibit the lessee from ever making
       any alterations to the property
    c. provide an extension of the term
       if the lessee requests it
    d. be a triple net lease

19. In a residential lease:

    a. pets should never be allowed
    b. the consequences of any breach of
       contract should be spelled out in advance
    c. guests of a tenant should not stay overnight
    d. tenants can make their own repairs
       whenever necessary

20. Peripheral issues relative to residential tenancy:

    a. are always in the standard lease agreement
    b. are rare and the property manager
       should not worry about them
    c. can be covered in letters and exhibits
       made part of the lease agreement
    d. can be dealt with later if they
       become a problem

# ANSWERS

1. *d*
2. *c*
3. *d*
4. *c*
5. *b*
6. *d*
7. *a*
8. *c*
9. *d*
10. *b*
11. *c*
12. *a*
13. *d*
14. *b*
15. *c*
16. *d*
17. *a*
18. *a*
19. *b*
20. *c*

# Tenant Relations

- **Establishing Relationships**
- **Some Specific Techniques**
- **When You Have To Get Them Out**
- **Not An Exact Science**

C H A P T E R **7**

# ESTABLISHING RELATIONSHIPS

If we're looking to make something happen in business, relationships help facilitate the objective. If we want our family to do something, good relationships within the family will allow it to come together. No one can force an objective on others. Relationships make it happen. The cooperative team approach is always best.

The landlord/tenant relationship is a business relationship. Make no mistake about that. It is not a friendship with the tenants. The property manager should be friendly in demeanor, but not be friends with the tenants. Although the landlord/tenant relationship is not a friendship, it is a relationship nevertheless. That means that each party has made certain commitments to the other. Each party has a certain confidence level towards the other party about the likelihood of their fulfilling their commitments.

The tenant is willing to move in because he or she believes the property manager will keep the premises safe and in good repair, and will provide a satisfying environment in which to live. The property manager is willing to accept the tenant because he or she believes the tenant most likely will pay the rent on time and will follow the rules. The trust and confidence each party has in the other is the basis for this business relationship.

The establishment of this business relationship is 100% the responsibility of the property manager. If a good business relationship is to be established with the tenants, it will be the doing of the property manager and no one else.

## First Impressions

The old saying, "You never get a second chance to make a first impression," is hard to refute. In this business relationship we seek to establish with our tenants, first impression is everything. If prospective tenants see an office that is messy and disorganized, subconsciously they lower their professional estimation of you. Although they may not be thinking this consciously, in their gut they're feeling that since you're a bit lax with your organization, they can afford to be a bit lax in the promptness of their payment and the tidiness of their rental space.

If they ask you about procedures for certain circumstances, such as needing repairs or having a problem with a neighbor, and you as the property manager don't have a system in place to handle such a problem—sort of making it up as you go along, they will sense your disorganization and lack of preparation. This is likely to carry over to their response to you in many areas, including paying the rent, maintaining their rental space and relations with other tenants.

If your demeanor with them is slap-happy, jovial and overly familiar, you will lose your advantage of control in the relationship. Your demeanor should be that of a police dog—watchful, polite and in control, but ready to take action if necessary. The action you might have to take is to reject their application if there are blemishes on their record you'd rather not accept. Or later in the process, if you've accepted them as tenants, you may have to approach them about obeying the rules of the complex or paying the rent on time. Your professional distance allows you to remain objective.

On the other hand, if tenants come into your office and see a neat, well-organized professional setting, they will expect to transact business efficiently. They will automatically expect that there will be standards and conditions to their acceptance as tenants. Without the words being spoken, they will expect that the rent must be paid on time and the rules must be obeyed. If they ask about a procedure such as request for repairs or a complaint against a neighbor, they will be very impressed when you show them a form for each of those circumstances.

They will say to themselves, "Boy, these guys are on top of things." As they see that you have systems and procedures in place, they will know that you enforce the rules and take care of business. It sets a whole different basis for your interacting together.

When they notice your police dog personality, they will perceive you as friendly but businesslike. They will know that you are fair but firm, that you apply the same standards to all and expect the same performance from all. If they are worthy of tenancy in your building, they will seek to live up to the standards because deep down inside they will know that anything less will not be tolerated. And if they know they are not credit worthy for whatever reason, they will not expect to be accepted, because they already understand you don't play games. You conduct sound business practices.

This kind of professionalism helps to establish the best kind of business relationship, where the tenant doesn't expect something for nothing. Tenants know there is no free lunch, but expect to be treated fairly. By conducting business in such a professional manner, the property manager smooths out the future by eliminating problems before they occur.

---

**Figure 7-1  Service Request**

Resident's name _____ Date_____

Apartment #_____ On-site manager's name _____

Phone # (home) _____ (work) _____

Repairs needed _____

_____

_____

_____

_____

_____

_____

Estimated Cost _____ Actual Cost _____

Date Completed _____

Completed By _____ Phone # _____

_____

Charge Resident _____ Charge Management _____

---

---

**Figure 7-2   Complaint Form**

Complaint Form

Resident_____Date_____

Apartment_____

Phone #_____

*******************************************************************

Offending Apartment_____ Date_____

Nature of Complaint_____

_____

_____

_____

_____

_____

_____

Signature:_____

## Second Impressions

Second impressions refer to the maintenance of the ongoing relationship after the applicant has been accepted for tenancy. Even after a careful qualifying process in which you have checked up on references and verified all parts of the application, you will find that you have two kinds of people living in your building—tenants and residents. These two terms have a technical distinction in that by using the term *tenant* some refer to the legal relationship of the lessee to the lessor, and by using the term *resident* they are referring to the human being living in the property.

But there is another distinction noticed by most property managers. There is a sense in which a *tenant* just occupies the unit. The *resident* considers the apartment complex home. It is not difficult to predict differences in attitudes and behavior between the two. The resident's unit is clean, in good repair and suffers little damage over time, other than normal wear and tear. The tenant's unit is not well-maintained and after moving out, significant repairs have to be made. The resident helps care for the entire complex, occasionally picking up trash that doesn't belong to him or her and pulling a weed or two just because it makes everything look better. The tenant uses the complex but doesn't contribute beyond what is required.

The resident respects the rights of other tenants, either keeps to oneself or gets along well with others, and has a vested interest in the quality of future residents. The tenant plays loud music, parks carelessly, litters and has conflicts with others. The resident stays in the complex for a long time, usually years. The tenant stays a much shorter time, usually months. It's just that the months *seem* like years. Residents rarely complain, and when they find it necessary to do so, they do it politely. Tenants complain frequently, and they do so loudly and rudely.

Since having your share of the two types of occupants is unavoidable, you must learn to deal with both. Be fair and always keep your promises to all tenants. There are at least three reasons for this. First, for legal reasons, you must keep your promises. If you promise something to prospective tenants that causes them to move into your complex, you have created what is called an *express warranty* and legally you must follow through. Second, your tenants will respect you for keeping your promises and this will enhance all of your dealings with them. And third, it's just the right thing to do.

## A Good Example

A property manager observed by this author years ago seemed to have captured the right balance between friendliness and professionalism. John was an on-site manager for a 40-unit complex. He also held a part time job to help make ends meet, but it never interfered with his duties as property manager. Several times a day John could be seen walking the grounds and the parking lot of the complex. He picked up trash, trimmed trees, picked weeds, watered and repaired external items as he came upon them. By caring for the complex, most of the residents felt that he was looking out for them.

If John observed a strange car parked on the property, he would check into it right away. If it was parked in a resident's reserved space, he would find out whose it was and have them move it. If he couldn't find who owned it, he would have it towed before the resident came home. If it was parked  in guest parking, he would take note of it and if not moved within 24 hours, and if he could not find the owner, he would have it removed. He was always mindful of strange cars driving through the complex. There was an occasional car break-in and theft, and John would talk to strangers to find out if they had a legitimate reason for being on the grounds. He would not hesitate to call the police if any person he observed seemed suspicious or was actually committing a crime.

John was a skilled airplane mechanic and was very handy with tools. He was always prompt and fair with his repairs in the apartment units. There wasn't anything he couldn't fix. This trait was a real plus for him as he took care of the complex and the interior of the individual units.

From a personality standpoint, John was low-key. He wasn't excitable; neither was he bashful. His communication was direct and with an economy of words. He told people what they needed to hear. He didn't avoid difficult tenants or situations, yet he was fair to everyone. John was in his late twenties and was an extremely responsible young man. He was well-liked by the residents of this apartment complex, and ownership must have appreciated him.

When it came time for John to move on, he was replaced by a married couple that proved to be an extreme contrast to the qualities the residents had come to take for granted in their on-site manager. The new couple was not available to the residents. The husband was always working his full-time job and the wife always stayed behind closed doors. The blinds would be drawn and she wouldn't answer the phone or the door. The care of the complex went down. Maintenance was slow or non-existent. If there was a crime or emergency on the property, the residents felt that management would be the last to know. Turnover increased as residents grew increasingly unhappy.

John built relationships with everyone. Each resident felt that he cared about the property and about them. The new managers built no relationships. Where John created a presence, the new managers created a void. They thought they could collect money and take care of a physical property without knowing or caring about the people who lived there. They were wrong. During their tenure as managers, vacancy increased from 2% to 8%. Car break-ins occurred more frequently and the physical appearance of the complex deteriorated as more and more deferred maintenance needed to be done. Safety was impaired as parking lots went dark and the walkways were not always free of obstructions. The quality of the occupants changed also. Many long time *residents* moved out to be replaced by short-term *tenants*. As you might expect, before too long all of this starts to have an impact on the net operating income, which directly impacts value.

# SOME SPECIFIC TECHNIQUES

Anyone dealing with people in business will get the best results if they like people. If you don't like people, they will sense it and offer resistance to whatever you want them to do. Also, if you don't like people you're missing out on some of the biggest joys of life. Such an attitude places you at great disadvantage. Here are some ways to improve your ability to gain cooperation rather than antagonism from the people you serve.

## Offer Sincere Appreciation

Start by calling people by name. In a very large complex this may be challenging, but start by adding one name per day. This shows that you recognize each resident as an individual, not just the "tenant in #208." If our society has a class system, one way it is divided is by property owners and renters. Renters receive the less esteem, but in the eyes of the law, all are equally important. So treat everyone with the dignity and respect they deserve. They are human beings, not just renters.

Find an aspect of their behavior that you can compliment. It might have to do with their following certain rules, paying the rent on time, helping a neighbor or the way they take care of their children. Mention it to them or send them a brief note expressing your appreciation. You will set yourself apart from any manager they ever had. Your purpose is not to be their friend, but to be the kind of human being who will engender cooperation. You do want them to like you and respect you, and this is best accomplished by being the type of person who exudes warmth and respect towards others. Incidentally, appreciating others and sincerely being warm and respectful to others is its own reward. It is not to be regarded as a manipulation, yet it almost never fails to create an attitude of cooperation as a by-product.

One on-site property manager in a large modern apartment complex, after showing the property to a mother and daughter and going through the approval process, handed them the key and said, "Now, here's the key. We don't need to call you, and you don't need to call us. Good bye!" How wonderful for human relations! How welcome the new residents must have felt! This property manager didn"t want to be bothered by anyone. Perhaps he had been burned so many times he was burned out. He could have used a course in some principles on human relations. If a property manager can maintain an attitude of service, help people and make the property the warmest and best functioning residential complex it can be, that benefits everyone. It meets obligations to ownership, engenders cooperation when needed and refreshes the manager, too.

When I was in Army basic training at Fort Polk, Louisiana, there were two platoon leaders with distinctly different leadership styles. Gary was one of the shorter men in the company, but treated each man under his command with respect. He did everything every other recruit had to do and led by example. He was well liked by his men and they did everything in their power to make his job easier.

Dar, on the other hand, was 6-foot 2-inches tall, handsome and looked every inch the leader. Dar had one problem—no respect for the men in his platoon. Because the drill sergeant appointed Dar as platoon leader, he thought he was better than everyone else. He ordered the men in his platoon to make his bunk in the morning and polish his boots and belt buckle. He found it too inconvenient to march to the rifle range, often rode in the back of a pickup truck with a smile on his face and displayed the "peace sign" in full view of his troops. He rarely got the head count correct in the morning formation, which usually resulted in extra duty for his men. Antagonism, not cooperation, was the result. In a hostile military environment, a rock hit him in the eye as he stood in an upstairs window and an attempt was made on his life with an ice pick as the weapon.

A condescending attitude will never elicit cooperation. If property managers project attitudes of superiority over their tenants, if they act like they don't want contact and don't want to live up to their part of the bargain, tenants will never go out of their way to do their share. It will result in an "us and them" attitude, resistance all the way. And whose job does this make harder? The tenant can move on, but the property manager will have to answer for the results of an inability to engender respect and cooperation.

A constructive way to express appreciation to a resident who has paid the rent on time for a year is to write a letter of commendation to his or her employer. Consider the following letter addressed to the resident's supervisor.

---

### Figure 7-3    Letter to Employer

May 22, 2001

XYZ Corporation
124 S. Main Street
Duncanville, OH 27092

Dear Mr. Johnson,

This letter is to commend to you one of your employees, Mr. Don Hoag. Mr. Hoag is a resident here at Garden Manor and is a real asset to our community.

In the year that he has lived here, he has always paid his rent on time and has always been cooperative in following the rules of the complex. We're happy to have Mr. Hoag as a resident of Garden Manor and hope he continues to live here for years into the future.

We wanted you to know of Mr. Hoag's excellent citizenship and hope that it will be taken into consideration the next time he is considered for a promotion.

Sincerely,
Joanne P. Wilson
Manager
Garden Manor Apartments

---

In addition to sending this letter to Mr. Hoag's employer, send Mr. Hoag a copy with a brief note letting him know you appreciate his prompt payments and good cooperation as a resident of Garden

Manor. You will probably set yourself apart from any other manager Mr. Hoag has ever had.

How will he feel about it? There could be a long list of feelings, but it's easy to see that everything will be positive. He'll feel appreciated. He will like you for taking the time and thought to do that. He will want to cooperate with you in the future, with rent, rules, everything! Why not strive to have a building full of residents who feel that way about living here and about you as manager? It couldn't hurt and it sure might make your job that much easier.

## See Things From Their Perspective

Not to agree with them, but to see where they're coming from. I like to eat ice cream, but when I go fishing, I don't try to put ice cream on the hook. I use worms. That's what the fish like. Bait the hook to suit the fish.

---

**Figure 7-4    Rent Collection—Letter A**

May 5, 2001

Rose Garden Apartments
123 First Ave.
Budville, FL 24094

Dear Tenant,

It is the 5th of the month and your rent has not been received. As property manager for the Rose Garden Apartments, I am charged with the responsibility of collecting the rents on time. I have responsibilities to ownership and many expenses and bills to pay.

It is imperative that you pay the rent immediately to avoid the start of eviction.

I hope to see you in my office no later than 6:00 p.m. tomorrow, May 6th.

Sincerely,
I. M. Dense
Property Manager

---

Consider Letters A and B, both intended to facilitate the collection of rent. Letter A **(Figure 7-4)** comes from the landlord's perspective. Let's observe the shortcomings.

Well, Letter A leaves a bit to be desired. Do you see how it comes only from the perspective of what the property manager's wants and concerns are? "I am charged with the responsibility of collecting the rents on time." Oh really? Such an important person! "I have responsibilities to ownership…" That's nice, but they're not the tenant's primary concern. "I have many expenses and bills to pay." No kidding! Why do you think the rent wasn't paid? Unexpected car repairs. Nagging doctor bills. The list never ends.

## Figure 7-5   Rent Collection—Letter B

May 5, 2001

Rose Garden Apartments
123 First Ave.
Budsville, FL 24094

Dear John,

I must ask you to do me a favor.

In three days I am required to send a report to ownership, naming any tenants who have not yet paid their rent for this month. From this report, they will instruct me to start eviction proceedings. I know from experience this can create an extreme hardship on the families involved, and make it very difficult to secure another rental.

As a valued resident in this complex, I don't want to see that happen to you. If your failure to pay is an oversight, please send the rent in right away. If you're having financial difficulties right now, as happens to almost everyone at one time or another, please contact me immediately to see if we can work something out.

I hope you'll be able to live here for a long time to come.

Sincerely,
I. Care
Property Manager

Letter A is likely to create resistance, resentment and defensiveness. People are mostly interested in their own circumstances, not someone else's. Your tenant could care less about *your* responsibilities, *your* obligations to management, *your* expenses and bills. All they can think of is their own. The letter was sent to help collect the rent, but more likely will create a staunchly resistant tenant—an angry one who will stall an eviction in every way possible.

Let's look at Letter B, which comes at the problem from a different perspective. Letter B **(Figure 7-5)** takes into account how the tenant likely is feeling.

First let me say, this tenant absolutely has to pay the rent, or leave. But doesn't it make sense to approach the tenant with a bit more empathy and concern? Don't we open the doors of communication if we express concern for his or her situation?

Notice we address the letter to the tenant by name, not just *tenant*. Again, we are seeing him as an individual, not a number. Secondly, when we ask him to do us a favor, we are making him feel important.

In this letter we are setting out what will happen if he fails to pay the rent. We are detaching ourselves from the process because the decision comes from ownership. We're simply caught in the middle. But the process will take place, nonetheless, and its consequences are serious indeed. All of this information has been presented in a backhanded way. The realities are plain, but it's not our fault. We're here to help if possible.

## Have a Profitable Discussion

Don't argue. Arguing makes the tenant defensive. You can't win an argument. Even if you're 100% right, you can't win. When people are backed into a corner, they defend their position at all costs. They can't see it any other way at that time. There's an old saying, "A man convinced against his will, is of the same opinion still." Arguing also hurts feelings which may never heal. Resentment can be carried for years. Arguing will never result in a profitable discussion.

Don't get angry. Don't get emotional. Don't get personal. Listen to the tenant. Hear that person out. People will sometimes talk themselves out and change their opinions simply because they've had the time to explore their positions. Let them do a lot of the talking and they'll appreciate the fact that you've allowed them to

 voice themselves without interruption. Do you know how rare that is in our society? When you talk to someone, how often are your sentences interrupted before you can finish them? The party thinks he or she knows where you're going and they finish the sentence for you, but they didn't understand or care to listen at all. How frustrating! Be different and hear that person out! It will be received as a kindness and it will soften the agitated party.

## Skillful Enforcement of the Rules

Use diplomacy and tact in all discussions, but do not compromise on what must be done. We know the tenant must pay the rent and obey the rules. There can be no compromise, but again, more can be accomplished with diplomacy and tact than with arrogance and force. If a tenant says, "I want my cousin to move in and if we make room for him to sleep on the floor in the living room, I don't see what difference that makes, whether he's on the lease or not," you have at least three choices. Number 1, you could let him, but this would be a mistake. Violating the use clause is never in the best interest of the other tenants, ownership or the building. Number 2, you could pull rank and authoritatively command, "Absolutely not. I'm the grand Pooh-Bah around here, and I say no!" Or Number 3, you could use in sales what is called the "feel, felt, found" method of closing. You could say something like this. "I understand how you feel. Ownership felt the same way at one time. But when they let too many people move in who weren't on the lease, they found that there were all sorts of problems in the complex. There were thefts, vandalism, parking problems, conflicts with other tenants, loud music, late rent and all sorts of problems. Sometimes the guest even ends up at odds with the family he's staying with. It's hard to have an extra family member living with you, you know. And I'm not saying any of this would happen with *your* cousin, but because of those bad experiences, they won't even consider it."

Here you've used diplomacy and tact. You've stated you understand how the tenant *feels*. Understanding is good. Even ownership *felt* that way at one time. But here's what they *found*. It doesn't work! And now *they* won't even consider it anymore. The answer is no, and it has nothing to do with them, and nothing to do with you. The decision is out of your hands. You're understanding, empathetic and compassionate. If you could accommodate them, you would. But you can't! If they continue to push, listen for a bit and then say, "Darn, I wish I could do something for you, but like

I say, it's out of my hands." Offer to help them find a place for him to stay: a shelter or the Salvation Army or a church. Then excuse yourself for an appointment or other work assignment. You've maintained the rules without destroying a relationship. And maybe you've just got your tenant thinking that you're actually saving him or her from an unpleasant situation anyway. Everyone's glad to have the relative move in until he's been here for a week or so. Maybe your way is best, and the tenant can turn his cousin down the same way you did. "I wish I could do something, but it's out of my hands!"

# WHEN YOU HAVE TO GET THEM OUT

Alright, you've done a good job of qualifying your tenants and you've done your best to build a good business relationship with them. Most of them like you and respect you and understand the nature of your relationship. But there's always going to be a small percentage of tenants who turn bad. It probably has nothing to do with you whatsoever. Their circumstances have changed and they can no longer pay the rent. Or perhaps they brought with them baggage from the past so far back and so remote that you had no possibility of discovering it, and now it's come home to roost. Anyway, you've got a problem tenant on your hands. It's time to employ the **3 I's formula**, in keeping, of course, with sound principles of human relations.

## #1: Interaction

That means talk to the tenants. Anything is more cost effective than eviction. You want cooperative tenants, especially on the way out. There are companies that help tenants delay the eviction process. They do this by helping the tenants invent complaints about the physical condition of the property. They encourage them to file bankruptcy. They'll do anything to help them delay eviction. Meanwhile, they collect a cash fee of $150 per month from the tenants while they stay for free in your building. Then other tenants hear about the system and the virus spreads quicker than cockroaches.

Talk to the tenants. Listen to their story about why they can't pay the rent. Use the *feel, felt* and *found* method. Talk about something they're interested in and find some common ground. Talk, talk, talk. Reiterate their story back to them by saying, "Let me see if I understand this right. Blah, blah, blah, blah." They say, "That's right." Then explain why that's not acceptable. Blame it on the owners. Keep the lines of communication open and try to work it out. If they don't have all of the money now, accept what they have and work out a payment plan, so long as the interruption of payments can be solved. Let them know the damage an eviction will do to their credit record. They will never again be able to answer "no" 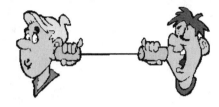 to the question on an application, "Have you ever been evicted?" They will find it very difficult to rent in a quality apartment complex. Have them sign an agreement and you may have saved a relationship and a vacancy.

---

### Figure 7-6    Payment Agreement

I, _____ am requesting to be allowed to pay my rent LATE for the month of _____ in the following method:

METHOD OF PAYMENT:

Amount $_____ Date:_____

Amount $_____ Date:_____

Amount $_____ Date:_____

Amount $_____ Date:_____

Reason for LATE payment is:_____

_____

My present home phone # is_____

I am now working at_____

_____

My present work phone # is_____

My spouse/roommate is now working at_____

_____

Their work phone # is_____

   I understand that I will be served a 3-Day Notice to Pay or Quit for the delinquent amount and should payment of the delinquent amount not be submitted by the dates indicated above, I will be served with an unlawful detainer action and be subject to eviction.

   I understand that this is not setting a precedent for my future rental payments. I further agree to pay my rent when it is due in the future as per my Lease Agreement with Rose Garden Apartments.

Address:_____

City:_____ State:_____ Zip:_____

Signature:_____ Date:_____

Signature:_____ Date:_____

---

If payments cannot be worked out, an agreement to vacate the apartment should be arranged. This is also accomplished by talking and negotiating. It may require the second "I".

# #2: Incentives

Because cooperation is always cheaper than force, offering an incentive for a tenant to vacate is usually a cost-effective thing to do. There are many ways to offer incentives. Offer to return what's left of their security deposit after you deduct for the past due rent. If they're evicted, they will owe beyond the amount of the security deposit plus have the eviction on their record. It's to their advantage to vacate early. They'll be ahead from a credit standpoint as well as a money standpoint.

Sweeten the offer by $100 or so. Most tenants won't move for less than that amount. Cut a $100 bill in half and give them one half. The other half is theirs when they turn in the key and have everything moved out. Offer to store their stuff for the first month while they get on their feet and find a new place to live. Or pay for the truck to move them. All of these items will cost around $100.

Or you might send them a note that reads something like this.

---

**Figure 7-7    Incentive Note**

Dear John and Suzie,

In the interest of helping you move and get on with your life, as well as avoid the legal hassles that accompany and follow an eviction, I have enclosed a crisp $100 bill. If you agree to move out in the next three days, you may keep it and use it to help with your expenses. Good luck.

Sincerely,
I. M. Generous
Property Manager

---

Send the note, but forget the $100 bill. If they're interested in that offer, they'll call you. Tell them you must have forgotten to enclose it. Have them stop by and sign an agreement to vacate and give them half of the $100 bill at that time, or just agree to have it for them when they turn in the keys.

**Figure 7-8   Agreement to Vacate**

I, _____ agree to vacate apartment

# _____ of the Rose Garden Apartments, 123 First Ave.,

Budsville, FL, 24094 on the following date: _____.

I understand that I will receive _____

_____

_____

_____

from management when I turn in the keys to the apartment.

I understand I must remove all of my possessions from the apartment

and leave the apartment in good condition to receive this incentive.

Any additional refund to which I may be entitled from my security

deposit will be returned to me no later than _____.

| _____ | _____ |
| Signature | Date |

| _____ | _____ |
| Signature | Date |

When offering incentives, it's important that the tenant understand two things. First, he or she must understand how it's advantageous to accept the incentive. People do what's in their best interest. We all do. So when an incentive is presented, they must understand what it will give them, and what it will help them avoid.

Second, offer the incentive in such a way that it will help the tenants save face. No one likes to be embarrassed or feel like a loser. If you've offered the $100 or the refund of the security deposit less the back rent, explain the benefits and then say something like, "That's what I'd do if I were in your situation." That way if they accept your offer, they're not sliding down the street on their bellies like some snake. They're being as smart as you would be and they can look you in the eye and hold up their heads as they take you up on your offer. Always give them a way out to feel good about themselves.

If none of these methods have worked and you're in for a long standoff, you may have to move to "I" Number 3.

## #3: Intimidation

Interacting with them didn't work. Offering incentives didn't work. It is time to try the last step before the legal process known as unlawful detainer—intimidation. Now intimidation doesn't mean you have any dangerous confrontations with them and it doesn't mean you hire any shady characters to change their attitudes. Nothing illegal or unsavory. But there are ways to get the point across that you are in the right and you will prevail. Though they are being uncooperative and are in possession of the unit for the time being, you are strong and you will not back down.

Let them see you taking photos of their parking area or damage they've done to their unit or to the exterior. Record their loud music on a tape recorder, noting the time and date. If they ask you what you're doing, tell them you're gathering evidence for court. Find out if you can have a uniformed law enforcement officer to serve them with their three-day notice.  In some jurisdictions off-duty law enforcement officers can wear their uniforms and serve such notices. Such service provides a bit of a more sobering effect and may convince the tenant to vacate before the entire eviction process has to be carried out. Law enforcement officers, in dealing with the unruly public, sometimes perform what they call a P-A-W-C. That's an acronym for *party advised, will cooperate*. If they could deliver a P-A-W-C along with the notice, so much the better.

## NOT AN EXACT SCIENCE

Establishing relationships and getting along with tenants is not an exact science, because human beings are not an exact science. But good principles of human relations will certainly help. We all like to be respected. We all like to feel that we count for something in the grand scheme of things. If you treat people like that, you will generally get better results and more cooperation. Cooperation is good.

There are many good books available on human relations, but one of the all-time classics is Dale Carnegie's, *How to Win Friends and Influence People*. When I mention this book to people, most say they've heard of it but have never read it. It's time to read it. This great book was written in 1936 and all of the examples, stories and illustrations took place a long time ago. But the principles are timeless and they are what we need to extract from this book. If we learn and apply only one idea from this book or others like it, we will establish better tenant relations and make our job that much easier.

## QUESTIONS

1. The best way to accomplish a business or personal objective is by:

    a. yourself
    b. with absolute authority
    c. the team approach
    d. having the law on your side

2. The landlord/tenant relationship is:

    a. a personal relationship
    b. a business relationship
    c. a friendship relationship
    d. a lessee/tenant relationship

3. The basis for the landlord/tenant relationship is:

    a. the trust and confidence each party
       has in the other
    b. the security deposit provided
       by the tenant
    c. the overseeing authority of the landlord
    d. the rental agreement

4. The first impression you seek to establish with
   your tenant is one of:

    a. professionalism
    b. fairness
    c. organization
    d. all of the above

5. In your relationship with a tenant you should
   seek to be:

    a. friends
    b. adversaries
    c. professional
    d. an authority figure

6. Your demeanor with tenants should be that of:

    a. a playful puppy
    b. a hound dog
    c. a bird dog
    d. a police dog

7. Your relationship with tenants could be
   characterized as:

    a. friendly but not friends
    b. firm but fair
    c. having a professional distance
       that allows you to stay in control
    d. all of the above

8. Your business office should project the image
   of a place that is:

    a. clean enough to be healthy but
       messy enough to be lived in
    b. a neat, well-organized setting where
       business can be conducted efficiently
    c. a friendly environment
    d. to be avoided

9. If you have designated paperwork for most circumstances that can arise, it shows that:

    a. you are organized and professional

    b. you are too detail-oriented

    c. you are aware of what can happen

    d. all of the above

10. In establishing good tenant relations it is important that the property manager:

    a. treat all tenants fairly

    b. have the highest property management educational designation possible

    c. file reports on time with ownership

    d. all of the above

11. The quality difference between a tenant and a resident is:

    a. tenants pay the rent on time

    b. residents regard the apartment complex as their home

    c. tenants stay longer

    d. residents are buyers, tenants are renters

12. If you make a promise to a tenant that causes him or her to move into the complex, you have created:

    a. an express warranty

    b. an implied warranty

    c. an actual guarantee

    d. an unenforceable covenant

13. Tenants' willingness to cooperate has a direct impact on:

    a. the timely payments of rent

    b. the desirability of the apartment complex

    c. the ease of the property manager's job

    d. all of the above

14. A letter commending a tenant to his or her employer is designed to:

    a. get the tenant a promotion

    b. express appreciation and engender a spirit of cooperation

    c. let the employer know of the employee's shortcomings

    d. all of the above

15. A letter to a tenant seeking to collect rent:

    a. should intimidate

    b. should be authoritative

    c. should express what management wants

    d. should acknowledge the tenant's perspective

16. An effective letter to a tenant would:

    a. address the tenant by name

    b. set out the consequences of not paying the rent

    c. express empathy

    d. all of the above

17. In order to have a profitable discussion with a tenant:

    a. don't argue unless you think you can win

    b. use anger to intimidate

    c. use diplomacy and tact

    d. use emotion to power your argument

18. The "feel, felt, found" method is designed to:

    a. tell the tenant how you feel

    b. start from a common understanding and move toward the desired position

    c. tell the tenant how ownership feels

    d. none of the above

19. A property manager should offer incentives to tenants to get them to move out because:

    a. it's cheaper than eviction
    b. it's a good way to show good will
    c. other tenants will like you
    d. the tenant will remember you fondly

20. Intimidation of tenants to get them to vacate an apartment:

    a. should never be used
    b. is heavy-handed and illegal
    c. puts the point across that you will prevail
    d. is sometimes accomplished by people impersonating a law enforcement officer

# ANSWERS

1. *c*
2. *b*
3. *a*
4. *d*
5. *c*
6. *d*
7. *d*
8. *b*
9. *d*
10. *a*
11. *b*
12. *a*
13. *d*
14. *b*
15. *d*
16 *d*
17. *c*
18. *b*
19. *a*
20. *c*

# Forms

- **Important Evidence**

C H A P T E R 8

# IMPORTANT EVIDENCE

This chapter is on forms. Actually, it is a collection of forms widely used in the renting of real property. Forms provide written evidence of agreement, activity and policy. Many standard forms are preprinted and are available through the various associations pertaining to the appropriate type of property. They can be filled in to denote the particular property and parties to which they refer, and can be customized as to details of management. Other forms can be originated for unique and unusual properties and functions.

The forms in this chapter emphasize residential housing and attempt to take us from the beginning of the relationship through to the end.

**Figure 8-1   Application to Rent**

# APPLICATION TO RENT

*(all sections must be completed)*        **Individual applications required from each adult occupant.**

| NAME | | | SOCIAL   SECURITY NUMBER |
|---|---|---|---|

| DATE OF BIRTH | DRIVER'S LICENSE NO | STATE | HOME·PHONE NUMBER |
|---|---|---|---|

**1**  PRESENT ADDRESS                                            ZIP CODE

| DATE IN | DATE OUT | OWNER/MGR NAME | OWNER/MGR PHONE NO. |
|---|---|---|---|

REASON FOR MOVING:

**2**  PREVIOUS ADDRESS                                            ZIP CODE

| DATE IN | DATE OUT | OWNER/MGR NAME | OWNER/MGR PHONE NO. |
|---|---|---|---|

REASON FOR MOVING:

**3**  NEXT PREVIOUS ADDRESS                                            ZIP CODE

| DATE IN | DATE OUT | OWNER/MGR NAME | OWNER/MGR PHONE NO. |
|---|---|---|---|

REASON FOR MOVING:

| PROPOSED OCCUPANTS | NAME | AGE | NAME | AGE |
|---|---|---|---|---|
| LIST ALL IN ADDITION TO YOURSELF | | | | |

| WILL YOU HAVE PETS? | DESCRIBE | WILL YOU HAVE LIQUID FILLED FURNITURE? | DESCRIBE |
|---|---|---|---|

*(continued on next page)*

## Figure 8-1 (cont'd)   Application to Rent

| A | PRESENT OCCUPATION | | EMPLOYER NAME | |
|---|---|---|---|---|
| | HOW LONG WITH THIS EMPLOYER? | | EMPLOYER ADDRESS | |
| | NAME OF YOUR SUPERVISOR | | EMPLOYER PHONE NO. | |
| B | PRIOR OCCUPATION | | EMPLOYER NAME | |
| | HOW LONG WITH THIS EMPLOYER? | | EMPLOYER ADDRESS | |
| | NAME OF YOUR SUPERVISOR | | EMPLOYER PHONE NO | |

CURRENT GROSS INCOME $ _____ PER

CHECK ONE: WEEK | MON. | YR.

**PLEASE LIST ALL OF YOUR FINANCIAL OBLIGATIONS BELOW**

| NAME OF YOUR BANK | BRANCH OR ADDRESS | ACCOUNT NUMBER | |
|---|---|---|---|
| | | CHECKING | |
| | | SAVINGS | |

| NAME OF CREDITOR | ADDRESS | PHONE NO. | MO. PYMT. AMT. |
|---|---|---|---|
| | | | |
| | | | |
| | | | |
| | | | |
| | | | |
| | | | |
| | | | |

| In case of emergency, notify: | Address | Phone | City | Relationship |
|---|---|---|---|---|
| 1. | | | | |
| 2. | | | | |
| Personal References | Address | Phone | Length of Acquaintance | Occupation |
| 1. | | | | |
| 2. | | | | |

Mother's maiden name _____

Automobile — Make _____ Model _____ Year _____ License Number _____

Automobile — Make _____ Model _____ Year _____ License Number _____

Motorcycles (other vehicles) _____

Applicant represents that all the above statements are true and correct and hereby authorizes verification of the above items including but not limited to the obtaining of a credit report and agrees to furnish additional credit references on request.

The undersigned makes application to rent housing accommodations designated as:

Apt. No. _____ Located at _____

the rental for which is $ _____ per _____ and upon approval of this application agrees to sign a rental or lease agreement and to pay all sums due, including required deposits, before occupancy.

Dated: _____ , 20 _____   _____ APPLICANT

## Figure 8-2    Statement of Condition

# STATEMENT OF CONDITION

PROPERTY _____ UNIT _____

Type of Unit _____ Occupant _____ Move in Date _____

    This move-in, move-out form is for your protection. When completing this form, be specific and check carefully. Among things you should look for are dust, dirt, grease, stains, burns, damages and wear. Use additional paper if necessary. California Civil Code 1950.5 stipulates that your security deposit is refundable to the extent not used for unpaid rent, damage and reasonable cleaning charges, normal wear and tear excepted.

| ITEMS | CONDITION | |
| --- | --- | --- |
| | MOVE-IN | MOVE-OUT |
| **Living Room & Dining Room** | | |
|   Doors and Locks | | |
|   Carpeting | | |
|   Floors and Baseboards | | |
|   Walls and Ceiling | | |
|   Draperies | | |
|   Electrical Fixtures | | |
|   Electrical Switches, Outlets | | |
|   Windows, Screens | | |
| Misc._____ | | |
| | | |
| | | |
| | | |
| | | |
| **Kitchen** | | |
|   Floors and Baseboards | | |
|   Walls and Ceiling | | |
|   Electrical Fixtures | | |
|   Electrical Switches, Outlets | | |
|   Range, Fan, Hood | | |
|   Oven | | |
|   Refrigerator | | |
|   Plumbing | | |
|   Sink & Disposer | | |
|   Cabinets, Counter Surfaces | | |
|   Windows, Screens | | |
|   Draperies / Curtains | | |
| Misc._____ | | |
| | | |
| | | |
| | | |
| | | |

# Figure 8-2 (cont'd.) Statement of Condition

| | CONDITION | | | |
|---|---|---|---|---|
| | MOVE-IN | | MOVE-OUT | |
| **Bedrooms** | #1 | #2 | #1 | #2 |
| Doors and Locks | | | | |
| Carpeting | | | | |
| Floors & Baseboards | | | | |
| Walls and Ceiling | | | | |
| Windows and Screens | | | | |
| Draperies | | | | |
| Electrical Fixtures | | | | |
| Electrical Switches, Outlets | | | | |
| Closets, Doors, Tracks | | | | |
| Misc. | | | | |

| | #3 | #4 or ____ | #3 | #4 or ____ |
|---|---|---|---|---|
| **Bedrooms** | | | | |
| Doors and Locks | | | | |
| Carpeting | | | | |
| Floors & Baseboards | | | | |
| Walls and Ceiling | | | | |
| Windows and Screens | | | | |
| Draperies | | | | |
| Electrical Fixtures | | | | |
| Electrical Switches, Outlets | | | | |
| Closets, Doors, Tracks | | | | |
| Misc. | | | | |

| | #1 | #2 | #1 | #2 |
|---|---|---|---|---|
| **Bathrooms** | | | | |
| Doors and Locks | | | | |
| Floors & Baseboards | | | | |
| Walls and Ceiling | | | | |
| Windows and Screens | | | | |
| Window Covering | | | | |
| Shower, Tub | | | | |
| Shower Door, Curtain | | | | |
| Toilet | | | | |
| Sink, Medicine Cabinet | | | | |
| Plumbing Fixtures | | | | |
| Electrical Fixtures, Fan | | | | |
| Electrical Switches, Outlets | | | | |
| Towel Racks | | | | |
| Misc. | | | | |

| | | | | |
|---|---|---|---|---|
| **Other Items** | | | | |
| Heating | | | | |
| Air Conditioning | | | | |
| Patio, Balcony | | | | |
| Yard Areas | | | | |
| Fencing | | | | |
| Garage or Carport | | | | |
| Misc. | | | | |

UNIT INSPECTED AND ACCEPTED AS NOTED      UNIT INSPECTED AND VACATED AS NOTED

Date _____      Date _____

Signature of Tenant            Signature of Tenant

Signature of Landlord / Agent      Signature of Landlord / Agent

## Figure 8-3    Rental Agreement: Month-To-Month

### RENTAL AGREEMENT
### (Month to Month)

THIS AGREEMENT entered into this _____ day of _____, 20 ____,

by and between _____, "Owner" (Landlord)

and _____, "Resident" (Tenant),

IN CONSIDERATION OF THEIR MUTUAL PROMISES AGREE AS FOLLOWS:

1.  Owner rents to the Resident and the Resident rents from the Owner for residential use only, the premises known as:

_____, CA.

2.  Rent is due in advance on the _____ day of each every month, at $_____ per month, beginning on the

_____ day of _____, 20 ____

3.  Except as prohibited by law, this agreement may be terminated by either party after service upon the other a written 30-day notice of termination of tenancy. Any holding over thereafter shall result in Resident being liable to Owner for "rental damages" at the fair rental value of $_____ per day.

4.  Premises shall be occupied only by the following named persons:

_____          _____

_____          _____

5.  Without Owner's prior written permission, no bird or animal, no water beds or liquid filled furniture, or

_____ shall be kept or allowed in or about said premises.

6.  Resident shall not violate any Governmental law in the use of the premises, commit waste or nuisance, annoy, molest or interfere with any other Resident or neighbor.

7.  Except as provided by law, no repairs, decorating or alterations shall be done by Resident, without Owner's prior written consent. Resident shall notify Owner in writing of any repairs or alterations contemplated. Decorations include, but are not limited to, painting, wallpapering, hanging of murals or posters. Resident shall hold Owner harmless as to any mechanics lien recordation or proceeding caused by Resident.

8.  Resident has inspected the premises, furnishings and equipment, and has found them to be satisfactory. All plumbing, heating and electrical systems are operative and deemed satisfactory.

9.  Except as prohibited by law, Resident shall keep the premises and furniture, furnishings and appliances, if any, and fixtures which are rented for Residents exclusive use in good order and condition. Resident shall pay Owner for costs to repair, replace or rebuild any portion of the premises damaged by the Resident, Resident's guests or invitees. Resident's personal property is not insured by Owner.

10.  Resident shall pay for all utilities, services and charges, if any, made payable by or predicated upon occupancy or Resident, except:

_____

*(continued)*

## Figure 8-3 (cont'd.)   Rental Agreement: Month-To-Month

11. The undersigned Resident(s), whether or not in actual possession of the premises, are jointly and severally liable for all obligations under this rental agreement, and shall indemnify owner for liability arising prior to the termination of the rental agreement for personal injuries or property damage caused or permitted by Resident(s), their guests and invitees. This does not waive "Owner's" duty of care to prevent personal injury or property damage where that duty is imposed by law.

12. Resident shall deposit with Owner, as a security deposit, the sum of $ _____,

payable _____. Owner may claim (withhold) of the security deposit only such amounts as are reasonably necessary to remedy tenant defaults as follows:
   (a) in the payment of rent, or
   (b) to repair damages to the premises caused by Resident, exclusive of ordinary wear and tear, or
   (c) to clean such premises, if necessary, upon termination of the tenancy.
   No later than two weeks (14 days) after the Resident has vacated the premises, the Owner shall furnish the Resident with an itemized written statement of the basis for, and the amount of, any security received and the disposition of such security and shall return any remaining portion of such security to the Residents.

13. If any legal action or proceeding be brought by either party to enforce any part of this Agreement, the prevailing party shall recover, in addition to all other relief, reasonable attorney's fees and costs.

14. Notice upon Owner may be served upon: _____

at: _____, CA.
Said person is authorized to accept legal service on behalf of Owner.

15. No portion of said premises shall be sublet nor this Agreement assigned. Any attempted subletting or assignment by the Resident, at the election of Owner, shall be an irremedial breach of this Agreement.

IF APPLICABLE:

A. House Rules:            By initialing as provided, Resident acknowledges receipt of a copy of house rules,
                           and has read them, a copy of which is attached hereto, marked as page _____,
                           and are incorporated herein by reference as though fully set forth at length. Said
            Initial_____ house rules shall be deemed covenants of this agreement.

B. Inventory:              By initialing as hereinafter provided, Resident acknowledges the subject
                           premises are furnished in accordance with the attached inventory and a copy
                           thereof is attached hereto, marked page _____, and is incorporated herein as
            Initial_____ though fully set forth at length.

C. Addendum:               By initialing as provided, Resident acknowledges that additional terms and
                           provisions have been agreed upon which are designated as an Addendum, a copy
                           of which is attached hereto, marked page _____, and is incorporated herein as
            Initial_____ though fully set forth at length.

The undersigned Resident acknowledges having read and understood the foregoing, and receipt of a duplicate original.


_____          _____
           OWNER                                    RESIDENT


_____          _____
     BY AUTHORIZED AGENT                            RESIDENT


                                         _____
                                                    RESIDENT

## Figure 8-4 Rental Agreement: Long-Form Lease

### RENTAL AGREEMENT
#### (Long Form Lease)

THIS AGREEMENT entered into this _____ day of _____ , 20 _____,

and between _____ , "Owner" (Landlord)

and _____ , "Resident" (Tenant)

IN CONSIDERATION OF THEIR MUTUAL PROMISES, THE PARTIES AGREE AS FOLLOWS:

1. Owner rents to the Resident, and the Resident rents from the Owner for residential use only, the premises known as:

_____

2. Rent is due in advance on the _____ day of each and every month, at $ _____ per month, beginning on the _____ day of _____ , 20 _____.

3. The term of this agreement is for _____ ,

beginning on the _____ day of _____ , and ending on the _____ day

of _____ , 20 _____, at which time the lease shall terminate without further notice. A "month to month" tenancy shall be created only if Owner accepts rent from Resident, thereafter.

4. Premises shall be occupied only by the following named persons:

_____

_____

5. Without Owner's prior written permission, no bird or animal, no water beds or liquid filled furniture, or _____ shall be kept or allowed in or about said premises.

6. Resident shall not violate any Governmental law in the use of the premises, commit waste or nuisance, annoy, molest or interfere with any other Resident or neighbor.

7. Except as provided by law, no repairs, decorating or alterations shall be done by Resident, without Owner's prior written consent. Resident shall notify Owner in writing of any repairs or alterations contemplated. Decorations include, but are not limited to, painting, wallpapering, hanging of murals or posters. Resident shall hold Owner harmless as to any mechanics lien recordation or proceeding caused by Resident.

8. Resident has inspected the premises, furnishings and equipment, and has found them to be satisfactory. All plumbing, heating and electrical systems are operative and are deemed satisfactory.

9. Except as provided by law, Resident shall keep the premises and furniture, furnishings and appliances, if any, and fixtures which are rented for Resident's exclusive use in good order and condition. Resident shall pay Owner for costs to repair, replace or rebuild any portion of the premises damaged by the Resident, Resident's guests or invitees. Resident's personal property is not insured by Owner.

10. Resident shall pay for all utilities, services and charges, if any, made payable by or predicated upon occupancy of Resident, except:

_____

11. The undersigned Residents, whether or not in actual possession of the premises, are jointly and severally liable for all obligations under this rental agreement, and shall indemnify owner for liability arising prior to the termination of the rental agreement for personal injuries or property damage caused or permitted by Resident(s), their guests and invitees. This does not waive Owner's duty of care to prevent personal injury or property damage where that duty is imposed by law.

12. Resident shall deposit with Owner, as a security deposit, the sum of $ _____, payable _____. Owner may claim (withhold) of the security deposit only such amounts as are reasonably necessary to remedy tenant defaults as follows:
  (a) in the payment of rent, or
  (b) to repair damages to the premises caused by Resident, exclusive of ordinary wear and tear, or
  (c) to clean such premises, if necessary, upon termination of the tenancy.

No later than two weeks (14 days) after the Resident has vacated the premises, the Owner shall furnish the Resident with an itemized written statement of the basis for, and the amount of, any security received and the disposition of such security and shall return any remaining portion of such security to the Resident.

13. If any legal action or proceeding be brought by either party to enforce any part of this Agreement, the prevailing party shall recover, in addition to all other relief, reasonable attorney's fees and costs.

## Figure 8-4 (cont'd.)  Rental Agreement: Long-Form Lease

14. Notice upon Owner may be served upon: _____

at _____ , CA.

15. Resident shall not sublet any portion of said premises nor assign this Agreement, without prior written consent of Owner. Owner shall not withhold consent unreasonably.

16. The waiver of either party of any breach shall not be construed to be a continuing waiver of any subsequent breach. The receipt by the Owner of the rent with the knowledge of any violation of a covenant or condition hereto shall not be deemed a waiver of such breach. No waiver by either party of the provisions herein shall be deemed to have been made unless expressed in writing and signed by all parties to this rental agreement.

17. The Resident shall not maintain, keep or allow to be kept or maintained upon said premises any item, or permit any acts to be done which will cause an increase in the rate of insurance upon, or endanger said premises.

18. The Owner or his agents or employees may enter the premises:
    (a) In case of emergency, or
    (b) When the Resident has abandoned or surrendered the premises, or to make necessary or agreed repairs, decorations, alterations or improvements, to supply necessary or agreed services, or to exhibit the dwelling unit to prospective or actual purchasers, lenders, residents, workmen or contractors, provided the Resident is given reasonable notice of Owner's intent to enter, with entrance during normal business hours (8:00 a.m. to 6:00 p.m., Monday through Saturday except holidays). Twenty-four hours shall be presumed to be reasonable notice, in absence of evidence to the contrary.

19. In the event that Resident breaches this rental Agreement, Owner shall be allowed at Owner's discretion, but not by way of limitation, to exercise any or all remedies provided Owner by California Civil Code Section 1951.2 and 1951.4. Damages the Owner "may recover" include the worth at the time of the award of the amount by which the unpaid rent for the balance of the term after the time of award, or for any shorter period of time specified in the rental agreement, exceeds the amount of such rental loss for the same period that the lessee proves could be reasonably avoided.

20. Within 10 days after written notice, Resident agrees to execute and deliver a certificate as submitted by Owner acknowledging that this rental Agreement is unmodified and in full force and effect, or in full force and effect as modified and stating the modifications. Failure to comply shall be deemed Resident's acknowledgement that the certificate as submitted by Owner is true and correct and may be relied upon by any lender or purchaser.

21. Each year on the anniversary date of the first rental monthly payment dates, the present rent shall be increased to that amount whereby the increase equals the average increase in Consumer Price Index for the published preceding twelve (12) calendar months.
    Consumer price index (CPI) means the consumer price index for all items for all Urban Consumers for the United States as compiled by the United States Department of Labor, Bureau of Labor Statistics, or if such index is unavailable, an equivalent standard.

22. IF APPLICABLE:

House Rules:
(A)

Initial _____  By initialing as provided, Resident acknowledges receipt of a copy of House Rules, and has read them, a copy of which is attached hereto, marked as page _____ and are incorporated herein by reference as though fully set forth at length. Said house rules shall be deemed covenants of this Agreement.

Inventory:
(B)

Initial _____  By initialing as hereinafter provided, Resident acknowledges the subject premises are furnished in accordance with the attached inventory and a copy thereof is attached hereto, marked page _____ and is incorporated herein as though fully set forth at length.

Addendum:
(C)

Initial _____  By initialing as provided, Resident acknowledges that additional terms and provisions have been agreed upon which are designated as an Addendum, a copy of which is attached hereto marked page _____, and is incorporated herein as though fully set forth at length.

The undersigned Resident(s) acknowledge(s) having read and understood the foregoing, and receipt of a duplicate original.

_____          _____
Owner                                                      Resident

_____          _____
Owner                                                      Resident

## Figure 8-5   Addendum to Rental Agreement and/or Lease

Page _____

# ADDENDUM TO RENTAL AGREEMENT AND/OR LEASE

THIS AGREEMENT is entered into this _____ day of _____ , 198 _____ , .

by and between _____ , "Owner" (Landlord)

and _____ , "Resident" (Tenant).

IN CONSIDERATION OF THEIR MUTUAL PROMISES OWNER and RESIDENT AGREE AS FOLLOWS:

1.  Resident is renting from Owner the premises located at:

_____ , CA

2.  This agreement is an Addendum and part of the Rental Agreement and/or Lease between Owner and Resident.

_____

_____

_____

_____

_____

_____

_____

_____

_____

_____

_____

_____

_____

3.  This addendum is to be effective as of _____ , 198 _____

_____         _____
Owner/Agent                                Resident

                                          _____
                                           Resident

**Figure 8-6    Smoke Detector Agreement**

## SMOKE DETECTOR AGREEMENT

THIS AGREEMENT is entered into this _____ day of _____ , 20 _____ ,

by and between _____ , "Owner" (Landlord),

and _____ , "Resident" (Tenant).

IN CONSIDERATION OF THEIR MUTUAL PROMISES, OWNER AND RESIDENT AGREE AS FOLLOWS:

1.  Resident is renting from Owner the premises located at:

    _____ , CA

2.  This agreement is an Addendum and part of the Rental Agreement and/or Lease between Owner and Resident.

3.  The premise(s) is/are equipped with a smoke detection device(s).

4.  The resident acknowledges the smoke detector(s) was tested and its operation explained by management in the presence of the Resident at time of initial occupancy and the detector(s) in the unit was working properly at that time.

5.  Each resident shall perform the manufacturer's recommended test to determine if the smoke detector(s) is (are) operating properly at least once a week.

6.  Initial ONLY if BATTERY OPERATED: _____    _____

    By initialing as provided, each Resident understands that said smoke detector(s) and alarm is a battery operated unit and it shall be each Resident's responsibility to:

    a.  ensure that the battery is in operating condition at all times;
    b.  replace the battery as needed (unless otherwise provided by law); and
    c.  if, after replacing the battery, the smoke detector(s) do not work, inform the Owner or authorized agent immediately in writing.

7.  Resident(s) must inform the owner or authorized agent immediately in writing of any defect, malfunction or failure of any detector(s).

8.  If local law requires the owner to test the smoke detector, the resident shall allow the owner or his agent access to the premises for that purpose.

_____        _____
*Owner/Agent*                            *Resident*

                                         _____
                                         *Resident*

**Figure 8-7   Waterbed Agreement**

### WATERBED AND/OR LIQUID FILLED FURNITURE AGREEMENT

THIS AGREEMENT entered into this _____ day of _____, 20 _____,

by and between _____, "Owner" (Landlord)

and _____, "Resident" (Tenant)

IN CONSIDERATION OF THEIR MUTUAL PROMISES AGREE AS FOLLOWS:

1. Resident is renting from Owner the premises located at:

_____, CA.

2. The Rental Agreement provides that without Owner's prior written consent, no waterbeds or liquid filled furniture shall be allowed in or about said premises.

3. Resident desires to keep the below described waterbed and/or liquid filled furniture hereinafter referred to as "said items":

_____

_____

4. This agreement is an Addendum and part of the Rental Agreement and/or Lease between Owner and Resident. In the event of default by Resident of any of the terms, Resident agrees, within three days after receiving written notice of default from Owner, to cure the default, or vacate the premises. Owner may revoke permission to keep said items on the premises by giving Resident written thirty (30) day notice.

5. As additional security, Resident agrees to pay Owner the sum of $_____ (receipt of which is hereby acknowledged). Owner may use therefrom such amount as is reasonably necessary to take care of any damages or cleaning caused by or in connection with said items. At the termination of this agreement, any balance shall be added to the rental agreement security deposit, and disbursed thereafter as required by law. Resident agrees to pay Owner for any excess damages or costs on demand.

6. Resident agrees to furnish Owner a valid copy or certificate of liability insurance policy with Owner named as insured before the placing of any said items in the premise and agrees to furnish additional copy of certificate of renewal insurance policy.

7. Resident agrees to comply with:
   (a)   governing Building Code Requirements;
   (b)   Health and Safety Codes;
   (c)   minimum component standards covering the manufacturing, testing and sale of said items, and
   (d)   all other applicable governmental laws and regulations.

8. As to any waterbed, Resident agrees to use a mattress, a safety liner and a frame. If a heater is provided by Resident and Owner pays for the utilities for said heater, Resident shall pay Owner the sum of $_____ per month on each rent payment date, as a special payment (not to be construed as rent) for the added utility costs.

9. Resident agrees to have qualified personnel install said items according to Manufacturers' specification. Cost of installation is the responsibility of Resident. At time of removal of said items, Resident shall use special care to dispose of water or liquid.

10. Resident shall be liable to Owner for all damages or expenses incurred by or in connection with said items, and shall hold Owner harmless for any and all damages or costs in connection thereto.

11. In an emergency, to prevent injury or damage, Resident agrees to immediately remove said items. If Resident fails to do so, Owner may remove said items.

_____          _____
Owner/Agent                                              Resident

                                                             _____
                                                             Resident

## Figure 8-8    Furniture Inventory

**FURNITURE INVENTORY**

The following furniture list is hereby acknowledged as part of your Lease/Rental Agreement:

| Quantity | Item | Move-in Condition | Move-out Condition |
|---|---|---|---|
| | Sofa | | |
| | Chair(s) | | |
| | Occasional Tables | | |
| | Living Room Lamps | | |
| | Desk | | |
| | Desk Chair | | |
| | Dinette Set | | |
| | Bookcases | | |
| | Twin Beds | | |
| | Full Beds | | |
| | Queen Beds | | |
| | Nightstands | | |
| | Dressers | | |
| | Chest of Drawers | | |
| | Mirrors | | |
| | Other | | |
| | | | |
| | | | |

SAMPLE

Receipt of above items is hereby acknowledged by Lessee    Move-in Inventory performed by:

Apartment No. _____ Date _____    _____
                                                                    (owner/agent)

Address _____    Move-out Inventory performed by:

Lessee (1) _____    _____
                                                                    (owner/agent)

Lessee (2) _____

                                              Date _____

### Figure 8-9   Co-Signer Agreement

CO-SIGNER AGREEMENT

The parties to this Agreement are_____

_____, herein called

Owner (or Agent) and_____

_____, herein called Co-Signer(s).

Co-Signer acknowledges that he has read the Agreement to Rent or

Lease entered into by Owner (or Agent) and _____

_____, herein called

Resident(s) and dated _____, and understands its terms.

Co-Signer agrees to personally guarantee the payment of any

monetary damages suffered by Owner including but not limited to

actual attorneys' fees incurred in the enforcement of said

Agreement to Rent or Lease and/or this Co-Signer Agreement.

Furthermore, Co-Signer acknowledges that he is not occupying the

premises leased pursuant to the Agreement to Rent or Lease, nor

is he entitled to service of any of the statutory notices

required by law to be provided occupants.

This Co-Signer Agreement shall continue in full force and effect
for:

    [ ] a period not to exceed_____.

    [ ] the entire term of Resident's tenancy including any
        extension, and any rental increases in effect during
        such tenancy.

OWNER/AGENT:                          CO-SIGNER:

_____      _____
Owner                        Signature              Date

_____      _____
By                           Signature              Date

_____
Title              Date

## Figure 8-10   Lease Extension Agreement

**LEASE EXTENSION AGREEMENT**

This is an agreement between Humphrey Property Company CA, Inc., (HPC) acting as the

Manager of the _____ Apartments

and _____ the Lessee

of Apartment #_____. HPC and Lessee agree to extend the Lease Agreement

dated _____ , 20____, for a period of _____

beginning _____ , 20____ and ending _____ , 20____,

at a monthly rental rate of $_____.

Lessee acknowledges that all other terms and conditions contained in the lease agreement

dated _____ stay in full force and effect.

If the term of the Lease Extension Agreement is not fulfilled, the Lessee will pay HPC for

any charges that are due under the terms of the original Agreement.

Executed in triplicate this _____ day of _____ , 20____

LESSEE:                                    LESSOR:

_____      Humphrey Property Company CA
                                          Inc., (HPC) solely as agent
_____
                                          By: _____

Rolodex _____

Ledger _____

**Figure 8-11   Cancellation Fee**

## ADDENDUM TO LEASE

CANCELLATION FEE/ LIQUIDATED DAMAGES

The undersigned resident(s) may cancel resident's obligation to pay the balance of rental owing for the lease term, by delivering in writing, a notice of intention to cancel this lease. Such notice will be deemed effective thirty (30) days from the date it is received by Owner/ Owner's Authorized Agent. Lessee further agrees to pay the sum of $_____ as a cancellation fee, releasing resident(s) only from further rental owing for the lease term. This amount is stipulated to be a fair and reasonable amount in the owner's damages are difficult to ascertain, but include lost rental profits, costs of rehabilitating the premises, premature advertising expense and management operating expenses incurred as a result of the premature cancellation of the lease. Owner thus waives any claim for rental damages pursuant to California Civil Code, Section 1950.5, and resident(s) waives any demand for mitigation of damages incident thereto.

This payment does not release resident from:

*   Damages and cleaning beyond normal wear and tear to the apartment or personal property.
*   Liability for all rent concessions used during the resident's occupancy.

Lessee:

X_____

X_____

X_____

Lessor:        Humphrey Residential Services, Inc.
               (HRS) solely as Agent

X_____

**Figure 8-12    Notice of Change in Terms**

NOTICE OF CHANGE OF TERMS OF TENANCY

(CIVIL CODE SECTION 827)

TO:_____

ALL TENANTS AND SUBTENANTS AND ALL OTHERS IN POSSESSION

ADDRESS:_____

CITY:_____ STATE:_____

PLEASE TAKE NOTICE that at the expiration of THIRTY (30)
DAYS after the service on you of this Notice, your month
to month tenancy of the premises described below and occupied
by you will be changed as follows:

Effective Date:_____

_____

_____

_____

_____

_____

_____

DATED:_____

_____        _____
        AGENT                                    OWNER

## Figure 8-13   Resident's Service Request

### RESIDENT'S SERVICE REQUEST

1. Resident(s) Name: _____ Time: _____ Date: _____ 20 ___

   Telephone (home) _____ (work or message) _____

   Address/unit _____ , CA

2. **SERVICE REQUESTED:** (describe trouble and special instructions)

3. **AUTHORIZATION:** Owner/Management/Service person(s) are authorized to enter unit if Resident(s) is not home unless instructions have been given above to the contrary.

   _____ If verbal, taken by: _____
   Signature of Resident(s)

4. **INSTRUCTIONS TO SERVICE PERSONNEL:**

5. **REPORT OF ACTION TAKEN**

   Upon completion, describe problem, work done and materials used:

   Time spent completing service request: Hours _____ Minutes _____
   Date Completed _____ We are unable to repair the problem because

   Estimated date of completion: _____ , 20 _____.

   Date: _____ 20 _____ _____
                          Signature of Service person

6. **CHARGE COSTS AS FOLLOWS:**

7. Resident(s) certifies that service request report is correct except as follows:

   Date: _____ 20 _____ _____
                          Signature of Resident(s)

**UNAUTHORIZED REPRODUCTION SHALL RENDER THIS FORM NULL AND VOID**

White copy for resident     Pink copy for office     Yellow copy returned to resident upon completion

SAMPLE

**Figure 8-14   Notice to Enter Dwelling Unit**

# NOTICE TO ENTER DWELLING UNIT
## (CC 1954)

PURSUANT TO CALIFORNIA CIVIL CODE SECTION 1954, OWNER DOES HEREBY GIVE NOTICE

TO: _____

_____, AND  ALL  PERSONS  IN  OCCUPANCY  OF  THE

PREMISES LOCATED AT: _____
STREET ADDRESS

APT. NO. _____ , _____ CALIFORNIA
CITY

THAT OWNER, OWNER'S AGENT OR OWNER'S EMPLOYEES WILL ENTER SAID PREMISES  ON

OR ABOUT THE _____ DAY OF _____ 20_____, DURING  NORMAL

BUSINESS  HOURS _____ FOR  THE  REASON  SET  FORTH  IN  THE  CHECKED  (✓)

NUMBERED ITEM(S) BELOW:

_____ 1.   TO MAKE NECESSARY OR AGREED REPAIRS.

_____ 2.   DECORATIONS.

_____ 3.   ALTERATIONS OR IMPROVEMENTS.

_____ 4.   SUPPLY NECESSARY OR AGREED SERVICES.

_____ 5.   TO EXHIBIT THE DWELLING UNIT TO PROSPECTIVE OR ACTUAL PURCHASERS.

_____ 6.   TO EXHIBIT THE DWELLING UNIT TO PROSPECTIVE OR ACTUAL MORTGAGEES
AND LENDERS.

_____ 7.   TO EXHIBIT THE DWELLING UNIT TO PROSPECTIVE OR ACTUAL TENANTS.

_____ 8.   TO EXHIBIT THE DWELLING UNIT TO PROSPECTIVE OR ACTUAL WORKMEN OR
CONTRACTORS.

_____ 9.   PURSUANT TO COURT ORDER.

_____ 10. TO INSPECT WATERBED OR LIQUID-FILLED FURNITURE

_____ 11. WHEN THE TENANT HAS ABANDONED OR SURRENDERED THE PREMISES.

DATED THIS _____ DAY OF _____ , 20 _____

_____        _____
(AGENT)                                    (OWNER)

**UNAUTHORIZED USE PROHIBITED**

EQUAL HOUSING
OPPORTUNITY

## Figure 8-15   Roommate Notice to Vacate

<u>ROOMMATE NOTICE TO VACATE AND SECURITY DEPOSIT RELEASE</u>

Date:(1)_____

TO:_____

    This will serve as my written notice to vacate the premises located at (3)_____ (address) apartment #(4)_____, on (5)_____(date).

    As of the above date I will no longer be responsible for any damage or rent due on the apartment I am vacating (providing I return the keys to the management).

    All responsibility is given to the remaining resident(s):

(6) _____ (name)

_____ (name)

    I (we), (7)_____
                **remaining resident signature**

        _____
                **remaining resident signature**

agree that (8)_____(vacating resident) is not responsible for any damage in the above referenced apartment.

    I agree to release the total security deposit paid on apartment #(9)_____ in the amount of  $(10)_____ to the above-named remaining roommate(s).

             (11)_____
                **vacating resident's signature**

Date received by management:(12)_____

Manager's signature_____

## Figure 8-16  Notice and Demand Regarding Dishonored Check

### NOTICE AND DEMAND REGARDING DISHONORED CHECK

To: _____

Address: _____ , CA.

The undersigned, by certified mail, hereby gives notice and demands as follows:

1. The check (draft or order) dated _____ , 20 _____ ,

   for the sum of: _____ dollars ( $ _____ )

   payable to: _____
   (bank, depository, person, firm or corporation)

   was not honored (not paid):

   (check (√) appropriate box)

   ☐ for lack of funds or credit to pay

   ☐ because the maker has no account with drawee

2. The undersigned demands payment within 30 days following this written demand delivered to the maker.

3. If not so paid, he shall be liable to the payee, in addition to the amount owed upon said check, draft or order, damages of treble the amount so owing, but in no case less than one hundred dollars ($100.00) and in no case more than five hundred dollars ($500.00).

Dated _____ , 20 _____   _____
                                              PAYEE/AGENT

#### AUTHORIZATION

California Civil Code Section 1719, effective January 1, 1984, states as follows:

"Notwithstanding any penal sanctions which may apply, any person who makes, utters, draws, or delivers any check, or draft, or order upon any bank or depository, or person, or firm, or corporation, for the payment of money, which refuses to honor the same for lack of funds or credit to pay, or because the maker has no account with the drawee, and who fails to pay the same amount in cash to the payee within 30 days following a written demand therefor delivered to the maker by certified mail, shall be liable to the payee, in addition to the amount owing upon said check or draft or order, damages of treble the amount so owing, but in no case less than one hundred dollars ($100.00), and in no case more than five hundred dollars ($500.00).

A cause of action under this section may be brought in small claims court, if it does not exceed the jurisdiction of that court, or in any other appropriate court."

## Figure 8-17   Notice of Intent to Vacate

### NOTICE OF INTENT TO VACATE

IN ACCORDANCE with California Civil Code, Section 1946, please accept this as the required 30-day notice of my intent to vacate Apartment No._____ at _____

on _____, 20_____.

UNDER THE TERMS of my lease dated _____, 20_____, representatives of management may enter my apartment during my presence for the purpose of showing it to prospective residents during this 30-day period.

MY REASONS FOR Vacating Are:

☐ Transferring from the area
   for business reasons
☐ Transferring from the area
   for personal reasons
☐ Have purchased a home
☐ Unable to afford the rent
☐ Too much noise
☐ Dislike the neighbors

☐ Dislike the manager
☐ Maintenance requests not taken care of promptly
☐ Not enough activity
☐ Dislike the location
☐ Premises untidy
☐ Other reasons:_____

_____

THE LEASE FOR my apartment expires (expired) on _____, 20_____.

I understand that any unused portion of my Security Deposit will be refunded to me promptly in accordance with the terms of my agreement with you.

MY FORWARDING ADDRESS will be: _____

_____

My phone no is: _____   _____

My apartment is located:   upstairs   downstairs (Please circle one)

My apartment is a: Studio   1 bedroom   2 bedroom   3 bedroom (circle 1)

My apartment has:   1 bath   2 bath   (Please circle one)

Signed:_____ Date:_____

Notice received by: _____

## Figure 8-18   Acknowledgement of Intent to Vacate

### ACKNOWLEDGEMENT OF RESIDENT(S) 30-DAY NOTICE OF INTENT TO VACATE

To Resident(s): _____

Address of Unit: _____ , CA.

1. Receipt of notice of intention to vacate the above unit, effective _____ , 20 _____ , is received.

2. Your tenancy is agreed to be terminated as of _____ , 20 _____ (stated date or thirty [30] days after service of the notice of intention to vacate, whichever is later).

3. Please note that you cannot apply the security deposit as "last month's rent." Rent is payable to the termination of the tenancy.

4. Rent must still be paid in advance on the normal rental date, prorated to the end of the tenancy as follows:

   From_____ , 20 _____ , to _____ , (for _____ days at $ _____ per day) equals $_____ .

5. Your security deposit is $ _____ shall, no later than 14 days after termination of tenancy, furnish the resident with an itemized written statement of the basis for, and the amount of, any security received and the disposition of the security and shall return any remaining portion of such security to Resident(s). The Owner may claim (withhold) of the security deposit only such amounts as are reasonably necessary to remedy tenant defaults as follows:

   a. in the payment of rent;
   b. to repair damages to the premises caused by Resident(s), exclusive of ordinary wear and tear; or
   c. to clean premises, if necessary, upon termination of tenancy.

6. California law further provides that Owner may exhibit the premises to prospective residents provided the Resident(s) is given reasonable notice of Owner's intent to enter, with entrance during normal business hours. (Twenty-four [24] hours shall be presumed to be reasonable notice, in absence of evidence to the contrary.)

7. Please arrange for an appointment with the Owner/management to check out "the condition of the premises" before you leave so that possible misunderstandings or problems can be resolved.

8. If you move earlier than the rental termination date, and if the Owner/management receives possession, Owner shall try to rent the unit. If successful in obtaining rent for a period prior to termination, resident will be given credit.

Dated _____ , 20 _____ _____
OWNER/AGENT

**Figure 8-19    Notice of Termination of Tenancy**

## NOTICE OF TERMINATION OF TENANCY

TO: _____
*All residents (tenants and subtenants) in possession (full name) and all others in possession*

PLEASE TAKE NOTICE that your tenancy of the below-described premises is terminated, effective

at the end of a thirty (30) day period after service on you of this notice, or _____
*(Date)*

whichever is later.

The purpose of this notice is to terminate your tenancy of the below-described premises.

If you fail to quit and deliver possession, legal proceedings will be instituted against you to obtain possession and such proceedings could result in a judgement against you which could include costs and necessary disbursements.

The premises herein referred to are situated in the city of _____

County of _____ , State of California, designated by the number and street

as _____ Apartment _____

Date: _____        _____
*Owner/Agent*

## Figure 8-20 House Rules and Regulations

### HOUSE RULES AND REGULATIONS

I. General
1. This agreement is an addendum and part of the rental agreement between Owner and Resident.
2. New rules and regulations or amendments to these rules may be adopted by Owner upon giving 30 days notice in writing. These rules and any changes or amendments have a legitimate purpose and are not intended to be arbitrary or work as a substantial modification of resident rights. They will not be unequally enforced. Resident is responsible for the conduct of guests and the adherence to these rules and regulations at all times.

II. Noise and Conduct
1. Resident shall not make or allow any disturbing noises in the unit by Resident, family or guests, nor do not permit anything by such persons which will interfere with the rights, comforts or conveniences of other persons.
2. All musical instruments, television sets, stereos, radios, etc., are to be played at a volume which will not disturb other persons.
3. The activities and conduct of resident and resident's guests outside of the unit on the common grounds, parking areas, or any recreation facilities must be reasonable at all times and not annoy or disturb other persons.
4. No lounging, visiting or loud talking that may be disturbing to other residents will be allowed in the common areas.
5. No resident shall keep, maintain or allow to remain on the premises for a period in excess of seven (7) days, any non-working, inoperable or non-functioning vehicle of any kind. The parties agree that the presence of any such vehicle on the premises for a period in excess of seven (7) days shall constitute a nuisance within the provisions of California Civil Code, Section 3479 and may, at owner's option, be the basis for terminating the tenancy herein.

III. Cleanliness and Trash
1. The unit must be kept clean, sanitary and free from objectionable odors.
2. Residents shall assist management in keeping the outside and common areas clean.
3. No littering of papers, cigarette butts or trash is allowed.
4. No trash or other materials may be accumulated which will cause a hazard or be in violation of any health, fire or safety ordinance or regulation.
5. Garbage is to be placed inside the containers provided and lids should not be slammed. Garbage should not be allowed to accumulate and should be placed in the outside containers on a daily basis. Items too large to fit in the trash containers should be placed neatly near the container.
6. Furniture must be kept inside the unit. Unsightly items must be kept out of vision.
7. Articles are not to be left in the hallways or other common areas.
8. Clothing, curtains, rugs, etc., shall not be shaken or hung outside of any window, ledge, or balcony.

IV. Safety
1. All doors must be locked during absence of the Resident.
2. All appliances must be turned off before leaving the unit.
3. When leaving for an extended period the resident shall notify management how long resident will be away.
4. When someone is to enter the resident's unit during resident's absence, resident shall give management permission beforehand to let any person in the unit and/or provide the name of person or company entering.
5. Smoking in bed is prohibited.
6. The use or storage of gasoline, cleaning solvent or other combustibles in the unit is prohibited.
7. The use of charcoal barbeques is prohibited unless consent is obtained from the owner.
8. No personal belongings, including bicycles, play equipment or other items may be placed in the halls, stairways or about the building.

V. Maintenance, Repairs and Alterations
1. If the unit is supplied with smoke detection devise(s) upon occupancy it shall be the responsibility of the resident to regularly test the detector(s) to ensure that the devices(s)is in operable condition. The resident will inform management immediately, in writing, of any defect, malfunction or failure of such smoke detector(s). Resident is responsible to replace smoke detector batteries, if any, as needed unless otherwise provided by law.
2. Resident shall advise management, in writing, of any items requiring repair (dripping faucets, light switches, etc.). Notification should be immediate in an emergency or for normal problems within business hours. Repair requests should be made as soon as the defect is noted.
3. Service requests should not be made to maintenance people or other such personnel.
4. Costs of repair or clearance of stoppages in waste pipes or drains, water pipes or plumbing fixtures caused by resident negligence or improper usage are the responsibility of the resident. Payment for corrective action must be paid by resident on demand.
5. No alterations or improvements shall be made by resident without the consent of management. Any article attached to the woodwork, walls, floors or ceilings shall be the sole responsibility of the resident. Resident shall be liable for any repairs necessary during or after residency to restore premises to the original condition. Glue or tape shall not be used to affix pictures or decorations.

The undersigned Resident(s) acknowledge having read and understood the foregoing, and receipt of a duplicate original.

_____
LESSOR

_____
LESSOR'S AGENT

_____
LESSEE

Dated this _____ day of _____ 20____

**Figure 8-21    Key Return Acknowledgement**

KEY RETURN ACKNOWLEDGEMENT


APARTMENT:_____HAS RETURNED

_____ APARTMENT KEYS

_____ MAILBOX KEYS

_____ OTHER


ON THIS DAY _____OF _____20,_____

SUNNYVALE MANOR

_____

RESIDENT:

BY:_____

_____

RESIDENT:


FORWARDING ADDRESS:

_____

_____

_____

**Figure 8-22   Installment Note**

INSTALLMENT NOTE

$ _____ $ _____
　　Dollars　　　　　　　　　　Written Dollar Amount

TOTAL DUE, _____, CALIFORNIA, _____ 20 ___
　　　　　　　　　City　　　　　　　　　　　　Month/Day

IN INSTALLMENTS AS HEREIN STATED,_____
　　　　　　　　　　　　　　　　　　Resident Name(s)

PROMISE TO PAY _____ THE AMOUNT
　　　　　　　　　　　Complex Name

STATED ABOVE FOR _____ INCURREC
　　　　　　　　Reason for Balance

ON _____ AT _____
　　　Date　　　　　　　　　　　　　Location

*************************************************************** ********
MONTHLY INSTALLMENTS
*************************************************************** ********

$ _____ FOR _____ MONTHS, BEGINNING ON _____ , 20 ___

FINAL PAYMENT DUE _____ IN THE AMOUNT OF $ _____

*FAILURE TO COMPLY WITH THE TERMS HEREIN STATED*
WILL RESULT IN LEGAL ACTION

_____　　_____

_____　　_____

Prepared by: _____

Approved by: _____

Entered by: _____

**Figure 8-23    Transfer of Security Deposit**

## TRANSFER OF SECURITY DEPOSIT

TO: Resident(s) _____

Effective _____ , 20 ____ , we will no longer manage/own the unit in which you reside,

located at _____ , California.

In accordance with the California Tenant/Landlord Civil Code, Section 1950.5, you are being informed that your

security deposit, in the amount of $ _____ , has been:

[ _____ ]    TRANSFERRED TO: _____

_____

_____

[ _____ ]    RETURNED TO YOU. _____
(Date)

YOUR PRESENT RENTAL AGREEMENT/LEASE WILL REMAIN IN EFFECT. FOR MORE INFORMATION ABOUT
YOUR NEW OWNER/AGENT, CONTACT:

_____

_____

_____

On _____ , 20 _____ , this Notice was:

[ _____ ]    Sent to you by certified mail; or

[ _____ ]    Personally delivered to you;

AND a copy of this Notice was mailed to the new owner/agent.

Dated _____ , 20 _____ .     _____
OWNER/AGENT

SAMPLE

## Figure 8-24   Itemized Disposition of Security Deposit

**ITEMIZED DISPOSITION OF SECURITY DEPOSIT**

Pursuant to Civil Code Section 1950.5, Owner, on the _____ day of _____, 20___, hereby furnished the following statement of disposition of security deposit monies to former resident(s):

_____
(Name(s))

for the premises located at: _____ California _____
(Address)                                                                    (Zip)

Itemized Damages: _____

_____

_____

_____

_____

_____

| TOTAL DAMAGES | $ |
|---|---|

Necessary cleaning of premises upon termination: _____

_____

_____

_____

_____

_____

| TOTAL CLEANING COSTS | $ |
|---|---|

Default in rent (explain): _____

_____

_____

_____

_____

| TOTAL RENT DUE | $ |
|---|---|

SAMPLE

**USE BACK OF FORM IF MORE SPACE IS NEEDED**

**SEND BALANCE DUE OWNER TO:**

NAME _____

ADDRESS _____

CITY, STATE, ZIP _____

| TOTAL CHARGES | $ |
|---|---|
| TOTAL SECURITY DEPOSITS RECEIVED | $ |
| BALANCE DUE OWNER PLEASE REMIT IMMEDIATELY | $ |
| BALANCE DUE RESIDENT PAID BY CHECK NO. | $ |

**FORMER RESIDENT'S NEW ADDRESS**

_____

_____

OWNER/AGENT

**Figure 8-25 Three-Day Notice to Pay Rent or Quit**

## NOTICE TO PAY RENT OR QUIT

TO: _____
<small>All residents (tenants and subtenants) in possession (full name) and all others in possession</small>

WITHIN THREE DAYS after the service on you of this notice, you are hereby required to pay to the under-

signed or_____, his authorized agent, the

rent of the premises hereinafter described, of which you now hold possession amounting to the sum of

_____ dollars ($ _____)

enumerated as follows:

$ _____ Due From _____ 20 _____ To _____ 20 _____

$ _____ Due From _____ 20 _____ To _____ 20 _____

$ _____ Due From _____ 20 _____ To _____ 20 _____

OR QUIT AND DELIVER UP THE POSSESSION OF THE PREMISES.

The premises herein referred to are situated in the city of _____,

County of _____, State of California, designated by the number

and street as _____, apt. _____.

YOU ARE FURTHER NOTIFIED THAT, the owner/landlord does hereby elect to declare the forfeiture of your lease or rental agreement under which you hold possession of the above-described premises and if you fail to perform or otherwise comply, will institute legal proceeding to recover rent and possession of said premises which could result in a judgement against you including costs and necessary disbursements together with treble damages as allowed by law for such unlawful detention.

DATE: _____        _____
                                        OWNER / AGENT

## Figure 8-26   Three-Day Notice to Perform Covenants and/or Conditions

# THREE DAY NOTICE TO PERFORM CONDITIONS
# AND/OR COVENANTS OR QUIT

TO: _____
      All residents (tenants and subtenants) in possession and all others in possession (full name).

PLEASE TAKE NOTICE that you are in violation of the terms of your rental agreement of the premises located at:

_____ , CA.

IN. THAT, the Rental Agreement/Lease condition(s) and/or covenants set forth below are being breached as follows:

  1.  Condition(s) and/or covenant(s) breached: _____

    _____

    _____

    _____

    _____

    _____

  2.  State specific facts of breach(s) and/or violation(s): _____

    _____

    _____

    _____

    _____

    _____

WITHIN THREE DAYS after the service on you of this notice, you are hereby required to perform or otherwise comply with the above-mentioned condition and/or covenant or QUIT AND DELIVER UP THE POSSESSION OF THE PREMISES.

YOU ARE FURTHER NOTIFIED that the Owner/Agent does hereby elect to declare the forfeiture of your rental agreement under which you hold possession of the above-described premises, and if you fail to perform or otherwise comply, will institute legal proceedings to recover rent and possession of said premises which could result in a judgment against you including costs and necessary disbursements together with treble damages as allowed by law for such unlawful detention.

Dated _____ , 20 _____  _____
                                        OWNER/AGENT

## Figure 8-27    Proof of Service

—PROOF OF SERVICE—

I served the within:

1. Name: _____

2. Person with whom left: title or relationship to person served:

   _____

3. Date and Time of Delivery: _____

4. Date of Mailing: _____ Place of Mailing: _____

5. Address, City and State (when required, indicate whether address is home or business): _____

6. Manner of Service (Check appropriate box):

   [ ]  A.  PERSONAL SERVICE:      By handing a copy to the person served.

   [ ]  B.  SUBSTITUTED SERVICE:   By leaving a copy at the dwelling, house, usual place of abode, of the person served in the presence of a competent member of the household, at least 18 years of age, who was informed of the general nature of the papers: and thereafter mailing (by first-class mail, postage prepaid) a copy to the person served at the place where a copy was left.

   [ ]  C.  SERVICE POSTING:       By posting a copy at a conspicuous place on the dwelling, house, usual place of abode pursuant to Section 1162(3); thereafter mailing (by first-class mail, postage prepaid) a copy to the person served to the posted address. At said time and place, _____ could not be found nor could a person of suitable age or discretion be found on the premises. At said time I was over the age of 18 years.

I declare under penalty of perjury that the foregoing is true and correct.

Executed on _____ 20 ___, at _____ California.

_____
(signature of declarant)

_____
(type or print name of declarant)

_____
(type or print address)

_____
(phone number)

# Figure 8-28    Cash Report

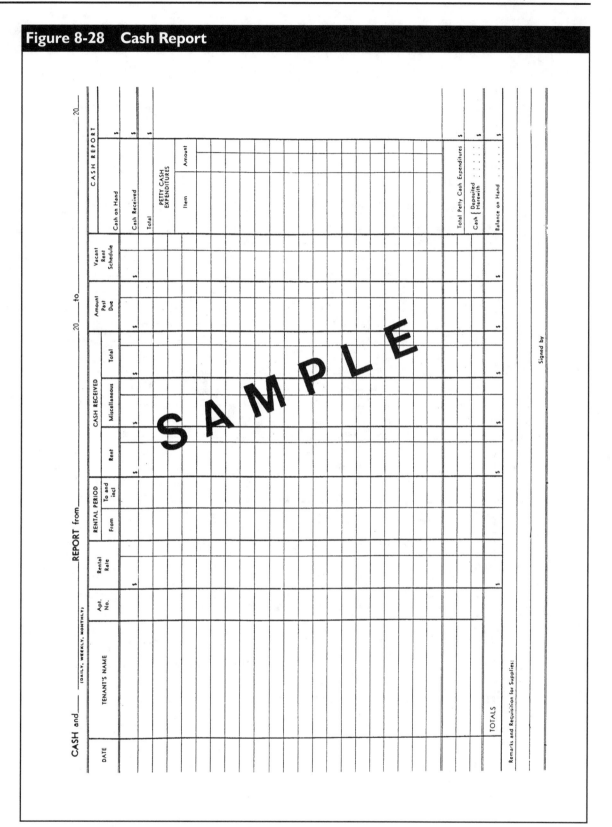

## Figure 8-29  Time Sheet

Note: This order required by Industrial Welfare Commission Order No.  5-80
To be filed with employer semi-monthly

### TIME SHEET - RECORD OF HOURS WORKED

EMPLOYEE_____

ADDRESS_____

CITY_____

ADDRESS OF EMPLOYMENT_____ CITY OF _____

| Date | | Detail of Time Spent on Apartment Business (Show fractions, thus: 8:30 - 9:30, 2:15 - 5:45) | Total Hours |
|---|---|---|---|
| Month | Day | | |
| | | | |
| | | | |
| | | | |
| | | | |
| | | | |
| | | | |
| | | | |
| | | | |
| | | | |
| | | | |
| | | | |
| | | | |
| | | | |
| | | | |
| | | | |

Total hours worked during period . . . . . . . . . . . . . . . . . . . . .

Note: Explain reason for any hours worked over those agreed upon in contract:

_____

_____

This will certify the above time record is complete and accurate.

Signed_____
                                        Employee

Employee NOT to use space below this line

Salary or wages for period (including allowance for use of apartment)   $ _____

Deductions:   Federal Old Age Insurance   $_____

Unemployment Insurance   _____

Other (                    )   _____   $ _____

NET Salary Paid   $ _____

## Figure 8-30    Resident Control Card

_____ APARTMENTS                    RESIDENT CONTROL CARD

TENANT:_____    FORMER ADDRESS:_____

_____    TELEPHONE NO._____

EMPLOYER:_____    BUS. PHONE:_____

RENT COMMENCES:                    MOVED IN:                    RENT EXPIRED:

| BEDROOMS | | | FURNITURE | | REFER. | | LOWER LEVEL | | UPPER LEVEL | | |
|---|---|---|---|---|---|---|---|---|---|---|---|
| ONE | TWO | THREE | YES | NO | YES | NO | FRONT | BACK | FRONT | BACK | |

| INITIAL RENTAL CHARGES AND DEPOSITS | RENT | | | | DEPOSITS | | TOTAL INITIAL AMOUNT |
|---|---|---|---|---|---|---|---|
| | APART. | FURN. | REFER. | OTHER | CLEANING | FINAL MO. | |
| | | | | | | | |

RECORD OF CASH RECEIVED

| DATE | RECEIPT NO. | RENTAL PERIOD | | RENT | | | | DEPOSITS | | TOTAL AMOUNT RECEIVED | CS CK |
|---|---|---|---|---|---|---|---|---|---|---|---|
| | | FROM | TO | APART. | FURN. | REFER. | OTHER | CLEANING | FINAL MO. | | |
| | | | | | | | | | | | |
| | | | | | | | | | | | |
| | | | | | | | | | | | |
| | | | | | | | | | | | |
| | | | | | | | | | | | |
| | | | | | | | | | | | |
| | | | | | | | | | | | |
| | | | | | | | | | | | |
| | | | | | | | | | | | |
| | | | | | | | | | | | |
| | | | | | | | | | | | |
| | | | | | | | | | | | |
| | | | | | | | | | | | |
| | | | | | | | | | | | |
| | | | | | | | | | | | |
| | | | | | | | | | | | |
| | | | | | | | | | | | |
| | | | | | | | | | | | |
| | | | | | | | | | | | |

SAMPLE

**Figure 8-31   Job Estimate and Worksheet**

<u>JOB ESTIMATE AND WORKSHEET</u>

PURPOSE AND INFORMATION: _____

_____

<u>PROSPECT</u>

NAME: _____ADDRESS: _____

PHONE: _____CONTACT: _____

GUARANTEES: _____PRICE: _____
_____

NEW: $ _____     USED: $ _____     REBUILT: $ _____

PARTS: $ _____     LABOR: $ _____     INSTALLATION: $ _____

PER SQ. FT: $ _____     PER SQ. YD: $ _____     PER WALL: $ _____

PER ROOM: $ _____     PER HOUR: $ _____     PER WINDOW: $ _____

ONE BEDRM: $ _____     TWO BEDRM: $ _____     THREE BED: $ _____
_____

MAXIMUM TIME: _____     MINIMUM TIME: _____

DELIVERY: _____     HOW LONG?: _____

OTHER: _____
_____

APPOINTMENT DATE: _____     TIME: _____

WITH WHOM: _____

APPROVED: _____

WORK STARTED: _____     DATE: _____

WORK FINISHED: _____     DATE: _____

INSPECTED: _____     DATE: _____

DELIVERED: _____     DATE: _____

PICKED-UP: _____     DATE: _____

INSTALLED: _____     DATE: _____

CALLED BACK: _____     DATE: _____

REDONE: _____     DATE: _____

OKAY FOR PAYMENT: _____     DATE: _____
_____

OVERCHARGE: $ _____     OKAY FOR PAYMENT: _____

REASON: _____

# QUESTIONS

1. Forms provide documentation of:

   a. agreement
   b. activity
   c. policy
   d. all of the above

2. The "Application to Rent" (Figure 8-1) may not require:

   a. social security number
   b. the race of the applicant
   c. income information
   d. employment information

3. A "Statement of Condition" (move-in/move-out) (Figure 8-2) signed by the tenant may be necessary to:

   a. refurbish the apartment after move-out
   b. collect from the tenant for normal wear and tear
   c. collect from the tenant for damage to the property
   d. none of the above

4. According to the "Rental Agreement: Month-to-Month" (Figure 8-3), in order to terminate this agreement, how much notice must be given?

   a. 7 days
   b. 14 days
   c. 30 days
   d. no notice is required

5. The "Rental Agreement: Long-Form Lease" (Figure 8-4) provides for an increase in lease payments:

   a. commensurate with the Consumer Price Index
   b. at a rate of 5% after one year
   c. to be determined by the lessor
   d. no increase is included

6. An "Addendum to Rental Agreement and/or Lease" (Figure 8-5):

    a. always increases the rent

    b. always adds tenants to the lease

    c. becomes part of the rental agreement

    d. is a unilateral agreement added to the original contract

7. The "Smoke Detector Agreement" (Figure 8-6) is designed to:

    a. make sure a tenant knows how a smoke detector works

    b. verify there is a smoke detector in each room

    c. let the tenant test the smoke detector

    d. none of the above

8. The "Waterbed Agreement" (Figure 8-7) may require the tenant to:

    a. give the landlord additional money as security

    b. furnish a certificate of liability insurance policy to owner

    c. pay additional money to owner to offset increased utility costs incurred by owner for heater

    d. all of the above

9. A co-signer in a rental agreement (Figure 8-9):

    a. may not occupy the unit

    b. stands behind the lessee but is not personally liable

    c. would not have to pay attorney's fees

    d. is entitled to the same statutory notices as any occupants

10. An addendum to a lease (Figure 8-11) providing for a cancellation fee for early termination:

    a. releases the tenant from any liability for rent concessions received during his or her tenancy

    b. holds the tenant accountable for normal wear and tear to the property

    c. requires the tenant to pay a fee to be relieved of any future lease payments

    d. does not require a 30-day notice

11. A "Notice of Change in Terms" (Figure 8-12) of tenancy:

    a. takes effect in 30 days
    b. does not require a 30-day notice
    c. can raise the rent before the expiration of the lease
    d. is a bilateral addendum to the contract

12. A "resident's Service Request" (Figure 8-13):

    a. enables management to serve the tenant more efficiently
    b. protects the rights of the tenant
    c. shields the landlord from liability
    d. all of the above

13. A "Roommate Notice to Vacate" (Figure 8-15):

    a. notifies a roommate to vacate the premises
    b. gives notice to management that one of the tenants is vacating
    c. does not relieve the vacating tenant of liability for any damage to the premises
    d. entitles the vacating tenant to receive his or her security deposit

14. When a tenant submits a "Notice of Intent to Vacate" (Figure 8-17):

    a. it must be done with two weeks notice
    b. it guarantees a full refund of his or her security deposit
    c. it allows management to show the unit prior to the tenant moving
    d. none of the above

15. An "Acknowledgement of Intent to Vacate" (Figure 8-18):

    a. allows the tenant to apply the security deposit as the last month's rent
    b. allows the landlord to apply part of the security deposit towards cleaning
    c. prohibits tenant from vacating the premises earlier than notice specifies
    d. relieves tenant from having to pay the rent in advance for the remainder of the agreement

16. The "Notice of Termination of Tenancy" (Figure 8-19):

     a. requires that valid reasons be given
     b. does not require that valid reasons be given
     c. is given from lessee to lessor
     d. can be given without reasons prior to expiration of a lease

17. The "House Rules and Regulations" (Figure 8-20) covers:

     a. noise and conduct
     b. safety
     c. maintenance and repairs
     d. all of the above

18. Deposits should be returned:

     a. before keys are returned
     b. before final inspection of the unit
     c. within the legal time limit of state law
     d. after final inspection of the unit but before the tenant drives away

19. A transfer of security deposit form (Figure 8-23) may be necessary in the event of:

     a. a transfer of an apartment to a different tenant
     b. a transfer of ownership of the building
     c. a transfer of lessees
     d. the assignment of the lease

20. All or part of a deposit (Figure 8-24) may be kept by the landlord for which of the following reasons:

     a. itemized damages to the premises
     b. necessary cleaning of the premises upon termination
     c. deficit in rent
     d. all of the above

# ANSWERS

1. *d*
2. *b*
3. *c*
4. *c*
5. *a*
6. *c*
7. *a*
8. *d*
9. *a*
10. *c*
11. *a*
12. *d*
13. *b*
14. *c*
15. *b*
16. *b*
17. *d*
18. *c*
19. *b*
20. *d*

# Apartment Management: Operations and Procedures

- Apartment Diversity
- Standard Operating Procedures (SOP)
- Insurance
- Computers
- Files And Record Keeping

C H A P T E R

9

# APARTMENT DIVERSITY

Apartments come in all shapes and sizes. Two- to four-unit buildings are apartments and so are multi-story buildings with elevators and everything in between. There are garden apartments, usually two-story affairs surrounding a courtyard emphasizing landscaping or sometimes a pool. Three-story walk-ups are popular in some urban areas and highrise luxury apartments cater to affluent urban and suburban districts. Some apartments are furnished—some unfurnished.  Some come with extensive amenities such as pools, tennis courts and gyms—others are bare-bones, laundry rooms being the extent of it.

The nature of the apartment building will dictate the workload of the manager. A complex with a pool will require watchful oversight every day. A highrise with elevators and lots of traffic will demand that the manager travel frequently the same route as the tenants to ensure the proper functioning of moving parts and a favorable presentation of the premises. A simpler structure with few amenities will render the manager's job more basic and allow time for office work and tenant relations.

# STANDARD OPERATING PROCEDURES (SOP)

Whatever the workload of the manager in relation to the configuration of the building and extent of the amenities, certain things are going to happen on a regular basis. These needs that recur and events that repeat themselves should spawn certain procedures so that things can be done the same way every time they happen. Since they are going to recur, there is no reason to be surprised and to waste time reinventing the wheel. So why not develop some standard procedures that will carry us through these events in the most efficient way possible? We call these *standard operating procedures*.

## Showing and Renting an Apartment

One property management company devised the following procedures for an on-site manager (OSM) in order to show and rent an apartment.

(1) All employees should be friendly and courteous to all clients.

(2) Telephone calls will be screened by the office first before referring them to the OSM or the cluster manager.

(3) A prospective tenant comes to the OSM to see the apartment; OSM will describe the apartment, show the apartment to the prospective tenant and answer all questions tenant may have about the apartment and the surrounding area.

(4) If a tenant walks in without an appointment set by the office, the tenant should fill out a rental application if the apartment is of interest. If an appointment was set, then no application is required.

(5) After the forms are complete, ask tenant for a $100.00 deposit and $25.00 for the credit check. Remind tenants that the $25.00 is non-refundable and after _____ (date), the deposit is non-refundable if they change their minds.

(6) Tell tenants you will get back to them after you have completed the credit check, called on their references from the applications, and all monies have cleared the bank (if they are checks). This would take a couple of days.

(7) Tenant may then come to pay the balance due on the security deposit and first month's rent; read, understand and sign the Residents Guide and Lease; witness the OSM inspect the apartment with MIMO (Move-in, Move-out form); sign an agreement; then receive keys to the apartment. The OSM tells tenants they will get a copy of the Residents Guide and the Lease.

This standard operating procedure ensures that all the bases are covered. The tenant is thoroughly investigated as to credit, character and ability to pay, and doesn't receive the keys or gain possession until he or she pays the required amount, understands and agrees to all of the terms. Sequence is important in this process and the SOP is presented in this manner to avoid mistakes. The OSM knows exactly what is expected.

## Vacancies

A similar process can be structured upon the occurrence of another regular event, the vacancy. The same property management company devised the following SOP for the OSM when a vacancy occurs.

(1) Change front door locks and make sure the Property Manager receives two sets of keys (one for the office) and the OSM has two sets (one for the tenant).

(2) Enter the vacant apartment and fill out the MIMO form. Make notes of the following items.

  a. Walls need to be painted

  b. Carpets/drapes need cleaning or replacement

  c. Doors and windows open/close easily—no damage

  d. Kitchen counters/cabinets—no damage/clean

  e. All appliances, fixtures and utilities are operating properly

(3) Report the outcome to the Property Manager, give an estimate of how much it would cost to ready the apartment and amount of time needed. Property Manager should then arrange for the work to be done.

(4) OSM lets workers into the apartment to do cleaning and/or repairs. When they claim to be done with the apartment, OSM must enter again and check the work to be sure it is satisfactory before dismissing the workers.

(5) OSM reports to the Property Manager that the apartment is ready to be inspected. If all checks out with the Property Manager, the apartment is ready to be shown. If it does not check out, the OSM must go back to the workers and have them complete it properly.

In many cases, of course, the OSM will be communicating directly with ownership. The arrangement described above is for a larger complex and provides a check and balance system to increase efficiency and eliminate waste and mistakes.

# Duties of the On-Site Manager

Duties of the OSM should be clearly stated so there are no misunderstandings. The following list was developed for the guidance of the OSM.

(1) Keep the complex quiet; handle unreasonable noise.

(2) Sweep the sidewalks and walkways. Pick up litter and inspect premises for signs of vandalism.

(3) Wash walkways and driveways down at least once a week.

(4) Inspect outside of complex for any damage that could cause trouble if unattended. Report this to Property Manager or ownership.

(5) Enforce the rules set forth in the Residents' Guide and the Lease.

(6) Enforce parking regulations; make sure tenants obey the signs.

(7) Be on a friendly basis with all tenants.

(8) Be responsible for cleaning, showing and renting any vacant unit. Screen tenants.

(9) Do light maintenance including cleaning the pool, ensuring that the sprinklers work, and various other tasks.

(10) Be able to handle such emergencies as fire, theft and injuries.

(11) Collect rents each month, report any late payments, hand out three-day notices and eviction notices. Be responsible for proper delivery of all forms and monies. Give a receipt to tenant for any monies collected and keep a record of all receipts.

(12) Conduct a regular six-month maintenance inspection with tenants present.

(13) Know where the water, gas and telephone lines are.

(14) Keep list of all phone numbers of each tenant.

(15) Report any deaths or arrests of any tenant to Property Manager or owner and follow instructions as to what should be done.

## Working with Tenant to Vacate

If the tenant leaves at the expiration of a lease or otherwise after giving notice, the following procedures are provided to ensure an orderly separation.

(1) Each tenant must give a 30-day notice from the first of any month which must be mailed and postmarked prior to the first of the month.

(2) OSM tells tenant the following. On moving day:

    a. Tenant must be present for final MIMO inspection.

    b. Tenant must return all keys before any deposit is refunded. If keys are not returned, a $20.00 fee is charged per key.

(3) OSM must make sure all appliances that were rented with apartment are still there and operating.

(4) OSM has tenant sign MIMO form.

(5) After tenant has left, OSM must make arrangements with the Cluster Manager to have necessary work done to the apartment the next day.

## In Case of Eviction

If the vacancy is created by eviction, these procedures should be followed.

(1) Before and after the tenant vacates, do a MIMO inspection on apartment. Tenant should be present for the "before" inspection. Have tenant sign MIMO form. If he or she won't sign, please make a note to that effect, date and initial it.

(2) OSM is to make sure all keys are collected from tenant before vacating. If keys are not returned, OSM should make a note to that effect, date and sign. Cluster Manager, Property Manager or owner should be notified immediately.

## SOP for Hiring On-Site Managers

The on-site manager is so important to the successful operation of an apartment building. Upper management and ownership should have standard operating procedures for effectively interviewing and hiring them. Here are some guidelines that have been developed.

### QUALIFICATIONS FOR OSMs

(1) Must be at least 21 years of age with a valid driver's license. Must get DMV printout.

(2) For couples only—one can work full time, but one of them must always be on the premises. Must always arrange backup for evenings and weekends when not there.

(3) Have some experience and/or excellent business and personal references.

(4) Must be able to handle light maintenance and have own tools to accomplish such tasks.

(5) Have no evictions or arrest record; can be trusted to handle monies.

(6) Have neat appearance and be responsible.

If qualifications are thought out in advance, they can be applied objectively when considering specific applicants. No matter how impressive applicants may be in an interview, if they don't meet the basic qualifications determined to be important for the position of on-site manager, they shouldn't be hired. A smooth operation can only be accomplished if the proper team members are in place. In addition to minimum qualifications, some thought should be given to qualities we would like to see in an on-site manager. The following guidelines have been developed.

**QUALITY GUIDELINES FOR OSMs**

(1) Fair

(2) Honest

(3) Reliable

(4) Used to dealing with people

(5) Intelligent

(6) Self-assured

(7) Unflappable

(8) Willing to learn

(9) Handy

(10) Helpful

(11) Modest

(12) Pleasant

(13) Patient

(14) Speak with air of authority

This list of qualities describes a person who would be pleasing to be around, but more importantly, would have the right balance of characteristics to deal effectively with a wide variety of people—namely, your tenants. This list of qualities has been carefully thought out by seasoned investors and property owners. Rather than scanning the list hurriedly, reflect on each quality to see how it applies to the OSM position. One particularly impressive quality on the list is *unflappable*, and proves that the list was composed with a great deal of thought behind it. Apartment houses are places where people live, and anything and everything happens where people live. OSMs most assuredly should be unflappable; that is, nothing should get to them. They take everything in stride and handle it with an air of emotional detachment.

When you find an OSM who is unflappable and has most of the rest of the above qualities, hold on to that person as a valuable employee—worth one's weight in gold to the smooth operation of your investment property. And if you *are* an OSM, you should aspire to attain a good measure of these qualities.

In addition to the above, some other characteristics and circumstances have been found to be valuable in an OSM.

(1) Previous experience (highly desirable)

(2) Marital status (married better than single)

(3) Age (younger may not stay long, mature person may be more settled)

(4) Cleanliness (home, auto, appearance)

(5) Rudimentary knowledge of construction (always helpful)

(6) Good working knowledge of home repair and fix-up

(7) A little salesmanship (never hurts; you don't want indifference!)

(8) Good public relations (OSM represents ownership —very important!)

(9) An understanding of bookkeeping

(10) Meticulous with details

(11) Good credit rating

## NOTES AND OBSERVATIONS TO MAKE DURING INTERVIEW

(1) Did they show up on time for the interview?

(2) Do they speak with a firm voice?

(3) Do they agree with whatever you say or do they take time to think and give their own answer and explanation?

(4) Would they be willing to learn?

(5) Intended time of service?

(6) Are they flexible or hardnosed?

(7) Do they look at you when you talk to them or when they talk to you?

(8) Do they have any nervous habits?

(9) How do they handle details in the following situations and questions?

**Question #1:** *Do you have any previous experience in managing apartments? If yes, please explain.*

Example situation:

(a) A prospective tenant comes to your door to rent a vacant apartment. What's the process from showing to renting?

(b) A tenant is making a lot of noise and disturbing neighbors at all hours of the day and night. What should you do?

(c) A tenant vacates a unit. What is the procedure to get the unit prepared and rented as soon as possible?

**Question #2:** *Have you had any type of sales experience or working with people? If yes, please explain.*

Example situation:

(a) A prospective tenant comes in and walks through a unit for rent. She points out details she does not like and is looking for something a little different. Do you accept no for an answer? What is your response?

See if the person mentions sending the tenant to another apartment owned or managed by the same group.

**Question #3:** *Are you married? Friend living with you? Any children? How many?*

This is to determine age of applicant. (Illegal to ask unless they offer.)

**Question #4:** *How long have you lived in the area? Do you know the surrounding community around XYZ Apartments?*

Examples: Shopping centers? Schools? Day-care centers? Hospital emergency room? Medical centers? Bus stops? Bus schedules and fares? Police station? Fire station? Emergency numbers?

**Question #5: *Where do you see yourself three years down the line? Five years?***

**Question #6: *What do you see as the profile for a "good tenant"?***

Example situations:

Appearance? Manner of speaking? Car they drive? Behavior of any child? Smoker/non-smoker? Cleanliness? Young marrieds? Male/female roommates?

**Question #7: *How do you fix the following?***

(a) A faucet is leaking—(make note as to whether or not they mention shutting water off under the sink, not at the main)

(b) Replacing a door—(type of door used: solid or hollow/door inside main door)

(c) A clogged sink or tub

(d) Baseboard that is coming off

(e) A 4-inch diameter hole in the wall

**Question #8: *How would you react to the following emergencies?***

(a) Someone's toaster oven catches fire and burns the wall

(b) Walking by a unit you smell gas leaking

(c) A medical emergency

**Question #9: *Have you had any bookkeeping experience?***

These questions and observations will give you a wealth of knowledge about the person being interviewed. You will develop a sense of whether or not the applicant "fits" the job description. You also will sense how well you can work with the person, and whether the individual is trustworthy and competent.

Consider some other areas of apartment management that lend themselves to *standard operating procedures*.

## Communication with Tenants

Communicating with tenants is a necessity for reasons of safety, security and profitability. Policies and procedures, rules and regulations all need to be clearly understood. Announcements and changes occur sometimes and need to be disseminated quickly and effectively to all tenants. Following are some of the possibilities.

### POSTED NOTICES

Flyers can be made up and posted in prominent locations around the complex. Bulletin boards, laundry rooms, mail boxes and various doors can all be designated message locations.

### NEWSLETTERS

These can be part of regular communication and can be a rapport builder, pulling together the apartment community into a tight knit group. The difficulty of this type of communication is that it is time consuming and demanding on the OSM. The regularity of the production schedule may beg for time the OSM doesn't have, and many in the position may not feel inclined to participate in this activity.

### RECORDINGS

Information that doesn't need to be disseminated immediately but over time can be left on a recording with the answering machine. When the OSM isn't available to answer the phone, the information will be given to those who call. Information of a more urgent nature would not be suitable for this method.

### PERSONAL DELIVERY

Notices and written correspondence can be personally delivered to a tenant's door. Information that needs to be promptly communicated can be handled in this direct fashion.

### PHONE CALLS

Phone calls are quick, direct and easily accomplished. Most people today have answering machines so if they're not home, they can still receive the information. Any message that has been left verbally in this manner should be followed with a written message, with verification that it has been received if necessary.

## Rules For Children

Rules and policies that apply to certain areas and circumstances can be posted in the pertinent locations as well as be acknowledged personally by each tenant, with appropriate copies in the file. Though a tenant has signed the *Pool Area Rules* and has received a copy of it, he or she will be more mindful of it if it is posted in a prominent spot around the pool.

If there are rules for children in the apartment complex, it is helpful to post them in a prominent location to remind parents of what the rules are, and also to make other tenants aware of what is expected of children. Heightened awareness of expected behavior from children will help accomplish the desired result. If on occasion results fall short due to parent negligence, posted policies and rules of management regarding the proper care of children may help indemnify ownership and management from liability in the event of accident or injury.

**Figure 9-1    Pool Area Rules**

### POOL AREA RULES

In order to make the best use of our pool and its equipment, and for the benefit of all our Residents, we ask your cooperation in complying with the following:

1.    The pool is provided for the convenience of the residents and occupants of the building ONLY.  While guests are permitted, they are limited to NO MORE THAN TWO (2) PERSONS PER UNIT.  Residents are REQUIRED to be at pool WITH guests.

2.    No charge is included in apartment rental or otherwise for the use of the pool area.  Users are expressly warned that pool and pool areas are dangerous and may be used ONLY under the condition that USER ASSUMES ALL RISKS of personal injury or property damage without qualification.

3.    Minors must be ACCOMPANIED by parent or adult, with the resident assuming all risks of personal injury, property damage and liability.

4.    The use of GLASS or CANS is prohibited in pool area.

5.    NO RUNNING, JUMPING, UNNECESSARY NOISE AND YELLING, SPLASHING of water or DIVING from balconies or other elevated areas is allowed.

6.    Residents and guests are responsible for items brought to the pool area. If items cause damage to pool or its filtering system, the resident will be charged for the repairs.  These items include: Body oils, suntan lotions, metal or glass objects, and cigarette ends.

7.    All pool equipment is to be cleaned and returned to its proper place. These items include: Tables, chairs, lounges, covers and life saving equipment.

8.    There shall be NO throwing of ANY OBJECTS into the pool.

9.    No person shall use the pool or pool area in improper dress.  Examples of such dress are: "G" Strings, Topless or Nude.

10.  Pool Hours:  _____ AM to _____ PM, Sunday thru Thursday

                 _____ AM to _____ PM, Friday and Saturday

11.  Management reserves the right to CLOSE POOL or to EXCLUDE or RESTRICT any person from the pool and its area at any time.

**Figure 9-2   Rules for Children**

### RULES FOR CHILDREN

1. Children will play in designated places on the premises, besides the inside of the rental unit.

2. Children are not allowed in, near, or around the pool without a consenting, supervising adult present with them.

3. Toys should be kept out of carports and streets, and away from public walkways at all times to prevent accidents. Tricycles, bigwheels and such should be used with the supervision of an adult on the premises.

4. Children should not be outside playing by themselves at night. An adult should be watching them if they are playing outside after dark.

5. Any adult suspected or caught abusing or molesting a child will be reported to the proper authorities and will be evicted.

6. After school, parents should make proper arrangements for their children to be met at the bus or supervised until parents are home.

7. Damage done by children in the complex or in the rental unit is the sole responsibility of the adult residents.

8. Any child caught stealing or being unnecessarily disruptive or violent towards other residents will result in an eviction of that family.

Other general rules for all residents can be posted in prominent locations to keep an awareness of what is expected in front of everyone. Even if the tenant has acknowledged and received a copy of the list of rules, it is a certainty that they do not take them out and review them periodically. Public posting is helpful.

---

**Figure 9-3   Residents' Guidelines**

### RESIDENTS' GUIDELINES

These are guidelines to ensure that Residents enjoy their living in XYZ Manor. Please be considerate of other people in all of your actions. If you have any questions, see the Manager. Remember that we have these rules so good Residents can enjoy their residency here. All of these rules can be summed up in one important phrase:

*Do unto others as you would have them do unto you.*

1. The activities and conduct of Resident, Residents' guests and minor children of Residents or guests, outside of the unit on the common grounds, parking areas, or any recreation facilities must be reasonable at all times and not annoy or disturb other persons. Residents are required to be particularly careful about noise before the hour of 8:00 a.m. and after 10:00 p.m. in consideration of other Residents. CHILDREN ON THE PREMISES MUST BE SUPERVISED BY A RESPONSIBLE ADULT AT ALL TIMES.

2. Residents agree not to use the premises for any commercial enterprise or for any purpose which is unlawful, against city ordinances, or which would injure the reputation of the building or its occupants in any way.

3. Guests are not to park on property. No boats, vans, trailers, trucks, etc. are to be parked without prior written permission from Manager or authorized agent. Abandoned cars, cars leaking oil, or inoperable cars are to be removed from premises. Residents are not to store gasoline or combustible materials on the premises.

4. If the unit is supplied with smoke detection devices upon occupancy it shall be the responsibility of the Resident to regularly test the detectors to ensure that the devices are in operable condition. The Resident will inform Management immediately in writing of any defect, malfunction or failure of such detectors.

5. Barbecuing, outside cooking, and picnicking are to be done only in approved areas.

*(continued)*

---

## Figure 9-3 (cont'd.) Residents' Guidelines

6. Roller skates, bikes, miniature autos, skateboards, etc. are not to be used within apartment grounds.

7. Clothing, curtains, rugs, etc., shall not be shaken or hung outside of any windows, ledge or balcony.

8. The Manager should be notified if a Resident is going to be absent from the building for a period of time. If someone is to enter Resident's unit during Resident's absence, Resident shall give management permission beforehand to let any person in the unit and/or provide the name of person or company entering.

9. In the event the Manager sets apart in the building a laundry room for the convenience of the Residents, Residents may, at their own risk, and without cost, use for the purpose of laundry. Agents of the Owner are prohibited as such in any way from moving or handling articles in or from the laundry room. If any such agent does, at the request of Resident, take part in moving, handling, opening or removing anything in or from such laundry room, he/she shall be the agent of the Resident and not the Manager. Resident assumes all risk of loss or damage to articles or things while in transit to or from such laundry room.

10. Agents of Manager are prohibited as such from receiving any packages or other articles delivered to the building for Resident or persons residing with Resident.

11. Manager will admit Residents who have been locked out of their unit but the following charge can be made: 8:00 a.m.–6:00 p.m.— $2.00; other hours—$5.00.

12. All notices to Management from Resident shall be in writing and in accordance with any time factor relating to notices. Management will comply with the same procedure on notices to Residents.

13. Resident shall place only normal disposable items in garbage disposals. Any disposal, plumbing damage or drain blockage that results from Resident misuse or abuse will be the responsibility of the Resident and costs will be charged to the Resident. Management will be responsible for normal wear and tear and repairs not relating from neglect.

14. All sidewalks, driveways, passages and common areas shall not be obstructed nor used for any other purpose than ingress and egress to and from units.

15. Resident agrees to keep premises both inside and outside including its equipment and contents in a reasonably clean and neat condition at all times. Items are not to be stored in front or outside Resident's unit.

## Collecting the Rent

With all of the work that goes into unit readiness, marketing and proper maintenance of an apartment complex, the day the rent comes in each month is a glorious one indeed. It represents the fruits of one's labor and enables the owner to pay the bills. Of all events that occur over the course of a month, it ought to be handled with precision and efficiency.

Let the tenant know what is expected from the beginning and facilitate his or her paying the rent as much as possible. Have a slotted and locked mail box available where the tenant can place the envelope. Some managers provide marked or preprinted envelopes for the duration of the tenant's lease. If the rent is due on the first of the month, let the tenant know it is expected on that day. Devise a specific procedure to follow if it is not received. Call the tenant by the third and inquire about the rent. Remind the tenant that if the rent is not received before the fifth of the month, a late charge is imposed. If the rent is received on the fifth, collect the late charge. If the rent is not received by the fifth of the month, serve a three-day notice to pay or quit on the sixth and if there is no response, follow through with the eviction process.

If a check bounces, have a procedure and follow it. Charge the tenant a penalty within the limits of what's allowed by law. If it happens a second time, charge the penalty again and charge a late charge if this causes the rent payment to be received late, as it probably will. After the second time tell the tenant that you will only accept certified funds from now on. If that's an inconvenience, that's too bad. The tenant didn't worry about inconveniencing you with insufficient funds. There's an old saying, "Fool me once, shame on you. Fool me twice, shame on me." This isn't about personal one upsmanship. This is about running a business efficiently and maintaining control.

There is something about establishing policies and procedures that helps people set priorities. It's like conditioning. We all need a place to live. Your tenants have a place to live in your apartment building. We establish our place to live by paying for it. If we think we can have the place to live without paying for it, we'll do that. It's human nature. If we think there's a chance for a free lunch, that we can live someplace by paying for it only when there is a surplus of money, or when we feel like it, that's what we'll do. If we become conditioned to know that if we do "A" then "B" happens, we develop a different understanding and different priorities.

If tenants understand that if they don't pay the rent on time, they have to pay even more money to continue to live there, that's not something they want to do. Better to pay on time and save the extra money. If they understand that failing to pay the rent at all for a given month means eviction, making life extremely difficult for a while, they will avoid that event by paying the rent. Again, it's a matter of priorities. Of the money that's available to the tenant, how shall he or she spend it? Well, since everyone needs a place to live, and since they won't have a place to live if they don't pay the rent, better pay the rent first and juggle the other items the best they can. It's conditioning, understanding and priorities.

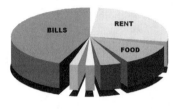

Of course, there are times when a tenant falls upon hard times, when due to illness or a job layoff there legitimately is no income to prioritize and pay the rent. These are unfortunate circumstances and all of us have been there. While we may feel sympathy for such an individual on a personal level, this is not personal. The individual no longer qualifies to live in the building because of a lack of ability to pay. This is a business decision, and policies and procedures must be followed. Detach from personal concerns and carry on with business.

One philosophical note on the personal side of things. If the persons you evict in these circumstances are negligent and not trying to help themselves, you won't change them. They will be the same way down the road and on into the future. You cannot afford to have them living in your building. If they are well-intentioned and trying to help themselves, they will not be harmed by vacating your premises. They may even agree to do so willingly. They will find a place to live with relatives or in a shelter and they will come through the hard times and be better in some ways for it. They will get on their feet again. But you will not be helping them by letting them stay for free, and they cannot help you in your business because they can't pay the rent. So a parting of the ways must take place. Wish them well and make it as amicable as possible.

When rent is received, the money must be handled properly. This means safely, efficiently and lawfully. Handling other people's money must be done with the utmost care and integrity. Check the requirements with the Department of Real Estate of your particular state. A good policy is to see that rental payments are deposited in the broker's trust account, a neutral escrow, or with the principal within one business day of receipt. Deposit records should be logged into a bookkeeping system or entered into the computer and tracked impeccably. A large apartment complex can handle hundreds of thousands of dollars per month and there should be no room for error.

In large apartment complexes, reports like monthly income and expenses should be prepared by one employee one month and verified by another. The next month different employees should perform the duties or at least the two should switch roles. This way all employees remain above suspicion and the most efficient procedure is attained.

## Maintenance

Facilities will be in need of repair continuously. How is this to be accomplished most efficiently? What is most cost effective and what is most expedient? Your particular property will have to be analyzed for its needs and standard operating procedures worked out.

First, if the apartment complex is large, there probably needs to be a chain of command to authorize repairs over a certain amount. The OSM will be the first to discover the need and a Property Manager, Cluster Manager or Supervisor will approve the expense. In a smaller development, the OSM probably will be authorized to make repairs and expenditures of items up to a certain amount, but would need authorization from ownership to spend more. Forms and paperwork should be designed to facilitate the process but should be kept as simple as possible. Remember that the forms are designed to serve us. When we become slaves to the forms and they slow us down, it's time to revise our system.

One of the desirable characteristics of the OSM is that he or she be handy. In a small development the OSM should be able to handle most routine repairs and maintenance. In a large complex, it will not be possible for the OSM to be quite so hands-on. Services may be contracted out or a full-time handyman may be hired for routine repairs and maintenance. The OSM must analyze the relative cost effectiveness of each method. In the large complex, some services may be so regular it is more cost effective to provide a full-time employee to render those services. Then supplies can be purchased wholesale and money can be saved. An example would be glass. In a very large complex, with hundreds of sliding glass doors and thousands of windows, it would cost a fortune to deal with a professional glass or window company. A skilled employee could be hired and a small workshop area maintained with the necessary tools and supplies.

The OSM and management might find that other services are more cost effective when subcontracted to professionals. Carpet might be such an area. When it comes to cleaning, carpet professionals have equipment that costs thousands of dollars. A skilled carpet cleaner can prolong the life of carpet and save the owner money. When we have found a skilled carpet person that we trust and can work with, we are probably better off to utilize their services than to try to duplicate the operation.

When we do maintenance and repairs on an apartment complex, how well shall we do it? How carefully shall we clean? How shall we decorate? We have said that we want our apartment complex to be inviting, to have a certain appeal. While this is true, we cannot afford to be lavish in our preparation. When we install a garbage disposal we are not going to choose the most expensive, industrial strength fishbone grinder on the market. But neither do we want the cheapest that is going to break down if the slightest resistance beyond water churns into its depths. We want to achieve a balance somewhere in the middle, an acceptable level of mediocrity.

Consider the McDonald's hamburger. I don't know what you think of it, but most would say it is not the greatest hamburger in the world—not a real gourmet feast for the hamburger aficionado. But it's not the worst either and families line up for them all over the world. They sell billions and billions of them. They generate quite a stream of income with their acceptable level of mediocrity. That's the way rental apartments should be. Safe, clean, acceptable. Expenses will be in line and the flow of income will be steady.

When it comes to cleaning, most management hires this service to be done. The job should be thorough, disinfecting and deodorizing, but probably will stop short of scrubbing the grout with a toothbrush. Because whoever hires the cleaning or does the work is not going to live there, they will leave such minutia to the fastidious tenant. That again, is ok. It is in keeping with cost effectiveness and an acceptable level.

Decorating should be done in a neutral fashion. Carpet should be beige or light brown in a medium grade and paint should be a nice off-white. It's less expensive than berber carpeting and custom three-color paint, but the main reason is any tenant's furnishings can be accommodated in such a decor. While one in 100 tenants might like chartreuse carpeting, the other 99 will go with the beige without resistance.

Sources of materials and supplies should be updated constantly. The OSM, as the eyes and ears of ownership, should always be on the lookout for a way to economize. Materials, supplies and services should be purchased for as close to wholesale cost as possible. Volume discounts can be obtained by managers of apartments in the hope of long-term continuous business. Relationships should be nurtured and loyalty should be the reward as merchants and suppliers work hard to accommodate our needs.

**"Just say no!"**

The OSM must resist, however, the temptation to accept incentives from a retailer to accept his or her goods. Suppose, for example, that a supplier of carpet has offered any buyer of 1,500 yards or more a free color television set. The OSM, enticed by this offer, decides that this is the carpeting that should be in the units. Six months later, when the carpeting is worn out and in need of replacement, the OSM has to try to explain to the owner how the incentive of the free color TV set that he's now watching had nothing to do with his decision to purchase that particular carpeting. If an incentive comes with a purchase, it belongs to the owner, whether the owner knows about it or not. This avoids any conflict of interest.

It is said that good management doesn't cost; it pays. This is proven over and over again in the area of controlling expenses and marketing. If the OSM can be cost effective in the area of maintenance and repairs and effective in marketing, it more than pays for the position.

## Safety and Security Issues

In matters of security as in health, prevention is the best cure. An apartment complex that is not secure will deteriorate rapidly, causing loss of income and value for the owner. A high level of security is attained by proper attention to the facility and the people.

Outside lighting should be functional. A darkened parking lot provides cover for criminals and anxiety for tenants. Some of the easiest burglaries a criminal commits are on automobiles, not apartments. Keep all outdoor areas well-lighted to cut down on the opportunity for criminal activity. Entryway and hallway lighting should also be functional in a building.

Start a campaign in the complex for residents to engrave all valuables with name, phone number and other identification. Engraved items are not nearly as easy for a burglar to sell, hence burglars often pass them by. The local police department can offer information about how to accomplish this for an entire apartment complex.

Be sure that all buildings and units are equipped with functional smoke alarms and fire extinguishers. Sometimes fire extinguishers can be mounted in hallways of buildings with interior entrances. Some owners and managers have chosen to mount smaller individual fire extinguishers on the walls of kitchens, the most likely location for the start of a fire.

If the configuration of the apartments does not allow the residents to see who is knocking at the door, a peephole can give the added assurance of knowing who's there before opening to a stranger. These items are inexpensive but can be just one more factor contributing to the sense of safety all residents want to have.

Neighborhood Watch is an activity that can make residents active participants in the safety of their community. Knowledge is power, and knowing what is taking place in a community in the way of criminal activity, what is being done to thwart criminal activity, and how each individual can contribute is a very helpful process. It makes the complex safer and draws the residents into a tightknit community.

Regarding security issues and people, let's consider three categories of people—tenants, guests of tenants and employees. You have the opportunity to check thoroughly the tenants' background before accepting them. Credit worthiness can tell you a lot about an individual's character and circumstances. A criminal background check is available to you; however, you cannot discriminate with criminal background checks. If you do not routinely obtain criminal background checks, you cannot selectively order them. You may invite a lawsuit for discrimination.

Guests of tenants visit at the pleasure of the tenants. They are responsible for obeying the rules and being courteous to other tenants just as a tenant is. Unsavory guests that create disturbances and arouse suspicion must be asked to leave. If the tenant persists in entertaining such guests and trouble continues, ask the tenant to leave. Illegal activities, disturbing the peace and violating the rules of the premises are certainly grounds for eviction.

The final category of people under discussion is employees. This category may be the last we would suspect of undermining security, but think of the opportunity. A maintenance worker or  other employee with access to all of the keys to a large complex could burglarize many units before getting caught, or commit crimes against a person. An OSM, office manager, property manager or bookkeeper would have access to an extraordinary flow of income. People with an intent to steal, harm or defraud may seek out such an advantageous position. Applicants for any role in property management should be checked out thoroughly with credit checks, reference checks and criminal history checks. We owe this to ownership and to the residents of a complex.

# INSURANCE

Part of the operation of an apartment complex is to make sure there is adequate insurance coverage. Insurance is available in many forms.

## Fire

Fire insurance is the most basic coverage. Every owner will want adequate fire insurance and every lender will demand it.

## Extended

Extended coverage policies can cover items such as water damage, explosions, storms, civil strife, smoke damage, malicious mischief and vandalism.

## Liability

Liability insurance can be written to cover numerous items and situations. If someone is injured on the property, liability insurance may save the owner from having to sell to pay a judgment. Liability insurance may also cover the property management company in the event of injury or illness to one of the company's employees. It is kind of an extended coverage beyond worker's compensation coverage. Another type of liability policy may cover owners guilty of certain types of pollution, though this type would most often apply to commercial and industrial properties.

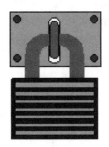

To avoid liability and prevent injuries, certain precautions should be taken. Keep the facilities in good repair. Never allow a loose step on a staircase. Fix any loose handrails immediately. Remove the diving board from the pool and always keep the gate to the pool locked. Don't allow pets that could attack anyone. Eliminate attractive nuisances as a danger to children. These could include deep holes in the ground, large mounds of dirt, construction underway or piles of lumber. If they can't be eliminated, secure them so no one can gain access. Post signs warning of any potential danger and clear any trash and debris from all walkways. Don't allow any slippery spots to remain on walkways, stairways and driveways.

## Loss of Rents

Loss of rent or occupancy insurance is available to cover these types of situations after an insured loss. If expenses and debts are high and the cash flow is tight, such insurance might be advisable.

## Renter's Insurance

The above types of insurance cover owners and management. Renter's insurance is for the tenant and covers items for which owners and managers are not responsible. One wise owner sent the following letter to his tenants to better inform them of the items for which they would need their own insurance coverage.

**Figure 9-4   Insurance Facts For Renters**

Dear Resident,

Apartment living has many advantages. Unfortunately it also carries some of the same risks faced by homeowners.

Read this list of possible costly misfortunes and see if you can pick out those which would probably be your legal responsibility as an apartment dweller.

(1)   Your babysitter is injured in your apartment.

(2)   You have a defective electrical extension cord. It starts a fire which causes considerable damage to the building and all of your personal possessions.

(3)   A friend helps you slide out your refrigerator so you can clean behind it, and suffers a back injury.

(4)   Your locked car is broken into at the supermarket and a camera is stolen.

(5)   You find a handyman from a classified ad and call him to fix your refrigerator. He slips on the wet kitchen floor and breaks his arm.

(6)   A burglar breaks your front door lock, or enters through a window, and steals your valuables.

(7)   Your five-year-old leaves a bicycle or toy at the foot of the stairs. Your next door neighbor falls over the bicycle and is severely injured.

Which items in the list do you think would be your expense? The answer, under the law, is probably all of them. Although most of the losses would not have been deliberately or even negligently caused by you, normally you would have to bear the cost just as you would if you were a homeowner.

Except under limited circumstances, the apartment owner is in most cases not legally responsible for loss to the tenant's property, and the owner's insurance does not cover these losses. However, Renter's Insurance can be purchased from any general insurance agent to cover fire, theft, liability and certain other perils. The cost is in the range of $10 to $15 per month. This is a low price for peace of mind and for the financial recovery if you have a loss.

Please note that this letter is not an attempt by the apartment owner to shift responsibility —that is already established by the legislature and the courts. However, we have found that some residents are unaware of the normal, everyday risks they live with, and believe that the owner pays for whatever happens. The purpose of this letter is to help inform you, so that you may better protect yourself if you wish.

# COMPUTERS

The state-of-the-art professional property management company today will be on the cutting edge of computer use. The complexities of law and accounting demand near flawless tracking of cash flow and documents responding to various circumstances. Computers assemble information more quickly and more accurately. They display the information in readable reports that meet the needs of both owners and the government for tax and legal purposes. Local apartment associations should be consulted to see what software programs are available.

The California Association of Realtors reports that a sophisticated property management software program will be capable of producing the following types of reports.

*(1) A list of delinquent rents and credit balances.* This report allows the manager to determine which units (or tenants) still owe rent or have overpaid on a daily basis. Late charges can be assessed and tenant statements can be sent out much faster than with a manual system.

*(2) Income register by individual property and total of all properties.* The income register shows all income received, including rents, laundry commissions and late charges. The report should also include tenant name, date of transaction, property and unit number or address.

*(3) Expense register by individual property and total of all properties.* The expense register details all expenses incurred and indicates property and unit, date of transaction, check number, amount of disbursement and account number or description from the chart of accounts.

*(4) Total transaction register by individual property and total of all properties.* This report lists all income and expenses in date order.

*(5) Income statement by individual properties.* The income statement includes a beginning cash balance, a list of income and expenses by category (from the chart of accounts) and an ending balance. Month-to-date and year-to-date columns are also very beneficial.

*(6) **Lists of properties by lease expiration date.*** This report is very useful in keeping track of lease expirations in order to renegotiate leases. The report may also include the date of the last rent increase, which is helpful when determining which rents are due to be increased.

*(7) **List of properties, including units and tenants, monthly rent and deposit held.*** Used as a master list, this can be referred to, updated and reprinted as needed.

*(8) **Tenant past-due rent statements.*** After late charges or other tenant charges have been posted, this option allows individual tenant statements to be printed, which can be mailed to notify tenants of past-due rent.

*(9) **List of cash balances by property and total cash balance.*** This report is quite beneficial and should be printed daily after entering transactions to determine the positive cash balance in each account. The report also provides a total to compare to the balance in a trust account.

*(10) **A chart of accounts.*** This list provides a description of each account number. The program should allow you the freedom to design your own chart of accounts, designating items as capital improvements, rent income, other income, security deposit, "owner deposit," expense and an "undefined" category.

*(11) **A list of management commissions by month and year-to-date.*** This report is helpful in keeping track of management fees paid and not paid.

*(12) **A vacancy list.*** This report indicates which units are vacant at the current date. All reports should include the current date, property address or property number.

# FILES AND RECORD KEEPING

In addition to the many files and reports generated by a sophisticated software program, it is still necessary to maintain certain hard copy files. Tenant files should be kept showing correspondence, notices, repairs and various forms of communication that have taken place. Vendor files are necessary to maintain receipts, guarantees and correspondence. Owner files should be kept with management contracts, correspondence, financial statements and reports, receipts, insurance and tax information. Employee files would maintain a record of hours worked, wages paid and other issues pertaining to employment. General correspondence files and check registers should also be maintained.

Many details must be attended to in the operation of an apartment building. The better these details can be organized into *standard operating procedures*, the less wasted time and effort. Knowing what to expect allows planning. Planning allows us to establish systems and procedures, and that creates efficiency. And that's what it's all about, isn't it?

# QUESTIONS

1. Garden apartments are:

    a. single-story apartments in agricultural areas

    b. three-story walk-up buildings with garden windows in the kitchen

    c. two-story buildings surrounding a courtyard

    d. none of the above

2. Factors that will determine the workload of the on-site manager are:

    a. the configuration and design of the buildings

    b. the number of amenities

    c. potential dangers to tenants

    d. all of the above

3. Standard operating procedures should be established:

    a. to improve the efficiency of operations

    b. for first-time nuisances

    c. because the more forms and systems, the better the operation

    d. uniformly for all apartment buildings regardless of size

4. Standard operating procedures should be established for:

    a. showing and renting an apartment

    b. handling a vacancy

    c. evictions

    d. all of the above

5. Duties of an on-site manager should be presented in *standard operating procedure* format:

    a. to keep the on-site manager busy

    b. to clarify exactly what is expected of the position

    c. to regulate the on-site manager's schedule

    d. to show tenants that he or she is "on the job"

6. The reason qualifications for an on-site manager should be established in advance is:

    a. they can be applied objectively to any hiring situation

    b. to be able to hire in advance of the need

    c. they provide evidence of organization

    d. qualifications for an on-site manager never change

7. All of the following qualities would be considered desirable for on-site managers except:

    a. self-assurance

    b. used to dealing with people

    c. dubious

    d. patient

8. "Unflappable" most nearly means:

    a. the person can take almost anything in stride while maintaining control

    b. a person who is unable to get excited about anything

    c. a person whose financial affairs are in order

    d. no wings

9. The reason on-site managers should have a good credit rating is:

    a. so they will be likely to pay the rent on time

    b. so they won't fall behind on their bills

    c. so they won't develop empathy with those who cannot pay the rent

    d. so they'll be likely to stay longer

10. Experience is desirable in an on-site manager for which of the following reasons:

    a. a wide variety of things can happen in an apartment complex

    b. being an effective on-site manager requires maturity

    c. being an on-site manager carries a lot of responsibility

    d. all of the above

11. A qualified on-site manager would be expected to fix all of the following except:

    a. an interior door with a hole in it

    b. a central air-conditioning unit

    c. a leaky faucet

    d. a clogged sink or tub

12. Collecting the rent should be handled:

    a. on a strict time line

    b. on a flexible time line allowing for tenants' problems

    c. with understanding on a case by case basis

    d. knowing that all of the tenants won't be able to pay on time, but collecting as much as you can

13. When rent is collected it can be placed in all of the following places except:

    a. a neutral escrow

    b. the broker's trust account

    c. the company safe

    d. the principal's hands

14. In the area of apartment maintenance:

    a. employees should be hired to do all of the work

    b. the work should always be sub-contracted to professionals

    c. the most cost effective procedure should be followed

    d. it should be put off as long as possible

15. Decorating and preparing a unit for rental should be done:

    a. in the cheapest way possible

    b. in a neutral decor to allow most tenants' furnishings to fit in

    c. according to the taste of the on-site manager

    d. according to the taste of the property supervisor

16. For cost effectiveness, the quality of a rental unit should be similar to:

    a. a compact and efficient condominium unit

    b. a McDonald's hamburger for its acceptable level of mediocrity

    c. a luxury car for its spacious interior

    d. a rental office for its efficiency

17. An on-site manager must not personally accept an incentive in buying items for an apartment building because:

    a. it would place the on-site manager in a conflict of interest

    b. the incentive might not be what he or she needs

    c. the incentive might not be top quality

    d. the on-site manager should select the lowest priced items only

18. People who can compromise the security of an apartment building are:

    a. tenants

    b. guests

    c. employees of the property management company

    d. all of the above

19. All apartment owners should purchase insurance on the following basis:

    a. buy all they can afford
    b. buy "loss of rent" insurance always
    c. buy based on likely need
    d. buy renter's insurance for all tenants

20. Sophisticated software programs and computers:

    a. eliminate the need for hard copy files
    b. make property management operations more efficient
    c. require more employee time
    d. deal with everything except management commissions

# ANSWERS

1. *c*
2. *d*
3. *a*
4. *d*
5 *b*
6. *a*
7. *c*
8. *a*
9. *c*
10. *d*
11. *b*
12. *a*
13. *c*
14. *c*
15. *b*
16. *b*
17. *a*
18. *d*
19. *c*
20. *b*

# Day-To-Day Operations

- **Sunnyvale Manor: A Case History**

C  H  A  P  T  E  R  **10**

# SUNNYVALE MANOR: A CASE HISTORY

Sunnyvale Manor is a 610 unit apartment complex located in the suburbs of Los Angeles. It covers a little over six acres of land. The style is a series of two-story garden apartments comprised of 61 buildings approximately 40 years old. Most of the buildings face a similar building, the two forming bookends and enclosing a courtyard. There is a laundry room for each pair of buildings and no pools in the complex. Managers and maintenance people have to travel the complex on golf carts because the community spans several city blocks. It has been owned by a partnership for approximately 20 years.

## Management at Sunnyvale Manor

Sunnyvale Manor is managed by the Humphrey Management Company, a large property management firm specializing in residential apartment units. Margaret Jones is one of the on-site managers of the complex that utilizes more than 20 full-time employees. Margaret is a mature woman in her 40s who lives in one of the units in the complex. She has prepared herself well for her current position, taking courses in property management from the local community college, taking the required courses to earn the Certified Apartment Manager (CAM) designation from the National Apartment Association (NAA), and attending Fair Housing meetings and legal workshops pertaining to property management. She is also in the process of getting her real estate license. Her preparation and maturity have earned her a "no nonsense" reputation and she is often assigned the more unpleasant duties for on-site managers, including handling tenant complaints and collecting the rent.

As Margaret reports to work at her office Tuesday morning the phone is already ringing and there are messages left with the answering service from the night before. Several prospects have called to inquire if there are any one-bedroom and two-bedroom units available. Two callers have left messages looking for a three-bedroom unit. Sunnyvale Manor doesn't have many more three-bedroom units. Some were divided and converted to a studio and a two-bedroom unit. Though the three-bedroom units are spacious and highly desirable, the conversion results in an additional $300 per unit over the three-bedroom rental price.

One message is from a prospective tenant who has already been approved for a two-bedroom unit. He needs to move in immediately but the unit has been slow to be made ready. Except for the few three-bedroom units, the turnover rate of two-bedroom units is the lowest because many families with children rent in the area. This prospective tenant has excellent credit and a good job, and Margaret doesn't want to lose him. Unable to raise the maintenance supervisor on the phone or the walkie talkie, Margaret decides to go and check on the unit herself.

She takes her golf cart out the back way past the carports and onto the alley between two rows of buildings. She notices a car in one of the resident's reserved spaces with the tires removed sitting with its rims on blocks. She makes a note of the parking space and will tag the car later, notifying the owner to move the car or make it operable, because the lease states that all inoperable cars will be removed from the premises. If the tenant does not respond within three days, Margaret will have the car removed on one of those new flatbed tow trucks.

## Maintenance-Ready

Margaret makes a right-hand turn down at the end of the alleyway, crosses a main street and makes a left-hand turn in the next alleyway. She is still on the property of Sunnyvale Manor and soon approaches the apartment's maintenance shop. Eleven full time  workers are employed at the shop. They handle their own carpentry, flooring, linoleum, screens, glass, and keys and lock work. They don't do their own air conditioner work and Margaret thinks they should add that trade to their repertoire. Two employees are used full time for maintenance of occupied units, two for painting, and two as porters to carry out trash and debris from vacated units.

For Sunnyvale Manor to have its own key shop is a wise decision indeed. Let's see, 610 units, times four keys for the door locks, plus a mailbox key for each unit. Well, you do the math. Not to mention the locks—610 door knob locks, 610 deadbolt locks, and laundry room locks all keyed so that the keys from one building will open the appropriate laundry room, plus master keys for management to be able enter any units in a given courtyard with just one key. Factor in the turnover rate and the charges per visit for a locksmith to change the pins and rekey the locks, and you get the idea. For cost effectiveness, it's one of those things you've just got to learn to do.

Margaret learned a long time ago the importance of having her keys properly labeled and her key ring with her anytime she made her rounds. A manager in a neighboring complex was making his rounds and did not use a master key system. He had a large key ring with him the size of one in the old western movies and the keys were unmarked. He noticed smoke coming from the window of one of the units. He fumbled with the keys for many minutes before the fire department arrived. Since he was unable to open the unit with a key, a fireman opened it with an  ax. Master keys easily labeled cost a few dollars. Fire damage and lost rental income cost thousands. It's really a no-brainer.

Margaret also insists on keeping the master keys, both her own personal set and the office's well hidden and under tight security. It would be a near disaster to have a burglar steal the master keys. All locks would have to be rekeyed and new keys issued to all tenants post haste. Such a situation must be avoided and prevented.

Hector, the maintenance supervisor, is not at the shop, and she is told that he is at number 268, the two bedroom she is checking on. She hurries down to that unit.

As Margaret pulls up to number 268 she is pleased to see her favorite carpet cleaning team working on the unit. Greg and Steve always do an excellent job and have surprised Margaret more than once by saving carpet that she thought would have to be replaced. Not only do they work miracles with stained, matted and smelly carpeting. Their prices are reasonable, too. Margaret uses them for all the carpet cleaning jobs in the complex.

Hector points out to Margaret that the interior of the unit has been painted, a window pane has been replaced, all appliances have been checked, the door has been rekeyed, heating and air conditioning are working and this afternoon the cleaning crew will come to put on the finishing touches. There's no reason a tenant cannot move in tomorrow. Margaret is delighted to hear this and hurries back to the office.

## Dealing with Tenants

Before she can call the new tenant about the two-bedroom unit, several tenants are waiting to see her. One wants to rent a video and she is accommodated first. Each month the office receives approximately 250 videos for a fee of about $250. The office can rent the videos to tenants and easily make a profit by charging one dollar for one day or night. The tenants appreciate the convenience and the good will, and the extra income is easily accomplished in the office.

A second tenant reports that he has lost three quarters in the coin-op laundry of his building. Margaret writes down the building number and makes a note to call maintenance to check out the problem. She refunds the three quarters immediately and thanks  the tenant for coming in. The third tenant has a complaint against a neighbor. Margaret asks if she is willing to put the complaint in writing and sign it. Margaret explains that she will not reveal to the tenant who filed the complaint, but that she doesn't do anything about a complaint unless the one complaining is willing to put it in writing. The tenant agrees to do that and Margaret gives her the proper form. While the tenant is filling out the complaint form, Margaret takes time to call the tenant for unit number 268. He is delighted and will come in tomorrow morning to sign the lease, make the first month's payment plus security deposit, make the move-in inspection with Margaret and pick up the keys.

## Collecting the Rent

The tenant continues to write her complaint when another tenant comes in. This tenant has lived in the complex with her husband and small child for just slightly over one month. Their rent is now four days overdue and Margaret has left a message on their phone answering machine. The wife has come in to say that her husband handles the paying of bills and she doesn't understand why he hasn't been able to pay. She asks Margaret to call her husband at his job.

Margaret calls him and is very firm. The husband says he has some back taxes to pay and that is the reason he's late. He wonders if he can make some arrangements for paying the rent. Margaret responds like this. "You don't have any track record with us. You haven't been here long enough. You haven't even been here 90 days and you're wanting to make special arrangements to pay the rent. Here's what you can do. You pay me $500 by the 20th of the month and the balance of the rent by the end of the month along with the full amount on the first for next month." The husband says, "So you'll give me a chance to work it out?" Margaret responds, "You've got your first and last chance right now, but you'll have to come in after work and sign a payment agreement."

Margaret is extremely effective at collecting the rent. Sunnyvale Manor's scheduled gross income is approximately $340,000 per month and most of the time collection losses are less than $3,000. That's less than one percent! She's had grown men sit at her desk and cry. She hands them a tissue and hammers out the problem. She's been cussed at and screamed at over her persistence in collecting the rent but she never takes it personally. Sunnyvale Manor is an integrated apartment complex. Margaret happens to be a Black woman, but she's been accused of discrimination by Blacks, Hispanics, Asians, Indians and Whites. She must be doing something right. She treats all people equally and she just keeps collecting the rent.

One time a man was quite upset with Margaret because she agreed to return his security deposit but wouldn't return his rent money which was rightfully due. He threatened to blow up the building. She called the management company and they called the man's employer. After some influence was brought to bear, the man realized he was fortunate not to have been arrested and came back and apologized to Margaret. There's not much she hasn't seen, and her knowledge and maturity continue to serve her well.

## More Tenant Issues

The tenant has finished filling out the complaint form, hands it to Margaret and makes a hasty retreat out of the office. Margaret reads the form.

---

Complaint Form

Date: _12/6_      Against Unit: _#748_

Nature of complaint: _Everytime those people go to bed and they have sex, they make a racket. She's screaming and there's all this huffing and puffing and the bed's crashing up against the wall. They never close their windows. It keeps us awake for hours._

---

Margaret prepares a three-day covenant notice. If the tenants in 748 don't comply, it could lead to eviction. People don't have the right to disturb the peace of others, no matter what they're doing. She'll serve the notice later in the day.

Margaret calls the tenant in unit 549. This tenant had requested that her parents be added to the lease and be allowed to move in with her and her son. Margaret has checked out the parents and has found that they are in the process of eviction. She calls and informs her tenant in 549 that her parents will not be allowed to move in with her. The tenant is not pleased and demands to know the reason. Margaret explains that her parents are in the process of eviction and if they were to apply to rent an apartment here on their own, they would be turned down. The tenant argues that that's not fair and that her parents should be allowed to live with her. Margaret stands firm on the position that no tenants will be accepted for residency in this complex who show an eviction on their record, even if they would be living with a roommate.

The subject of roommates has caused management no small amount of grief in the past few months. Margaret has followed the policy that if there are to be two or three roommates in an apartment, the income of each one has to be sufficient to qualify for occupancy on one's own. Many can't understand that and think it's unfair, but the reason is that roommates can move out and leave the others high and dry, so each roommate must be able to pay the full amount of the rent.

Another problem arises when roommates give the rent to the designated rent payer and the rent payer does something else with the money. Or when the various roommates *claim* that they gave their share of the rent money to the designated rent payer but really didn't. No matter what their stories, if the full amount of rent doesn't come in, all of them will be evicted.

A deaf woman lived in the apartments with her teenage son. He regularly played his music too loud but his mother had no way of knowing. After numerous complaints by neighbors the mother was finally informed. She was quite embarrassed and tired of living with her son. She asked Margaret if she would evict just the son! Margaret explained if there were to be an eviction, both of them would have to go.

## Memories

Margaret hops on her golf cart and leaves the phones to Peggy, the office manager. She's going to post that covenant notice on 748 and stop by the maintenance shop to talk to Hector about the availability of more one-bedroom units. As she scoots through a back parking lot, she passes the spot where a year earlier one of their porters had been severely beaten by several tenants. He had honked at them to get them to move so he could park in his parking space. They took exception and actually fractured the man's skull. He spent some time in the hospital and never did come back to work.

Police reports were filed but for some reason no charges ever materialized. Margaret went ahead with eviction proceedings against those accused and they complained to the Department of Fair Employment and Housing. They asserted that they were being discriminated against because of their race. A representative of the Department visited the apartment complex and basically took the tenants' side. When other instances were cited of their bullying and taunting other tenants, the representative asked, "How do you know they were talking to *them*?" Margaret learned that though the intent of Fair Housing Laws is good, these laws are not always used as intended. The undesirables finally moved out on their own to make trouble elsewhere.

Margaret rolls past a storage unit in the alley that had been the last resting place of a transient a couple of months earlier. The odor caused nearby residents to contact her, and she called the police. The man had been seen in the area before, but to her knowledge, no identification had been made.

## Management Supervision

Margaret mulls over in her mind some of the concerns she has about the apartment complex. The person they call the Business Manager, what we have termed Property Manager, is a young woman with a real estate license but not much training or experience in property management. She oversees the entire complex, but based on her lack of experience, hasn't made good decisions. A month ago she put the courtesy patrol, a security service, in charge of parking. This led to her having three residents' cars towed away, one for an expired registration, one for being dirty, and one for having oxidized paint. It cost one man a day's pay and all were extremely angry. Margaret knows that all of the tenants could have sued because the only grounds for having a car towed away according to the lease is that it's inoperable and the tenant doesn't respond to a 72-hour notice to remove it.

This Business Manager took away another tenant's parking space because his engine was too loud. She made him park on the street, which resulted in his T-top being stolen from his convertible car. Again, the apartment complex could be held liable for such actions. With Margaret's training and education, she always asks herself the following questions before taking any action. "What are my grounds for doing this? Can I be sued for this action?" This type of thinking has resulted in more responsible decisions. Everyone may not like her all of the time, and there are few who don't respect her, but her decisions are usually vindicated in the long term.

## Dangerous Practice

Margaret passes a courtyard where a maintenance worker is giving a ride to two children on the back of a golf cart. She stops and approaches the golf cart and tells the children they must get off the golf cart now so they won't get hurt. She addresses them in a very sweet tone of voice, appropriate for communication with children. Margaret is a caring and conscientious person and makes transitions from dealing with adults to children very naturally. As the children run to play, her attention turns to the maintenance worker. She is much more firm in warning him of the dangers posed to the children and the exposure of liability to the apartment complex, should one of them fall off and get hurt. Responsibility for stopping this reckless behavior lies with the Business Manager, but although she's been told about it, she hasn't taken any action. Margaret makes an effort to have an influence in the right direction even if she's not backed up by her superiors.

## Maintaining the Landscaping

 While in the courtyard, Margaret notices that the numerous children playing have nearly destroyed the foliage. They play tag, and hide and seek, and chase after balls. They're not doing anything wrong, they're just doing what comes naturally to children. They expend a lot of energy. But it takes its toll on the landscaping. Margaret will announce later in the week, by circulating fliers

throughout the entire complex, a program that she has just had accepted by upper levels of management. It is a courtyard beautification project, designed to involve the children and have them take an interest in their courtyard. The program will provide flower seeds, small potted plants, fertilizer, gardening tools and instruction on how to plant and care for flowers and other foliage. Each

 month the complex will be divided into quarters and there will be a contest within each quarter to judge which courtyard is the most beautiful. The winning courtyard will receive a free barbecue, compliments of management with hot dogs, hamburgers, buns and all the trimmings.

Margaret is no fool. She knows that she could get tough with these kids and demand that they be careful of the plants. She could spend thousands of dollars restoring the landscaping. But she also knows that the only result would be bad feelings from the parents, resistance from the kids and the spending of more thousands of dollars to restore the landscaping again and again. She also might lose some tenants. This way it costs less, everybody's motivated to solve the problem, and everybody's pulling together. *There's a saying that good management doesn't cost, it pays.* Sometimes ownership doesn't realize this because good management pays by helping ownership avoid costs and expenses that would otherwise occur. By handling this problem poorly, the appearance of the complex deteriorates. To correct it costs a lot of money that probably will have to be spent on a recurring basis. To allow deterioration in the appearance of the complex is to attract the wrong kind of tenant, gradually see the net operating income go down, and consequently the value. This is one on-site manager who could be worth her weight in gold!

## Readying Vacant Units

Margaret arrives at unit 748 and posts her three-day covenant notice. She swings back around to the maintenance shop to speak to Hector about the progress in making ready some 18 one-bedroom units that have been vacant for more than 30 days. Hector explains that all of those units have been inspected by him and that they are in various states of repair. Only two of them have been ready for occupancy and two more are ready as of today. Several more would be ready except they need an inspection by a refrigeration company and the air conditioning units need to be fixed. Because of the hot weather, all of the refrigeration companies in the area have been booked and are slow to respond.

For these units to be vacant when tenants are standing in line for them is a foolish waste of money. Margaret has felt for a long time that the maintenance shop should expand to include its own refrigeration services. The effect of having to wait for servicing on the air conditioning units has been a lack of urgency when it comes  to other repair items. Since some of the units can't be rented until the refrigeration company comes out, the full-time employees who work for the apartment complex reason that there's no hurry in performing the other repairs. Since the maintenance shop is run by the management company, Margaret will talk to upper management about the possibility of adding this service.

## Scheduling

Margaret arrives back at the office and finds things quiet for the moment. She has about an hour before she will steal away for a few minutes to take a well-deserved lunch. She usually lunches in her own apartment to save time. After lunch she'll submit some credit applications and call on some references for those who have made application to live in the apartment complex. Then at 3:00 p.m. she has an appointment to show an apartment to a young couple. At 5:00 p.m. she has a move-in inspection with a tenant in one of the one-bedroom units.

## Community Involvement

Now, however, while the office is quiet, she takes a few moments to make some notes on the talk she is scheduled to give tonight at a local sheriff's substation as part of what's called the Nuisance Abatement Program. The meeting will be attended by local deputy sheriffs, property managers, owners and other interested parties. Margaret is the local organizer of the Neighborhood Watch program in the complex and has been very effective at getting the community and the sheriff's department involved in fighting crime in the area. Before Margaret arrived on the scene two years ago, crime was a serious problem at Sunnyvale Manor. People were afraid to go outside, but Margaret did not hesitate to call the sheriff's station whenever something was wrong.

Margaret has encouraged others to calls the sheriff's station as well. "If you don't want to call the sheriff," Margaret tells them, "then call me and *I'll* call the sheriff." Margaret believes that if people don't ask for help, they won't get any help. Now all of the local sheriff deputies know Margaret and they know she doesn't cry wolf. When Margaret calls, they come running. The result is that incidents of crime have been cut by more than half.

Now Margaret has not only the respect of those interested in community affairs and neighborhood safety, she has their ear. When Margaret has something to say, people figure it's worth listening to. Margaret pulls no punches. What she wants to tell people tonight is that they can make a difference. Even one person not afraid to speak out can make a difference. Everyone but criminals wants to reduce criminal activity. Good neighbors, residents, management and law enforcement are all happy when a criminal is removed from the community. So why not work together and accomplish more of that? Margaret doesn't get extra pay for activities such as tonight's, but she knows the satisfaction of giving her all, helping others, and making a real difference in her community. Margaret truly is an uncommon individual.

## An Alarming Call

The phone rings and a resident of the complex reports that there may be a problem in apartment 187. The elderly gentleman who lives in that apartment is hard of hearing and is regularly heard loudly talking on the phone near his kitchen window. His voice in the courtyard has been strangely absent over the past three or four days, and several tenants have reported a foul odor coming from the apartment. Margaret knows what that could mean. She calls her friends at the sheriff's station and they meet her at her office. Together they walk to apartment 187 where a handful of curious tenants are gathered outside in the courtyard, a safe distance from the door. The coroner's office is called and the body of the elderly man is wheeled down the stairs on a gurney. No foul play is suspected but an autopsy will reveal the cause of death. Margaret thanks the deputies for responding so quickly. She wants to begin cleaning the man's apartment but must wait for a determination of the cause of death and a release from the sheriff's office.

Margaret goes to her apartment to grab a quick bite of lunch, but the foul odor of 187 lingers in her mind. The smell of death is difficult to erase. Though she doesn't usually allow any aspects of her job to affect her personally, she doesn't feel much like eating lunch. She sips from a cool glass of water and relaxes for a few moments before going back to the office.

## A Hub of Activity

As Margaret returns to the office, activity is picking up again. Another on-site manager is at his desk handling all that he can, but Margaret jumps into the middle of it to help. A tenant from one of the units calls to complain about a neighbor who is leaving a smelly cat litter box outside by her front door. Margaret tells her to come in and fill out a complaint form. In the back of her mind, she is thinking that the courtyard beautification project may help to resolve a problem like that.

## Credit Approvals

Humphrey Management Company calls to tell Margaret that two of the applications that have been submitted have checked out OK for credit and that she can go ahead and approve the applicants. She asks how far back the credit was checked and she is told, "Two years." She accepts what her superiors tell her, but she has concerns about it. Previously they checked credit for the past five years. When they did that, they seemed to get a better qualified tenant. With the credit being checked only for the past two years, an individual can overcome an eviction or bankruptcy very quickly. She would rather see a more stringent screening process, eliminating potential problems before they occur. Margaret has concerns over the applicants' appearances and the cars they drive. They don't appear reliable, but upper management is making the decision to be more lenient on qualifying and reduce the vacancy rate. That's a strategy that may increase the bottom line initially, but sometimes creates more work for Margaret in higher tenant complaints, breaches of contract and turnover rate. "Oh well," Margaret reasons. She'll do the best job she can and implement the decisions and policies of her employer, whether she agrees with all of them or not.

## Eviction

The legal firm of Chenowith and Howe calls to discuss the eviction of the tenant in apartment 536. The three-day notice/nuisance has been filed and the court hearing is next week. They want to be sure they understand all of the details. Humphrey Management Company uses this legal firm for all of its evictions because the firm wants this process done right the first time. Chenowith and Howe specializes in evictions and knows the process better than anyone else in the area. It's just not worth the time of the management company to dabble in such a highly specialized legal process and take the chance of making a mistake.

The tenant in unit 536, a Ms. Epson, had a male guest over one night and they were playing loud music. One of her neighbors asked them to turn it down and the visitor took exception to this request and pulled a gun on the neighbor. This resulted in the sheriff's department being called and the arrest of Ms. Epson's guest. Since it is not only illegal, but also against the rules of the complex to pull a gun on a tenant, and since a tenant is basically responsible for the actions of her guest, Sunnyvale Manor has asked Ms. Epson to move out. She has refused, hence the eviction process.

Margaret gives the eviction firm all of the information it requests and marks the date on her calendar next week when she may have to make a brief court appearance.

## Showing a Vacant Unit

Margaret's one o'clock appointment arrives and they take a golf cart out into the complex. The prospective tenants are a young couple recently married. Both work and their combined income well qualifies them for being able to afford the apartment. Because they're married, their income is not divided and treated like they're roommates. It's much easier for roommates to separate than marriage partners. In this area, a tenant must gross three times the amount of the monthly rent to qualify. That way, no more than one third of income is used for housing expenses. In this case, the tenants make a little over four times the monthly rental amount. Margaret feels good about their ability to pay.

On the way to one of the upper one-bedroom apartments, they pass through a nearby courtyard. The music is deafening. Margaret thinks of dueling banjos. From one side of the courtyard Mexican  music is blaring. From the other side, rap. Margaret stops the golf cart momentarily and excuses herself. She walks up the stairs to the apartment that is playing the rap music and asks them to turn it down. They comply immediately. She walks to the other side of the courtyard, up the stairs to the apartment playing the Mexican music. She gets their cooperation immediately as well. She returns to the golf cart, enjoying the momentary quiet.

As they continue on their way, the young wife asks Margaret why she had the tenants turn down their music. Margaret explains that it was too loud and that it was an annoyance. The young lady said she doesn't see why that's a problem. Margaret explains that no one has the right to disturb the peace of others and that it is her job to see to it that the rights of all the tenants are protected. The young lady says, "Well, I would expect to be able to play my music as loud as I want." Margaret says, "Well, I would be the first to come over and tell you to turn it down."

Margaret makes a U-turn at the end of the alley and heads back to the office. They pass through the courtyard where the loud music had been playing and all is quiet still. They pull into Margaret's golf cart parking space and get off. The husband smiles sheepishly and thanks Margaret for the ride. The couple strides off and Margaret shakes her head. Just when you think you've heard it all!

## Readying Vacant Units Now!

Having two new accepted applicants and more inquiries coming in for one-bedroom units, Margaret decides to go over to the maintenance shop and see for herself exactly how close some of them are to being ready for occupancy. She and Hector tour some of the units. In one, the bathroom floor shows water damage. In an effort to save money, earlier management decisions placed new tub liners over old tubs that they didn't fit just right. The seal couldn't be made to be water tight, and the result was leaks. Now they had to replace linoleum and possibly subflooring.

**TIME IS MONEY**

Margaret has learned that the best dollar spent in apartment maintenance is the one that fixes a problem right the first time and prevents further damage from arising. Margaret suggests not only fixing the floor but replacing the tub rather than trying to seal two pieces that were not made to fit. But that decision will have to be approved by the management company.

Margaret and Hector inspect another unit. This one has not been made ready because it needs an electrical inspection. The last electric bill was five times what it normally should have been. Management has to be aware of excesses like that. The tenant who moved out recently says she didn't use excessively the air conditioning, lights or electrical appliances. The unit will be checked next Friday.

Margaret tries to impress upon Hector the importance of getting vacant units ready as soon as possible. She explains that it's like a restaurant with customers waiting in the lobby and some choice booths have been vacated. The tables must be bussed immediately so someone else can occupy the space and pay for the services the establishment offers. The overhead does not diminish when there are vacancies, only the cash flow. If the maintenance supervisor can have this overview of the apartment complex, he can more effectively see his role and the importance of it in keeping the cash flowing. Many workers do not develop this responsible view, however, and must be approached with an incentive program that directly affects their income. Margaret deals with the budget and various reports that are produced to inform ownership of how the apartment complex is doing compared to its goals and its competition. Her job performance is directly related to how well the complex is doing overall, so she sees the big picture. She will continue to make every effort to increase the cash flow and minimize expenses.

## A Busy Office

Margaret goes back to the office and finds that the level of activity has not relented. All of the staff is on the phone, but other lines are still ringing. Margaret picks up one and asks the caller to hold. She picks up the second line and talks to that caller. It is another inquiry about a two-bedroom unit. She takes the caller's name and phone number and says she will call when one becomes available.

## A Wet Emergency

Margaret gets back to the line that was put on hold. The tenant on the line is frantic. She lives in apartment number 341, a downstairs one-bedroom unit, and water is beaded up on her bedroom ceiling and is dripping on her bed. Margaret tells her she'll be right there. She pushes the accelerator on her golf cart to the floor and goes no faster than she did before, but at least she feels that she's making the effort. She pulls up in front of 341 and runs up the stairs to 441 above it. She knocks on the door firmly and when there is no answer, she immediately opens the door with her master key. She glances at the kitchen but walks directly to the bathroom to see if the sink or tub is overflowing. Everything looks normal. She walks into the bedroom and there it is—a collapsed waterbed sitting in a puddle. The carpet and subflooring is, of course, soaked as well as the ceiling damage in the unit below, plus possible damage to personal property below. This is why Sunnyvale Manor requires the tenants to have insurance if they're going to have a waterbed. Insurance is good and necessary, but Margaret has been trying to get upper management to establish a policy that waterbeds can only be used in downstairs units. That would have prevented this problem.

A copy of the insurance rider for the water bed is in the tenant's file in the office. Margaret calls Hector on the walkie-talkie and asks him to send over a cleanup crew right away to unit 441. She inspects the damage in apartment 341, assures the tenant that her upstairs neighbor carries insurance to cover problems like this and that she'll call her with a phone number to the insurance company and the policy number.

## Welcoming a New Tenant

Margaret goes back to her office like the Greyhound bus driver who was trained to expect only the unexpected. It's almost five o'clock and the new tenant who will inspect her apartment with Margaret is happily waiting in the office. Finally, something goes off without a hitch. The apartment is inspected and everything is in good condition. The tenant initials the move-in/move-out (MIMO) form, comes back to the office to sign the lease, goes over the residents' rules and accepts and understands all terms and conditions, pays her money and receives her keys. No surprises. No exceptions. Sometimes it happens.

## After-Hours

It's nearly 6:00 p.m. now and Margaret's thoughts turn to getting changed and driving over to the sheriff's substation for her presentation. She is tired but has been looking forward to this occasion for several weeks and expects it to be an enjoyable experience. She is about to get up from her desk when the husband from unit 748 walks into the office, three-day covenant notice in his hand. Margaret had worded the complaint carefully and professionally, referring to excessive noise and disturbance from "perceived sexual activity." The man is not irate, more perplexed, and tells Margaret that there must be some mistake. He works nights and is at work at the time of the alleged activity. It could not possibly be coming from his apartment. Margaret thought she had already seen the toughest part of her day, but calmly informs the man that she has a signed complaint from a tenant whose name she cannot reveal and that there is no mistake. The man from unit 748 assures her that the disturbance will stop and somberly walks out of the apartment.

Margaret gets in her car, refreshed and with a change of clothes, looking forward to seeing friends and having a stimulating evening talking about the challenges of managing residential real estate. One thing is certain. No two days are ever identical. They may be similar, but there are always surprises. Even though she thinks she reads people well, sometimes they'll do the unexpected. Human nature doesn't change, and human nature always comes through in people's behavior. The best help for Margaret in her job is policies and procedures that establish some sense of order to the entire process of dealing with the people who rent her properties. That and the support of her superiors and colleagues in the business of managing real property. Tomorrow will be another day, but for Margaret, it will be a little different than any other.

# QUESTIONS

1. Sunnyvale Manor is a:

   a. series of four-plexes

   b. complex of multi-story buildings

   c. series of garden apartments with courtyards

   d. complex of high-rise luxury apartments

2. Sunnyvale Manor has:

   a. more than 20 full-time employees

   b. 10 full-time employees

   c. less than five full-time employees

   d. no full-time employees

3. Amenities at Sunnyvale Manor include:

   a. pools

   b. laundry rooms

   c. gym facilities

   d. none of the above

4. Sunnyvale Manor is owned by a (an):

    a. trust

    b. individual

    c. partnership

    d. bank

5. Workers travel Sunnyvale Manor by:

    a. car

    b. foot

    c. bicycle

    d. golf cart

6. Sunnyvale Manor is managed by:

    a. the owners

    b. a large property management company

    c. Margaret Jones

    d. the National Apartment Association (NAA)

7. At Sunnyvale Manor, Margaret Jones holds the position of:

    a. property manager

    b. business manager

    c. office manager

    d. on-site manager

8. Margaret Jones has prepared herself for her property management job by:

    a. earning the Certified Apartment Manager (CAM) designation

    b. taking college courses

    c. going to legal workshops

    d. all of the above

9. Margaret's management style is best described as:

    a. no nonsense and direct

    b. tentative

    c. dictatorial and intolerant

    d. manipulative

10. Sunnyvale Manor's approach to the three-bedroom unit is that:

    a. it's popular so let's have as many as we can
    b. it's not needed
    c. it's more profitable to make two units out of them
    d. it's a wise use of space

11. Sunnyvale Manor's qualifying policies for new tenants have been in the direction of:

    a. reducing vacancies
    b. stringency
    c. caution
    d. reducing turnover

12. Right now Sunnyvale Manor's delays in getting units ready to rent are due to:

    a. not having enough full-time workers
    b. a complacency on the part of its maintenance workers
    c. having to wait for outside contractors
    d. b and c above

13. According to Sunnyvale Manor's leases, a car can be towed from the premises for the following reasons:

    a. expired registration
    b. inoperable
    c. dirty
    d. paint is oxidized

14. Sunnyvale Manor provides all of the following services itself except:

    a. keys and locks
    b. linoleum
    c. refrigeration servicing
    d. glass

15. Disturbing the peace would result in the offending tenant receiving a:

    a. three-day nuisance notice
    b. three-day covenant notice
    c. three-day waste notice
    d. three-day notice to quit

16. If a tenant can't pay the rent on time, Margaret Jones will likely:

    a. evict the tenant right away
    b. wait to see how long it's going to take for the tenant to pay
    c. refuse a partial payment
    d. work out a payment plan but firmly warn the tenant

17. Sunnyvale Manor's policy regarding roommates is that:

    a. the roommates' combined income must be three times the monthly rent
    b. the roommates' combined income must be four times the monthly rent
    c. each roommate must qualify on one's own
    d. Sunnyvale Manor does not allow roommates

18. The reason Margaret Jones speaks at special neighborhood programs is:

    a. for the fees involved
    b. to encourage other owners and managers to make a difference
    c. to become better known in the community
    d. to pass the time

19. In response to the deterioration of the courtyards, Margaret Jones devised:

    a. a courtyard beautification project
    b. stricter rules
    c. increased security patrol
    d. tougher eviction policies

20. Sunnyvale Manor utilizes the services of an eviction company because:

    a. it is more efficient
    b. it is cost effective
    c. management doesn't want to risk making a mistake
    d. all of the above

# ANSWERS

1. *c*
2. *a*
3. *b*
4. *c*
5. *d*
6. *b*
7. *d*
8. *d*
9. *a*
10. *c*
11. *a*
12. *d*
13. *b*
14. *c*
15. *b*
16. *d*
17. *c*
18. *b*
19. *a*
20. *d*

# Systems and Reports

- **Let Technology Help**
- **Project Operating Report**
- **Cash Flow Statement**
- **Balance Sheet**
- **General Ledger**
- **Market Survey**

C H A P T E R

*11*

# LET TECHNOLOGY HELP

Sophisticated software programs keep a close watch on the financial operations of an apartment complex. Based on daily input and accurate record keeping of the managers and bookkeepers, reports are produced regularly and systematically that give an overall view of the monetary well being of the property. The systems are also designed to analyze the results of the reporting and offer plausible explanations for any variances from budget that may occur, based on the information made available to them. Consider the following types of analyses.

# PROJECT OPERATING REPORT

The project operating report breaks the income and expenses down into many specific categories and reports them according to budget and actual, current month, and year to date. It also produces a variance analysis when an item varies significantly from the budget. The project operating report looks like this, section by section.

**Project Operating Report**
**Current Month**

| Description | Acct | Budget | Actual | Variance | % of Budget |
|---|---|---|---|---|---|
| Standard Rent Roll | | 349,084-* | 327,116- | 21,968- | 6.3%- |
| | | | | | |
| Income | | | | | |
| Gross Rental Inc | 0178 | 370,144- | 384,144- | 14,000 | 3.8% |
| Loss: Old Leases | 0196 | 13,560 | 57,028 | 43,468- | 320.6%- |
| Loss: Vacancy | 0157 | 29,000 | 39,460 | 10,460- | 36.1%- |
| Loss: Model Apts | 0168 | 2,350 | | 2,350 | 100.0% |
| Loss: Lease Conc** | 0154 | 7,500 | | 7,500 | 100.0% |
| EOM*** Delinq | 0176 | 6,100 | 44,988- | 51,088 | 837.5% |
| Writeoffs | 0198 | 259 | | 259 | 100.0% |
| | | | | | |
| Total Rental Income | | 311,375- | 332,644- | 21,269 | 6.8% |

\* "-" Following a Figure = *Favorable*
\*\* Conc = Concessions
\*\*\* EOM = End-Of-Month

(continued on next page)

**Project Operating Report**
**Year-To-Date**

| Description | Acct | Budget | Actual | Variance | % of Budget |
|---|---|---|---|---|---|
| Standard Rent Roll | | 1,052,852- | 691,087- | 361,765- | 34.4%- |
| | | | | | |
| Income | | | | | |
| Gross Rental Inc | 0178 | 1,098,432- | 768,288- | 330,144- | 30.1%- |
| Loss: Old Leases | 0196 | 22,680 | 77,201 | 54,521- | 240.4% |
| Loss: Vacancy | 0157 | 116,700 | 63,149 | 53,551 | 45.9% |
| Loss: Model Apts | 0168 | 7,050 | | 7,050 | 100.0% |
| Loss: Lease Conc | 0154 | 22,900 | | 22,900 | 100.0% |
| EOM Delinq | 0176 | 21,424 | 41,940- | 63,364 | 295.8% |
| Writeoffs | 0198 | 777 | | 777 | 100.0% |
| | | | | | |
| Total Rental Income | | 906,901- | 664,348- | 242,553- | 26.8%- |

The report then expands to include other forms of income.

**Project Operating Report (cont'd.)**
**Current Month**

| Description | Acct | Budget | Actual | Variance | % of Budget |
|---|---|---|---|---|---|
| Appl* Lease Income | 1234 | 100- | | 100- | 100.0% |
| Forfeited Deposits | 1235 | 462- | 112- | 350- | 75.8%- |
| Cleaning Reimbmnt | 1236 | 1,387- | 1,185- | 202- | 14.6%- |
| Credit App** | 1238 | 1,275- | | 1,275 | 100.0% |
| Vending Machines | 1239 | | | | |
| Cleaning Fees | 1240 | | 1,295- | 1,295 | |
| General | 1241 | | 301- | 301 | |
| Laundry | 1242 | 716- | 1,405- | 689 | 96.2% |
| Late Rent Fees | 1243 | 1,000- | 1,200- | 200 | 20.0% |
| Other: NSF*** Fees | 1244 | 150- | 198- | 48 | 32.0% |
| Storage Room Rent | 1245 | 75- | | 75- | 100.0% |
| Application Fee | 1246 | | 560- | 560 | |
| Washer/Dryer Rent | 1247 | | | | |
| Tenant Damage Pmt[†] | 1248 | 225- | | 225- | 100.0% |
| | | | | | |
| Total Other Income | | 5,390- | 6,256- | 866 | 16.1% |
| | | | | | |
| Total Income | | 316,765- | 338,900 | 22,135 | 7.0% |

　\* Appl = Appliance
　\*\* App = Application
\*\*\* NSF = Non-Sufficient Funds
　† Pmt = Payment

*(continued on next page)*

**Project Operating Report (cont'd.)**
**Year-To-Date**

| Description | Acct | Budget | Actual | Variance | % of Budget |
|---|---|---|---|---|---|
| Appl Lease Income | 1234 | 300- | | 300- | 100.0%- |
| Forfeited Deposits | 1235 | 1,386- | 112- | 1,274- | 91.9%- |
| Cleaning Reimbmnt | 1236 | 4,161- | 1,980- | 2,181- | 52.4%- |
| Credit App | 1238 | 3,825- | | 3,825- | 100.0%- |
| Vending Machines | 1239 | | 200- | 200 | |
| Cleaning Fees | 1240 | | 1,295- | 1,295 | |
| General | 1241 | | 301- | 301 | |
| Laundry | 1242 | 2,148- | 1,722- | 426- | 19.8%- |
| Late Rent Fees | 1243 | 3,000- | 2,270- | 730- | 24.3%- |
| Other: NSF Fees | 1244 | 450- | 1,078- | 628 | 139.6% |
| Storage Room Rent | 1245 | 225- | | 225- | 100.0%- |
| Application Fee | 1246 | | 864- | 864 | |
| Washer/Dryer Rent | 1247 | | 160- | 160 | |
| Tenant Damage Pmt | 1248 | 675- | | 675- | 100.0%- |
| | | | | | |
| Total Other Income | | 16,170- | 9,982- | 6,188- | 38.3%- |
| | | | | | |
| Total Income | | 923,071- | 674,330- | 248,741- | 27.0%- |

The report now expands into salary expenses.

**Project Operating Report (cont'd.)**
**Current Month**

| Description | Acct | Budget | Actual | Variance | % of Budget |
|---|---|---|---|---|---|
| Salaries | | | | | |
| Management | 1011 | 13,338 | 1,399 | 11,939 | 89.5% |
| Management: Bonus | 1012 | 2,867 | 2,046 | 821 | 28.6% |
| Asst Manager | 1013 | | 7,558 | 7,558- | |
| Apt Manager | 1014 | 2,754 | | 2,754 | 100.0% |
| Leasing Agent | 1015 | | 628 | 628- | |
| Gen Maint | 1016 | | 6,094 | 6,094- | |
| Maint: Porters | 1017 | | 2,856 | 2,856- | |
| Maint: Painters | 1018 | | 2,398 | 2,398- | |
| Maint: Foreman | 1019 | 2,000 | 340 | 1,660 | 83.0% |
| Maint: Assistant | 1020 | 13,057 | 1,628 | 11,429 | 87.5% |
| Maint: Bonus | 1021 | | 83 | 83- | |
| Maint: Apt | 1022 | 2,746 | 6,860 | 4,114- | 149.8% |
| Mgt* Related Exp** | 1023 | 4,001 | 540 | 3,461 | 86.5% |
| Mgt Related Exp | 1024 | 860 | 593 | 267 | 31.1% |
| Asst Related Exp | 1025 | | 2,192 | | |

*(continued on next page)*

**Current Month (cont'd.)**

| Description | Acct | Budget | Actual | Variance | % of Budget |
|---|---|---|---|---|---|
| Leasing Rel*** Exp | 1026 | | 182 | 182- | |
| Maint Rel Exp | 1027 | | 1,767 | 1,767- | |
| Maint Rel Exp | 1028 | | 828 | 828- | |
| Maint Rel Exp | 1029 | | 695 | 695- | |
| Maint Rel Exp | 1030 | 600 | 99 | 501 | 83.5% |
| Maint Rel Exp | 1031 | 3,917 | 472 | 3,445 | 88.0% |
| Maint Rel Exp | 1032 | | 24 | 24- | |
| Total Salaries | | 46,140 | 39,282 | 6,858 | 14.9% |

* Mgt = Management
** Exp = Expenses
*** Rel = Related

**Year-To-Date**

| Description | Acct | Budget | Actual | Variance | % of Budget |
|---|---|---|---|---|---|
| Salaries | | | | | |
| Management | 1011 | 40,014 | 3,686 | 36,328 | 90.8% |
| Management: Bonus | 1012 | 8,601 | 2,046 | 6,555 | 76.2% |
| Asst Manager | 1013 | | 10,447 | 10,447- | |
| Apt Manager | 1014 | 8,262 | | 8,262 | 100.0% |
| Leasing Agent | 1015 | | 848 | 848- | |
| Gen Maint | 1016 | | 8,522 | 8,522- | |
| Maint: Porters | 1017 | | 3,705 | 3,705- | |
| Maint: Painters | 1018 | | 4,505 | 4,505- | |
| Maint: Foreman | 1019 | 4,000 | 1,191 | 2,809 | 70.2% |
| Maint: Assistant | 1020 | 39,171 | 2,212 | 36,959 | 94.4% |
| Maint: Bonus | 1021 | | 83 | 83- | |
| Maint: Apt | 1022 | 8,238 | 6,860 | 1,378 | 16.7% |
| Mgt Related Exp | 1023 | 12,003 | 1,203 | 10,800 | 90.0% |
| Mgt Related Exp | 1024 | 2,580 | 593 | 1,987 | 77.0% |
| Asst Related Exp | 1025 | | 3,030 | 3,030 | |
| Leasing Rel Exp | 1026 | | 246 | 246- | |
| Maint Rel Exp | 1027 | | 2,471 | 2,471- | |
| Maint Rel Exp | 1028 | | 1,074 | 1,074- | |
| Maint Rel Exp | 1029 | | 1,306 | 1,306- | |
| Maint Rel Exp | 1030 | 1,200 | 345 | 855 | 71.3% |
| Maint Rel Exp | 1031 | 11,751 | 641 | 11,110 | 94.6% |
| Maint Rel Exp | 1032 | | 24 | 24- | |
| Total Salaries | | 135,820 | 55,038 | 80,782 | 59.5% |

The report now expands into advertising and promotion.

## Project Operating Report (cont'd.)
### Current Month

| Description | Acct | Budget | Actual | Variance | % of Budget |
|---|---|---|---|---|---|
| Adv*/Promo | | | | | |
| Advertising | 1201 | 2,600 | 5,986 | 3,386- | 130.2%- |
| Promotion | 1202 | 100 | 1,097 | 997- | 997.0%- |
| Signs | 1203 | 800 | | 800 | 100.0% |
| Brochures | 1204 | 500 | | 500 | 100.0% |
| Model Acc**/Lab | 1205 | | 400 | 400- | |
| Newspaper | 1206 | 500 | | 500 | 100.0% |
| Other Media | 1207 | 500 | | 500 | 100.0% |
| Humphrey Lifestyle | 1208 | | 18 | 18- | |
| Referral Fee | 1209 | 1,400 | | 1,400 | 100.0% |
| Res*** Retention Fee | 1210 | 400 | 274 | 126 | 31.6% |
| Total Adv/Promo | | 6,800 | 7,775 | 975- | 14.3%- |

```
  *  Adv = Advertising
 **  Acc = Accessories
***  Res = Resident
```

### Year-To-Date

| Description | Acct | Budget | Actual | Variance | % of Budget |
|---|---|---|---|---|---|
| Adv/Promo | | | | | |
| Advertising | 1201 | 5,800 | 8,644 | 2,844- | 49.0%- |
| Promotion | 1202 | 500 | 1,107 | 607- | 121.4%- |
| Signs | 1203 | 2,400 | 272 | 2,128 | 88.7% |
| Brochures | 1204 | 1,500 | | 1,500 | 100.0% |
| Model Acc/Lab | 1205 | | 400 | 400- | |
| Newspaper | 1206 | 1,500 | | 1,500 | 100.0% |
| Other Media | 1207 | 1,500 | | 1,500 | 100.0% |
| Humphrey Lifestyle | 1208 | | 18 | 18- | |
| Referral Fee | 1209 | 4,200 | | 4,200 | 100.0% |
| Res Retention Fee | 1210 | 1,200 | 274 | 926 | 77.2% |
| Total Adv/Promo | | 18,600 | 10,715 | 7,885 | 42.4% |

The report now expands into maintenance expenses.

**Project Operating Report (cont'd.)**
**Current Month**

| Description | Acct | Budget | Actual | Variance | % of Budget |
|---|---|---|---|---|---|
| Maintenance | | | | | |
| Plumbing | 2100 | 750 | 750 | | 0.0% |
| Air Conditioning | 2101 | 110 | 124 | 14- | 12.7%- |
| Electrical | 2102 | 735 | 447 | 288 | 39.2% |
| Carpet | 2103 | 60 | 60 | | 0.0% |
| Drapery | 2104 | 25 | | 25 | 100.0% |
| Yard/Landscaping | 2105 | 5,150 | 5,131 | 19 | 0.4% |
| Appliances | 2106 | 130 | 155 | 25- | 19.2%- |
| Roof | 2107 | 50 | | 50 | 100.0% |
| Exterminating | 2108 | 1,025 | 146 | 879 | 85.8% |
| Uniform Rental | 2109 | 185 | | 185 | 100.0% |
| Painting | 2110 | 1,150 | | 1,150 | 100.0% |
| Proj* Vehicle Exp | 2111 | 200 | 310 | 110- | 55.0%- |
| Sprinkler Repair | 2112 | 250 | | 250 | 100.0% |
| | | | | | |
| General | | | | | |
| Fire Ext**/Smoke Al*** | 2113 | 100 | | 100 | 100.0% |
| Lock and Keys | 2114 | 530 | 1 | 529 | 99.8% |
| Light Blbs†/Ballast | 2115 | 300 | 9 | 291 | 97.0% |
| Pkg‡ Lot/Sidewalk | 2116 | 200 | | 200 | 100.0% |
| Contract Labor | 2117 | | 2,857 | 2,857- | |
| Equip Repair | 2118 | 125 | | 125 | 100.0% |
| Glass Repair | 2119 | 2,550 | 168 | 2,382 | 93.4% |
| Cleaning Supplies | 2120 | 140 | 110 | 30 | 21.4% |
| Hardware & Tools | 2121 | 220 | 316 | 96- | 43.6%- |
| Interior Repairs | 2122 | 1,200 | 26 | 1,174 | 97.8% |
| Exterior Repairs | 2123 | 1,000 | | 1,000 | 100.0% |
| Carpet Shampoo | 2124 | 100 | | 100 | 100.0% |
| Vinyl | 2125 | 100 | | 100 | 100.0% |
| Rehab Interiors | 2126 | 3,750 | | 3,750 | 100.0% |
| New Counter Tops | 2127 | 300 | | 300 | 100.0% |
| Turn Cost: Carpet | 2128 | 1,875 | 3,523 | 1,648- | 87.9%- |
| Turn Cost: Paint | 2129 | 4,825 | 5,063 | 238- | 4.9%- |
| Turn Cost: Cleaning | 2130 | 2,265 | 4,135 | 1,870- | 82.6%- |
| Turn Cost: Blinds | 2131 | 100 | | 100 | 100.0% |
| Turn Cost: Plumbing | 2132 | | 1,404 | 1,404- | |
| | | | | | |
| Total Maintenance Exp | | 29,500 | 24,735 | 4,765 | 16.2% |

```
  *  Proj = Project
 ** Ext = Extinguisher
*** Al = Alarm
  † Blbs = Bulbs
  ‡ Pkg = Parking
```

*(continued on next page)*

**Project Operating Report (cont'd.)**
**Year-To-Date**

| Description | Acct | Budget | Actual | Variance | % of Budget |
|---|---|---|---|---|---|
| Maintenance | | | | | |
| Plumbing | 2100 | 2,250 | 2,667 | 417- | 18.5%- |
| Air Conditioning | 2101 | 330 | 194 | 136 | 41.2% |
| Electrical | 2102 | 2,205 | 923 | 1,282 | 58.1% |
| Carpet | 2103 | 180 | 60 | 120 | 66.7% |
| Drapery | 2104 | 75 | | 75 | 100.0% |
| Yard/Landscaping | 2105 | 15,450 | 5,131 | 10,319 | 66.8% |
| Appliances | 2106 | 390 | 402 | 12- | 3.1%- |
| Roof | 2107 | 150 | | 150 | 100.0% |
| Exterminating | 2108 | 3,075 | 1,496 | 1,579 | 51.4% |
| Uniform Rental | 2109 | 655 | | 655 | 100.0% |
| Painting | 2110 | 3,450 | | 3,450 | 100.0% |
| Proj Vehicle Exp | 2111 | 600 | 374 | 226 | 37.7% |
| Sprinkler Repair | 2112 | 750 | | 750 | 100.0% |
| | | | | | |
| General | | | 166 | 166- | |
| Fire Ext/Smoke Al | 2113 | 1,200 | 326 | 874 | 72.8% |
| Lock and Keys | 2114 | 1,590 | 1,201 | 389 | 24.5% |
| Light Blbs/Ballast | 2115 | 900 | 446 | 454 | 50.4% |
| Pkg Lot/Sidewalk | 2116 | 600 | | 600 | 100.0% |
| Contract Labor | 2117 | | 2,857 | 2,857- | |
| Equip Repair | 2118 | 375 | | 375 | 100.0% |
| Glass Repair | 2119 | 7,650 | 285 | 7,365 | 96.3% |
| Cleaning Supplies | 2120 | 420 | 110 | 310 | 73.8% |
| Hardware & Tools | 2121 | 660 | 1,805 | 1,145- | 173.5%- |
| Interior Repairs | 2122 | 3,600 | 30 | 3,570 | 99.2% |
| Exterior Repairs | 2123 | 3,000 | | 3,000 | 100.0% |
| Carpet Shampoo | 2124 | 300 | | 300 | 100.0% |
| Vinyl | 2125 | 300 | | 300 | 100.0% |
| Rehab Interiors | 2126 | 11,250 | | 11,250 | 100.0% |
| New Counter Tops | 2127 | 900 | | 900 | 100.0% |
| Turn Cost: Carpet | 2128 | 5,625 | 3,523 | 2,102 | 37.4% |
| Turn Cost: Paint | 2129 | 14,475 | 6,590 | 7,885 | 54.5% |
| Turn Cost: Cleaning | 2130 | 6,795 | 4,135 | 2,660 | 39.2% |
| Turn Cost: Blinds | 2131 | 300 | | 300 | 100.0% |
| Turn Cost: Plumbing | 2132 | | 3,628 | 3,628- | |
| | | | | | |
| Total Maintenance Exp | | 89,500 | 36,349 | 53,151 | 59.4% |

The report now expands into administrative costs.

**Project Operating Report (cont'd.)**
**Current Month**

| Description | Acct | Budget | Actual | Variance | % of Budget |
|---|---|---|---|---|---|
| **Administrative Costs** | | | | | |
| Management Fee | 3100 | 9,455 | 10,161 | 706- | 7.5%- |
| Office Supplies | 3101 | 500 | 804 | 304- | 60.8%- |
| Postage | 3102 | 175 | 78 | 97 | 55.4% |
| Professional Fees | 3103 | 1,750 | 672- | 2,422 | 138.4% |
| Office Rent Exp | 3104 | | | | |
| Security Patrol | 3105 | 5,840 | 12,000 | 6,160- | 105.5%- |
| Telephone | 3106 | 1,075 | 1,362 | 287- | 26.7%- |
| Answering Service | 3107 | 75 | 346 | 271- | 361.3%- |
| General | 3108 | | 16 | 16- | |
| Credit Verif* | 3109 | 1,275 | 3,782 | 2,507- | 196.6%- |
| Employee Training | 3110 | 200 | 13 | 187 | 93.5% |
| Fed Express/Other | 3111 | 66 | 65 | 1 | 1.5% |
| Recruiting Exp | 3112 | 150 | 2,075 | 1,925- | 283.3%- |
| Automotive | 3113 | 25 | | 25 | 100.0% |
| Printing/Dupl** | 3114 | 200 | 19 | 181 | 90.5% |
| Social/Recreation | 3115 | 200 | 231 | 31- | 15.5%- |
| Mgt Overhead | 3116 | 6,375 | 6,819 | 444- | 7.0%- |
| Dues/Subscriptions | 3117 | | | | |
| Temp*** Services | 3118 | | 5,795 | 5,795- | |
| Leased Equip | 3119 | 500 | 340 | 160 | 32.0% |
| Comp Software | 3120 | 1,750 | 19 | 1,731 | 98.9% |
| Banking Cost | 3121 | 100 | | 100 | 100.0% |
| Parking | 3122 | | | | |
| Total Adm† Costs | | 29,711 | 43,253 | 13,542- | 45.6%- |

```
  * Verif = Verification
 ** Dupl  = Duplication
*** Temp  = Temporary
  † Adm   = Administrative
```

**Year-To-Date**

| Description | Acct | Budget | Actual | Variance | % of Budget |
|---|---|---|---|---|---|
| **Administrative Costs** | | | | | |
| Management Fee | 3100 | 27,548 | 20,390 | 7,158 | 26.0% |
| Office Supplies | 3101 | 1,500 | 1,607 | 107- | 7.1%- |
| Postage | 3102 | 525 | 361 | 164 | 31.2% |
| Professional Fees | 3103 | 5,250 | 339- | 5,589 | 106.5% |

*(continued on next page)*

**Project Operating Report (cont'd.)**
**Year-To-Date**

| Description | Acct | Budget | Actual | Variance | % of Budget |
|---|---|---|---|---|---|
| Administrative Costs (cont'd.) | | | | | |
| Office Rent Exp | 3104 | | 2,420 | 2,420- | |
| Security Patrol | 3105 | 17,520 | 12,000 | 5,520 | 31.5% |
| Telephone | 3106 | 3,225 | 2,484 | 741 | 23.0% |
| Answering Service | 3107 | 225 | 563 | 338- | 150.2%- |
| General | 3108 | | 16 | 16- | |
| Credit Verif | 3109 | 3,825 | 5,012 | 1,187- | 31.0%- |
| Employee Training | 3110 | 600 | 59 | 541 | 90.2% |
| Fed Express/Other | 3111 | 198 | 109 | 89 | 45.0% |
| Recruiting Exp | 3112 | 450 | 2,165 | 1,715- | 381.1%- |
| Automotive | 3113 | 75 | 48 | 27 | 36.0% |
| Printing/Dupl | 3114 | 600 | 1,131 | 531- | 88.5%- |
| Social/Recreation | 3115 | 600 | 363 | 237 | 39.5% |
| Mgt Overhead | 3116 | 12,653 | 6,819 | 5,834 | 46.1% |
| Dues/Subscriptions | 3117 | 300 | 415 | 115- | 38.3%- |
| Temp Services | 3118 | | 28,418 | 28,418- | |
| Leased Equip | 3119 | 1,500 | 469 | 1,031 | 68.7% |
| Comp Software | 3120 | 1,750 | 45 | 1,705 | 97.4% |
| Banking Cost | 3121 | 300 | | 300 | 100.0% |
| Parking | 3122 | 1,970 | | 1,970 | 100.0% |
| Total Adm Costs | | 80,614 | 84,555 | 3,941- | 4.9%- |

The report now expands into utility expenses.

**Project Operating Report (cont'd.)**
**Current Month**

| Description | Acct | Budget | Actual | Variance | % of Budget |
|---|---|---|---|---|---|
| Utilities | | | | | |
| Electricity | 4100 | | 3,804 | 3,804- | |
| Gas | 4101 | | 2,895 | 2,895- | |
| Water | 4102 | | 10,723 | 10,723- | |
| Water & Sewer | 4103 | 6,590 | | 6,590 | 100.0% |
| Elec*/Common Area | 4104 | 4,600 | 1,570 | 3,030 | 65.9% |
| Garbage Collection | 4105 | 4,035 | 4,381 | 346- | 8.6%- |
| Gas/Common Area | 4106 | 1,445 | | 1,445 | 100.0% |
| Elec/Mgt Service | 4107 | | | | |
| Total Utilities | | 16,670 | 23,373 | 6,703- | 40.2%- |

\* Elec = Electricity

(continued on next page)

**Project Operating Report (cont'd.)**
**Year-To-Date**

| Description | Acct | Budget | Actual | Variance | % of Budget |
|---|---|---|---|---|---|
| Utilities | | | | | |
| Electricity | 4100 | | 5,807 | 5,807- | |
| Gas | 4101 | | 4,132 | 4,132- | |
| Water | 4102 | | 20,381 | 20,381- | |
| Water & Sewer | 4103 | 19,770 | | 19,770 | 100.0% |
| Elec/Common Area | 4104 | 13,800 | 5,416 | 8,384 | 60.8% |
| Garbage Collection | 4105 | 12,105 | 8,719 | 3,386 | 28.0% |
| Gas/Common Area | 4106 | 4,335 | | 4,335 | 100.0% |
| Elec/Mgt Service | 4107 | | 554 | 554- | |
| | | | | | |
| Total Utilities | | 50,010 | 45,009 | 5,001 | 10.0% |

The report expands to real estate taxes and insurance, deducts the total expenses from effective gross income, and reveals the net operating income.

**Project Operating Report Cont'd)**
**Current Month**

| Description | Acct | Budget | Actual | Variance | % of Budget |
|---|---|---|---|---|---|
| Real Estate Taxes | 0001 | 23,362 | | 23,362 | 100.0% |
| Insurance Premiums | 0002 | | 4,011 | 4,011 | |
| Ins* Premiums/Trust | 0003 | 4,081 | | 4,081 | 100.0% |
| | | | | | |
| Total Insurance | | 4,081 | 4,011 | 70 | 1.7% |
| | | | | | |
| Total Expense | | 156,264 | 142,429 | 13,835 | 8.9% |
| | | | | | |
| Net Operating Income | | 160,501- | 196,471- | 35,970 | 22.4% |

\* Ins = Insurance

*(continued on next page)*

## Project Operating Report (cont'd.)
### Year-To-Date

| Description | Acct | Budget | Actual | Variance | % of Budget |
|---|---|---|---|---|---|
| Real Estate Taxes | 0001 | 70,086 | | 70,086 | 100.0% |
| Insurance Premiums | 0002 | | 20,891 | 20,891- | |
| Ins Premiums/Trust | 0003 | 16,881 | | 16,881 | 100.0% |
| Total Insurance | | 16,881 | 20,891 | 4,010- | 23.0%- |
| Total Expense | | 461,511 | 252,557 | 208,954 | 45.3% |
| Net Operating Income (-) or Loss | | 461,560- | 421,773- | 39,787- | 8.6%- |

One final Project Operating Report deals with capital expenditures, and total cash flow before debt service.

## Project Operating Report (cont'd.)
### Current Month

| Description | Acct | Budget | Actual | Variance | % of Budget |
|---|---|---|---|---|---|
| Capital Expenditures | | | | | |
| Drapes/Blinds | 5100 | | 712 | 712- | |
| Carpet | 5101 | 5,500 | 1,036 | 4,464 | 81.2% |
| Appliances | 5102 | 1,000 | 2,247 | 1,247- | 124.7%- |
| Cabinets/Counters | 5103 | 2,000 | | 2,000 | 100.0% |
| Plumbing | 5104 | 350 | 552 | 202- | 57.7%- |
| Heating/AC | 5105 | 150 | 1,022 | 872- | 581.3%- |
| Furniture | 5106 | | 300 | 300- | |
| Vinyl & Tile | 5107 | 2,700 | | 2,700 | 100.0% |
| Light Fixtures | 5108 | 1,000 | 30 | 970 | 97.0% |
| Equipment | 5109 | | 106 | 106- | |
| Signs | 5110 | | 37 | 37- | |
| Painting | 5111 | 7,000 | | 7,000 | 100.0% |
| Office Equipment | 5112 | 2,500 | 59 | 2,441 | 97.6% |
| Total Capital Expenditures | | 22,200 | 6,101 | 16,099 | 72.5% |
| Total Cash Flow Before Debt Service | | 138,301- | 190,370- | 52,069 | 37.7% |

*(continued on next page)*

**Project Operating Report (cont'd.)**
**Year-To-Date**

| Description | Acct | Budget | Actual | Variance | % of Budget |
|---|---|---|---|---|---|
| Capital Expenditures | | | | | |
| Drapes/Blinds | 5100 | 1,000 | 712 | 288 | 28.8% |
| Carpet | 5101 | 12,500 | 1,507 | 10,993 | 87.9% |
| Appliances | 5102 | 3,000 | 3,255 | 255- | 8.5%- |
| Cabinets/Counters | 5103 | 2,000 | | 2,000 | 100.0% |
| Plumbing | 5104 | 1,050 | 852 | 198 | 18.9% |
| Heating/AC | 5105 | 450 | 1,022 | 572- | 127.1%- |
| Furniture | 5106 | | 300 | 300- | |
| Vinyl & Tile | 5107 | 6,400 | | 6,400 | 100.0% |
| Light Fixtures | 5108 | 1,000 | 580 | 420 | 42.0% |
| Equipment | 5109 | | 106 | 106- | |
| Signs | 5110 | | 37 | 37- | |
| Painting | 5111 | 7,000 | | 7,000 | 100.0% |
| Office Equipment | 5112 | 2,500 | 59 | 2,441 | 97.6% |
| | | | | | |
| Total Capital Expenditures | | 36,900 | 8,430 | 28,470 | 77.2% |
| | | | | | |
| Total Cash Flow Before | | | | | |
| Debt Service | | 424,660- | 413,343- | 11,317- | 2.7%- |

# Interpretations Provided by Software

The best explanation of the previous reports comes from the analysis provided by the software program, in a section called *Variance Analysis*.

### STANDARD RENT ROLL

For the Standard Rent Roll, note the following numbers:

Budget: $349,084          Variance: $21,968
Actual: $327,116     % of Variance: 6.3

*Explanation:* Unfavorable variance due to the actual occupancy being lower than the projected number, as well as current residents being below the market rate.

### TOTAL RENTAL INCOME

Budget: $311,375          Variance: $21,269
Actual: $332,644     % of Variance: 6.8

*Explanation:* Favorable variance largely due to the funds transfer to the community needed to pay previously due invoices.

## TOTAL OTHER INCOME

Budget: $5,390          Variance: $866
Actual: $6,256          % of Variance: 16.1

*Explanation:* Favorable variance due to actual cleaning fees charged to residents upon moveout exceeding the budgeted amount, and laundry income exceeding the projected amount. There were insignificant variances in all other subaccounts.

## TOTAL SALARIES

Budget: $46,140         Variance: $6,858
Actual: $39,282         % of Variance: 14.9

*Explanation:* Favorable variance due to manager and maintenance supervisor's salaries being coded incorrectly to Temp Service and Contract Labor. These line items will be corrected and will reflect in next month's report.

## ADVERTISING AND PROMOTION

Budget: $6,800          Variance: $975
Actual: $7,775          % of Variance: 14.3

*Explanation:* Unfavorable variance due to prior invoices being paid during the current billing cycle for *For Rent Magazine* and *The Press Telegram.*

## TOTAL MAINTENANCE EXPENSES

Budget: $29,500         Variance: $4,765
Actual: $24,735         % of Variance: 16.2

*Explanation:* Favorable variance due to the following: (1) Savings in painting, $1,150; (2) The non-receipt of the extermination invoice during the current cycle, $879; (3) Savings in glass repair, $2,382; (4) There were insignificant variances in all other subaccounts.

**ADMINISTRATIVE COSTS**

Budget: $20,256          Variance: $12,836
Actual: $33,092          % of Variance: 63.4

*Explanation:* Unfavorable variance due to the following: (1) Past due Security Patrol invoices being paid during the current cycle, $6,160; (2) Manager's salary being miscoded to Temp Services, $5,795; (3) Past due Office Supply invoices being paid during the current cycle, $304; (4) There were insignificant variances in all other subaccounts.

**TOTAL UTILITIES**

Budget: $16,670          Variance: $6,703
Actual: $23,373          % of Variance: 40.2

*Explanation:* Unfavorable variance due to both February and March gas, water and electricity invoices being paid during the current billing cycle, $6,356.

**CAPITAL EXPENDITURES**

Budget: $22,200          Variance: $16,099
Actual: $6,101          % of Variance: 72.5

*Explanation:* Favorable variance due to savings in the following: (1) Carpet, $4,464; (2) Cabinets/Countertops, $2,000; (3) Vinyl, $2,700; (4) Painting, $7,000; (5) There were insignificant variances in all other subaccounts.

# CASH FLOW STATEMENT

Another report produced by the software very similar to the Project Operating Report is the Cash Flow Statement. Due to its similarity it will not be reproduced here, but it summarizes the various categories of income and expense, includes debt service after net operating income, capital expenditures and other depreciable assets, and the cash flow after these distributions. It also analyzes according to current month, year to date, budget, actual and variances.

The Cash Flow Statement produces a Cash Sources and Uses Statement depicted here.

### Cash Sources and Uses

| Cash Reconciliation | | March 31, 2001 |
|---|---|---|
| Beginning Cash Balance | $154,203.30 | |
| **Current Month Sources and Uses** | | |
| Cash Flow per Cash Flow Statement | $12,202.25 | |
| Change in Prepaid | ⟨4,454.83⟩ | |
| Change in Escrowed Real Estate Taxes | ⟨15,105.28⟩ | |
| Change in Accummulated Development Improvement | ⟨687.85⟩ | |
| Change in Security Deposits Liability | ⟨625.00⟩ | |
| **Ending Cash Balance** | | **$145,532.59** |
| **Proof of Cash** | | |
| **Ending Cash Balance** | | **$145,532.59** |

Another report generated by the Cash Flow Statement is a Management Fee Calculation Statement depicted here.

### Management Fee Calculation
### Year-To-Date

| | | | |
|---|---|---|---|
| **Total Income** | | $674,328.89 | |
| Adjustments | | | |
| Employee Rent | | 5,530.00 | |
| Income Base for Management Fee | | $679,858.89 | |
| Management Fee | | | |
| Greater of: 3% | $20,395.77 | | |
| or $2,500 per month | 5,000.00 | | |
| Management Fee | | | $20,395.77 |
| **Total Project Fee Expense Per Calculation** | | | **$20,395.77** |
| **Total Project Fee Expense Per General Ledger** | | | $20,389.57 |
| Adjustment for Previous Month | | | ⟨32.70⟩ |
| Adjust Management Fee | | | 38.90 |
| **Management Fee** | | | **$20,395.77** |

# BALANCE SHEET

The software program also produces a balance sheet, essential to the operation of any business. A balance sheet shows the assets of the business, the liabilities and the net worth. The balance sheet would be considered to reflect the operation of the business of renting the real property known as Sunnyvale Manor, not the equity or value of the real estate itself. It would be similar to running a balance sheet on a restaurant. It would not reflect the equity or value of the real estate.

**Balance Sheet**

| | Current Month | Year-To-Date |
|---|---|---|
| **Assets** | | |
| Cash | 8,770.71CR | 146,432.59 |
| Intercompany Receivable | 332,768.05 | 304,854.38 |
| Buildings & Improvements | 6,040.65 | 8,370.46 |
| Accumulated Depreciation | 687.85 | 687.85 |
| Furniture, Equipment and Vehicles | 59.28 | 59.28 |
| Escrowed Taxes and Insurance | 15,105.28 | 25,508.62 |
| **Total Assets** | **317,976.73** | **485,913.18** |
| **Liabilities and Capital** | | |
| Intercompany Payable | 27,913.67 | |
| Notes Payable: Mortgage | 8,816.50 | 17,610.69 |
| Security Deposits | 625.00 | 555.66 |
| Clearing & Suspense | 328,213.22CR | 370,172.22CR |
| **Total Liabilities** | **290,858.05CR** | **352,005.87CR** |
| **Total Liabilities and Capital** | **317,976.73CR** | **485,913.18CR** |

# GENERAL LEDGER

Property Management software also produces a General Ledger (not shown here), with an accounting of all debits and credits going through the business bank account for various periods of time (month-by-month, and Year-To-Date). Based on this information, it produces a bank reconciliation statement which can be compared to the regular monthly bank statements received from the bank. This is another way to keep track of the flow of cash through the business of renting real property.

# MARKET SURVEY

An important service provided by Property Management software is a market survey, comparing the subject property to competing properties in the area. The program breaks the data down by unit, bedrooms, square footage, age, lease terms, deposits, discounts, fees and percent occupied. This enables an owner or manager to know how the property ranks in all of these categories with the competing units in the community.

The following charts were printed out for the subject property.

## Figure 11-1  Market Survey

MARKET SURVEY

MONTH OF:  APRIL, 2002

| | PROPERTY SUNNYVALE MANOR | COMPETITOR #1 | COMPETITOR #2 | COMPETITOR #3 | COMPETITOR #4 | COMPETITOR #5 | COMPETITOR #6 | MARKET AVERAGES |
|---|---|---|---|---|---|---|---|---|
| Age | 1958 | 1972 | 1967 | 1972 | 1960 | 1972 | 1988 | |
| Units | 610 | 192 | 420 | 149 | 358 | 200 | 153 | |
| Utilities | W/T | W/T | W/T/G | W/T | W/T/G | W/G | W/T | |
| Lease Terms | 3,6,12,MTM | 6, MTM | 6,12,MTM | 6,12,MTM | 12,MTM | 6,12,MTM | 6,MTM | |
| Deposits | $200-300 | $300 | $300 | $399 | $350 | $150 | $99 O.A.C. | |
| Fees | $25 app. fee | | | | | | | |
| % Occupied | 93% | 92% | 96% | 95% | 20% | 94% | 74% | |

**STUDIO FLOORPLAN**

| | Subject | Comp #1 | Comp #2 | Comp #3 | Comp #4 | Comp #5 | Comp #6 | Market Avg |
|---|---|---|---|---|---|---|---|---|
| Mkt. Rent | 450 | | | | | 580 | 450 | 515 |
| Sq.Ft | 400 | | | | | 525 | 500 | |
| Rent/Sq.Ft | 1.13 | | | | | 1.10 | 0.90 | |
| Discount | 0 | | | | | 81 | 33 | 57 |
| Grid | | | | | | | | $0 |
| Net Rent | 450 | | | | | 499 | 417 | Disc.Rent $458 / Net Rent $458 |

**1X1 FLOORPLAN**

| | Subject | Comp #1 | Comp #2 | Comp #3 | Comp #4 | Comp #5 | Comp #6 | Market Avg |
|---|---|---|---|---|---|---|---|---|
| Mkt. Rent | 550 | 640 | 675 | 770 | 650 | 680 | 595 | 668 |
| Sq.Ft | 638 | 640 | 700 | 756 | 900 | 680 | 756 | |
| Rent/Sq.Ft | 0.86 | 1.00 | 0.96 | 1.02 | 0.72 | 1.00 | 0.79 | |
| Discount | 0 | 65 | 50 | 62 | 76 | 81 | 33 | 61 |
| Grid | | | | | | | | $0 |
| Net Rent | 550 | 575 | 625 | 708 | 574 | 599 | 562 | Disc.Rent $607 / Net Rent $607 |

**2x1 FLOORPLAN**

| | Subject | Comp #1 | Comp #2 | Comp #3 | Comp #4 | Comp #5 | Comp #6 | Market Avg |
|---|---|---|---|---|---|---|---|---|
| Mkt. Rent | 650 | 790 | 785 | 870 | 650 | | | 773.75 |
| Sq.Ft | 871 | 885 | 830 | 923 | 800 | | | |
| Rent/Sq.Ft | 0.75 | 0.89 | 0.95 | 0.94 | 0.81 | | | |
| Discount | 0 | 25 | 50 | 79 | 76 | | | 57.5 |
| Grid | | | | | | | | $0 |
| Net Rent | 650 | 765 | 735 | 791 | 574 | | | Disc.Rent $716 / Net Rent $716 |

**2x2 FLOORPLAN**

| | Subject | Comp #1 | Comp #2 | Comp #3 | Comp #4 | Comp #5 | Comp #6 | Market Avg |
|---|---|---|---|---|---|---|---|---|
| Mkt. Rent | 795 | | 805 | 900 | 770 | 785 | | 815 |
| Sq.Ft | 935 | | 884 | 923 | 1200 | 1016 | | |
| Rent/Sq.Ft | 0.85 | | 0.91 | 0.98 | 0.64 | 0.77 | | |
| Discount | 0 | | 50 | 84 | 96 | 33 | | 65.75 |
| Grid | | | | | | | | $0 |
| Net Rent | 795 | | 755 | 816 | 674 | 752 | | Disc.Rent 749.25 / Net Rent 749.25 |

**3x1 FLOORPLAN**

| | Subject | Comp #1 | Comp #2 | Comp #3 | Comp #4 | Comp #5 | Comp #6 | Market Avg |
|---|---|---|---|---|---|---|---|---|
| Mkt. Rent | 835 | | 895 | | 895 | | | 895 |
| Sq.Ft | 1092 | | 1032 | | 1300 | | | |
| Rent/Sq.Ft | 0.76 | | 0.87 | | 0.69 | | | |
| Discount | 0 | | 50 | | 117 | | | 83.5 |
| Grid | | | | | | | | $0 |
| Net Rent | 835 | | 845 | | 778 | | | Disc.Rent 811.5 / Net Rent 811.5 |

**CONCESSIONS:**

- **Subject:** None.
- **Competitor #1:** $250 = 1st month's rent on the 1 Bedrooms. $150 off 1st month's rent on the 2 Bedrooms.
- **Competitor #2:** $300 off of 1st month's rent on all floorplans on a 6 mo. lease.
- **Competitor #3:** $399 Move-In Special on a 6 month lease.
- **Competitor #4:** $195 = 1st month's rent on a 12 month lease.
- **Competitor #5:** $81 off each month on a 6 month lease.
- **Competitor #6:** $200 off 1st month's rent on a 6 month lease.

**ADDRESS:**

## Figure 11-2   Rent Rankings: Studio

### HUMPHREY MANAGEMENT SERVICES

#### RENT RANKINGS
(Highest to Lowest)

DATE:   Apr-02

NAME   SUNNYVALE MANOR          UNIT TYPE  STUDIO          SQUARE FOOTAGE   400

| | MARKET RENT | (1) Monthly Rent | DISCOUNTED RENT (Market Rent Less Concessions) | (2) Monthly Conc. | (3) Monthly Rent | ADJUSTED & DISCOUNTED RENT (Market Rent Less Conc. & Amenity Adjustment) | (4) Amenity Adjust. | (5) Net Rent |
|---|---|---|---|---|---|---|---|---|
| | COMMUNITY | | COMMUNITY | | | | | |
| 1 | COMPETITOR #5 | 580 | COMPETITOR #5 | 81 | 499 | COMPETITOR #5 | 0 | 499 |
| 2 | SUNNYVALE MANOR | 450 | SUNNYVALE MANOR | 0 | 450 | SUNNYVALE MANOR | 0 | 450 |
| 3 | COMPETITOR #6 | 450 | COMPETITOR #6 | 33 | 417 | COMPETITOR #6 | 0 | 417 |
| 4 | | | | | | | | |
| 5 | | | | | | | | |
| | AVERAGE | 493 | AVERAGE | 38 | 455 | AVERAGE | 0 | 455 |

(1)  Market Rent - No deductions for discounts
(2)  Average monthly concessions/discounts
(3)  (1) minus (2) (Market Rent minus Monthly Concessions)
(4)  Grid Amenity Adjustment (+ or -)
(5)  (3) plus or minus (4) (Discount Rent + or - Amenity Adjustment)

## Figure 11-3   Rent Rankings: 1 Bedroom/1 Bath

### HUMPHREY MANAGEMENT SERVICES

#### RENT RANKINGS
(Highest to Lowest)

DATE:   Apr-02

NAME   SUNNYVALE MANOR          UNIT TYPE   1X1          SQUARE FOOTAGE   638

| | MARKET RENT | (1) Monthly Rent | DISCOUNTED RENT (Market Rent Less Concessions) | (2) Monthly Conc. | (3) Monthly Rent | ADJUSTED & DISCOUNTED RENT (Market Rent Less Conc. & Amenity Adjustment) | (4) Amenity Adjust. | (5) Net Rent |
|---|---|---|---|---|---|---|---|---|
| | COMMUNITY | | COMMUNITY | | | | | |
| 1 | COMPETITOR #3 | 770 | COMPETITOR #3 | 62 | 708 | COMPETITOR #3 | 0 | 708 |
| 2 | COMPETITOR #5 | 680 | COMPETITOR #2 | 50 | 625 | COMPETITOR #2 | 0 | 625 |
| 3 | COMPETITOR #2 | 675 | COMPETITOR #5 | 81 | 599 | COMPETITOR #5 | 0 | 599 |
| 4 | COMPETITOR #4 | 650 | COMPETITOR #1 | 65 | 575 | COMPETITOR #1 | 0 | 575 |
| 5 | COMPETITOR #1 | 640 | COMPETITOR #4 | 76 | 574 | COMPETITOR #4 | 0 | 574 |
| 6 | COMPETITOR #6 | 595 | COMPETITOR #6 | 33 | 562 | COMPETITOR #6 | 0 | 562 |
| 7 | SUNNYVALE MANOR | 550 | SUNNYVALE MANOR | 0 | 550 | SUNNYVALE MANOR | 0 | 550 |
| 8 | | | | | | | | |
| | AVERAGE | 651 | AVERAGE | 52 | 599 | AVERAGE | 0 | 599 |

(1)  Market Rent - No deductions for discounts
(2)  Average monthly concessions/discounts
(3)  (1) minus (2) (Market Rent minus Monthly Concessions)
(4)  Grid Amenity Adjustment (+ or -)
(5)  (3) plus or minus (4) (Discount Rent + or - Amenity Adjustment)

## Figure 11-4   Rent Rankings: 2 Bedroom/1 Bath

HUMPHREY MANAGEMENT SERVICES

### RENT RANKINGS
(Highest to Lowest)

DATE:   Apr- 02

NAME ___SUNNYVALE MANOR___          UNIT TYPE ___2X1___          SQUARE FOOTAGE ___871___

| | MARKET RENT | (1) Monthly Rent | DISCOUNTED RENT (Market Rent Less Concessions) | (2) Monthly Conc. | (3) Monthly Rent | ADJUSTED & DISCOUNTED RENT (Market Rent Less Conc. & Amenity Adjustment) | (4) Amenity Adjust. | (5) Net Rent |
|---|---|---|---|---|---|---|---|---|
| | COMMUNITY | | COMMUNITY | | | | | |
| 1 | COMPETITOR #3 | 870 | COMPETITOR #3 | 79 | 791 | COMPETITOR #3 | 0 | 791 |
| 2 | COMPETITOR #1 | 790 | COMPETITOR #1 | 25 | 765 | COMPETITOR #1 | 0 | 765 |
| 3 | COMPETITOR #2 | 785 | COMPETITOR #2 | 50 | 735 | COMPETITOR #2 | 0 | 735 |
| 4 | SUNNYVALE MANOR | 650 | SUNNYVALE MANOR | 0 | 650 | SUNNYVALE MANOR | 0 | 650 |
| 5 | COMPETITOR #4 | 650 | COMPETITOR #4 | 76 | 574 | COMPETITOR #4 | 0 | 574 |
| 6 | | | | | | | | |
| 7 | | | | | | | | |
| 8 | | | | | | | | |
| 9 | | | | | | | | |
| 10 | | | | | | | | |
| 11 | | | | | | | | |
| 12 | | | | | | | | |
| 13 | | | | | | | | |
| | AVERAGE | 749 | AVERAGE | 46 | 703 | AVERAGE | 0 | 703 |

(1)  Market Rent - No deductions for discounts
(2)  Average monthly concessions/discounts
(3)  (1) minus (2) (Market Rent minus Monthly Concessions)
(4)  Grid Amenity Adjustment (+ or -)
(5)  (3) plus or minus (4) (Discount Rent + or - Amenity Adjustment)

## Figure 11-5   Rent Rankings: 2 Bedroom/2 Bath

HUMPHREY MANAGEMENT SERVICES

### RENT RANKINGS
(Highest to Lowest)

DATE:   Apr- 02

NAME ___SUNNYVALE MANOR___          UNIT TYPE ___2X2___          SQUARE FOOTAGE ___935___

| | MARKET RENT | (1) Monthly Rent | DISCOUNTED RENT (Market Rent Less Concessions) | (2) Monthly Conc. | (3) Monthly Rent | ADJUSTED & DISCOUNTED RENT (Market Rent Less Conc. & Amenity Adjustment) | (4) Amenity Adjust. | (5) Net Rent |
|---|---|---|---|---|---|---|---|---|
| | COMMUNITY | | COMMUNITY | | | | | |
| 1 | COMPETITOR #3 | 900 | COMPETITOR #3 | 84 | 816 | COMPETITOR #3 | 0 | 816 |
| 2 | COMPETITOR #2 | 805 | SUNNYVALE MANOR | 0 | 795 | SUNNYVALE MANOR | 0 | 795 |
| 3 | SUNNYVALE MANOR | 795 | COMPETITOR #2 | 50 | 755 | COMPETITOR #2 | 0 | 755 |
| 4 | COMPETITOR #6 | 785 | COMPETITOR #6 | 33 | 752 | COMPETITOR #6 | 0 | 752 |
| 5 | COMPETITOR #4 | 770 | COMPETITOR #4 | 96 | 674 | COMPETITOR #4 | 0 | 674 |
| 6 | | | | | | | | |
| 7 | | | | | | | | |
| | AVERAGE | 811 | AVERAGE | 53 | 758 | AVERAGE | 0 | 758 |

(1)  Market Rent - No deductions for discounts
(2)  Average monthly concessions/discounts
(3)  (1) minus (2) (Market Rent minus Monthly Concessions)
(4)  Grid Amenity Adjustment (+ or -)
(5)  (3) plus or minus (4) (Discount Rent + or - Amenity Adjustment)

## Figure 11-6 Rent Rankings: 3 Bedroom/1 Bath

**HUMPHREY MANAGEMENT SERVICES**

**RENT RANKINGS**
(Highest to Lowest)

DATE: Apr-02

NAME    SUNNYVALE MANOR            UNIT TYPE    3X1            SQUARE FOOTAGE    1,092

| | MARKET RENT | (1) Monthly Rent | DISCOUNTED RENT (Market Rent Less Concessions) | (2) Monthly Conc. | (3) Monthly Rent | ADJUSTED & DISCOUNTED RENT (Market Rent Less Conc. & Amenity Adjustment) | (4) Amenity Adjust. | (5) Net Rent |
|---|---|---|---|---|---|---|---|---|
| | COMMUNITY | | COMMUNITY | | | | | |
| 1 | COMPETITOR #2 | 895 | COMPETITOR #2 | 50 | 845 | COMPETITOR #2 | 0 | 845 |
| 2 | COMPETITOR #4 | 895 | SUNNYVALE MANOR | 0 | 835 | SUNNYVALE MANOR | 0 | 835 |
| 3 | SUNNYVALE MANOR | 835 | COMPETITOR #4 | 117 | 778 | COMPETITOR #4 | 0 | 778 |
| 4 | | | | | | | | |
| 5 | | | | | | | | |
| | AVERAGE | 875 | AVERAGE | 56 | 819 | AVERAGE | 0 | 819 |

(1)  Market Rent - No deductions for discounts
(2)  Average monthly concessions/discounts
(3)  (1) minus (2) (Market Rent minus Monthly Concessions)
(4)  Grid Amenity Adjustment (+ or -)
(5)  (3) plus or minus (4) (Discount Rent + or - Amenity Adjustment)

This market survey and rent rankings allow management to see that Sunnyvale Manor is on the low end regarding rental prices. There is room for an increase assuming Sunnyvale Manor's amenities are comparable to higher priced units in the area. The reports also reveal that Sunnyvale Manor offers no rent concessions, whereas all of the competing properties do. If the net rental income after concessions is still higher than the subject property, Sunnyvale Manor may want to consider offering rent concessions to attract new tenants and reap a higher net income.

The systems and reports in this chapter show how much money is coming in and where it's going. It helps a property management company report to ownership on the critical issues they will want to see. It also helps ownership report to the government for tax purposes. It allows ownership and management to plan for improvements and changes. It offers understanding of why variances have occurred and how to correct them. It also offers a view of where the subject property stands in the entire competing marketplace according to key property characteristics. Such systems and reports are invaluable in guiding an income producing property to its maximum performance.

# QUESTIONS

1. Sophisticated software programs exist in property management in order to:

   a. assist property management companies in reporting on vital issues to ownership

   b. assist ownership in reporting to the government for tax purposes

   c. track cash flow

   d. all of the above

2. One thing even a sophisticated software program can't do is:

   a. provide an analysis of why variances occur

   b. give reasons for overages and shortages

   c. give output without input

   d. provide an indication of when a variance is considered significant

3. A Project Operating Report does all of the following except:

   a. compares budget items to actual

   b. offers general ledger accounting

   c. produces a variance analysis

   d. breaks down cash flow into specific categories

4. A Project Operating Report breaks down income into all of the following categories except:

   a. vending machines

   b. general maintenance

   c. laundry

   d. NSF fees

5. Sources of loss of income could come from:

   a. vacancies due to model apartments

   b. late rent fees

   c. forfeited deposits

   d. tenant damage payment

6. Salary expenses can include all of the following except:

    a. management fees
    b. advertising/promotional fees
    c. leasing agent fees
    d. general maintenance fees

7. Maintenance expenses involve which of the following personnel:

    a. porters
    b. managers
    c. leasing agents
    d. security patrol

8. Advertising/promotional expenses could include:

    a. newspaper advertising
    b. brochures
    c. referral fees
    d. all of the above

9. Expenses for hardware and tools would come from which category of expense:

    a. management
    b. maintenance
    c. advertising/promotional
    d. fixed expenses

10. Administrative costs include all of the following except:

    a. office supplies
    b. credit verification fees
    c. turnover costs of blinds
    d. automotive

11. The highest utility expense year to date in Sunnyvale Manor is:

    a. electricity
    b. gas
    c. garbage collection
    d. water

12. Capital expenditures at Sunnyvale Manor include all of the following except:

    a. vinyl and tile
    b. swimming pool
    c. painting
    d. office equipment

13. Actual rent roll figures are less than expected in the budget because:

    a. actual occupancy is higher than the projected number
    b. too many vacancies
    c. not enough rent is being collected from tenants
    d. too many expenses

14. Actual rental income is more than budget because:

    a. funds were transferred to pay previously due invoices
    b. the vacancy rate virtually disappeared
    c. of rental increases
    d. there were no defaults

15. Total salaries varied below budget by 14.9% due to:

    a. one employee quitting
    b. temporary service employees dominating the first quarter
    c. a bookkeeping error of incorrect coding
    d. giving no salary increases

16. Sometimes variances are caused by:

    a. failure to receive an invoice
    b. paying an invoice out of cycle
    c. bookkeeping errors
    d. all of the above

17. A Cash Flow Statement:

    a. states cash flow after debt service, capital expenditures and depreciation
    b. breaks income and expenses down in more detail than a Project Operating Report
    c. ignores current month figures
    d. states cash flow after debt service only

18. A Cash Sources and Uses Statement shows:

    a. beginning cash balance
    b. changes in cash on hand
    c. ending cash balance
    d. all of the above

19. A Balance Sheet shows:

    a. the value of the buildings
    b. the net worth of the business
    c. the equity in the property
    d. the value of the improvements
       and land combined

20. The Market Survey shows:

    a. what competing properties
       charge for rent
    b. where the subject property ranks
       in comparison to competing rentals
    c. comparisons in a number of categories
    d. all of the above

# ANSWERS

1. *d*
2. *c*
3. *b*
4. *b*
5. *a*
6. *b*
7. *a*
8. *d*
9. *b*
10. *c*
11. *d*
12. *b*
13. *b*
14. *a*
15. *c*
16. *d*
17. *a*
18. *d*
19. *b*
20. *d*

# Managing Commercial Property

- What Is Commercial?
- The Marketing Process
- Qualifying The Tenant
- The Lease
- Reports

C H A P T E R 12

# WHAT IS COMMERCIAL?

Commercial property is defined as real property where services are offered or performed. This is in distinction to residential property where people reside, and industrial property where people work. For the purposes of this chapter we will consider both office buildings and retail establishments the main topics of discussion.

## Office Properties

Office buildings can consist of several office units for small businesses or a small professional practice, or they can be high-rise luxury buildings like the World Trade Center in New York.

Modern office buildings today are more than giant file cabinets. They are equipped with systems to facilitate services and communication. The earliest innovations along this line were buildings with automated lighting systems, elevators, safety and security systems. The entire building is wired to accomplish these services.

A more advanced innovation is in the area of telecommunications. Some buildings allow for the reception and transmission of voice and data at the same time. Satellite dishes receive signals from both microwave and satellites. This type of communication can be important for international corporations with satellite offices in various parts of the world.

Another recent development facilitates the communication and transmission of data and word processing within the building. When these services are available in a commercial office building, tenants can be attracted by savings in traditional telephone billing and the appeal of being a part of a state-of-the-art office complex. Technology of this type changes rapidly and unless a property manager works within these technical fields on a daily basis, it's difficult to keep up. Check with colleagues within property management and also computer and technical consultants to stay abreast of new developments in this area of expertise.

Some of the more elaborate office buildings and complexes will have a building or facilities manager on-site who works for the occupying company. This position will coordinate all required services for management and maintenance of the building. If such a complex is occupied by multiple tenants, an on-site facilities manager may have to be put in place by the property management company.

## Retail Centers

Over the years retail centers have changed, with the development of the automobile. In early times the biggest retail centers used to be in the downtown part of the city, at the hub of public transportation systems. As the mobility of the public increased due to the automobile, people began moving to the suburbs for recreation and for places to live. Retail centers of all sizes began to spring up to offer the commercial support facilities that were needed. Now—although commercial and financial districts may co-exist in downtown areas—many people never travel there except to work or visit specific businesses or agencies.

The *strip center* is the smallest of such retail centers. It is located in the suburbs and at the outskirts of the big city areas. It may have half-a-dozen to a dozen small stores of various kinds, usually with a small food mart or liquor store where basic food items can be purchased at 150% of their retail price in most grocery stores. Yet the system works. Why? Convenience! People will spend more money for items they really want right away rather than endure time delays. So the strip center is popular. Other stores in a strip center might be a donut shop or a sandwich shop, where you can pick up something to eat quickly and without hassle. Others might be a dry cleaners or a hardware store. Parking is usually perpendicular right in front of the store, so a quick in and out is the appeal. Strip centers can be one row of stores or they can be in an "L" shape taking up a corner location.

The *neighborhood center* is the next largest size of retail center. The neighborhood center services a neighborhood where a thousand or so households will support it. It has what is called an *anchor store*, usually a grocery store that offers the main reason for patronage, with a supporting cast of more than a dozen other compatible stores. Drug stores, 99-cent stores, dry cleaners, real estate offices, stationery stores and in and out fast food establishments offer a lot of reasons for domestic shopping.

The next largest size of retail center is the *community center*. The community center is anchored by a small department store and is supported by sometimes more than 50 other smaller stores. In addition to general household stores, shoppers can find clothing, food, basic services and specialty shops like gift stores, book stores and music stores. Shoppers for a community center will come from five miles or more and it is generally held that at least 5,000 households are required to support a community center.

A *regional center* is the next largest size of retail center. The term *mall* would apply here and it would offer half a dozen major department stores along with 100 to 200 or more general merchandise and specialty shops. Regional centers also usually include banks, restaurants, food courts and many times theaters. Bakeries and candy shops appeal to a customer's impulsive palate. The wide variety of stores and merchandise offer customers many reasons to come to the mall. Merchants know that if they can display  their merchandise effectively they will benefit from the impulsive purchases of customers who did not know about their establishment. The appeal of the mall is broad and draws many customers, benefiting all merchants. Regional centers of this size draw customers from as far as 50 miles and are usually supported by 50,000 to 150,000 households.

A good-sized regional center is sometimes topped by a *super mall* or *mega center*. The Mall of America in Minnesota or the Edmonton Mall in Edmonton, Alberta, Canada, would be examples of these. They are practically cities under cover of roof and attract shoppers from hundreds of miles around, as well as one-time shoppers who are traveling or vacationing in the area.

# THE MARKETING PROCESS

As in all property management, marketing is a key ingredient in establishing the flow of income in commercial property. Good marketing is done with a thorough understanding of the property, the marketing area and the type of client that will be best suited to the property.

# Property Analysis

Office buildings and retail centers vary widely in characteristics and amenities, which should be clearly understood by the property manager. Your office building may have certain special features that set it apart from many other properties in the area, making it a good match for a business looking for space. For example, if your building offers shared tenant services and has the technological innovations mentioned earlier in this chapter, those features may indeed make it different from other buildings in the marketplace.

Any prospective tenant will be looking for a certain amount of square footage and this should be determined as precisely as possible. The age of the building may be important to tenants. Some tenants will not want an older building with many functional deficiencies. They will insist on state-of-the-art heating and air conditioning systems, modern restroom facilities, elevators and appealing lobbies. Some of this preference will be due to their own desire for comfort for themselves and their employees. Some will be due to the desire to appeal to a certain clientele and to make the right impression. Obviously, the property you have will either match their expectations or it will not. But you must know the amenities and advantages you have to describe them clearly.

Location of office space will be important as it is for all types of real estate. The purpose of an office is to conduct business and the location of the business must be accessible to clients. High

visibility and a prestigious area will help to attract the right type of clientele for certain businesses. For some, location at the juncture of a freeway will make sense, as well as convenient and ample parking. If public transportation is convenient to the area, many clients may take advantage of it, as in New York City, where *not* having a car may be an advantage. The high-rise office buildings of Wall Street suffer no lack of clientele due to a paucity of parking.

Not only must clients find easy access to a commercial office building, there must be a supply of available workers. Is the building near such a work force? Will employees have easy access to the property? Are the amenities of the building sufficiently attractive that workers will want to be employed there? These are factors that must be assessed and presented when marketing the space available in the building.

Safety issues of the building must be analyzed as well. When inviting prospective tenants to view an office building and ultimately occupy it, have you first checked for any physical aspects of the building that might present a safety hazard? Do these have to do with design and items of functional obsolescence, or are parts of the building in various states of disrepair? Safety issues should be resolved before a prospective tenant views the property. Any desirable prospect wants a safe environment for his or her workers and would eliminate any building that would not meet this minimum requirement.

A property manager must also analyze retail centers well. Know the type of retail center that it is and the size of the market area it serves. Know the physical characteristics of the center. Is it an older center or is it modern with state-of-the-art facilities and services? What is the square footage of the available units? What type of client would likely occupy these types of stores? What draws the customers to the center? Is the center highly visible and easily accessible for its type? Are parking accommodations adequate?

Are there too many vacancies in a retail center for it to be appealing to a prospective tenant? A mall that is only half occupied is not very appealing to customers. It bespeaks that something is wrong. Merchants who would be tenants sense this, too. Incentives must be offered to decrease the vacancy rate because the appearance of a fully occupied mall is much more inviting than empty space every other store.

If the retail center is a mall, how is the mall perceived in the community? Is it perceived as a family oriented place that is safe to patronize any time of the day or night? Or have there been problems with crime? All retail establishments experience shoplifting, but there are other types of crimes—shootings, muggings, violent crimes that keep people away in droves. It's not difficult to see if a mall has an undesirable reputation. If so, it may become a hangout for patrons that will not spend the money necessary to support the merchants. They'll use the services of the food courts, restrooms and benches to loiter and intimidate other patrons. But they will not buy clothing, books and appliances.

In this kind of situation, a serious campaign needs to be undertaken to make the center safe *and* change its image. Notice that this is a combination of substance and style. In the above situation, safety and security cannot be denied as an issue. Security and the visibility of security must be increased inside the mall and outside in the parking lot. Prosecutions must take place and perpetrators of crime must come to understand that this particular retail center is not a place where they can expect to get by with criminal behavior.

But secondly, once results are in progress and crime is being reduced, a campaign to change the image of the center must be launched. Perception is everything! The mall could be the safest one in the country, but if the popular perception is that it's a place of trouble, consumers who have money to spend will go elsewhere. That spells a lack of success for the merchants in the mall, which snowballs into the failure of the entire center. Security should establish a presence that bolsters confidence in the safety of the mall. Advertising at bus stops and in the print media should emphasize the family orientation that the mall wishes to promote. Individual merchants should plan family offerings. Collectively the merchants should establish attractions for children and families in the common areas of the mall. The image of the mall can be turned around gradually and prosperity for the tenants and owners of the center can increase. Remember that in any kind of property, failure breeds more failure and success more success.

As a property manager you must look at your property objectively. You are not the owner. You are a professional who must be unbiased in your analysis. You must understand the relative strengths and weaknesses of your property so you can correct what is correctable and market the best you can what is not correctable. But you must know the property.

## Market Analysis

When the property itself is clearly understood, you must analyze the marketplace. What properties are you competing against for tenants? What can you do to make your property more appealing? How can you win the qualified tenant? How does supply and demand stack up relative to your type of property? If we are dealing with commercial office space, how much is available relative to the demand in your community? What is the absorption rate? How long will it take for the marketplace to absorb the available square footage of space? This is determined by past performance in the area. Divide the number of square feet of office space available by how many square feet have been leased in a year and this will give you the number of years supply. Are there any mitigating factors present in today's marketplace that would increase the absorption rate? If supply outpaces demand by a large margin, an aggressive marketing campaign will have to be mounted and incentives may have to be offered. It is important to know the supply and demand for your property type in your area.

What about the economy of the area? Is the unemployment rate high or low? Are businesses moving into the area or away from the area? Are consumers spending more money or are they holding on to what they've got? Do consumers have confidence in the economy or are they cautious of parting with the dollar? How is the business cycle doing? Is the Gross National Product up or down? How's Wall Street doing? What other economic indicators are telling you how business is doing? The economics of property management is going to tell you the affordability of your commercial space in this marketplace at this time.

Economic indicators, of course, must be looked at nationally but also locally. If all indicators appear to be optimistic nationally but there are valid reasons for a local recession, it's the local recession you have to deal with. When new businesses are forming to provide services that are in demand, office space will not stay vacant in the marketplace for long. When consumer demand for goods is high and spending is brisk, merchants will open stores to sell their goods and large corporations will expand their retailing network to take advantage of the consumers' buying pace.

At these times, demand for commercial space will be high. At other times of recession, the renting of commercial space will be sluggish. The market analysis is important so that ownership can be well informed and appropriate strategies for marketing can be developed and implemented.

## Choosing Strategies

If the property we're managing is clearly understood and the global and local marketplace has been accurately assessed, we're ready to adopt an appropriate marketing strategy. We know if it needs to be aggressive or if a routine, systematic approach will get the job done. The best methods historically for marketing commercial property are discussed here.

### SIGNS

Office buildings should have signs placed on the premises. Business owners looking for office space frequently drive by the areas they consider desirable, with the most appealing properties. Having a sign in place is a golden opportunity to let a prospective tenant know that a property is available. Signs for tenants in retail centers will vary. A strip center visible from the street or a neigh-borhood retail center occupying a corner will benefit from a billboard type sign close to the street. This will usually state the size of the space available with a name and phone number. In a regional retail center such as a mall, outside signage looking for new tenants may not be appropriate or effective since marketing is more often a process of targeting a particular type of tenant rather than making a universal appeal, but smaller signs inside the mall may indicate that particular storefront space is available.

### BROCHURES

Brochures are effective in marketing office space because moving the location of a business is an expensive proposition. Businesses are likely to lease for a minimum of three years and there may be a number of owners and managers participate in the decision. The brochure offers the opportunity to make a tasteful and lingering sales presentation to all of the decision makers. For the retail center, brochures also serve to make a dignified presentation of its amenities. The brochure can be targeted to prospective tenants of the type needed in the center and to leasing agents. Rates and lease types should not be offered in the brochure. These can be offered later in person after the advantages of the amenities are established.

**Figure 12-1    Brochure**

# BUILDINGS&FEATURES

FOR THE PROFESSIONAL TENANT LOOKING FOR AN EFFICIENT AND WELL-ORGANIZED WORKING ENVIRONMENT, STANLEY FOLB BUILDINGS OFFER A HOST OF FEATURES. THESE INCLUDE INDIVIDUALLY-ZONED AREAS OF HEATING AND AIR CONDITIONING, NON-GLARE, ENERGY EFFICIENT LIGHTING AND WINDOW TREATMENTS, KEYED FLOOR RESTROOMS AND ATTRACTIVE LANDSCAPING. IN ADDITION, STRICT FIRE CODE CONSTRUCTION WITH COMPLETE SPRINKLER SYSTEM AND EARTHQUAKE CODE COMPLIANCE ENSURE PEACE OF MIND FOR BOTH PEOPLE AND PROPERTY. STEEL CURTAINWALL CONSTRUCTION FURTHER MAXIMIZES INTERIOR SPACE AND OFFERS FLEXIBLE FLOOR PLANS. AS A BONUS, WE'RE LOCATED IN THE LARGEST TOLL-FREE DIALING AREA IN LOS ANGELES.

STANLEY FOLB DEVELOPERS & CONTRACTORS

**Figure 12-2   Brochure**

SUITE OPTIONS

THE EXPERIENCED DESIGN STAFF AT STANLEY FOLB DEVELOPERS CAN CREATE FUNCTIONAL OFFICE SPACE TO APPEAL TO ANY TASTE AND CREATE WHATEVER AMBIANCE THE TENANT DESIRES. A TYPICAL RECEPTION AREA CAN PROVIDE A COMFORTABLE ENVIRONMENT THROUGH THE USE OF SOFT FABRICS, SPOTLIGHTS WITH DIMMERS, NATURAL LIGHTING, COLOR COORDINATED MINI-BLINDS AND PASTEL COLORS. FOR A DIFFERENT LOOK, RECEPTION AREAS CAN BE ACCENTED WITH FRENCH DOORS AND WINDOWS, INCANDESCENT LIGHTING AND ANTIQUE FURNITURE TO PROVIDE A MODERN OFFICE WITH AN EVOCATIVE AMBIANCE. AN EXECUTIVE OFFICE COULD INCLUDE THE USE OF FINE WOOD, PLUSH CARPETING OR FLOOR LENGTH DESIGNER DRAPERIES WITH BLACKOUT DRAPERIES. KITCHENS AND KITCHENETTES FEATURE CUSTOM CABINETRY, PORCELAIN OR STAINLESS STEEL SINKS, CONVENTIONAL OR MICROWAVE OVENS, DISHWASHERS, VENDING MACHINES, BUILT-IN COFFEE SERVICE, IN-LINE WATER FILTERS OR BUILT-IN BOTTLE WATER DISPENSERS.

STANLEY FOLB DEVELOPERS & CONTRACTORS

### PRINT MEDIA ADVERTISING

Display advertising in newspapers can be effective in marketing both office space and space in retail centers. The display advertising should be placed in the major financial newspaper of a local area, in the business or financial section. Managers and executives are likely to read these sections of the paper. If the office complex or retail center is of major size, the property manager could advertise in papers of national distribution, such as *Investors Business Daily* or the *Wall Street Journal*. The display could be similar to the picture on a brochure with some key words highlighting major advantages of the complex. Just enough information should be given to entice the executive to call, not so much that he or she could eliminate the property from contention before even seeing it.

### PRESS RELEASE

In addition to paid display advertising, a media press release is free of charge and can be most effective. Interest the real estate editor of the local newspaper in the renovation or changes that are occurring with your facility, write up an article describing it, and you will generate valuable publicity to your center or building.

### RELATIONSHIPS

So long as quality of service is present, nothing beats relationships. If current tenants, employees of the Chamber of Commerce, utility employees and other managers and executives are willing to refer you and your facility to other business people, that's effective advertising that money can't buy. Some effort should be made on the part of the property manager to be a part of community relations and business organizations, and to stay in touch with contacts. Don't just breeze by people on your way to somewhere. Value them and build relationships. It will help in your business and just make life that much more worthwhile.

### DIRECT MAIL

Direct mail is an effective way to find just the right tenant for an office building or retail center. By watching the newspapers and reading business journals, you can keep abreast of which businesses are moving or expanding and might be in need of new office space. Target them with a letter and a brochure, along with an invitation to preview the property. It is even more essential in a retail center that you have a good mix of retail businesses. One complements another and actually helps the business of the other, while too many

of the same kind diminish the prospects of success. With direct mail you can target the kind of retailer you need in your center who will actually enhance the business of others and stand the best chance for success.

### TELEPHONE

Canvassing by telephone is another way of targeting the exact prospects you're interested in. Again, target businesses that are on the move through growth and expansion. In an office building it is less essential to orchestrate the mix of tenants in your building than it is in a retail center. So for the retail center, target precisely  the types of businesses that will benefit other businesses and the center as a whole. Go to the library and find business directories and reference books for the kind of retailer you're seeking. If you systematically make 20 phone calls a day, you'll make 100 in a week. You're bound to stir up some activity!

### LEASING AGENTS

For retail centers and office space, outside leasing agents can increase the exposure of your facility. You will have to offer them a commission for their services, but how much is vacant space costing you and your clients? Leasing agents are in touch with many qualified prospects and can greatly enhance your possibilities. Call them on the phone. Send them a letter with your commitment to a commission stating the percentage, a specification (spec) sheet detailing the property and the space you have available, and brochures to help in their marketing.

### THE RIGHT MIX

Just a word on the right mix of tenants. Certain businesses are compatible with each other. Drug stores are good to have in the same center as a grocery store. People buy both their products on the same shopping trip and like the convenience of having both stores side by side. It's also convenient if an office building can offer complementary services, though not essential. If a building has attorneys, perhaps accounting services and private investigators would be compatible in the same facility. In a retail center, however, the right mix of merchants is essential to the success of the whole. Too many men's clothing stores dilute the market so that none are profitable. One or two men's clothing stores will work, but they will benefit by the existence of several shoe stores to complement their offerings. A high-tech computer store would benefit from the nearby stationery store providing paper and office supplies. This is why it's important for the property manager to take charge of the situation and market space in a deliberate, targeted manner to ensure that the tenant mix is most beneficial.

## QUALIFYING THE TENANT

Qualifying the tenant for commercial space is the same in principle as qualifying a residential tenant, but the details are different. You want to locate a tenant who will pay the rent on time. But in addition, you want a tenant who will prosper at your location and will enhance the experience of other tenants in the facility.

If the tenant has been in business a long time, it's easy to check his or her references. What are the financial strengths of the tenant? Is the business growing and prospering or is it marginally profitable? Does it offer the kind of business that will thrive in your facility? What is the business's track record of paying the rent in its previous facility? Who are the principals and what is their collective track record?

For a new business you want to be sure there is enough capital behind the business so it will survive during the early, lean periods. Do the principals have enough experience to make the business work? Does the business make sense? Does it embrace a good and progressive idea? Does it provide an essential product or service or is it likely to be doomed from the outset? Property managers can be wrong on this type of assessment, but it must be made. Wild exceptions occur in business, but that's  not the way to bet. Put your money (and your reputation) on the business that is fundamentally sound and stands the best chance of success, as well as enhancing the success of your current collection of businesses and retailers.

## THE LEASE

One thing about commercial tenants that is different from residential tenants is that the commercial tenant, by and large, is a professional client. He or she is renting your space to make

money. They're not just trying to find space to live, they're trying to find space to produce a livelihood. For the most part, that puts them on a different level. You usually don't have to worry about them destroying the property, because that would destroy their ability to produce a livelihood. It would affect their clients and their business, so it wouldn't make sense that they would do that. It's not in their best interest. Sometimes a business will take what appears to be the easy way out when it comes to disposing of pollutants, the expedient way as they see it, and this can cause harm for the property and other tenants. But barring this temporary loss of perspective, commercial tenants usually conduct themselves professionally and in such a manner as to benefit their business.

Because of this, after the selection and qualifying of the right tenant, the most important thing you have to do is secure that tenant to the proper lease terms. Since it's in their best interest to take care of the property and remain in the property on a long term basis, all you need is to set in order the basis for this long term relationship and everything should work.

There aren't too many juicy stories about commercial tenants. One property manager said that they come in with a bang and they go out with a bang, kind of like owning a boat. You've heard the old adage about the two biggest days in boat owners' lives—the day they got their boat and the day they sold it? A lot of stuff happens in between to change their attitudes, but the purpose of the lease is to order the relationship between tenant and owner and all of its details.

One of the important issues of the lease is on what basis shall the tenant pay for the space? Office space is usually rented on a square-foot basis with the tenant paying none, some or all of the expenses of the building. Review the chapter on leases to see the differences here. Whichever way the lease goes in this regard should be clearly spelled out.

Retail space is usually paid on the basis of a minimum rent for the space and location of the tenant and a percentage of the gross. The percentage must be equitable for tenants, that is—it must be within their ability to pay and it must not hit them the hardest when times are tough. Percentage of gross usually meets these requirements. The percentage of gross will vary according to the type of business. An independent drug store will typically pay four to six percent of the gross, a grocery store one percent and a theater as high as 12 percent. It all depends on the type of business. Of course, any combination of base and/or percentage lease can be devised, but always remember that it must be mutually beneficial. Greed on one side or the other will destroy the entire system. If the tenant tries to get something for nothing, the facility will not be able

to provide essential services for the overall prospering of the complex. And if the facility tries to take too much from the business, it destroys the goose that lays the golden egg. We must create a symbiotic relationship, not a parasitic one.

In addition to method of payment, determine important issues such as landlord services, method of dividing the common area and paying for property taxes, which services are paid for by tenant and landlord, what will be allowable uses of the property, insurance, who pays for damage and/or alteration of the property, what happens in the event of default, is the lease assignable, and many other details. The lease on the following pages is illustrative of a general commercial lease and sets forth the terms of many of these issues.

---

**Figure 12-3    Commercial Lease**

# COMMERCIAL LEASE
### (General Form)

1. PARTIES.
   This Lease is made and entered into this _____ of _____,

20____ by and between _____

_____ (hereinafter referred to as ''Landlord'') and

_____

_____ (hereinafter referred to as ''Tenant'').

2. PREMISES.
   Landlord hereby leases to Tenant and Tenant hereby leases from Landlord, on the terms and conditions hereinafter set forth, that certain

real property and the building and other improvements located thereon situated in the City of _____,

County of _____, State of _____, commonly known as

_____
(here insert address)

and described as _____
(here insert legal description)

_____

said real property is hereinafter called the ''Premises'').
3. TERM.
   The term of this Lease shall be for _____, commencing on _____,
                                         (months/years)
and ending on _____, unless sooner terminated as hereinafter provided.
   4. RENT.
   Tenant shall pay to Landlord as rent for the Premises the following sums per month, in advance on the first day of each month during the term of this Lease:

## Figure 12-3 (cont'd.)   Commercial Lease

During the first through _____ year of the term of this Lease, the sum of _____
(e.g. 5th)

_____ ($_____) dollars per month;

During the _____ year through the _____ year of the term of this Lease, the sum of _____
(e.g. 6th)                          (e.g. 10th)

_____ ($_____) dollars per month.

During the _____ year through the _____ year of the term of this Lease, the sum of _____
(e.g. 16th)                         (e.g. 20th)

_____ ($_____) dollars per month.

enant shall pay to Landlord upon the execution of this Lease the sum of _____

$_____) dollars as rent for _____
lent for any period during the term of this Lease which is for less than one (1) month shall be a prorata portion of the monthly installment. Rent shall be payable without notice or demand and without any deduction, off-set, or abatement in lawful money of the United States to the Landlord at the address stated herein for otices or to such other persons or such other places as the Landlord may designate to Tenant in writing.

5. SECURITY DEPOSIT.

Tenant shall deposit with Landlord upon the execution of this Lease the sum of _____

$_____) dollars as a security deposit for the Tenant's faithful performance of the provisions of this Lease. If Tenant fails to pay rent r other charges due hereunder, or otherwise defaults with respect to any provision of this Lease, Landlord may use the security deposit, or any portion of it, to ure the default or compensate Landlord for all damages sustained by Landlord resulting from Tenant's default. Tenant shall immediately on demand pay to andlord the sum equal to that portion of the security deposit expended or applied by Landlord which was provided for in this paragraph so as to maintain the ecurity deposit in the sum initially deposited with Landlord. Landlord shall not be required to keep the security deposit separate from its general account nor shall andlord be required to pay Tenant any interest on the security deposit. If Tenant performs all of Tenant's obligations under this Lease, the security deposit or that ortion thereof which has not previously been applied by the Landlord, shall be returned to Tenant within fourteen (14) days after the expiration of the term of this ease, or after Tenant has vacated the Premises, whichever is later.

6. USE.

Tenant shall use the Premises only for _____

_____

_____

and for no other purpose without the Landlord's prior written consent.

Tenant shall not do, bring or keep anything in or about the Premises that will cause a cancellation of any insurance covering the Premises or the building in which the Premises are located. If the rate of any insurance carried by the Landlord is increased as a result of Tenant's use, Tenant shall pay to Landlord within ten (10) days after written demand from Landlord, the amount of any such increase. Tenant shall comply with all laws concerning the Premises or Tenant's use of the Premises, ncluding without limitation, the obligation at Tenant's cost to alter, maintain, or restore the Premises in compliance and conformity with all laws relating to the :ondition, use, or occupancy of the Premises by Tenant during the term of this Lease. Tenant shall not use or permit the use of the Premises in any manner that will end to create waste or a nuisance or, if there shall be more than one tenant of the building containing the Premises, which shall unreasonably disturb any other tenant.

Tenant hereby accepts the Premises in their condition existing as of the date that Tenant possesses the Premises, subject to all applicable zoning, municipal, :ounty and state laws, ordinances, regulations governing or regulating the use of the Premises and accepts this Lease subject thereto and to all matters disclosed hereby. Tenant hereby acknowledges that neither the Landlord nor the Landlord's agent has made any representation or warranty to Tenant as to the suitability of he Premises for the conduct of Tenant's business.

7. TAXES.

(a) Real Property Taxes.

_____ shall pay all real property taxes and general assessments levied and assessed against the Premises during the term of this Lease. If it shall be Tenant's obligation to pay such real property taxes and assessments hereunder, Landlord shall use its best efforts to cause the Premises to be separately assessed from other real property owned by the Landlord. If Landlord is unable to obtain such a separate assessment, the assessor's evaluation based on the building and other improvements that are a part of the Premises shall be used to determine the real property taxes. If this evaluation is not available, the parties shall equitably allocate the property taxes between the building and other improvements that are a part of the Premises and all buildings and other improvements included in the tax bill. In making the allocation, the parties shall reasonably evaluate the factors to determine the amount of the real property taxes so that the allocation of the building and other improvements that are a part of the Premises will not be less than the ratio of the total number of square feet of the building and other improvements that are a part of the Premises bear to the total number of square feet in all buildings and other improvements included in the tax bill. Real property taxes attributable to land in the Premises shall be determined by the ratio that the total number of square feet in the Premises bears to the total number of square feet of land included in the tax bill.

(b) Personal Property Taxes.

Tenant shall pay prior to the delinquency all taxes assessed against and levied upon the trade fixtures, furnishings, equipment and other personal property of Tenant contained in the Premises. Tenant shall endeavor to cause such trade fixtures, furnishings and equipment and all other personal property to be assessed and billed separately from the property of the Landlord. If any of Tenant's said personal property shall be assessed with Landlord's property, Tenant shall pay to Landlord the taxes attributable to Tenant within ten (10) days after receipt of a written statement from Landlord setting forth the taxes applicable to Tenant's property.

8. UTILITIES.

Tenant shall make all arrangements and pay for all water, gas, heat, light, power, telephone and other utility services supplied to the Premises together with any taxes thereon and for all connection charges. If any such services are not separately metered to Tenant, the Tenant shall pay a reasonable proportion, to be determined by Landlord, of all charges jointly metered with other premises.

9. MAINTENANCE AND REPAIRS.

(a) Landlord's Obligations.

Except as provided in Article 12, and except for damaged caused by any negligent or intentional act or omission of Tenant, Tenant's agents, employees, or invitees, Landlord at its sole cost and expense shall keep in good condition and repair the foundations, exterior walls, and exterior roof of the Premises. Landlord shall also maintain the unexposed electrical, plumbing and sewage systems including, without limitation, those portions of the systems lying outside the Premises; window frames, gutters and down spouts on the building, all sidewalks, landscaping and other improvements that are a part of the Premises or of which the Premises are a part. The Landlord shall also maintain the heating, ventilating and air-conditioning systems servicing the Premises. Landlord shall resurface and restripe the parking area on or adjacent to the Premises when necessary. Landlord shall have thirty (30) days after notice from Tenant to commence to perform its obligations under this Article 9, except that Landlord shall perform its obligations immediately if the nature of the problem presents a hazard or emergency situation. If the Landlord does not perform its obligations within the time limit set forth in this paragraph, Tenant can perform said obligations and shall have the right to be reimbursed for the amount that Tenant actually expends in the performance of Landlord's obligations. If Landlord does not reimburse Tenant within thirty (30) days after demand from Tenant, Tenant's sole remedy shall be to institute suit against the Landlord, and Tenant shall not have the right to withhold from future rent the sums Tenant has expended.

(b) Tenant's Obligations.

Subject to the provisions of Sub-paragraph (a) above and Article 12, Tenant at Tenant's sole cost and expense shall keep in good order, condition and repair the Premises and every part thereof, including, without limitation, all Tenant's personal property, fixtures, signs, store fronts, plate glass, show windows, doors, nterior walls, interior ceiling, and lighting facilities.

If Tenant fails to perform Tenant's obligations as stated herein, Landlord may at its option (but shall not be required to), enter the Premises, after ten (10) lays prior to written notice to Tenant, put the same in good order, condition and repair, and the costs thereof together with interest thereon at the rate of ten (10%) )ercent per annum shall become due and payable as additional rental to Landlord together with Tenant's next rental installment.

## Figure 12-3 (cont'd.)  Commercial Lease

### 10. ALTERATIONS AND ADDITIONS.

(a) Tenant shall not, without the Landlord's prior written consent, make any alterations, improvements or additions in or about the Premises except for non-structural work which does not exceed $1,000.00 in cost. As a condition to giving any such consent, the Landlord may require the Tenant to remove any such alterations, improvements, or additions at the expiration of the term, and to restore the Premises to their prior condition by giving Tenant thirty (30) days written notice prior to the expiration of the term that Landlord requires Tenant to remove any such alterations, improvements or additions that Tenant has made to the Premises. If Landlord so elects, Tenant at its sole cost shall restore the Premises to the condition designated by Landlord in its election before the last day of the term of the Lease.

Before commencing any work relating to the alterations, additions, or improvements affecting the Premises, Tenant shall notify Landlord in writing of the expected date of the commencement of such work so that Landlord can post and record the appropriate notices of non-responsibility to protect Landlord from any mechanic's liens, materialman liens, or any other liens. In any event, Tenant shall pay, when due, all claims for labor and materials furnished to or for Tenant at or for use in the Premises. Tenant shall not permit any mechanic's liens or materialmen's liens to be levied against the Premises for any labor or material furnished to Tenant or claimed to have been furnished to Tenant or Tenant's agents or contractors in connection with work of any character performed or claimed to have been performed on the Premises by or at the direction of Tenant. Tenant shall have the right to assess the validity of any such lien if, immediately on demand by Landlord, Tenant procures and records a lien release bond meeting the requirements of California Civil Code Section 3143 and shall provide for the payment of any sum that the claimant may recover on the claim (together with the costs of suit, if it is recovered in the action).

Unless the Landlord requires their removal as set forth above, all alterations, improvements or additions which are made on the Premises by the Tenant shall become the property of the Landlord and remain upon and be surrendered with the Premises at the expiration of the term. Notwithstanding the provisions of this paragraph, Tenant's trade fixtures, furniture, equipment and other machinery, other than that which is affixed to the Premises so that it cannot be removed without material or structural damage to the Premises, shall remain the property of the Tenant and removed by Tenant at the expiration of the term of this Lease.

### 11. INSURANCE; INDEMNITY.

(a) Fire Insurance.

_____ at its cost shall maintain during the term of this Lease on the Premises a policy or policies of standard fire and extended coverage insurance to the extent of at least ninety (90%) percent of full replacement value thereof. Said insurance policies shall be issued in the names of Landlord and Tenant, as their interests may appear.

Tenant at its cost shall maintain during the term of this Lease on all its personal property, Tenant's improvements, and alterations in or about the Premises, a policy of standard fire and extended coverage insurance, with vandalism and malicious mischief endorsements, to the extent of their full replacement value. The proceeds from any such policy shall be used by Tenant for the replacement of personal property or the restoration of Tenant's improvements or alterations.

(b) Liability Insurance.

Tenant at its sole cost and expense shall maintain during the term of this Lease public liability and property damage insurance with a single combined liability limit of five hundred thousand ($500,000.00) dollars, and property damage limits of not less than one hundred thousand ($100,000.00) dollars, insuring against all liability of Tenant and its authorized representatives arising out of and in connection with Tenant's use or occupancy of the Premises. Both public liability insurance and property damage insurance shall insure performance by Tenant of the indemnity provisions in Sub-paragraph (d) below, but the limits of such insurance shall not, however, limit the liability of Tenant hereunder. Both Landlord and Tenant shall be named as additional insureds, and the policies shall contain cross-liability endorsements. If Tenant shall fail to procure and maintain such insurance the Landlord may, but shall not be required to, procure and maintain same at the expense of Tenant and the cost thereof, together with interest thereon at the rate of ten (10%) percent per annum, shall become due and payable as additional rental to Landlord together with Tenant's next rental installment.

(c) Waiver of Subrogation.

Tenant and Landlord each waives any and all rights of recovery against the other, or against the officers, employees, agents, and representatives of the other, for loss of or damage to such waiving party or its property or the property of others under its control, where such loss or damage is insured against under any insurance policy in force at the time of such loss or damage. Each party shall cause each insurance policy obtained by it hereunder to provide that the insurance company waives all right of recovery by way of subrogation against either party in connection with any damage covered by any such policy

(d) Hold Harmless.

Tenant shall indemnify and hold Landlord harmless from and against any and all claims arising from Tenant's use or occupancy of the Premises or from the conduct of its business or from any activity, work, or things which may be permitted or suffered by Tenant in or about the Premises including all damage, costs, attorney's fees, expenses and liabilities incurred in the defense of any claim or action or proceeding arising therefrom. Except for Landlord's willful or grossly negligent conduct, Tenant hereby assumes all risk of damage to property or injury to person in or about the Premises from any cause, and Tenant hereby waives all claims in respect thereof against Landlord.

(e) Exemption of Landlord from Liability.

Except for Landlord's willful or grossly negligent conduct, Tenant hereby agrees that Landlord shall not be liable for any injury to Tenant's business or loss of income therefrom or for damage to the goods, wares, merchandise, or other property of Tenant, Tenant's employees, invitees, customers or any other person in or about the Premises; nor shall Landlord be liable for injury to the person of Tenant, Tenant's employees, agents, contractors, or invitees, whether such damage or injury is caused by or results from fire, steam, electricity, gas, water or rain, or from the breakage, leakage, obstruction or other defects of pipes, sprinklers, wires, appliances, plumbing, air-conditioning, or lighting fixtures, or from any other cause, whether such damage results from conditions arising upon the Premises or upon other portions of the building in which the Premises are a part, or from any other sources or places. Landlord shall not be liable to Tenant for any damages arising from any act or neglect of any other tenant, if any, of the building in which the Premises are located.

### 12. DAMAGE OR DESTRUCTION.

(a) Damage - Insured.

If, during the term of this Lease, the Premises and/or the building and other improvements in which the Premises are located are totally or partially destroyed rendering the Premises totally or partially inaccesible or unusable, and such damage or destruction was caused by a casualty covered under an insurance policy required to be maintained hereunder, Landlord shall restore the Premises and/or the building and other improvements in which the Premises are located into substantially the same condition as they were in immediately before such damage or destruction, provided that the restoration can be made under the existing laws and can be completed within one hundred twenty (120) working days after the date of such destruction or damage. Such destruction or damage shall not terminate this Lease.

If the restoration cannot be made in said 120 day period, then within fifteen (15) days after the parties hereto determine that the restoration cannot be made in the time stated in this paragraph, Tenant may terminate this Lease immediately by giving notice to Landlord and the Lease will be deemed cancelled as of the date of such damage or destruction. If Tenant fails to terminate this Lease and the restoration is permitted under the existing laws, Landlord, at its option, may terminate this Lease or restore the Premises and/or any other improvements in which the Premises are located within a reasonable time and this Lease shall continue in full force and effect. If the existing laws do not permit the restoration, either party can terminate this Lease immediately by giving notice to the other party.

Notwithstanding the above, if the Tenant is the insuring party and if the insurance proceeds received by Landlord are not sufficient to effect such repair, Landlord shall give notice to Tenant of the amount required in addition to the insurance proceeds to effect such repair. Tenant may, at Tenant's option, contribute the required amount, but upon failure to do so within thirty (30) days following such notice, Landlord's sole remedy shall be, at Landlord's option and with no liability to Tenant, to cancel and terminate this Lease. If Tenant shall contribute such amount to Landlord within said thirty (30) day period, Landlord shall make such repairs as soon as reasonably possible and this Lease shall continue in full force and effect. Tenant shall in no event have any right to reimbursement for any amount so contributed.

(b) Damage - Uninsured.

In the event that the Premises are damaged or destroyed by a casualty which is not covered by the fire and extended coverage insurance which is required to be carried by the party designated in Article 11(a) above, then Landlord shall restore the same; provided that if the damage or destruction is to an extent greater than ten (10%) percent of the then replacement cost of the improvements on the Premises (exclusive of Tenant's trade fixtures and equipment and exclusive of foundations and footings), then Landlord may elect not to restore and to terminate this Lease. Landlord must give to Tenant written notice of its intention not to restore within thirty (30) days from the date of such damage or destruction and, if not given, Landlord shall be deemed to have elected to restore and in such event shall repair any damage as soon as reasonably possible. In the event that Landlord elects to give such notice of Landlord's intention to cancel and terminate this Lease, Tenant shall have the right, within ten (10) days after receipt of such notice, to give written notice to Landlord of Tenant's intention to repair such damage at Tenant's expense, without reimbursement from Landlord, in which event the Lease shall continue in full force and effect and Tenant shall proceed to make such repairs as soon as reasonably possible. If the Tenant does not give such notice within such 10 day period, this Lease shall be cancelled and be deemed terminated as of the date of the occurrence of such damage or destruction.

## Figure 12-3 (cont'd.)   Commercial Lease

(c) Damage Near the End of the Term.

If the Premises are totally or partially destroyed or damaged during the last twelve (12) months of the term of this Lease, Landlord may, at Landlord's option, cancel and terminate this Lease as of the date of the cause of such damage by given written notice to Tenant of Landlord's election to do so within 30 days after the date of the occurrence of such damage; provided, however, that, if the damage or destruction occurs within the last 12 months of the term and if within fifteen (15) days after the date of such damage or destruction Tenant exercises any option to extend the term provided herein, Landlord shall restore the Premises if obligated to do so as provided in subparagraph (a) or (b) above.

(d) Abatement of Rent.

If the Premises are partially or totally destroyed or damaged and Landlord or Tenant repairs or restores them pursuant to the provisions of this Article 12, the rent payable hereunder for the period during which such damage, repair or restoration continues shall be abated in proportion to the degree to which Tenant's reasonable use of the Premises is impaired. Except for the abatement of rent, if any, Tenant shall have no claim against Landlord for any damages suffered by reason of any such damage, destruction, repair or restoration.

(e) Trade Fixtures and Equipment.

If Landlord is required or elects to restore the Premises as provided in this Article, Landlord shall not be required to restore Tenant's improvements, trade fixtures, equipment or alterations made by Tenant, such excluded items being the sole responsibility of Tenant to restore hereunder.

(f) Total Destruction—Multitenant Building.

If the Premises are a part of a multitenant building and there is destruction to the Premises and/or the building of which the Premises are a part that exceeds fifty (50%) percent of the then replacement value of the Premises and/or the building in which the Premises are a part from any cause whether or not covered by the insurance described in Article II above, Landlord may, at its option, elect to terminate this Lease (whether or not the Premises are destroyed) so long as Landlord terminates the leases of all other tenants in the building of which the Premises are a part, effective as of the date of such damage or destruction.

### 13. CONDEMNATION.

If the Premises or any portion thereof are taken by the power of eminent domain, or sold by Landlord under the threat of exercise of said power (all of which is herein referred to as "condemnation"), this Lease shall terminate as to the part so taken as of the date the condemning authority takes title or possession, whichever occurs first. If more than twenty (20%) percent of the floor area of any buildings on the Premises, or more than twenty (20%) percent of the land area of the Premises not covered with buildings, is taken by condemnation, either Landlord or Tenant may terminate this Lease as of the date the condemning authority takes possession by notice in writing of such election within twenty (20) days after Landlord shall have notified Tenant of such taking or, in the absence of such notice, then within twenty (20) days after the condemning authority shall have taken possession.

If this Lease is not terminated by either Landlord or Tenant as provided hereinabove, then it shall remain in full force and effect as to the portion of the Premises remaining, provided that the rental shall be reduced in proportion to the floor area of the buildings taken within the Premises as bears to the total floor area of all buildings located on the Premises. In the event this Lease is not so terminated, then Landlord agrees at Landlord's sole cost and expense, to as soon as reasonably possible restore the Premises to a complete unit of like quality and character as existed prior to the condemnation.

All awards for the taking of any part of the Premises or any payment made under the threat of the exercise of the power of eminent domain shall be the property of the Landlord, whether made as compensation for the diminution of the value of the leasehold or for the taking of the fee or as severance damages; provided, however, that Tenant shall be entitled to any award for loss of or damage to Tenant's trade fixtures and removable personal property.

Each party hereby waives the provisions of Code of Civil Procedure 1265.130 allowing either party to petition the Superior Court to terminate this Lease in the event of a partial taking of the Premises.

Rent shall be abated or reduced during the period from the date of taking until the completion of restoration by Landlord, but all other obligations of Tenant under this Lease shall remain in full force and effect. The abatement or reduction of the rent shall be based on the extent to which the restoration interferes with Tenant's use of the Premises.

### 14. ASSIGNMENT AND SUBLETTING.

Tenant shall not voluntarily or by operation of law assign, transfer, sublet, mortgage, or otherwise transfer or encumber all or any part of Tenant's interest in this Lease or in the Premises without Landlord's prior written consent which consent shall not be unreasonably withheld. Any attempted assignment, transfer, mortgage, encumbrance, or subletting without such consent shall be void and shall constitute a breach of this Lease. If Tenant is a corporation, any dissolution, merger, consolidation or other reorganization of Tenant, or the sale or other transfer of a controlling percentage of the capital stock of Tenant, or the sale of at least fifty-one (51%) percent of the value of the assets of Tenant, shall be deemed a voluntary assignment. The phrase "controlling percentage" means the ownership of, and the right to vote, stock possessing at least fifty-one (51%) percent of the total combined voting power of all classes of Tenant's capital stock issued, outstanding, and entitled to vote for the election of directors. This paragraph shall not apply to corporations the stock of which is traded through an exchange or over the counter.

Regardless of Landlord's consent, no subletting or assignment shall release Tenant of Tenant's obligation to pay the rent and to perform all other obligations to be performed by Tenant hereunder for the term of this Lease. The acceptance of rent by Landlord from any other person shall not be deemed a waiver by Landlord of any provision hereof. Consent to one assignment or subletting shall not be deemed consent to any subsequent assignment or subletting.

### 15. DEFAULT.

(a) Events of Default.

The occurrence of any one or more of the following events shall constitute a default and breach of this Lease by Tenant:

(1) Failure to pay rent when due, if the failure continues for five (5) days after written notice has been given to Tenant.

(2) Abandonment and vacation of the Premises (failure to occupy the Premises for fourteen (14) consecutive days shall be deemed an abandonment and vacation).

(3) Failure to perform any other provision of this Lease if the failure to perform is not cured within thirty (30) days after written notice thereof has been given to Tenant by Landlord. If the default cannot reasonably be cured within said thirty (30) day period, Tenant shall not be in default under this Lease if Tenant commences to cure the default within the thirty (30) day period and diligently prosecutes the same to completion.

(4) The making by Tenant of any general assignment, or general arrangement for the benefit of creditors; the filing by or against Tenant of a petition to have Tenant adjudged a bankrupt or a petition for reorganization or arrangement under any law relating to bankruptcy unless the same is dismissed within sixty (60) days; the appointment of a trustee or receiver to take possession of substantially all of Tenant's assets located at the Premises or of Tenant's interest in the Lease, where possession is not restored to Tenant within thirty (30) days; or the attachment, execution or other judicial seizure of substantially all of Tenant's assets located at the Premises or of Tenant's interest in the Lease, where such seizure is not discharged within thirty (30) days.

Notices given under this paragraph shall specify the alleged default and the applicable lease provisions, and shall demand that Tenant perform the provisions of this Lease of pay the rent that is in arrears as the case may be, within the applicable period of time. No such notice shall be deemed a forfeiture or a termination of this Lease unless Landlord so elects in the notice.

(b) Landlord's Remedies.

The Landlord shall have the following remedies if Tenant commits a default under this Lease. These remedies are not exclusive but are cumulative and in addition to any remedies now or hereafter allowed by law.

Landlord can continue this Lease in full force and effect, and the Lease will continue in effect so long as Landlord does not terminate Tenant's right to possession, and the Landlord shall have the right to collect rent when due. During the period that Tenant is in default, Landlord can enter the Premises and relet them, or any part of them, to third parties for Tenant's account. Tenant shall be liable immediately to the Landlord for all costs the Landlord incurs in reletting the Premises, including, without limitation, brokers' commissions, expenses of remodeling the Premises required by the reletting, and like costs. Reletting can be for a period shorter or longer than the remaining term of this Lease. Tenant shall pay to Landlord the rent due under this Lease on the dates the rent is due, less the rent Landlord receives from any reletting. No act by Landlord allowed by this paragraph shall terminate this Lease unless Landlord notifies Tenant that Landlord elects to terminate this Lease. After Tenant's default and for so long as Landlord has not terminated Tenant's right to possession of the Premises, if Tenant obtains Landlord's consent, Tenant shall have the right to assume or sublet its interest in the Lease, but Tenant shall not be released from liability. Landlord's consent to the proposed assignment or subletting shall not be unreasonably withheld.

If Landlord elects to relet the Premises as provided in this paragraph, any rent that Landlord receives from such reletting shall apply first to the payment of any indebtedness from Tenant to Landlord other than the rent due from Tenant to Landlord; secondly, to all costs, including maintenance, incurred by Landlord in such reletting; and third, to any rent due and unpaid under this Lease. After deducting the payments referred to in this paragraph, any sum remaining from the rent Landlord receives from such reletting shall be held by Landlord and applied in payment of future rent as rent becomes due under this Lease. In no event shall tenant be entitled to any excess rent received by Landlord. If, on the date rent is due under this Lease, the rent received from the reletting is less than the rent due on that date, Tenant shall pay to Landlord, in addition to the remaining rent due, all costs, including maintenance, that Landlord shall have incurred in reletting that remain after applying the rent received from the reletting as provided in this paragraph.

Landlord can, at its option, terminate Tenant's right to possession of the Premises at any time. No act by Landlord other than giving written notice to Tenant shall terminate this Lease. Acts of maintenance, efforts to relet the Premises, or the appointment of a receiver on Landlord's initiative to protect Landlord's interest in this Lease shall not constitute a termination of Tenant's right to possession. In the event of such termination, Landlord has the right to recover from Tenant:

## Figure 12-3 (cont'd.)   Commercial Lease

(1) The worth, at the time of the award, of the unpaid rent that had been earned at the time of the termination of this Lease;

(2) The worth, at the time of the award, of the amount by which the unpaid rent that would have been earned after the date of the termination of this Lease until the time of the award exceeds the amount of the loss of rent that Tenant proves could have been reasonably avoided;

(3) The worth, at the time of the award, of the amount by which the unpaid rent for the balance of the term after the time of the award exceeds the amount of the loss of rent that Tenant proves could have been reasonably avoided; and

(4) Any other amount, including court costs, necessary to compensate Landlord for all detriment proximately caused by Tenant's default.

"The worth at the time of the award," as used in (1) and (2) of this paragraph is to be computed by allowing interest at the maximum rate an individual is permitted by law to charge. "The worth at the time of the award" as referred to in (3) of this paragraph is to be computed by discounting the amount at the discount rate of the Federal Reserve Bank of San Francisco at the time of the award, plus one (1%) percent.

If Tenant is in default under the terms of this Lease, Landlord shall have the additional right to have a receiver appointed to collect rent and conduct Tenant's business. Neither the filing of a petition for the appointment of a receiver nor the appointment itself shall constitute an election by Landlord to terminate this Lease.

Landlord at any time after Tenant commits a default, can cure the default at Tenant's cost and expense. If Landlord at any time, by reason of Tenant's default, pays any sum or does any act that requires the payment of any sum, the sum paid by Landlord shall be due immediately from Tenant to Landlord at the time the sum is paid, and if paid at a later date shall bear interest at the maximum rate an individual is permitted by law to charge from the date the sum is paid by Landlord until Landlord is reimbursed by Tenant. The sum, together with interest thereon, shall be considered additional rent.

**16. SIGNS.**

Tenant shall not have the right to place, construct or maintain any sign, advertisement, awning, banner, or other exterior decorations on the building or other improvements that are a part of the Premises without Landlord's prior, written consent, which consent shall not be unreasonably withheld.

**17. EARLY POSSESSION.**

In the event that the Landlord shall permit Tenant to occupy the Premises prior to the commencement date of the term of this Lease, such occupancy shall be subject to all the provisions of this Lease. Said early possession shall not advance the termination date of this Lease.

**18. SUBORDINATION.**

This Lease, at Landlord's option, shall be subordinate to any ground lease, mortgage, deed of trust, or any other hypothication for security now or hereafter placed upon the real property of which the Premises are a part and to any and all advances made on the security thereof and to all renewal, modifications, and extensions thereof. Notwithstanding any such subordination, Tenant's right to quiet possession of the Premises shall not be disturbed if Tenant is not in default and so long as Tenant shall pay the rent and observe and perform all the other provisions of this Lease, unless this Lease is otherwise terminated pursuant to its terms. If any mortgagee, trustee, or ground lessor shall elect to have this Lease prior to the lien of its mortgage or deed of trust or ground lease, and shall give written notice thereof to Tenant, this Lease shall be deemed prior to such mortgage, deed of trust or ground lease, whether this Lease is dated prior to or subsequent to the date of such mortgage, deed of trust or ground lease, or the date of recording thereof. Tenant agrees to execute any documents required to effect such subordination or to make this Lease prior to the lien of any mortgage, deed of trust, or ground lease, as the case may be, and failing to do so within ten (10) days after written demand from Landlord does hereby make, constitute and irrevocably appoint Landlord as Tenant's attorney in fact and in Tenant's name, place and stead to do so.

**19. SURRENDER.**

On the last day of the term hereof, or on any sooner termination, Tenant shall surrender the Premises to Landlord in good condition, broom clean, ordinary wear and tear accepted. Tenant shall repair any damage to the Premises occasioned by its use thereof, or by the removal of Tenant's trade fixtures, furnishings and equipment which repair shall include the patching and filling of holes and repair of structural damage. Tenant shall remove all of its personal property and fixtures on the Premises prior to the expiration of the term of this Lease and if required by Landlord pursuant to Article 10(a) above, any alterations, improvements or additions made by Tenant to the Premises. If Tenant fails to surrender the Premises to Landlord on the expiration of the Lease as required by this paragraph, Tenant shall hold Landlord harmless from all damages resulting from Tenant's failure to vacate the Premises, including, without limitation, claims made by any succeeding tenant resulting from Tenant's failure to surrender the Premises.

**20. HOLDING OVER.**

If the Tenant, with the Landlord's consent, remains in possession of the Premises after the expiration or termination of the term of this Lease, such possession by Tenant shall be deemed to be a tenancy from month-to-month at a rental in the amount of the last monthly rental plus all other charges payable hereunder, upon all the provisions of this Lease applicable to month-to-month tenancy.

**21. BINDING ON SUCCESSORS AND ASSIGNS.**

The terms, conditions and covenants of this Lease shall be binding upon and shall inure to the benefit of each of the parties hereto, their heirs, personal representatives, successors and assigns.

**22. NOTICES.**

Whenever under this Lease a provision is made for any demand, notice or declaration of any kind, it shall be in writing and served either personally or sent by registered or certified United States mail, postage prepaid, addressed at the addresses as set forth below:

TO LANDLORD AT: _____

_____

_____

_____

TO TENANT AT: _____

_____

_____

_____

Such notice shall be deemed to be received within forty-eight (48) hours from the time of mailing, if mailed as provided for in this paragraph.

**23. LANDLORD'S RIGHT TO INSPECTIONS.**

Landlord and Landlord's agent shall have the right to enter the Premises at reasonable times for the purpose of inspecting same, showing the same to prospective purchasers or lenders, and making such alterations, repairs, improvements or additions to the Premises or to the building of which the Premises are a part as Landlord may deem necessary or desirable. Landlord may at any time place on or about the Premises any ordinary "For Sale" signs and Landlord may at any time during the last one hundred twenty (120) days of the term of this Lease place on or about the Premises any ordinary "For Sale or Lease" signs, all without rebate of rent or liability to Tenant.

**24. CHOICE OF LAW.**

This Lease shall be governed by the laws of the state where the Premises are located.

**25. ATTORNEY'S FEES.**

If either Landlord or Tenant becomes a party to any litigation or arbitration concerning this Lease, the Premises, or the building or other improvements in which the Premises are located, by reason of any act or omission of the other party or its authorized representatives, and not by reason of any act or omission of the party that becomes a party to that litigation or any act or omission of its authorized representatives, the party that causes the other party to become involved in the litigation shall be liable to that party for reasonable attorney's fees and court costs incurred by it in the litigation.

If either party commences an action against the other party arising out of or in connection with this Lease, the prevailing party shall be entitled to have and recover from the losing party reasonable attorney's fees and costs of suit.

**26. LANDLORD'S LIABILITY.**

The term "Landlord" as used in this Lease shall mean only the owner or owners at the time in question of the fee title or a Lessee's interest in a ground lease of the Premises, and in the event of any transfer of such title or interest, Landlord herein named (and in case of any subsequent transfers to the then successor) shall be relieved from and after the date of such transfer of all liability in respect to Landlord's obligations thereafter to be performed. The obligations contained in this Lease to be performed by Landlord shall be binding upon the Landlord's successors and assigns, only during their respective periods of ownership.

**27. WAIVERS.**

No waiver by Landlord of any provision hereof shall be deemed a waiver of any other provision hereof or of any subsequent breach by Tenant of the same or any other provision. Landlord's consent to or approval of any act shall not be deemed to render unnecessary the obtaining of Landlord's consent to or approval of any subsequent act by Tenant. The acceptance of rent hereunder by Landlord shall not be a waiver of any preceding breach by Tenant of any provision hereof, other than the failure of Tenant to pay the particular rent so accepted, regardless of Landlord's knowledge of such preceding breach at the time of its acceptance of such rent.

## Figure 12-3 (cont'd.) Commercial Lease

28. INCORPORATION OF PRIOR AGREEMENTS.

This Lease contains all agreements of the parties with respect to any matter mentioned herein. No prior agreement or understanding pertaining to any such matter shall be effective. This Lease may be modified only in writing, and signed by the parties in interest at the time of such modification.

29. TIME.

Time is of the essence of this Lease.

30. SEVERABILITY.

The unenforceability, invalidity, or illegality of any provision of this Lease shall not render the other provisions hereof unenforceable, invalid or illegal.

31. ESTOPPEL CERTIFICATES.

Each party, within ten (10) days after notice from the other party, shall execute and deliver to the other party a certificate stating that this Lease is unmodified and in full force and effect, or in full force and effect as modified, and stating the modification. The certificate shall also state the amount of minimum monthly rent, the dates to which rent has been paid in advance, and the amount of any security deposit or prepaid rent, if any, as well as acknowledging that there are not, to that party's knowledge, any uncured defaults on the part of the other party, or specifying such defaults, if any, which are claimed. Failure to deliver such a certificate within the ten (10) day period shall be conclusive upon the party failing to deliver the certificate to the benefit of the party requesting the certificate that this Lease is in full force and effect, that there are no uncured defaults hereunder, and has not been modified except as may be represented by the party requesting the certificate.

32. COVENANTS AND CONDITIONS.

Each provision of this Lease performable by Tenant shall be deemed both a covenant and a condition.

33. SINGULAR AND PLURAL.

When required by the context of this Lease, the singular shall include the plural.

34. JOINT AND SEVERAL OBLIGATIONS.

"Party" shall mean Landlord and Tenant; and if more than one person or entity is the Landlord or Tenant, the obligations imposed on that party shall be joint and several.

35. OPTION TO EXTEND.

Provided that Tenant shall not then be in default hereunder, Tenant shall have the option to extend the term of this Lease for _____ additional _____ year periods upon the same terms and conditions herein contained, except for fixed minimum monthly rentals, upon delivery by Tenant to Landlord of written notice of its election to exercise such option(s) at least ninety (90) days prior to the expiration of the original (or extended) term hereof. The parties hereto shall have thirty (30) days after the Landlord receives the option notice in which to agree on the minimum monthly rental during the extended term(s). If the parties agree on the minimum monthly rent for the extended term(s) during the period, they shall immediately execute an amendment to this Lease stating the minimum monthly rent. In the event that there is more than one option to extend the term of this Lease, the parties hereto shall negotiate the minimum monthly rent as set forth herein for each extended term of this Lease. If the parties hereto are unable to agree on the minimum monthly rent for the extended term(s) within said thirty (30) day period, the option notice shall be of no effect and this Lease shall expire at the end of the term. Neither party to this Lease shall have the right to have a court or other third party set the minimum monthly rent.

36. ADDENDUM.

Any addendum attached hereto and either signed or initialled by the parties shall be deemed a part hereof and shall supersede any conflicting terms or provisions contained in this Lease.

The parties hereto have executed this Lease on the date first above written.

LANDLORD:

By: _____

By: _____

TENANT:

By: _____

By: _____

Once a commercial facility is fully leased, the property manager's job is not over. The manager must watch the functioning and well being of the facility. Are the businesses flourishing together? Are they complementing one another? How does the facility look? Is it attracting clientele for the tenants as it should? How is its condition? Are there repairs or maintenance that need to be performed? Are there changes in the environment or marketplace to which the facility needs to respond?

Most retail centers of any size have some sort of merchant association and members promote their facility in an organized and systematic fashion. Does the promotion of the facility need to be changed in some way? Anything the property manager can do to help the tenants prosper not only will be appreciated, it will reflect on the success of the facility and the manager's ability to create success.

# REPORTS

As with any property, regular reports must be generated to ownership to show the cash flow and the operation of the property. Project operating reports breaking down income and expenses give management and ownership information relating to budget and variance from budget. Computerized analyses are performed to offer understanding and insight into the variances. Cash flow statements and cash reconciliation statements are facilitated by the software program. Monthly balance sheets are prepared and year-to-date figures are presented regarding assets and liabilities. Market surveys are also performed based on information provided for the computer and pertaining to competing properties, amenities, rental rates and demand in the area.

# QUESTIONS

1. Commercial property is defined as:

    a. property where people reside
    b. property where manufacturing takes place
    c. property where services are provided
    d. property where products are assembled

2. Modern office buildings today can best be described as:

    a. giant file cabinets
    b. buildings wired to facilitate communications
    c. obsolete
    d. overpriced

3. A facilities manager in a building:

    a. always works for the occupying company
    b. always works for the property management company
    c. coordinates all required services for management and maintenance
    d. works in an off-site office

4. An influence changing the location and nature of retail centers has been:

    a. the development of the automobile
    b. the development of the electric elevator
    c. the proliferation of the credit card
    d. automatic doors

5. The smallest type of retail center is the:

    a. neighborhood center
    b. community center
    c. strip center
    d. corner gas station and mini-mart

6. A regional center:

    a. is comprised of five or six major department stores plus more than 100 smaller stores
    b. draws customers from as far as 50 miles away
    c. is supported by a minimum of 50,000 households
    d. all of the above

7. An anchor store in a retail center is:

    a. a store that deals in boating supplies

    b. a major name recognized store that provides the primary attraction to the center

    c. the least popular store in the center

    d. a store on the bottom floor of a multi-story center

8. For office space to successfully attract clientele it must:

    a. be accessible to the automobile

    b. have ample parking

    c. be accessible to some effective form of transportation

    d. have valet service

9. Tenants in a retail center must be well chosen because:

    a. certain types of retailers complement other types of retailers

    b. the clientele attracted to one retailer helps support another retailer

    c. the goods and services of one retailer may be compatible with those of another retailer

    d. all of the above

10. If a mall has a reputation as being an unsafe place:

    a. there's not much a manager can do

    b. a promotional campaign to change the image must be started immediately

    c. measures must be taken to increase security and reduce crime

    d. people will still shop there because there aren't very many malls

11. Market analysis for commercial property is important because:

    a. a manager must understand if his or her property is in demand or if it is part of an oversupply
    b. a manager must understand what the client is looking for
    c. a manager must understand where the business cycle is as it reflects on demand
    d. all of the above

12. Absorption rate is:

    a. the rate at which water will leach up into the walls of properties located near the coast or in a flood control channel
    b. the ounce per square-foot ratio of water to the industrial mop
    c. a measure of how long the marketplace will take to rent up available square footage of commercial space
    d. the capacity of industrial sponges

13. Marketing commercial property would historically include all of the following methods except:

    a. direct mail
    b. open house
    c. display ads
    d. signs

14. The advantage of a press release over a display ad is:

    a. it carries the endorsement of the media
    b. it is free
    c. it runs continuously
    d. it contains pictures

15. The reason brochures can be effective in marketing office space is:

    a. there may be several executives and managers who will have input into the decision
    b. the move isn't likely to be long-term
    c. they're cheap to print up
    d. b and c above

16. The advantage of using direct mail in marketing retail space is:

    a. a postage stamp is cheap
    b. you can target the kind of tenant you need
    c. the contact with the prospect is accomplished quickly
    d. the prospect responds right away

17. Retail space is usually rented out on the basis of:

    a. price per square foot plus a percentage of the gross
    b. price per cubic foot plus a percentage of the net
    c. price per front foot plus a premium for the location
    d. none of the above

18. The commercial lease is important in order to:

    a. guarantee that the tenant will pay
    b. ensure that there will be no damage to the property
    c. set in order the relationship between landlord and tenant
    d. allow the landlord to keep the security deposit

19. The purpose of a merchant association in a retail center is:

    a. to systematically promote the center
    b. to keep undesirable tenants out
    c. to keep undesirable customers out
    d. to keep the premises clean

20. Software-generated reports on commercial property can do all of the following except:

    a. offer cash flow analysis
    b. compare the property to competition in the marketplace
    c. make economic forecasts
    d. offer balance sheets

# ANSWERS

1. *c*
2. *b*
3. *c*
4. *a*
5. *c*
6. *d*
7. *b*
8. *c*
9. *d*
10. *c*
11. *d*
12. *c*
13. *b*
14. *b*
15. *a*
16. *b*
17. *a*
18. *c*
19. *a*
20. *c*

# Hotels and Motels

- **Hotels—A Brief History**
- **Motels—An Overview**
- **Classifications Of Lodging Establishments**
- **Careers In Hotel/Motel Management**
- **The American Hotel & Motel Association (AH&MA)**

C H A P T E R

**13**

# HOTELS—A BRIEF HISTORY

Places of commercial lodging have existed since times of antiquity. In the days of the Roman Empire before the time of Christ, inns and taverns punctuated the trade routes and roadways, offering weary travelers rest from their journeys and food for their stomachs. At first the accommodations were basic and primitive. A place for shelter, a few winks of sleep, a bit of food—these were all a traveler hoped for far from home. As transportation routes expanded, the inns and taverns followed in anticipation of meeting a basic human need and earning compensation. Taverns with common sleeping areas gradually expanded to inns offering private rooms for the very rich. By the mid-1600s travelers found shelter at hospices, abbeys and other places of worship. The Reformation brought a desire for culture and refinement. The proliferation of roads throughout England in the mid-1600s brought a need for formal *post houses* or inns to accommodate travelers. Again, a common sleeping area was offered to the peasant with private rooms for the rich surrounding a courtyard below.

THE STAR INN :
ALFRISTON:SUSSEX

The proliferation of lodging establishments has always followed the expansion of transportation routes. By the mid-1700s royalty and upper class were traveling to the great cities of Europe including Paris, London, Venice and Rome. They desired sumptuous lodging accommodations, so large structures such as monasteries were converted to lavish hotels with private rooms, ballrooms, gardens, stores and theaters. The Royal Hotel in Plymouth, England, was built with 50 rooms, a theater, ballroom, dining area, lounge and library. This hotel was more luxurious than any that had come before and included the customary large courtyard for the care of horses and coaches. Common bathing facilities were located some distance from the rooms.

In North America, taverns and inns sprang up as needed at the great seaports. Locations such as Boston Harbor and New York Harbor accommodated business and political travelers. As travel inland increased, inns sprang up along the major rivers and roadways. Sometimes they were large private residences with extra rooms where the owner became the proprietor and offered food in addition to lodging.

After the Revolution, the United States became the scene of the development of true *hotels*. The term *hotel* (from the French *hostel* or the Latin *hospitale*) was not a term in wide usage as yet, but the commercial establishment built solely for the purpose of accommodating travelers was coming into its own, as opposed to the temporary conversion of a large house into an inn. The City Hotel in New York was the scene of the first presidential inaugural ball and was expanded from *tavern* status in 1794. In 1809 a 200-room hotel in Boston called the Exchange Coffee House captured the attention of wealthy travelers. In 1826 another impressive hotel was built in Baltimore—Barnum's City Hotel—and received international acclaim.

METROPOLITAN HOTEL

A major step forward in the development of the modern hotel occurred when architect Isaiah Rogers designed the Tremont Hotel in Boston. The Tremont was a 170-room hotel and the first to have a lobby or reception area. Previously occupants would check in at the bar. The Tremont offered gas lights in public areas, an a la carte restaurant, door locks on single and double rooms and indoor private baths equipped with pitchers, soap and wash cloths. The Tremont offered advances in privacy, service and convenience.

Another important innovation of the Tremont Hotel was the method of financing. The Tremont was built on the sale of stock to investors, and this signaled an important method of being able to raise capital for real estate development. Now the size and expense of a large establishment did not have to be forbidding but could be accomplished through a joint effort of investors pooling their capital, a process that would be duplicated many times in the future.

Large hotels continued to flourish, arising in many prominent American and European cities. These hotels grew larger and more luxurious, and were designed to cater to the desires of the affluent. John Jacob Astor of New York, once the wealthiest man in the world from his real estate investments, hired Isaiah Rogers in 1836 to design the Astor House, a five-story, 309-room hotel. As luxurious hotels continued to be built, more and more innovations were added. Emphasis was placed on dining rooms, banquet halls and meeting rooms. Every conceivable amenity was provided to tickle the fancies of guests.

With the advent of the elevator, hotel structures were built taller and the importance of views from the top floors was clearly established. Some people began to live in hotels on a permanent or semi-permanent basis, and suites were established for this purpose. Retail stores were incorporated into the architecture and were visible from the street. Every service that was thought to be of interest to a guest was made available—shoe-shine booths, newspaper sales, transportation services—all of this the lavish end of the scale.

For the more modest traveler, simpler accommodations were still available—the roadway inns, the large homes with rooms to let, the taverns with rooms on the side. The basic and more economical means of lodging existed then and to this day, and rightfully earn their share of the market.

But the luxury hotel was blazing new trails in development, location and elegance—not only for the hotel industry, but for commercial real estate in general. Technological advances were incorporated into luxury hotels before they appeared in other types of commercial properties. Hotels installed the gaslight in private rooms in 1835, central heating in its buildings in 1846, electric lights in public areas in 1882, private bathrooms for each guest room in 1888 and guest room telephones in 1894.

Gas jet

In the 1800s two structural innovations allowed hotels and all commercial edifices to be built larger—elevators and steel frame construction. Elevators were known as *vertical railways* and had been used in the hotel industry for 20 years to transport baggage before they were used for passengers. Just as in office buildings and apartment buildings, this allowed people to conveniently reach the upper floors of a tall structure.

But the structures could not have been made taller had it not been for the new steel-framed construction techniques. Wood-frame buildings had limitations on heights due to lack of stability, and many burned to the ground. Steel-framed skyscrapers built at the turn of the century stand today as a testament to the durability of the new methods. As demand has increased, transportation has expanded, construction methods have been perfected and financing has been made more readily available. Nothing has stood in the way of the proliferation of luxury hotels.

# MOTELS—AN OVERVIEW

As lodging establishments have followed transportation routes and have tried to meet the needs of travelers, it was only a matter of time before some sort of basic accommodations would appear in outlying areas. Between large cities and off major highways, motorists would need a place to stay. America's love affair with the automobile would create a tremendous demand for such lodging. These kinds of accommodations would cater not to the rich, but to middle-America, the vacationing family, the average person who could afford a car and had the time to drive it away from home. The *motel* (a hybrid of *motor* and *hotel*) was born.

The motel was essentially the equivalent of the old post-road inn of the 1800s. In the early 1900s farmers had erected tourist cabins along the first highways to be built. The cabins were built in linear fashion, side by side. In the 1950s, with the automobile in full popularity, some lodging entrepreneurs amplified the concept with automobile travel in mind.

Luxury would not be the object of these establishments. Rather, they would seek efficiency, practicality and simplicity. The motorist would be able to exit and re-enter the highway quickly and conveniently. The car would be parked right near the motel room door for ease in loading and unloading. Rooms would be equipped with the essential conveniences—two double beds, dresser, phone, fully equipped bath, table and chairs. Many motels would have pools. Though motels range in prices and quality, appointments are basically simple, absent the costly amenities that drive up the prices in the luxury hotel.

In addition to the simple appointments characteristic of motels, another reason costs can be kept at a minimum is the relatively low cost of land. Luxury hotels are built where the action is—in the big cities and in resort areas where the land is most expensive. Motels make their home out in the middle of nowhere, where motorists find themselves in transit. Land in these locations is cheaper, allowing owners to cut costs and keep prices lower.

 Other services that naturally cluster around motels are automobile service stations and restaurants. Sometimes motel owners will operate a restaurant in conjunction with the motel, but more often than not this is a separate establishment, willingly offered by an experienced entrepreneur eager to take advantage of the built-in demand of one or more busy motels. Service stations, sometimes combined with mini-marts and/or fast food establishments, also usually stand by themselves, strategically located in close proximity to a cluster of motels, but not operated by the same entrepreneur. These kinds of establishments help one another obtain business. The restaurants and service stations obviously feed off the guests in the motel, but sometimes the reverse is true as well. A motorist may stop for gasoline or food, and after getting out of the car for awhile, decide to stay and rest for the night.

Motels can be operated by a single independent entrepreneur, but many have become part of large nationwide chains. Franchises and chains allow for a standardized management plan and a duplication of marketing and operations procedures that have been proven to be effective. They also benefit from combined marketing efforts and the name recognition that comes from being nationally known.

Franchise name recognition has proven effective in many types of businesses all over the world including fast food, printing, plumbing and cleaning services, and last but not least, lodging. The appeal to the buying public seems to be a familiarity with the product and services even though the customer may be in a different part of the country or world. There is a sense with the public that if the motel bears a familiar name, the guest knows what to expect in terms of quality, cleanliness and service. There is built-in confidence through pre-selling and experience, and this pays off on the road.

Alliance with various associations for quality assurance and marketing purposes is another way for a motel to achieve acceptance with the traveling public. Organizations like the Automobile Association of America (AAA) inspect motels and publish their names and rates in a special catalog provided for their members when a certain standard of quality is met. Inclusion in the catalog is like a recommendation from a trusted friend, and as with franchise name recognition, travelers feel a little more confident with the referral. They also receive a discount upon presentation of their membership card.

While independent entrepreneurs can benefit from membership in these kinds of associations, the vast majority of commercial motels are franchise operations. It's difficult to compete with automatic name recognition.

# CLASSIFICATIONS OF LODGING ESTABLISHMENTS

In the not too distant past, it used to be fairly easy to classify lodging establishments. They were divided as follows.

## Commercial

These types cater to the transient clients, the business travelers, salespeople, tourists and commercial travelers.

## Residential

These hotels provide lodging for permanent and semi-permanent residents.

## Resort

These types of hotels are large and lavish, catering to the wealthy vacationer or business person. They began largely as spas that attracted wealthy vacationers in the summer. Their share of the market has expanded, however, and today they emphasize one or more forms of recreation, such as a golf course, swimming, boating, dancing, horseback riding or fishing. To attract the business and corporate client, they often are equipped with state-of-the-art conference rooms offering computer, audio-visual and other technical services.

## Blended Classifications

The difficulty now in classifying lodging establishments is that so many have blended their marketing and their amenities. The goal of hotel managers is to minimize the seasonal fluctuation in their business. One way to do that is to cross markets. When one category of clientele is not available, make sure that another is. Many hotels that previously would have been classified as *commercial* have allocated part of their rooms to permanent and semi-permanent residents, crossing classifications and increasing their market.

Corporations are often attracted to the resort hotel for business conferences so that business and recreation can be accomplished at the same time. Resort hotels that offer state-of-the-art conference rooms have responded to this demand. Commercial hotels catering to the transient population but not offering recreational amenities lose much of their corporate clientele.

When classifying hotels today, several criteria are taken into consideration.

### FACILITIES

What facilities does the hotel have? How many rooms? What kind of rooms are they? Suites? Single bedrooms? Double rooms? What is the conference room capacity? How many restaurants does a hotel have and what is their capacity? What is the overall meeting space? What is the size of the ballroom? Are the grounds designed to accommodate certain activities? Is there a golf course? Is the landscaping lavish? Does the hotel sport a distinguished art collection?

### LEVEL OF SERVICE

What is the level of service offered by the hotel? If full service, the hotel offers room service, bellmen, concierge, restaurants, a conference center for business clients, banquet rooms and transportation services. Other hotels find that full service is beyond the scope of what they can offer and they have limitations on what they offer—sometimes imposed by limited facilities, sometimes by budget and personnel. These hotels may offer only a simple room and little more.

## LOCATION

Location is another criteria for the classification of hotels. Is the hotel located near a major airport? Is it in a resort community, such as a seaside or mountain location? Is it in a downtown area or in a suburban location? Whatever the attraction is for the location will help determine the clientele it attracts and the services it offers.

# Modern-Day Hybrids

These criteria blend together to form more than 100 classification systems used around the world. In addition to the previously mentioned basic three classifications, the following hybrids have emerged.

### THE AIRPORT HOTEL

The airport hotel used to be a simple accommodation to meet travelers' needs at the beginning or end of a journey. They have now expanded, however, to include conference rooms, fitness centers and restaurants to serve as the destination point for business meetings and conferences rather than just a way station. They are usually part of large commercial real estate developments with clusters of hotels and office buildings. An airport hotel today would often have 300 to 400 rooms, be 10 or 20 stories high and be considered a full-service hotel.

### THE SUBURBAN HOTEL

The suburban hotel is within driving distance of the downtown area of a large city, but is located out on the highway amongst the smaller suburban cities surrounding the major population center. In close proximity to the suburban hotel are office buildings. The hotel will attract business clientele with its complete array of business services including conference rooms, computer hookups, audio-visual equipment and communication capabilities. This type of hotel is also positioned to attract the casual vacationer traveling the highways in the area.

### THE DOWNTOWN HOTEL

The downtown hotel is usually older and somewhat limited in space. Though it may modernize to the extent of offering state-of-the-art communications systems for the business traveler, it is difficult in a downtown location to expand facilities to include large banquet halls or conference rooms when that space has not already been allocated. Consequently, the downtown hotel may offer luxury amenities for the individual traveler, but its ability to appeal to groups is limited.

### THE CONVENTION HOTEL

As the name suggests, the convention hotel is large, designed to accommodate several thousand guests for attendance at conventions. This type of hotel will have large banquet facilities, conference rooms, lobby areas and extra elevator capacity. Its design is to move large amounts of people around the hotel for meetings, dining, entertainment and lodging and to do that with ease and convenience. These types of hotels, including some large chains such as Marriott, Sheraton and Hilton, have found conventions to be a significant profit center and have targeted this specific market.

### THE ALL-SUITE HOTEL

This classification is named primarily because of its facilities. It offers full suites to guests, similar to a furnished one-bedroom apartment, some with mini-kitchens. The suites are approximately 500 square feet in size and there may be 200 or 300 suites per good-sized, first class hotel. These hotels cater to extended-stay residents, business and vacation travelers. They are located in suburban areas within driving distance from heavy population centers. Because most of the square footage is devoted to private room space, there is a minimum of public area. Lobbies are small and the facility may be supported with the services of a single restaurant.

## Distinct Specialties

With blended services and combined market shares among many hotel facilities, some distinct specialties still exist within the lodging industry.

### THE BED AND BREAKFAST INN

The bed and breakfast inn is usually converted from a large home or older hotel in a secluded area. The purpose is to offer a change of pace, a get-away experience generally for a couple while affording comfortable surroundings and maximum privacy. Breakfast is usually served in a nicely furnished dining room and the guests are left to themselves for the rest of the day. They can travel in the local area or just relax and enjoy the ambiance of the inn. B&B's, as they're called, usually capture a certain style or period, such as Colonial, Renaissance, Country or New England. The atmosphere is supported by the authenticity of the architecture, furnishings and artwork.

## PERIOD HOTELS AND INNS

The purpose of some hotels and inns is to convey the sense of a particular period of time in history. While their services are more extensive in scope than those of the bed & breakfast inn, the sense of culture and history is paramount to the experience of enjoying the hotel. Furnishings, architecture, artwork and even uniforms worn by hotel workers help reinforce the total cultural experience. The Bellevue-Stratford Hotel in Philadelphia, built in the 19th Century, was carefully restored to capture that period. The Hotel del Coronado in San Diego County captures the Victorian Age and attracts vacationers interested in experiencing that period in history.

## TOURIST HOUSES

Tourist houses are situated in suburban and rural areas to accommodate tourists seeking to economize. They may be on a bus tour or touring by private automobile, taking in a large area of the country and needing affordable lodging. Accommodations are found in private homes with rooms to rent. Meals are usually served in the dining room and the tourist saves money over more commercial lodging establishments. At the same time guests see first hand the culture of a part of the world heretofore unfamiliar to them.

## MOTOR CAMPS

Across the country there are chains of campgrounds such as KOA where motorists and recreational vehicle drivers can pull in for the night or for an extended stay. They can hook up their campers or RVs to power sources, service their vehicles and rest for any period of time. Many motor travelers plan their route according to the location of these camps. Economical and efficient, practical and with no frills, they offer the traveler the necessities and the respite needed after long hard hours on the road.

### GUEST RANCHES

Guest ranches, previously called "dude ranches," provide a unique vacation experience as guests live on a ranch property for a week to two weeks while participating in ranch life. The guest voluntarily engages in "work" style activities such as herding cattle, branding calves, riding horses, feeding the livestock and going on cattle drives. This is a change of pace for the guest and usually is considered rehabilitative, while the ranch hand probably vacations in the city. Food is an important part of the experience and generally is plentiful and well prepared. The immersion in an entire new lifestyle offers the rejuvenation the vacationer seeks.

### TIMESHARES

A specialized type of resort hotel is the timeshare. Owners of a timeshare purchase the right to occupy the space, whether a condominium or a hotel room, for a certain period of time during the year. Timeshares are usually sold by the week, but an individual or family could own multiple weeks. The properties are usually located in desirable vacation spots, such as beaches, lakes or mountains. Timeshare sales in the United States are up by 17% in the last five years due to the stable performance of existing time share management companies and the entrance into the market of well-known lodging companies such as Disney, Marriott, Sheraton, Hilton and Hyatt.

# CAREERS IN HOTEL/MOTEL MANAGEMENT

Career opportunities in the hotel/motel industry are clearly a reflection of the size and growth rate of the industry. The hotel/motel industry takes in more than a billion dollars a day in the United States alone. In 1998 there were approximately 46,000 hotels and motels offering about 3.5 million guest rooms. Most of the rooms are found in motels and suburban hotels, with 80% of the rooms in the suburbs and along the highways.

When the general public thinks of hotels, it may think of the large luxury hotels with thousands of rooms. While these are certainly in demand in resort areas, many career opportunities exist in a much smaller work environment. A breakdown of the U.S. properties and rooms follows.

## Figure 13-1   U.S. Property/Room Breakdown: 1998

| By Type of Facility | Property | Rooms |
|---|---|---|
| Urban | 5.4% | 14.3% |
| Suburban | 40.4% | 35.1% |
| Highway | 47.7% | 33.6% |
| Airport | 2.6% | 6.4% |
| Resort | 3.9% | 10.6% |

| By Rate | Property | Rooms |
|---|---|---|
| Under $30.00 | 26.8% | 8.2% |
| $30 – $44.99 | 28.0% | 17.1% |
| $45 – $59.99 | 16.3% | 17.9% |
| $60 – $85 | 15.1% | 22.0% |
| Over $85 | 13.0% | 34.8% |

| By Size | Property | Rooms |
|---|---|---|
| Under 75 rooms | 66.8% | 25.5% |
| 75 – 149 rooms | 21.5% | 30.8% |
| 150 – 299 rooms | 8.6% | 22.6% |
| Over 299 rooms | 3.1% | 21.4% |

Worldwide, in 1994 there were approximately 11.3 million hotel rooms with 70% of them in the United States and Europe. The number increases approximately 2% per year. Large chains dominate the hotel industry. In 1996, the five leading worldwide hotel chains controlled more than 13% of the rooms available.

The lodging industry is one of the world's largest. According to the American Hotel & Motel Association, travel and tourism (lodging plus related service businesses such as restaurants, airlines, cruise lines, car rental firms, travel agents and tour operators) *is* the world's largest industry, producing $3.6 trillion of gross output in 1998 and generating 10.7% of the world's gross domestic product. The industry employs 225 million workers worldwide and expects to add another 130 million jobs by the year 2006. More than 1 billion people are expected to be traveling worldwide by that year, and international tourism receipts are expected to increase to $7.1 trillion.

According to the U.S. Department of Labor, the total number of people employed by the lodging industry in this country in 2005 is expected to be nearly 2 million, up from 1.6 million in 1998.

A survey by the American Hotel & Motel Association indicates that there are about 30 employees per hotel in smaller properties of about 100 rooms, and about 55 employees per hotel in larger properties with 150 rooms or more. The median is 42 full- and part-time employees per 100 rooms, and this matches the national average.

With so many positions available within the scope of the industry, any employee can be assured of the opportunity for a rewarding career and rapid advancement. Positions are available part-time or full-time, day, swing or night shift, skilled or unskilled, technical or non-technical and seasonal or year-round in any type of lodging available. Consider the following partial list of positions available.

### Positions in the Hotel Industry

| | |
|---|---|
| General Manager | Assistant Manager |
| Banquet Director | Housekeeper |
| Reservation Clerk | Room Clerk |
| Rack Clerk | Key Clerk |
| Mail Clerk | Floor Clerk |
| Superintendent of Service | Bell Captain |
| Bellhop | Concierge |
| Door Attendant | Porter |
| Page | Washroom Attendant |
| Valet | Elevator Operator |

## Positions Defined

A brief definition of the functions of the above positions follows.

### GENERAL MANAGER

The general manager is in charge of all of the departments of the hotel. He or she is over each department manager and must ensure that each department interacts and coordinates with other departments as appropriate. The financial management of the entire hotel is in the hands of the general manager, who reports to ownership or the management company operating the hotel.

## ASSISTANT MANAGER

The assistant manager relieves the general manager of any duties so directed by the general manager. The assistant manager interfaces with department heads and reports directly to the general manager. Assistant managers are grooming themselves to become general managers.

## BANQUET DIRECTOR

The banquet director is in charge of all of the physical aspects of a banquet room's availability, food service, tables, chairs, linens, waiters and waitresses. Such an individual would rise through the ranks of food service.

## SUPERINTENDENT OF SERVICE

The superintendent of service is the supervisor of all front office service personnel, including bellhops, porters, door attendants, elevator operators and various kinds of support staff. The superintendent conducts interviews, hires, fires and performs the duties of a personnel director for service personnel.

## CLERK

There are many detailed functions that need attention, and the larger the facility, the more specialized clerk functions there would be. In a large hotel, some clerks are needed for reservations, some for the delivery of mail, some to keep track of keys, some for the coat rack and some for floor activities. Being a clerk in charge of a specific function is an opportunity to prove oneself in service to others, to learn much about the operation of a hotel, and to position oneself for advancement.

## BELL CAPTAIN

The bell captain is the second ranking job in the service department. The bell captain is in charge of the bellhops, assigns bellhops to calls, instructs and critiques them, interviews, and has an influence in the hiring and firing. He or she also investigates customers' complaints.

### BELLHOP

This position is one of the most important contacts a guest may have at the hotel, as first impressions are generally lasting ones. The bellhop ushers the guests to their rooms, transports their baggage, hangs clothes in closets, ensures that the thermostat is properly set, and provides information about the local area.

### DOOR ATTENDANT

In large, formal hotels the door attendant assists guests through entrances and exits, keeps foot traffic moving, and provides directions and information to any guests who ask. In addition, this person is an ambassador of good will for the hotel.

### PORTER

A porter is a baggage handler, one who rushes luggage to rooms via freight elevators and sees to it that large amounts of luggage or heavy pieces are not lost, but promptly delivered.

### PAGE

In a large, formal hotel, a page is an employee who delivers a message or summons a guest from a crowded hotel lobby.

### WASHROOM ATTENDANT

In a large, formal hotel, a washroom attendant is an employee whose constant attention ensures that the facilities are clean and properly supplied, and that the guest's every need is met.

### CONCIERGE

Originally a hospitality service, the concierge makes special arrangements for guests, including procuring tickets for entertainment events, arranging for limousine service and handling other special request items.

### VALET

The valet receives a guest's automobile at the front door, parks it safely and retrieves it when the guest is ready to leave.

**HOUSEKEEPER**

The housekeeper cleans the rooms, changes linens and towels, replenishes supplies and generally makes the room ready for its next guests.

**ELEVATOR OPERATOR**

Still an integral part of some of the larger and older hotel operations, the elevator operator's main function is to keep traffic moving through the hotel as quickly as possible.

The smaller the hotel, the fewer employees it will have. The functions necessary to accomplish its range of service will be consolidated into the job descriptions that it has. Thus, the assistant manager may find himself or herself functioning as the page, porter, bell captain, clerk and concierge all at the same time.

The larger the hotel, the more employees it will need. Thus, each position mentioned may have numerous employees filling it and have various supervisors and assistants helping to carry off the function well. The prior list barely scratches the surface for a large hotel.

In addition to salaried in-house positions, there are numerous related trades and professions that service the lodging industry. Some of these services are provided in-house in some of the larger establishments. Other facilities find it more feasible to sub-contract the services and bring them in when needed. Listed here are some of these related fields.

**Related Trades and Professions**

| | |
|---|---|
| Entertainment | Chefs |
| Sales | Printing |
| Computers | Transportation |
| Telecommunications | Contractors |
| Skilled Labor | Architects |
| Travel Agents | Communications Systems |
| Engineers | Accounting |
| Legal Services | Environmental |
| Advertising | Public Relations |

# Characteristics of Employees

With such a large industry integrating the services of so many fields, an ambitious person cannot help but see opportunity. But an employee who would be successful in the lodging industry must have certain characteristics. Consider the ones listed here.

### LIKE PEOPLE

To have a successful career in the lodging industry an individual must like people. People are what it's all about. In any lodging establishment you will constantly be surrounded by people—guests and co-workers. You will interact with all kinds of people—happy people and sad people, smiling people and angry people, English-speaking people and non-English-speaking people. People, people, people. One assistant hotel manager, when asked what she liked most about her job, responded simply, "People!" If you don't like people, there are other careers you could develop, like an actuary or a statistician. But to work in the hotel industry, you must find people interesting, stimulating and likeable.

### DESIRE TO SERVE

Working in a hotel serving people is an opportunity to make a real difference in guests' experiences on their journey. Helping them get to their room, helping them find a piece of lost luggage, helping them secure transportation, helping them find their destination—all of these may seem routine after years of working in the industry, but they mean a lot to a guest who is far from home and on a tight schedule or budget. A hotel manager, when asked what the biggest challenge of his job was, answered, "Taking a bad situation and making a good one out of it." Therein lies not only the biggest challenge, but also the greatest satisfaction. That's service.

### ATTITUDE

Attitude is everything in everything. It's no different in the hotel business. If your attitude is to give, serve and work hard, there is a great career ahead for you in lodging. If you're willing to go the extra mile for people, the world is at your feet. If your approach to this work is to withhold, resist, and get by with as little as you can do, you will not last long in the hotel business. A great attitude brings great rewards.

## ATTENTION TO DETAIL

Attention to detail is important in the hotel business. Guests are sometimes most upset over the little things—special requests that were forgotten, a missing glass, the taxi that wasn't called on time, the food order that left out a small but important item. Attention to detail will win praise and compliments. Inattention to it will ensure that guests will not return.

## GROOMING AND NEATNESS

A hotel employee must present himself or herself to be neat and well-groomed. The hotel facilities look sharp and clean, don't they? Each employee must exemplify the same characteristics. An unkempt and sloppy employee would look out of place in the lobby of an elegant hotel and such a presence would send a mixed message to guests. Neatness and good grooming counts!

## A READY SMILE

A smile brightens every face! The entire countenance changes when a smile breaks forth! A smiling employee says nonverbally, "I'm glad you're here. I'm happy to serve you, and I'll do my very best to see to it that your every need is met." For a successful career in the hotel industry, make smiling a habit!

## RESERVED MANNER

A hotel employee assisting guests should be friendly, but have a reserved manner. This allows the guest every opportunity to communicate and make his or her needs known. It also makes the guest feel safe to make requests and ask questions. The employee should do more listening than talking. An employee who is too talkative or imposes his or her will on the guest with an overbearing personality will not be able to render the desirable level of service.

## UNDERSTANDING AND TOLERANCE

A hotel employee must be understanding and tolerant. Remember, the object is to serve people, and those people will come from all geographical areas and cultural backgrounds. Customs and expectations may be different where they come from. Being understanding and tolerant will help the employee to meet the guests' needs and resolve any problems.

## SELF-STARTER

In the hotel business, an employee must be a self-starter. He or she must be intelligent enough to grasp the scope of the position and respond quickly and sometimes even anticipate the demands. If employees wait to be told everything that must be done, it's too late.

### WILLING TO LEARN

There are many things that must be learned in the hotel industry to be an effective and useful employee. First, an employee should learn every aspect of his or her current job and how it relates to other departments in the hotel. They should keep abreast of the industry changes and trends. Taking courses at a local college or through the Educational Institute of the American Hotel & Motel Association would assist in this knowledge. Learning a second language would be extremely useful. Spanish is widely spoken in the western hemisphere and French is an international language. Knowledge of world geography, politics and history also would be helpful in relating to guests from all over the world.

## Benefits of a Lodging Industry Career

The benefits of a successful career in the lodging industry are too numerous and too individual to ever compile a complete list. The list here represents some reasons others have found such a career rewarding.

### FAST-PACED

No one can deny that working in a hotel or motel is fast paced. These establishments are open 24 hours a day, seven days a week. There's a lot of work to be done, and with people coming and going, you never know what's going to challenge you next. That appeals to a lot of people.

### SERVE PEOPLE

The opportunity to offer service to people, many feel, is the greatest reason to pursue a career.

### MEET PEOPLE

The opportunity to meet interesting people from all over the world is one that is not available in every career.

### TRAVEL

Remember that the hotel/motel industry is dominated by chains. Establish a good work record, learn another language, make yourself valuable and you could live and work in any part of the world you desire. You also might attain a position that afforded you the opportunity to visit hotels all over the world—if that's your wish!

### PLEASANT SURROUNDINGS

The opportunity to work in elegant surroundings where the marble entry way sparkles, sunlight glistens through the giant windows of a majestic atrium, courtyards effuse lush green leaves and bright flowers, this opportunity doesn't come to everyone. But it could be yours if you choose to work in a luxury hotel. Somebody has to—it might as well be you!

### ADVANCEMENT

Few industries are so wide open for advancement as the lodging industry. If you're willing to work hard and learn, nothing can hold you back. Over a million jobs and constant turnover assures opportunity for anyone who wants it.

### FRINGE BENEFITS

Many positions offer full benefit packages. In addition to insurance and retirement plans, some employees receive a complimentary meal each day and a room. Added to a competitive salary and tips (for some positions) the compensation package is quite beneficial.

### FLEXIBLE HOURS

For someone starting out in the hotel industry, part-time work is available with three different shifts to choose from. An individual can go to school and arrange hours compatible with a family and school schedule to see if he or she likes hotel work.

# THE AMERICAN HOTEL & MOTEL ASSOCIATION (AH&MA)

The American Hotel & Motel Association (AH&MA) is the only trade association representing the lodging industry. It was founded in Chicago in 1910 and is a federation of hotel and motel associations located in the 50 states, the District of Columbia, Puerto Rico and the U.S. Virgin Islands.

# The American Hotel & Motel Association

1201 New York Avenue, NW, #600
Washington, D.C. 20005-3931
(202) 289-3100 Voice
(202) 289-3199 Fax

Web site address: **http://www.ahma.com**

The AH&MA establishes a strong presence in Washington, D.C., lobbying Congress on issues that affect the lodging industry. The organization believes that the biggest danger to the industry is government interference and its leaders are dedicated to preventing it. The group is organized with departments for communications, government affairs, conventions, corporate relations, allied membership, information and member relations.

The AH&MA also has over 30 committees that provide leadership and guidance in developing programs and activities of value to association members. They focus both on the problems and opportunities of the lodging industry, such as communications, economy lodging, information processing and related technology, marketing, research and property safety and security.

A press release from the AH&MA highlights the Educational Institute (EI), an affiliate of AH&MA. The Educational Institute supports educational and institutional research for the lodging industry. EI was established in 1952 as a nonprofit educational foundation and is the world's largest source of training and educational materials for the lodging industry.

Students serious about advancing in knowledge about the hotel industry should contact AH&MA, EI, and their state hotel and motel association.

# The Educational Institute (EI)

P. O. Box 1240
East Lansing, MI 48826-1240
(517) 353-5500 Voice      (517) 353-5527 Fax

Web site address: **http://www.ei-ahma.org**

# QUESTIONS

1. Historically the proliferation of lodging establishments has always followed the expansion of:

    a. transportation routes
    b. communications systems
    c. gold mining towns
    d. advertising

2. Early hotels were converted from:

    a. warehouses
    b. monasteries
    c. caves
    d. castles

3. The term *hotel* is derived from:

    a. the English *hot*
    b. the French *hostel*
    c. the Greek *hoete*
    d. the Latin *hosete*

4. One of the inventions that helped hotels grow taller was:

    a. the escalator
    b. the elevator
    c. the pulley
    d. the dumbwaiter

5. The Tremont Hotel in Boston was the first hotel financed by:

    a. trading other land holdings
    b. John Jacob Astor
    c. the sale of stock to investors
    d. the trust department of a bank

6. An innovation that helped hotels to become larger was:

    a. steel-framed construction techniques
    b. interlocking parts
    c. interchangeable parts
    d. heat tempered nails

7. Motels had their origin in:

    a. the old post-road inns of the 1800s

    b. tourist cabins erected by farmers in the early 1900s

    c. suburban hotels

    d. both a and b

8. Motels exemplify:

    a. luxury

    b. practicality

    c. high rates

    d. high cost of land

9. Which of the following statements regarding motels is true:

    a. affiliated services such as restaurants and service stations benefit from the presence of a motel, but the opposite is never true

    b. it is easier to depreciate motel land than urban hotel land because motel land is cheaper

    c. the majority of motels are independent establishments not connected with any chain

    d. the average motel has less than 75 rooms

10. The former way of classifying lodging establishments took into account the following characteristics:

    a. commercial, residential, resort

    b. urban, suburban, remote

    c. large, medium, small

    d. full service, less than full service

11. Blended classifications of today include:

    a. facilities

    b. level of service

    c. location

    d. all of the above

12. The airport hotel today:

    a. accommodates the business traveler at the beginning or end of a journey

    b. is not often a destination point for business meetings

    c. is in a densely populated area and rarely has space for more than 200 rooms

    d. is usually isolated from other commercial properties

13. The downtown hotel:

    a. appeals to the individual traveler

    b. is usually newer in age

    c. has plenty of space

    d. attracts large groups

14. The all-suite hotel:

    a. has plenty of lobby space

    b. is located downtown

    c. caters to extended stay residents

    d. averages 75 suites or less

15. Which of the following terms would apply to the bed and breakfast inn?

    a. large converted house

    b. secluded area

    c. maximum privacy

    d. all of the above

16. In the United States, the majority of lodging establishments are:

    a. highway

    b. urban

    c. suburban

    d. resort

17. In the United States, most lodging establishments offer:

    a. under 75 rooms

    b. 75-149 rooms

    c. 150-299 rooms

    d. 300 or more rooms

18. The average number of employees per 100 rooms in the United States is:

    a. 10
    b. 20
    c. 30
    d. 40

19. The opportunity for advancement in the hotel/motel industry is:

    a. small
    b. great
    c. marginal
    d. it takes a long time to advance in the hotel industry because there's so much to learn

20. The AH&MA is located in:

    a. New York
    b. Washington
    c. New Jersey
    d. Washington D.C.

# ANSWERS

1. *a*
2. *b*
3. *b*
4. *b*
5. *c*
6. *a*
7. *d*
8. *b*
9. *d*
10. *a*
11. *d*
12. *a*
13. *a*
14. *c*
15. *d*
16. *a*
17. *a*
18. *c*
19. *b*
20. *d*

# Hotel Business Operations

- **Operations Overview**
- **Challenges In The Hotel Business**
- **Front Of The House**
- **Back Of The House**
- **Trends In Hotel/Motel Operation**

C H A P T E R **14**

# OPERATIONS OVERVIEW

A hotel or motel is a type of income producing property. All properties of this type are cash flow generating machines. Each has certain characteristics, fulfills a particular need in our society, and requires specific management techniques. The better these properties meet the needs of people, the more successful they are at generating cash flow. The more effective the management techniques, the more likely people's needs will be met.

One of the peculiar characteristics of hotels and motels is the fast-paced nature of the business. Meeting needs in the hotel/motel business is about keeping people on the move. People at business conventions are in a hurry to get from one location in the hotel to another. People on their way in or out of town are in a hurry to reach their next destination. To accomplish this objective in the hotel business, operations must be professional, efficient and thoroughly coordinated.

# CHALLENGES IN THE HOTEL BUSINESS

No business is without challenges. Depending on the pace of the business, unmet challenges can send a business in the wrong direction in a hurry. Due to its fast pace, the hotel business is particularly prone to the adverse effects of delays and neglect. Consider the following urgent challenges of the hotel business.

## Room Turnover

Rooms must be made ready for occupancy not in 30 days as with an apartment building, but in a matter of hours. If checkout time is 11:00 a.m. and that's when a guest vacates the room, the next guest may be checking in at 2:00 p.m. Multiply that by 75 rooms, or in the case of much larger facilities, hundreds or thousands of rooms, and you realize the enormity of the task. Most managers allocate approximately 30 minutes for housekeeping to prepare a room for the next guest. That means the trash must be removed, dusting and vacuuming accomplished, beds changed, bathrooms cleaned and restocked, and air-freshener applied to the room. The operation must be efficient with labor, linens, supplies and cleaning equipment readily available.

Imagine the cost of a large block of rooms not being available when new guests arrive. The guests either move to another hotel or wait unhappily in the lobby while the room is prepared. In either case, they probably won't return to your establishment.

The best-case scenario for room turnover occurs in some motels located on an interstate highway. Sometimes a traveler (trucker or other business person) stops in to catch a few hours of sleep and leaves the same day. If the room is made ready quickly, it can be rented again later in the day. This would result in an income greater than the potential gross income for that particular room. Of course, this will not be accomplished all of the time and for every room, but it definitely helps offset downtime suffered at other times of the month or in the off-season.

## Supplies

Adequate supplies must be kept on hand to accomplish the work that needs to be done. This includes cleaning supplies for the rooms, lobbies and other common areas; paper supplies such as toilet paper and paper towels; linens for the rooms and banquet

halls; uniforms; cleaning equipment; light bulbs; forms for reports and evaluations; food and beverage supplies; and countless other items for specific locations and functions. These supplies, of course, would be ordered by specific managers or their assistants who are familiar with the needs of their respective departments.

## Coordination of All Departments

There are many functions to the operation of a hotel and many departments to carry out those functions in a large hotel. The general manager is responsible for coordinating the communication and services of all of these departments. The left hand needs to know what the right hand is doing. The marketing department needs to inform the front desk what marketing campaigns are underway, from what sources reservations may be expected and in what volume. Advertising may be considered part of the marketing department, but sometimes the functions may be different. Advertising may be a marketing effort with the general public, but specific marketing techniques may be employed with previous guests and corporate clients. Advertising and marketing should be a concerted effort, with each department knowing what effort is being expended on the part of the other. Reservations must communicate with food service so demand can be anticipated and met. For one department to generate business that another department is not ready to serve would be disastrous. A reliable system of communication must be developed between the departments.

## Overcoming Vacancies

Some hotels and motels are less affected by slow seasons than others. An airport hotel located near a busy airport and well-equipped for business meetings may not experience as much fluctuation in business as a resort hotel affected by changing temperatures and seasons. Also, a resort hotel in Hawaii may not experience the fluctuation in business that the same type of hotel in Florida experiences. Depending on the type of lodging facility and the location, a hotel may have a significant challenge to put heads in the beds during an off-season.

This situation is a marketing challenge. It is incumbent on the hotel, if it is to be a successful cash flow generator, to meet that challenge and expand its market. First, it must know its source of clientele. It must develop a guest profile analysis. A recent survey by the American Hotel & Motel Association revealed a breakdown of its membership according to the following categories.

| Figure 14-1 Guest Profile Analysis: 1998 (AH&MA) | |
|---|---|
| **Percentage of Guest Nights** | |
| **Booked by Source** | **Mean** |
| Travel Agents | 12 |
| Walk-in | 21 |
| Direct Call to Property | 51 |
| Central Reservation System | 14 |
| On-Line with PC | 0 |
| Other | 2 |
| | |
| **Percentage of Guest Nights** | |
| **Sold by Source** | **Mean** |
| Business | 25 |
| Leisure | 36 |
| Group/Convention | 13 |
| Government | 5 |
| Other | 21 |

---

**Figure 14-1 (cont'd.)  Guest Profile Analysis: 1998 (AH&MA)**

| Percentage Method of Payment | Mean |
|---|---|
| Cash | 23 |
| Credit Sales | 68 |
| Other Credit Sales | 9 |

| Percentage of Guests by Average Length of Stay | Mean |
|---|---|
| One Night | 38 |
| Two Nights | 30 |
| Three Nights | 16 |
| Four to Seven Nights | 11 |
| Eight or More Nights | 5 |

| Percentage of Guests by Gender | Mean |
|---|---|
| Male | 58 |
| Female | 42 |

| Percentage of Guests by Nationality | Mean |
|---|---|
| Domestic | 82 |
| International | 18 |

The tabulation on the preceding pages measures the guest profile analysis for hotels that are members of the AH&MA. A similar type of analysis must be performed by each hotel that is interested in capturing a larger market.

For instance, assume for the moment that the survey results from the previous pages were data from a single hotel. The category of information that indicates the source of bookings reveals that 51% of the guests for this period of time made a direct call themselves to the hotel to book a reservation, 21% just walked in, 14% used a central reservation system, and 12% utilized the services of a travel agent. This hotel is fairly well known so that 72% of its guests take it upon themselves to either walk in or call to arrange a stay in the hotel. It would be interesting to know what percentage of guests were repeat visitors to the hotel—probably a high amount. What would happen if hotel management reached out more to central reservation systems and to travel agents? If management could increase the percentage of reservations that came from these sources, it would not diminish the number of guests that came from direct calls or walk-ins, only the percentages. The overall numbers would increase, as more first-time guests would be booked at the subject hotel.

The percentage of guest nights sold by source refers to the group to which the guest belongs. It is broken down into *business, leisure, group/convention*, and *government* travelers, as well as a significant percentage attributed to *other*. If these figures represented a single hotel, they would indicate to management that the majority (36%) of its guests were here for leisure (vacation) pur-

poses. The next largest group was business (25%), followed by other (21%), then group or convention (13%), and government (5%). Without wanting to lose any guests who stay at the hotel for vacationing and business purposes, management would obviously look to groups and conventions as well as government travelers as a source of increased business. If a hotel can accommodate some groups and conventions, it can obviously accommodate more of them. Groups and conventions are profitable, with large blocks of rooms being occupied and a lot of food being consumed in restaurants and banquet halls. Management should analyze the timing of the vacancy and increase marketing for groups and conventions to reduce that vacancy. It should be determined if marketing to government travelers would be worthwhile. If the market exists, it should be tapped. Also, the category labeled *other* should be broken down to determine what component parts can be increased.

The information regarding the percentage method of payment revealed credit sales of 68%, cash sales of 23% and other credit sales of 9%. The key is to make payment methods flexible and easy for the guest. So long as a complete array of payment plans are available, management can be assured that it has set up no barriers to receiving guests. The vast majority of hotels and motels accept credit cards, but occasionally a traveler encounters one that accepts cash only. This facility offers a great deal of resistance to receiving guests and relegates itself to a tran-

sient and non-affluent guest population. This restriction on payment methods should be overturned as soon as possible.

Regarding the average length of stay, 38% of the guests stay one night, 30% two nights, 16% three nights, 11% four to seven nights, and 5% eight or more nights. Obviously the more nights a guest stays, the less vacancy and more income a hotel receives. But the length of stay may be the most difficult area to change. Vacations, conferences and business trips are often locked in for the duration and there is little the hotel can do to extend them. Even if specials are offered giving one night free for a number of paid nights, the income from the additional night is lost. Realizing that the majority of the guests stay only one or two nights, management's best strategy may be to capitalize on the time the guest is present and make the stay pleasant and memorable. There's only a short time to make a good impression. The likelihood of the guest returning for another or longer stay is enhanced if the first brief stay goes well.

The survey reveals that 58% of the guests are male, 42% female. Most business travelers are probably still male, which may account for the slight disparity. This would probably not be a critical area of information that management could adjust.

The last category of information presented the percentage of guests by nationality and revealed 82% were domestic and 18% international. For a single hotel, this should be an area of attention. Since the majority of guests at the present time are vacationers and the second category is business, why not seek more guests from the international arena for both purposes? Tapping into central reservation systems and travel agents may help accomplish this. Contacting foreign cities, chambers of commerce and consulates may be beneficial. Training a staff to expect and accommodate foreign visitors can project a special interest in the international traveler and encourage many to return.

With all of the above analyses, of course, must be an awareness of the vacancy rate and the timing of such vacancies. Is there a distinct off season or are the vacancies spread throughout the year? If there is a distinct off season, is there an alternative use for the facility or area that would appeal to guests? Is there a particular demographic group to which marketing could appeal? Would some modifications to the facilities, services or management policies be in order to help facilitate the appeal to a new market? These and other questions have to be addressed to determine strategies that will lower the vacancy rates at a hotel.

## People Problems

It should be extremely important to all management personnel and all workers at a hotel that a guest have a pleasant and satisfying experience. That is the essence of a hotel worker's job. To arrange objects but not be concerned about how one's service has impacted people is to miss the entire purpose of one's work. When asked what is the greatest source of satisfaction on the job, one hotel assistant manager responded, "Turning a bad situation into a good one." This means customer satisfaction.

If a guest complains that there aren't enough towels or that a glass isn't clean, the response of hotel personnel is critical to that guest's impression of the hotel. If the situation is rectified quickly, with a sincere apology and a smile, the guest is likely to overlook the mistake and continue to have positive feelings about the hotel. If it takes a long time to correct the mistake, or if it is done grudgingly and with excuses, the guest will look for greener pastures the next time he or she is in the area.

If the concierge fails to secure tickets or reservations for a theater event or fails to accomplish some other objective for the guest, more than just disappointment may result. If business connections fail to materialize, presentations don't get made and contracts are not signed, a trip may be considered disastrous from a business standpoint. If the reason can be attributed to the lodging facility, a customer is lost. Sometimes connections are made because a concierge has taken the time to develop relationships. When they extend themselves personally for others, then others will do the same for them. Often an objective is reached on behalf of a guest due to attention to detail. It is the concierge's willingness to go the extra mile to accomplish what needs to be done.

There are many retail businesses that excel in customer service. They stand head and shoulders above their competition. They do so because they believe in the importance of excellent customer service. They have identified the principles of strong customer service that are applicable to their particular type of business and they have taken the time to train their employees in the techniques that make them stand out. They have emphasized a customer-focused approach. In many retail businesses, employees are very friendly—to each other. They talk readily to each other about their personal activities, break time, weekends and so forth, while the customer stands idly by awaiting some attention.

Successful retail businesses have also changed the employees' vocabulary when necessary. Disneyland had a training program for new employees who were to come into regular contact with guests. During those two days of training, they wanted all employees to come up to a consistent level of customer service. Part of that consistency was to eliminate certain words from one's vocabulary, and to replace them with the preferred word selected by Disneyland. One of those word substitutions was *attraction* for *ride*. Disneyland does not have *rides*, they have *attractions*. *Attraction* connotes glamour, while every other amusement park in the world has *rides*.

One summer when my daughter was about five years old, Alice (from Walt Disney's *Alice in Wonderland*) approached her near Main Street in Disneyland. As she knelt down to talk to her, I thought she would ask her name and ask her if she was having fun at Disneyland today. Instead, Alice went into some dialogue from the story, *Alice in Wonderland*. She went on and on spinning the tale of the queen and her court much to my daughter's obvious delight. She was developing the fantasy of the theme park and enhancing the experience of Disneyland.

So it must be in the service of guests at a hotel. Employees must be customer-focused, dedicated to providing the most excellent customer service possible and to creating a most pleasurable lodging experience. Language and vocabulary need not be stilted, but certainly should be upscale and first class. Friendliness and helpfulness should be the mood in the hotel with emphasis on the guest, not the employee. One guest at a luxury hotel asked that a shirt be pressed and returned to him by 10:00 a.m. The bellman suggested the shirt would be ready by 1:00 p.m., that such timing would be better. Better for whom? If all other aspects of service were perfect, the guest would likely remember this inconvenience in getting his shirt pressed. Every effort should be made to accommodate the needs of the guest.

# FRONT OF THE HOUSE

Front of the house is a term that refers to operations of the hotel business that deal directly with the guests. The quality of interaction between these personnel and the guests is what will form the first impression of the hotel and lead to the lasting

memories the guest will keep. Most top management positions and all executive positions are found in the front of the house.

*Back of the house* operations refers to those functions that take place behind the scenes that the guest usually does not observe. It's the preparation that makes the front of the house look good. One small, privately owned motel with only 14 rooms had its operation naturally divided by its husband and wife owners into *front of the house* and *back of the house*. The wife was the one who answered the phone, took reservations, worked the front desk and checked guests in. She also arranged for and supervised housekeeping, kept the books and performed the accounting operations. The husband secured supplies and did all necessary maintenance on the motel. She was smiling in front of the public. He was sweating behind the scenes. It was a natural division of labor and worked well for them.

A large hotel is a much more complex integration of departments. Let's consider some of the more significant parts of a *front of the house* operation.

## Service

By service we mean all assistance offered to guests upon arrival and departure from the hotel, as well as special needs and requests between those times. It begins by being picked up at the airport and driven to the hotel. It includes contact with bellhops, doormen, restroom attendants, baggage porters and the concierge. These are the contact personnel that will connect the guest to the *back of the house*, although most guests will not know it. These employees, by and large, will determine the guests' first impressions and lasting memories of the hotel. Consequently, the conduct of these employees is crucial to the satisfaction of guests and their willingness to return.

## Front Office

The front office is an integral part of the hotel operation. The front office is charged with the responsibility of processing reservations, keeping track of the availability of rooms and being certain not to overbook, receiving payment and dispersing keys. These personnel also handle room complaints, supply guests with information about local events and points of interest, and receive and distribute faxes and mail for guests.

The front office is staffed with a front office manager, responsible for all of the employees and functions of the front office. In larger hotels there will be an assistant manager, an individual whose presence on the floor of the lobby is as a good will ambassador, an employee who knows the operations of the hotel very well and can coordinate its services to solve problems for guests. Other positions in the front office include the various clerks and office workers subdividing the duties as dictated by size of the hotel and need.

# Accounting

While this process obviously is not directly observed by guests, it is usually included in the *front of the house* operations because the controller or chief accountant reports directly to the manager of the hotel. Accounting operations are such an integral part of hotel operations that many of its managers rise to prominent positions of management in the hotel.

In a small hotel or motel even today, some accounting operations have not been converted to a computer. They keep a simple set of books and undergo periodic audits and reports. In most hotels or motels of any size, however, and certainly those that are part of a chain, computer programs rule the scene. Under the direction of the controller, software programs will generate many types of reports, including monthly and annual profit and loss statements, balance sheets and other financial statements for the hotel at large and individual departments. Budget checks, fiscal policy and planning are all possible thanks to the accounting department.

For marketing purposes, computer generated reports will segment the market, indicating how much money is taken in and from what source. A room rate posting report is produced to ensure that what is supposed to be posted from each room has actually been received and charged. Credit reports are produced showing what each guest has spent and in what category. Expense reports are generated and then budget checks are run, matching computer records to budget items. Checks and balances are run for each department and for the facility as a whole. Accounts receivable, accounts payable and payroll are also important functions of the accounting department. The accounting department is at the heart and soul of the hotel operation. A controller or chief accountant has a thorough understanding of how the hotel operates, and it is for this reason that so many top executives emerge from the accounting department.

## Credit Department

The credit department handles everything associated with credit cards. It determines a guest's credit limits, whether or not credit is approved, and verifies that correct charges have been posted against credit card accounts. The credit department attempts to prevent fraudulent use of credit cards by securing proper identification of the credit card holder and ensuring that the user is the owner of the card. It also follows up on delinquent accounts and keeps files on all credit business.

Since a majority of hotel business is paid for by credit cards, special guest reference files are often made available to marketing. Special requests made by guests are cross referenced so extraordinary needs can be anticipated on subsequent visits. This helps housekeeping to be ready and enables the hotel to provide an extra level of personal service for guests. Also, any credit problems or delinquencies can be picked up immediately should a guest call for a reservation.

## Banquets

There are aspects of food ordering and preparation that belong to the *back of the house*, but there are also aspects that belong to the *front of the house*. The banquet manager interfaces with the public in arranging the services that groups want. From business groups to civic groups to private parties, each banquet function must be customized to meet the needs of the group. The banquet manager answers to both the catering manager and the director of sales because his or her job involves both food and sales. Their knowledge of food and the profit margins of various items helps to compile the menu, and their ability to relate to the customer helps to sell the event. Banquet manager is a key position attained only after many years of experience in food service.

## Public Relations

Public relations personnel speak for executive management. The position is important because the wealth of the hotel is the service it has to offer, and the service is only as good as it is perceived to be. An individual representing the hotel in public relations must have a thorough working knowledge of the hotel business, personnel positions and duties, budgets and costs as well as hotel policies and procedures. Such an employee becomes the face of the hotel and represents the substance behind the name. He or she may be asked to interface with international business groups, or prepare a program for a visiting chess club, or publicize the entertainment for a podiatrist's convention. The tasks are many and varied and a good formal education as well as broad experience in the lodging industry are helpful in carrying out these duties.

## Advertising

Advertising may be considered an activity occurring behind the scenes and in a sense it is. The fruits of its labors, however, are highly visible in and around the hotel. Advertising copy is submitted to local newspapers as well as international magazines. In the lobby, strategically placed easels may display news of special entertainment or events. Attractions may be heralded in window or elevator displays. Table cards in the dining room may announce special offers or events. In addition, advertising personnel will supervise the production of all printed material including menus and programs. Successful implementation of the advertising program requires a thorough knowledge of activities and the budget as it impacts advertising.

## Sales and Marketing

The sales department markets convention space and banquet facilities to groups. It is responsible for a great deal of money coming into the hotel. Consequently its function is regarded as extremely important to the profitability of the hotel. Sales managers must decide which groups to approach as well as how and when. Sales personnel are well paid and when effective, often receive bonuses or incentive rate increases. Sales and marketing must be in close communication with public relations, banquets and the advertising departments. Effective sales managers often earn the opportunity for advancement into the upper ranks of executive management.

# Hotel Management

Management is the engine that runs the machine. Though generally considered part of the *front of the house*, management affects the *back of the house* as well. Consider the responsibilities of different levels of management.

## RESIDENT MANAGERS

Resident managers are the on-site managers in charge of day-to-day operations. They are in charge of all department heads and meet regularly with them, informing them of changing policies, procedures and plans. The resident managers are integrally involved in human resource management and will participate in the hiring, firing, counseling and disciplining of all employees. They also will participate in negotiations with labor unions and other employee groups. There is usually one resident manager per hotel—not one per shift. During the various shifts when the resident manager is not on duty, the assistant manager would have the authority to implement policies. Resident managers should be closely acquainted with the operations of each of the departments under their supervision, even to the extent of maintenance and engineering issues. Resident managers are not expected to be experts in the repair of specialized equipment, but they are expected to be familiar enough with kitchen equipment, water heaters, furnaces and laundry machinery to know how to keep them running without wasting money. Resident managers are usually promoted to their positions from the ranks of the various department heads, depending on their overall experience, knowledge and abilities.

## EXECUTIVE MANAGEMENT

Executive management is not only *front of the house*, but *top of the house* as well. It may be represented by an individual—sometimes called a managing director or president of a hotel corporation or management company. More often executive management is actually similar to the executive branch of the government, but comprised of more than just one individual. It may be represented by a management committee or a board of directors made up of executives of a bank or insurance company that has a financial interest in the hotel. The main concern of executive management is to ensure the profitability of the hotel. As with all income producing property, they are concerned not only with current income but with the durability of that income. This brings executive management into the areas of legal issues, capital improvements, investments, financing and major changes in operations. The executive position oversees the resident manager and meets with him or her regularly to ensure that major concerns are carried out.

# BACK OF THE HOUSE

The *back of the house* is that part of a hotel operation that the resident manager doesn't want the guests to see or think about. It is the countless hours of work expended in buying, preparing, fixing, studying and getting ready for guests so that their stay and activities at the hotel go off without a hitch. The *front of the house* works hard as well and probably will garner either the blame or the praise, but the *back of the house* makes it all possible. Experience at the *back of the house* makes advancement to and within the *front of the house* a greater likelihood. Consider the following departments in the *back of the house*.

## Purchasing

Some would consider purchasing to be in the *front of the house* because of its connection to many *front of the house* departments, but clearly it is done behind the scenes and for the purposes of our discussion, will be considered a *back of the house* operation. Efficient purchasing procedures can be integral to the profitability of a hotel. The purchasing agent or manager will interview salespersons, change vendors as deemed necessary, sign contracts and purchase needed items in the proper quantity—of the appropriate quality and at the right price. Depending on the size of the hotel, the purchasing agent will purchase items and supplies for the entire hotel or for designated departments, leaving other personnel the task of purchasing for their respective departments. The importance of a quality purchasing agent cannot be overestimated, and an individual can rise to that position only after considerable experience in the appropriate departments.

A significant area of experience for purchasing agents is food service. They must know profit margins, freshness factors for various items, demand and acceptance at the dining table for different foods and a host of other considerations relating to food. While courses and formal education in hotel management are always desirable, there is no substitute for experience in the area of food service and production. One cannot advance to purchaser without extensive knowledge and experience in food.

Wine is a department of its own in some hotels and requires such expertise and knowledge that only a wine steward can perform the function of purchasing wine. Departments that require such specialization would rely only on the designated experts in their field. The purchasing agent for a large hotel will be no less busy.

## Food Operation

The importance of quality food at a lodging establishment cannot be overstated. Many guests who have experienced an average room will depart happy and enthusiastic about the hotel if they have enjoyed a good quality meal at a fair price. The food operation department offers entry level positions with no previous experience necessary. An individual could start as a helper and rise to the position of master chef, with the proper training and experience. Experience in food operation also can open doors to management and other areas of hotel work. So key is the proper operation of food controls, ordering, preparation and service that an extensive knowledge of these operations makes an individual invaluable while advancing up the management ladder.

Successful food operations function within narrow and precise profit margins. They are like other manufacturing and marketing procedures with much shorter deadlines due to spoilage and shelf life. Food operations must procure the raw materials (before they spoil or begin to deteriorate), fashion them into a finished product that is attractive to the palate and the eye, and place the product on the market in the restaurant or bakery. A high degree of precision in purchasing, preparation and service is required for a profitable operation.

## Housekeeping

An efficient housekeeping operation contributes to the good reputation of a hotel. Crisp linens, clean rooms and sparkling mirrors, windows and porcelain make a guest feel glad to be there. This makes it easy for the bellhop to take the guests to their room and to introduce the room to them. The bellhop receives the praise for a job well done by the *back of the house*.

In a small motel operation known to the author, the facility is old but the maintenance and housekeeping are excellent. The light green porcelain from a different era shines when one enters the bathroom. Beds are clean and tight, wood paneling sparkles and dirt or neglect can be found nowhere. The room is inviting and says, "Glad you're here. Come back soon!" The owner told me she gets many compliments on the housekeeping and is grateful for the family-owned service she employs. She often allows more than the standard time for these services because she knows she's getting quality and that it contributes to the profitability of the motel.

Turnover in housekeeping services is usually high, which means there are frequent openings. An individual can be hired in housekeeping with no previous experience and be trained for the job. This experience in a *back of the house* department can lead to transfer and promotion to other departments and on up the ladder. As always, a willingness to work hard and to learn are important requisites.

## Personnel

Personnel matters are sometimes considered *front of the house* issues, but because they are undertaken behind the scenes we include them here. Personnel issues include hiring, firing, training and disciplining employees. It involves determining job descriptions and commensurate requirements for positions created. The personnel department will keep employees' files—including records of time worked for verification with payroll, vacations, time off and overtime. An employee's file also will contain evaluations, consideration for promotion, disciplinary records and educational records.

Managers of the personnel department are sometimes hired from within and pushed up in the ranks. Other times managers are hired from outside, people with human resources experience in another industry. Either way, when sufficient hotel personnel experience is obtained, the personnel manager may be a candidate for further advancement up the management ranks.

## Engineering

Maintenance of the physical plant is an important function of *back of the house* operations. Almost every hotel of any size will have to have a full time maintenance engineer. An ample supply of hot water must be available 24 hours a day. Electricity must be supplied safely and consistently. Kitchen equipment must be functioning properly so the incessant demand for food can be met uninterrupted. Boiler rooms and engine rooms must be operated and properly maintained. Air conditioning must be functioning, as well as security systems, fire alarms and sprinkler systems. Also under the purview of the engineering department are carpenters, plumbers, electricians, painters and compression workers. Which specialists would be employees and which services would be contracted out would be based on the size and needs of the hotel. The most valuable qualifications for these positions are expertise in the respective trades. Previous hotel experience is not necessary.

## Technology

Modern hotels are on the cutting edge of technology. Some require full time technicians to maintain communication systems, computer systems and high-tech electronics within the facility. A malfunction of any of these systems can result in a shut-down of operations, which no hotel can afford. The size and sophistication of the hotel will determine if consultants and technicians are on call, or if they are employees.

# TRENDS IN HOTEL/MOTEL OPERATION

A survey by the AH&MA in 1998 processed information from approximately 2,300 of its members. The typical respondent was the operator of a full-service hotel or motel with fewer than 150 rooms in the mid-price category as defined by Smith Travel Research. Note the following areas of information.

| Figure 14-2  Property Operations | |
|---|---|
| **Number of Employees** | **Median** |
| Total Number of Employees | 45 |
| Number of Full-Time Employees | 28 |
| Number of Part-Time Employees | 15 |
| Number of Full-Time Equivalents | 40 |

## Figure 14-2 (cont'd.)   Property Operations

| | Percentage of Respondents Answering "Yes" |
|---|---|
| Employees Allowed to Accept Tips | 93.1 |
| Property Franchised | 42.3 |
| Property Managed by Independent Management Company | 36.3 |
| Plan to Renovate Over Next 12 Months | 58.8 |
| Renovated Over Past 12 Months | 64.5 |
| Have a Property Management System | 65.7 |
| Plan to Install a Property Management System | 22.5 |
| Connected to a Central Reservation System | 64.3 |
| Hotel Management Access to E-Mail | 43.7 |
| Hotel Management Access to World Wide Web | 37.8 |

# Property Operation

According to the AH&MA, nearly two-thirds of the respondents' properties had been renovated during the past 12 months. The median age of the hotels was 20 years, with 25% of them 31 or more years old. Many owners are planning renovation this year. The AH&MA reports that there were about 30 employees per 100 rooms in the smaller properties and 55 employees per 100 rooms in the hotels with 150 rooms or more. Professional Property Management Systems are in use in two-thirds of the hotels in the survey, an increase of nearly 60% from two years ago. Now 64% of the hotels are connected to a central reservation system, a 38% increase from two years ago. In 44% of the hotels, management has access to e-mail, and 38% are tied to the World Wide Web.

## Dining and Entertainment

Smith Travel Research reports in the U.S. Lodging Census database that 40% of hotels have an integrated food and beverage facility. The AH&MA survey, however, revealed a much higher percentage—62%. Most food and beverage services, according to the AH&MA survey are owner operated (83%), one out of six is leased, and only 6% of those with food and beverage facilities had a contract for an on-site concession. Many owners are tapping the profit source of operating their own food service, but there is room for growth.

| Figure 14-3   Dining and Entertainment | Percentage of Respondents Answering "Yes" |
|---|---|
| Physically Integrated Food and Beverage Facility | 62.0 |
| Food and Beverage Facility Owned/Operated or Leased | 82.7 |
| National Food Concessions Contract | 8.0 |
| Complimentary Breakfast | 51.8 |
| Catering Services | 64.6 |
| Room Service | 56.4 |
| 24-Hour Room Service | 17.3 |
| Special Dietary Requests | 53.8 |
| Full Service Bar/Nightclub | 57.1 |

## Services and Amenities

Extra services and special amenities vary widely and are offered for increasing profitability and developing return business. Certain trends are interesting. There seems to be a move toward healthful practices, with 90% of respondents stocking bottled water in their mini-bars, a greater percentage than even beer or candy, although those items are high on the list as well. Exercise rooms are provided by nearly half of the respondents, and more than half give attention to recycling. More profit centers are available as only a small percentage of respondents offer pay-per-view movies, video rentals, video games or VCRs.

| **Figure 14-4  Special Services and Amenities** | |
|---|---|
| | Percentage of Respondents Answering "Yes" |
| On-Site Business Center | 21.7 |
| In-House Laundry Service | 44.3 |
| Coin-Operated Laundry Service | 40.8 |
| Concierge Service | 29.7 |
| Beauty Salon | 9.9 |
| VIP/Club Floor | 12.5 |
| Smoke Detectors in Guest Rooms | 95.5 |
| Green Rooms | 9.9 |
| Irons/Ironing Boards | 84.5 |
| Hair Dryers | 67.6 |
| Makeup Mirrors | 21.3 |
| In-Room Coffee Makers | 47.7 |
| Indoor Pool | 26.7 |
| Outdoor Pool | 55.3 |
| Free Guest Parking | 84.5 |
| Valet Parking | 15.8 |
| In-Room Exercising Equipment | 6.5 |
| In-Room Safety Material | 55.7 |
| Bed Turndown Service | 22.7 |
| Leave a Mint or Other Goodie | 25.9 |
| Airport Shuttle Service | 34.4 |
| Other Shuttle Service | 33.2 |

## Figure 14-4 (cont'd.)   Special Services and Amenities

|  | Percentages of Respondents Answering "Yes" |
|---|---|
| **Religious Materials** | |
| Provide Religious Reading Material | 75.3 |
| Bible Provided | 97.3 |
| Teachings of Buddha Provided | 1.9 |
| Book of Mormon Provided | 5.2 |
| | |
| **Facilities** | |
| Allow Pets in Guest Rooms | 44.4 |
| Staffed Health/Fitness Facility | 14.0 |
| Exercise Room | 43.7 |
| | |
| **Recycling** | |
| Property Has Recycling Program | 58.7 |
| Glass | 86.1 |
| Newspaper | 90.5 |
| Paper | 92.3 |
| Plastic | 77.8 |
| Aluminum | 92.2 |
| | |
| **In-Room Entertainment** | |
| Cable/Satellite TV | 90.5 |
| Pay-Per-View Movies | 35.3 |
| Interactive Services | 4.5 |
| Video Games | 8.9 |
| VCR Rental | 24.1 |
| Movie Rentals | 19.2 |

| Figure 14-4 (cont'd.)   Special Services and Amenities | |
|---|---|
| | Percentage of Respondents Answering "Yes" |
| **Mini-Bars** | |
| Mini-Bars Available in Guest Rooms | 10.9 |
| Items Included in Mini-Bar: | |
|     Beer | 79.7 |
|     Candy | 85.9 |
|     Wine | 75.9 |
|     Healthful Foods | 64.7 |
|     Spirits | 73.9 |
|     Cameras | 23.7 |
|     Bottled Water | 90.0 |
|     Suntan Lotion | 9.1 |

The objective of professional hotel management is to maximize occupancy, make sure that guests are satisfied, and see to it that the hotel is run as efficiently and as profitably as possible. This is always a work in progress. As society changes, so must the hotel change. When more emphasis is placed on fitness, hotels must respond with bottles of water and exercise facilities. As technology and communication advances, fax machines and computer connections must be available. By anticipating and meeting the needs of guests, hotels will successfully compete for their share of the market and entice return visitors.

# QUESTIONS

1. One special demand that is unique to the hotel business is:

   a. accounting procedures

   b. a much more rapid turnover time

   c. the need for customer service

   d. it is a people business

2. Which of the following hotels is most likely to suffer a seasonal downturn in occupancy levels?

   a.  a Florida resort hotel

   b.  a Hawaiian resort hotel

   c.  an airport hotel

   d.  a suburban hotel

3. If hotel management discovered that the majority of their guests arranged their stays through their own direct call to the property or by just walking in, one way to increase occupancy levels would be to:

   a.  do a marketing outreach to travel agents

   b.  tap into a central reservation system

   c.  offer more payment options through more credit cards

   d.  both a and b

4. The way to increase the number of nights guests stay at a hotel is:

   a.  offer two-for-one specials

   b.  extend their vacation

   c.  there may be little you can do

   d.  offer entertainment in the lounge

5. A hotel or motel that doesn't accept credit cards for payment is:

   a.  restricting its market

   b.  losing business

   c.  suffering from obsolete business practices

   d.  all of the above

6. In general, hotel management should make the payment of money from the guest to the hotel:

   a.  take place upon arrival

   b.  as easy and flexible as possible

   c.  take place early in the day

   d.  conditioned on stringent safety requirements

7. To increase the percentage of international visitors to a hotel, management would:

    a. seek more reservations from a central reservation system or travel agent

    b. advertise in domestic newspapers

    c. make inquiries to domestic chambers of commerce

    d. hire multi-lingual hotel workers in the front office

8. In the case of an off-season, what can hotel management do to increase profitability?

    a. investigate an alternative use for the facility

    b. determine if there is a particular demographic group to which marketing can appeal

    c. decide if modifications to facilities, services or policies would attract a new market

    d. all of the above

9. In customer service, the most important thing is:

    a. that the employees feel they have done their jobs

    b. that the employees abide by the policies in the book

    c. customer satisfaction

    d. obtaining the full amount of money for services rendered

10. Effective customer service training in any retail business must change the employee's:

    a. focus

    b. attitude

    c. vocabulary

    d. all of the above

11. The *front of the house* in the hotel business refers to:

    a. the area where the doorman stands

    b. operations in the hotel that deal directly with guests

    c. the front desk

    d. the portion of the hotel's gross income that goes to pay its employees

12. All of the following are considered *front of the house* operations except:

    a. front office

    b. service

    c. public relations

    d. housekeeping

13. The resident manager of a hotel:

    a. is in charge of all department heads

    b. answers to the executive manager

    c. is responsible for the day-to-day operations

    d. all of the above

14. The *back of the house* in the hotel business refers to:

    a. the area of the hotel where supplies are delivered

    b. operations behind the scenes that don't affect the guests

    c. work activities done at the end of the day

    d. areas of work that guests seldom see

15. *Back of the house* operations:

    a. provide a great training ground for *front of the house* operations

    b. are less important than *front of the house* operations

    c. are often commented on by guests

    d. include accounting services

16. Working in food operations in a large hotel:

    a. requires a lot of experience

    b. can provide valuable expertise that can lead to advancement

    c. is irrelevant to the important operations in the *front of the house*

    d. requires knowledge of broad profit margins

17. According to the 1998 AH&MA member survey, what percentage of respondents have an integrated food and beverage facility in their hotels?

    a. 40%
    b. 62%
    c. 75%
    d. 33-1/3%

18. According to the 1998 AH&MA member survey, what is the highest percentage of respondents to offer the following amenities?

    a. laundry service
    b. airport shuttle service
    c. smoke detectors in guests' rooms
    d. free guest parking

19. According to the 1998 AH&MA member survey, what is the item most likely to appear in members' mini-bars?

    a. bottled water
    b. beer
    c. candy
    d. health food

20. According to the 1998 AH&MA member survey, what is one area of service that hotel owners might look to increase in order to add to the margin of profitability?

    a. cable/satellite TV
    b. candy
    c. movie rentals
    d. wine

# ANSWERS

1. *b*
2. *a*
3. *d*
4. *c*
5. *d*
6. *b*
7. *a*
8. *d*
9. *c*
10. *d*
11. *b*
12. *d*
13. *d*
14. *d*
15. *a*
16. *b*
17. *b*
18. *c*
19. *a*
20. *c*

# Current Issues In Hotel/Motel Management

- Elements For Success
- Economic Issues
- Consumer Issues
- Industry Issues
- Conclusion

C H A P T E R  **15**

# ELEMENTS FOR SUCCESS

To be successful, hotel owner/operators must pay attention to the economic issues that affect their area. They must also be aware of the issues that are important to consumers. Owner/operators have to understand how to meet their customers' needs and appeal to their preferences. Finally, it is necessary that hoteliers have a grasp on issues affecting the lodging industry as a whole so they can respond appropriately and remain competitive. Follow these issues through this chapter as we develop their relevance to the lodging entrepreneur.

# ECONOMIC ISSUES

People who are not prosperous are not frequent travelers. People who are prosperous travel often for business and pleasure. The lodging industry in this country is affected by worldwide economic conditions, bringing visitors from across the globe—subject to fluctuations on the international business scene.

## International Tourism

The United States is the most popular destination in the world for international tourists. According to the American Hotel & Motel Association, in 1989 the U.S. share of world tourism receipts was 13.7%. In 1990 it climbed to 14.8% and in 1991, 16.5%. The rate stayed at 16.5% in 1992 and then rose to 18.1% in 1993. In 1994 there was a slight decrease to 17.8% and then a jump to 18.3% in 1995. In 1996 and 1997 the rate dropped to 17.4%, accounting for $80 billion in income.

International arrivals to the United States totaled 43.4 million in 1997, a decrease of 3% from 1996 when the total was 44.7 million. It is believed that about one-third of the visitors are here on business. Overall, international arrivals were up 4% in 1997. The Office of Tourism In-  dustries estimates the number of visitors will continue to increase through the turn of the century with 48 million in 2000 and 49.8 million in 2001. Total travel receipts that year are expected to top $100 billion.

At the present time, most of the tourists come from Japan, the United Kingdom and Germany. The biggest drop-off of inbound tourists was from Mexico and the greatest increase came from Asia and the Middle East. The fastest growing inbound markets are expected to be Brazil, South Korea and Taiwan.

Spending from international travel in 1997 totaled $61.1 billion, an increase of 5% from 1996. This created an estimated U.S. travel and trade surplus of $19.5 billion, a 4% increase over 1996. According to the AH&MA, these visitors were directly responsible for supporting a U.S. payroll of $16 billion and 970,000 jobs, and generating more than $8.2 billion in federal, state and local tax revenue.

Overseas arrivals to the United States (excluding Canada and Mexico) totaled 20.6 million in 1997, an increase of 12% from 1996. This is expected to grow 6% per year on the average each year through 2001. In 1997, 65% of overseas travelers arrived in the U.S. for a vacation (travel holiday), 26% were here on business, 25% visited friends, 8% attended a convention, and 6% came for educational purposes. Eighty-two percent of overseas visitors to the United States stayed in hotels and motels an average of 8.3 nights and spent an average of $357 on lodging per trip.

The top destination state in the U.S. is Florida (5.3 million), followed by California, New York, Hawaii and Nevada. New York City was the top city for overseas visitors, followed by Los Angeles, Miami and Orlando.

This information provided by the AH&MA is significant for the owner or manager of a hotel/motel. Especially if one's lodging establishment is located in one of the most frequently visited states, the owner/manager would want to be sure of capturing one's share of the market. A significant share of one's market in those states should be from the international arena. If a market analysis shows this to be lacking, steps can be taken to increase that share of the international market. The owner/manager should see to it that the establishment is on the map for international travel agents, has a place on the World Wide Web, has on-line reservation capabilities, participates in a central reservation system, has an advertising presence in magazines and other

international publications, and offers accommodations that will meet the needs of international travelers—including employees who speak a variety of languages. These steps can help a lodging establishment capture its share of the international market and maximize profitability.

## Occupancy Levels and Rates

Smith Travel Research (STR) indicates that room occupancy for the first seven months of 1998 was 1.1% above the same period in 1997. The average daily rate continues to increase faster than anticipated. A significant statistic tracked by STR is revenue per available room (RevPAR), and it is reported as 1.2% higher for this period than expected.

Room revenue for the first seven months of 1996 was over $33.6 billion, nearly 10% above the first seven months of 1995. The number of rooms rented in the commercial and resort category continued to rise at a much more rapid rate in the first seven months of 1996 than for those rooms serving both categories, despite the effect of the 1996 Olympics in Atlanta.

There was actually a decline in room occupancy in July 1998 and also for the 12-month periods ending in that month during the past five years. Since 1995, the increase in the supply of rooms has absorbed larger portions of the change in demand. If sharp room rate increases had not occurred over the past several years, higher levels of room revenue and RevPAR could not have occurred.

Research by STR is designed to compare statistics of current periods of time with past periods and to make predictions about the future. STR also attempts to explain the reasons for any changes so that hotel/motel operators can respond to the market. STR reveals that over the past 10 years 49% of the total annual room revenue received by the lodging industry is received in the first six months of the year. The first half of 1998 shows more than 50% of the anticipated room revenue has been received in the first six months, pushing projections to $57.5 billion, 2% more than their initial estimate.

The following facts are presented to help explain the increased revenue. They apply to the first six months of 1998 in the United States.

## TOTAL UNITED STATES

- The increase in room occupancy was 26% less than the average rate of change during each six-month period over the previous four years.

- Although the rate of increase in rooms sold (demand) was the same as between 1993 and 1997, new properties were added at nearly double the rate of the previous periods.

- The number of rooms vacant daily declined at a combined rate of 1.4% in the previous periods; in 1998 the drop was less than 1%.

- The increase in the average room rate of 6.2% was double the variance in the previous six-month period resulting in a 33% increase in the rate of change in the revenue per available room (RevPAR).

## REGIONS

- The four STR regions in the Central and Mountain time zones showed accelerating changes in the number of new properties and the rate of increase in daily vacancies.

- Significant declines in demand occurred in the East and West North Carolina regions although the number of rooms available rose at a higher rate in 1998 than in the previous periods.

- The average number of daily vacancies increased by over 5% in the East South Central and West North Central regions as a result of adding new properties.

- In the Mountain region the rate of change in daily vacancies went from an average decline of 3.4% to an increase of nearly 5% in 1998.

## PRICE LEVEL

- The increase in new properties nearly doubled in 1998 in the STR Upscale and Midprice groups.

- Although the rate of change in vacancies dropped in the Economy group, there was an increase in the variation of rooms sold in 1998.

- From average declines in the number of vacant rooms of nearly 2% in the Upscale and Midprice segments, the rate of increase rose by over 1%.

## LOCATION

- The rate of adding new properties was double the previous average in 1998 in Highway locations.
- The number of daily vacancies in Suburban locations rose from a decline of 1.4% to an increase by the same ratio.

## Interpretation of Statistics

STR concludes that the performance of the lodging industry in the first six months of 1998 compared favorably with similar previous periods only because operators were able to double the increase in the average room rate. The development of New Upscale and Mid-Price properties in Suburban and Highway locations in the Mountain and four Central regions (where the rise in demand was inadequate to absorb the additional rooms) has resulted in the leveling of industry-wide occupancies.

So the supply of available rooms is up. Rates are up. Demand is up. Occupancy overall has leveled off, but the end result is that revenue is up. And when all is said and done, hotel/motel operators still have to contend with the factors that impact their particular market area. As always the name of the game is to increase occupancy levels, minimize expenses and optimize net income.

**Case History**             **Hotel Conglomerate**

The large hotel/entertainment company, Harrah's Inc., is borrowing marketing tactics from the airlines and the giant consumer products companies. The firm is adding personal information to the database of customer information that it already has. Some 6 million guests are in Harrah's database and the company expects to add data to about 1 million files per year. Information like what guests dined on, the kind of gambling they like to do, what they bought at the gift shop, how much money they spent and how long they stayed—emotional and personal data that will help Harrah's personalize marketing offers to its clients for their next visit. The system will also chronicle whether or not the guests were happy on their last visit, noting whether there were any complaints or difficulties such as faulty air conditioning or bad service. In connection with this program, Harrah's is issuing a "Total Gold" card that will allow a guest to accumulate "points," as in a frequent flyer program with an airline. The hotel's hope is that guests will gamble more often at Harrah's to accumulate points—and that they will feed the database by using their electronic Total Gold card and credit cards at Harrah's hotels, shops and restaurants.

**Case History**  **Independent Hotel Operator**

An independent hotel operator in the Midwest met the challenges of his market in a unique way. His market is not a high demand market in comparison to New York or Florida, and many of the hotels/motels in his area were rundown and not profitable. He entered the market to save money on his personal income taxes.

The first thing he did upon buying his first motel was fix it up. Rundown motels don't command a very high rate and don't make the guest feel like returning. He also insisted on excellent services so that the rooms and common areas were very clean. This makes the guest feel better about being there and makes them want to return. In addition, the owner instilled in his employees basic concepts of good customer service. Complaints were handled quickly and with consideration for the guest. It was obvious to the guests that the employees cared and were really trying to give good service and create a favorable experience for them. The difference came through.

This entrepreneur also observed that many hotels/motels in the Midwest area were simply too big to be profitable in that marketplace. Hotels and motels were certainly needed for the highway traveler, but the huge demand that exists in California, New York and Florida was just not there. After acquiring his first several hotels/motels, he began to build his own. Instead of building hotels/motels that had 100 rooms like many in the area did, he built establishments that contained an average of 60 rooms. This way, it would be easier to reach a profitable occupancy level, and as an extra bonus, that level actually decreased for the smaller hotel/motel. Another side benefit was that start-up capital was less. So his plan made sense.

This hotel/motel operator decided to build "no-frills" establishments. He observed that many of the hotels in the area tried to offer too many extra services that were not always utilized by their guests and offering these services made it more difficult to be profitable. He felt that many guests in his particular market didn't care about the frills. What they wanted was friendly and helpful employees, clean rooms and good rates. He even eliminated food service and doesn't operate a restaurant in any of his more than 200 lodging establishments. Occasionally a guest will wish there were a restaurant in the hotel, but overall this system is working and the guests continue to return.

With an eye to minimize building expenses, this hotel entrepreneur created and operates his own construction company. It enables him to build a hotel room for an average of $30,000, about an 18% savings. From the inception of a new establishment he can operate with less debt and greater cash flow.

In addition to saving building expenses, this imaginative entrepreneur has instituted other innovations that save operating expenses, make the entire function more efficient and raise the spirits of his employees. For example, he offers a free stay on Thanksgiving and Christmas to guests who are visiting friends or family in the hospital. He also pays his cleaning staff by the room cleaned, not by the hour. It gives them a greater incentive to do an excellent job and rewards them for efficiency by shortening their work day. One head housekeeper says that if they were paid by the hour, they would lose money. With great incentives and high morale, employees tend to stay longer. Less turnover contributes to more efficiency.

Another innovation employed by this entrepreneur is that he moved the laundry rooms to a new location—behind the front desks in his hotels. That way his night clerks can stay busy during the slow times and it saves him more than $1.25 million per year throughout his hotel empire.

These examples put us on notice that money-saving, service-enhancing and marketing innovations are the result of experience and imagination. They are out there, as we say, and there are many that have not yet been devised, implemented or come to the attention of owners/operators of hotels and motels. That's exciting because it reminds us that the field of hotel/motel operation is not static and boring, but is dynamic, imaginative and creative. Consequently, the rewards from such a field can be great.

# CONSUMER ISSUES

Hotel owner/operators who do not have a sense of what consumers want or how to reach them do not have a firm grasp on their stream of income. As in most businesses, the customer is king. Lodging entrepreneurs must understand the consumer and give them what they want.

## Improvements

Hoteliers who are members of the AH&MA revealed in a recent survey that one of their top priorities is to fix up their properties and to improve services and amenities for their guests. Most lodging entrepreneurs are constantly looking to improve aspects of the following areas.

- Operations
- Dining
- Entertainment
- Services
- Amenities

## Traveler Safety

According to the Travel Industry Association of America, domestic travelers are less likely to be victims of crimes than the United States population at large. The difference is significant. The crime rate against U.S. travelers was 40% lower than those who stayed home. One reason for the decrease in crime against domestic travelers is that rental car license plates can no longer be distinguished from privately-owned automobiles. There was a time when rental cars leaving an airport were targeted by criminals, but this is no longer a significant factor.

Secondly, the AH&MA launched the National Traveler Safety Campaign in March of 1993. Since then the group has conveyed a "play it safe" method to more than 200 million consumers providing valuable information and raising the consciousness of crime by the following methods.

- Tip cards
- In-room public safety announcements
- Meeting planner's checklists

## Family Market

The family market is a growth one for U.S. lodging establishments, making up more than 50% of leisure market travelers. In 1997, three out of 10 adults took at least one vacation with their children, according to the 1998 Travel Monitor. Marketing to families is becoming a major focus for many lodging companies, with hotels engaging in some of the following marketing activities.

- Offering and supervising children's activities
- Providing giveaways for kids
- Family-oriented suites
- A kids' frequent guest program
- Children's or reduced-price menus
- Special check-in packets
- Tips on local family attractions
- Child-care references
- Family discount coupons

## Self-Service Check-In

Hotels, in an effort to shorten guests' check-in time, are experimenting with portable, interactive, touch-screen information kiosks that are placed in the lobby and public areas. Guests access the kiosk with the same credit card used to make the reservation. Details of the guest's stay are then pulled up, a registration card and key are produced, and directions to the guestroom and information on hotel amenities and services are provided. The kiosks even maintain a guest comment card system. As guests become more accustomed to the technology, industry watchdogs expect the number of these kiosks to increase as properties better integrate front desk personnel with the check-in process.

## Internet

Lodging chains continue to improve and expand ways their home pages can be utilized by the traveling public. Sites feature on-line booking capabilities that specify all rates, promotions and pack-ages available through the company's central reservation system, and data on affiliated international properties, including photos, local maps and meeting rooms. In addition, lodging chains are more aggressively marketing their on-line capabilities and adding new dimensions to their booking capabilities. Future innovations to sites include cancellation functions, and booking special services such as massages and tee times. The percentage of Internet bookings is currently small; however, hoteliers are expecting this number to grow significantly by the start of the next century.

## Frequent Stay Programs

Since 1983, lodging chains have used frequent stay programs to reward brand loyalty. Although costly, these programs increase market share, and provide a valuable database in which chains can track individual customers. Many hotels have revised their programs to offer guest service and recognition benefits coupled with cost-effective awards.

## Business Rooms and Services

According to an American Express survey, business travelers spent nearly $33 billion on the lodging industry in 1998. According to the Travel Industry Association of America, 275 million business trips were taken in 1997. As a result, hotels continue to respond to the needs of this lucrative market. Most hotels already provide the in-room coffee machine, iron and complimentary continental breakfast, but more lodging establishments are adding the following amenities.

- A large working desk
- Improved lighting
- A dataport
- A two-line phone with voice mail
- A comfortable chair

- Office supplies
- Fax machine, on premises if not in-room
- Laser printer
- Copy machine

## In-Room Technology

Hotels are going high-tech, positioning themselves for the 21st Century. Consider some of the following innovations that are appearing in the most forward-thinking hotels.

- Internet hookups
- Fax machines that double as scanners
- Two-inch-thick plasma screen televisions that hang from the wall like a picture
- Business link phone systems that offer cellular service at the same number as the guestroom
- Microcameras that provide a view of a person at the door via in-room monitors or through the television set
- Computer-controlled wall vaults that identify the user and grant access while recording how long the vault was open and who opened it
- Speech recognition devices that control the telephone, lighting, drapes, climate, television, entertainment center, and other appliances such as the bathtub

# INDUSTRY ISSUES

Issues and trends that impact the entire lodging industry are important because they affect the way individual hoteliers and large conglomerates interact with the government, comply with and help influence legislation, and ultimately, how they will run their businesses.

## Mergers

One method of operating more efficiently and enhancing bottom line profits is seen as creating alliances and mergers of major hotel/motel chains. The major advantage of mergers, however, is to create rapid expansion of a hotel company without the painstaking construction of new establishments one by one. According to the AH&MA, investment companies across the country are buying up independent lodging establishments and chains at an unprecedented pace. The industry is rebounding from overbuilding in the 1980s and mergers are recording record profits. New companies that are well-funded are active in this market and are expected to bring some of the old established names in the industry significant competition in coming years.

Doubletree Corporation and Promus Hotel Corporation recently announced that they will merge in a $2.14 billion stock swap, creating the world's third-largest hotel company. This merger includes such well-known brand names as Embassy Suites, Hampton Inn and Red Lion.

A newspaper article in the *Orange County* (California) *Register* goes on to say, "The deal combines two of the fastest growing companies in the $58 billion-a-year U.S. industry. Promus's expertise at franchising hotels combined with Doubletree's management and upscale chains will forge a rival to Hilton Hotels Corporation, ITT Corporation's Sheraton and Marriott International Inc., analysts said."

"They are ideally positioned because they are in the fastest growing, most profitable segment of the industry," according to an analyst at Independence Investment Associates.

The combined company will control 1,136 hotels with 172,000 rooms and 40,000 employees in the United States. Its system-wide revenue of $5 billion puts it behind only Holiday Inn owned by Bass PLC and Marriott. Promus currently operates the Embassy Suites, Hampton Inn and Homewood Suites, Embassy Vacation Resort and Hampton Vacation Resort chains. Doubletree currently has the Doubletree Hotels, Doubletree Guest Suites, Club Hotels by Doubletree and Red Lion.

Analysts feel that the two companies complement one another more than compete head-on. Promus was created out of the old Holiday Inns of America, which sold that chain to Bass PLC in 1988. The company then spun off its casino operations in a separate company called Harrah's Entertainment Inc. in 1996.

Doubletree, which went public in 1994, was one of the few independent premiere hotel brands left after a series of mergers and acquisitions. In 1996, the company almost doubled its number of hotel rooms.

According to *The Register*, the new company will be able to combine Promus' profitable Embassy Suites upscale hotels with Doubletree's Guest Suites. It also gives the two companies a larger presence in the rapidly growing market for longer-stay hotels, combining Doubletree's Candlewood Hotels and Promus's Homewood Suites.

The companies report that the combination will save $15 million to $20 million per year in overhead, technology and financing costs, while creating opportunities for marketing between the brands. The combined company will have $740 million in debt. Promus's President Raymond Schultz says that their ability to cross-sell and cross-market their brands will be key to future growth and profitability. As appropriate mergers promote rapid expansion and economic rewards, more are expected in the near future, involving among others the hotel real estate investment trust Starwood Lodging, Westin Hotels and Resorts, Wyndham, Omni and Holiday Inn.

# Sales

Lodging sales are brisk with prices per room averaging $22,956 in 1998, an eight-year high according to the AH&MA. Even at these prices there is room for increases because the per-room average lags behind replacement cost. Entrepreneurs have recognized the tremendous profit potential in the lodging industry.

The year 1998 was the most successful thus far in the industry with more than $79 billion in sales, according to the AH&MA. Properties worldwide reported higher occupancies and rates (expected to increase by nearly 4% in 1999) pushing gross operating profits to 29.4% of total sales, an increase from 1997's 25.7%. Properties in North America report that more than 65% of total revenue came from room sales. Average operating profits are estimated to grow to $1,307 per available room in 1999. Industry volume has increased to 97.8 million room nights since the recession of the 1980s, according to the AH&MA.

# Jobs

The travel industry will continue to create more jobs than any other industry in the United States as we turn the century. A growth rate of more than 18% is expected by the year 2005, accounting for more than a million additional jobs, according to the Travel

Industry Association of America. The travel and tourism industry will account for 262 million jobs worldwide this year, or 10.5% of the total, according to the World Travel and Tourism Council. The industry continues to be the world's largest, producing more than 10% of the world's gross domestic product.

## Workforce

The travel industry is so vast, it is not surprising that its workforce has become increasingly diversified with more nationalities than ever now represented at the average hotel. The AH&MA also reports that high employee turnover rates, which have always plagued the industry, appear to be leveling off. Overall employee turnover has gone from 46.8% in 1985 to 53.2% in 1995. According to a 1995 AH&MA survey, average annual turnover is just under 60% for non-management employees and 20% for management. Diverse job descriptions and ample turnover contribute to the abundant opportunities in the travel industry.

## U.S. National Tourism Organization, Inc. (USNTO)

The U.S. National Tourism Organization, Inc. (USNTO) was created in 1996 to market tourism to the United States. The board of this organization, appointed by the AH&MA, will provide within one year of its first meeting a report to the Senate Committee on Commerce, Science and Transportation and the House Committee on Commerce for long-term funding for the organization. AH&MA will lobby Congress to appropriate funds for the USNTO.

## Reform of the Fair Labor Standards Act (FLSA)

The Fair Labor Standards Act (FLSA) was enacted during the depression when times and circumstances were certainly different. The law set minimum wage requirements, guaranteed employees overtime payments for time worked over 40 hours, and defined which types of jobs were exempt from overtime requirements. Revision of that law is now being considered by Congress. Industry officials support reforms that would reflect the modern workplace, including:

- Allowing compensatory time off in lieu of mandatory overtime payments
- Flexible scheduling

- New definitions for executive, administrative and professional positions

## Telecommunications

The year 1996 saw the passage of a far-reaching overhaul of telecommunications laws and practices. The lodging industry is faced with increasingly complex and potentially costly decisions about products and services. The industry seeks to meet guests' desires for more services but must also hold down costs. Other issues challenging the industry in the area of telecommunications include:

- Toll fraud issues
- Additional regulations
- Hearing aid compatibility
- Enhanced 911 access
- Long-distance access

## Technology

Advancing technology is forcing major changes on the lodging industry. Hoteliers are spending millions of dollars on hardware and technology that allow them to improve their operational efficiency and provide better customer service. AH&MA has launched a sweeping initiative to create computer interfacing standards designed to accelerate the lodging industry's technology usage and lower automation costs by connecting disparate computerized hospitality systems.

## Room Taxes

Local and state room taxes have been on the increase and that trend is not expected to reverse itself anytime soon. These taxes are generally used for tourism funding, but they have been increasingly used for funding sports stadium construction and renovation, and the construction of convention centers. AH&MA is opposed to any tax that adversely affects the lodging industry and will continue to track legislation of this nature.

## Green Properties

AH&MA has initiated a three-part environmental campaign for the lodging industry that includes in-room "Good Earthkeeping" guest cards, a workbook entitled *The Environmental Action Pack for Hotels*, and an educational video, "Shaping Change and Changing Minds: Environmental Management for the Lodging Industry." Benefits of this program to hoteliers include:

- Increased profit margins
- Meeting and exceeding guests' service expectations
- Reducing costs of energy, water and solid waste disposal

## Travel Agents

Travel agents continue to play a larger role in the lodging industry. Rising revenues mean higher travel agent commissions. Electronic hotel bookings rose from 55% in 1996 to 61% in 1997. Hotel bookings via global distribution systems in 1997 increased by almost 40% over 1996 bookings, totaling more than 26 million hotel reservations, according to a survey conducted by the Hotel Electronic Distribution Network Association. Lodging companies have been making more rates available in central reservation systems and actively encouraging bookings. As an added benefit, centralized commission payment offerings have made it easier for agencies to collect their fees.

## Meetings and Conventions

In 1998 statistics showed that there were fewer meetings at convention hotels, but with greater attendance and spending. The industry was predicted to grow by 39% in 1999 according to a 1999 Meetings Outlook Survey. PKF Consulting projects that convention hotels will experience the most growth in occupancy in the near future, followed by resort properties.

## Construction

Since the building boom of the 1980s, there has been an obvious reduction in the number of new rooms added (70,000 in 1996 compared to 185,000 in 1985). Cities, lenders and lodging companies themselves are placing heavy financial support behind new projects. In the United States, much of the new building is in limited-service and extended-stay hotels. The average size of a new property has dropped from 125-plus rooms in 1992 to fewer than 80 rooms in 1997. Properties are being built in tertiary markets that never experienced the building boom of the 1980s.

The larger trend to acquire existing hotels, renovate and reflag them is expected to continue to dominate the market. In 1996, acquisition costs averaged about 70% of replacement costs. Conversions of other types of commercial properties, such as offices and even prisons, is a popular concept and continues to be practiced.

## Food and Beverage Services

Just as occupancy in rooms is up, hotel restaurants are enjoying record occupancies. Annual food and beverage sales amount to more than $17.8 billion, and the market has had a com-  pounded growth rate of 4.3% since 1996. Hotel restaurants have become independent profit centers and food has become a major contributor to bottom-line performance. The latest trends include:

- Mediterranean dishes increase in popularity

- Room service menus match the casual main restaurant

- Wines continue to help drive the beverage business

- Ready-made licensed food courts or food stores replace hotel restaurants

## Extended Stay Properties

The extended-stay market has become one of the hottest in the industry, with travelers staying five or more nights accounting for 30% of all room nights. In 1997, these properties generated an estimated $3.5 billion (or 5%) in total revenue. In 1998, more than 10 lodging companies introduced extended-stay brands. As of 1999, there are 861 properties affiliated with major chains containing 127,000 suites, representing 3.6 of the guestrooms in the industry. Occupancy and average room rates at these properties are predicted to be much higher than the industry at large.

# CONCLUSION

There is no denying that the hotel industry is a growing and dynamic one. For hotel operators to be successful, they must know their market and keep up with the latest trends in marketing, customer service and technology. They also must be energetic and imaginative in meeting the challenges of the industry. Where there is demand, there is great opportunity for the supplier.

# QUESTIONS

1. The most popular destination in the world for international tourists is:

    a. Great Britain
    b. the United States
    c. Canada
    d. France

2. Most tourists to the United States originate from:

    a. Australia, New Zealand and South America
    b. Africa, France and Spain
    c. Great Britain, Japan and Germany
    d. Russia, China and Taiwan

3. The leading destination state in the United States is:

    a. California
    b. Florida
    c. New York
    d. Hawaii

4. If hotel operators see that their portion of the international market is less than it should be, one of the steps they can take is:

    a. place a home page on the World Wide Web with on-line reservation capabilities
    b. participate in a central reservation system
    c. advertise in international publications
    d. all of the above

5. In general, an hotel operator seeks to:

   a. increase occupancy levels

   b. minimize expenses

   c. maximize profitability

   d. all of the above

6. The entrepreneur who built lodging establishments in the Midwest of smaller size than his predecessors found that:

   a. it required less start-up capital

   b. it was more difficult to achieve an acceptable occupancy level

   c. the occupancy level needed to reach profitability was higher

   d. none of the above

7. The main advantage of hotel companies to merge is:

   a. conserve start-up capital

   b. eliminate competition

   c. save money

   d. create rapid expansion

8. When considering building new lodging establishments vs. acquiring existing ones:

   a. acquisition costs are less than the cost of building

   b. acquisition costs are about the same as the cost of building

   c. acquisition costs have been running slightly more than the cost of building

   d. it's better to build new because then the hotel operator can design what he or she wants

9. Statistics show that domestic travelers are less likely to become victims of crime than those who stay home. The reason for this is:

 a. domestic travelers are more familiar with the area
 b. domestic travelers stay in their lodging establishment which is secure
 c. domestic travelers have a higher level of crime consciousness
 d. domestic travelers travel without much cash

10. The accommodation of children in the lodging industry:

 a. is a main focal point for many hotels
 b. is not an issue because few children travel
 c. is approached in an indifferent manner by most hotels
 d. is not very important because it doesn't contribute to profitability

11. Self-service check-in kiosks are an innovation designed to:

 a. give employees more free time
 b. shorten guests' check-in time
 c. afford guests more privacy at check-in time
 d. save guests money

12. Hotel home pages on the Internet offer which of the following advantages:

 a. on-line booking capabilities for reservations
 b. dispense information on rates, promotions and packages
 c. on-line booking capabilities for special services like massages
 d. all of the above

13. The purpose of "frequent-stay" programs is to:

 a. increase market share
 b. save money
 c. be able to offer contests
 d. compete with the airlines

14. Special business room accommodations for guests would include:

    a. a two-line phone with voice mail

    b. a fax machine

    c. improved lighting

    d. all of the above

15. A new organization implemented to promote tourism to the United States is the:

    a. National Association of Tourism Offices (NATO)

    b. U.S. Association of Tourism (USAT)

    c. U.S. National Tourism Organization, Inc. (USNTO)

    d. Tourism Company of America (TCA)

16. High-tech in-room advances include:

    a. two-inch-thick plasma screen televisions that hang from the wall like a picture

    b. speech recognition devices that control the telephone

    c. internet hookups

    d. all of the above

17. Lodging industry officials believe that the Fair Labor Standards Act (FLSA) needs to be revised because:

    a. it was originally enacted during the depression

    b. its regulations regarding overtime may not fit today's hotel

    c. laws need to reflect the needs of the modern workplace

    d. all of the above

18. "Green properties" refers to:

    a. hotels that are new in the marketplace

    b. hotels that are making a lot of money

    c. hotels that are environmentally efficient

    d. hotels that are painted green

19. Changes in telecommunications laws create complex challenges for the hotel industry. Among these challenges are:

    a. seeing-eye dogs
    b. toll fraud
    c. pager regulations
    d. all of the above

20. Food and beverage services at hotels are:

    a. a profit center of their own
    b. increasingly important and a major contributor to the bottom line
    c. not that important to profitability
    d. both a and b

# ANSWERS

1. *b*
2. *c*
3. *b*
4. *d*
5. *d*
6. *a*
7. *d*
8. *a*
9. *c*
10. *a*
11. *b*
12. *d*
13. *a*
14. *d*
15. *c*
16. *d*
17. *d*
18. *c*
19. *b*
20. *d*

# Legal Issues In Property Management

• **Building A Foundation**
• **Americans With Disabilities Act (ADA)**
• **Fair Housing Laws**
• **The Process of Eviction**
• **Environmental And Safety Issues**
• **Landlord/Tenant Relations**
• **Homeowners' Associations**
• **Conclusion**

# BUILDING A FOUNDATION

We are a nation of laws. In the area of personal rights and property rights, we do not act whimsically nor with prejudice. We act in consideration of the rights of others and with an eye to the law. It is a matter of authority. With every act that the property manager takes, he or she must consider the law. What authority does the law give me to do this? Could I be sued for taking this action? This is the foundation of our actions in the practice of property management.

When we manage real property, it is obvious we are also managing people. We permit people to do this—we restrict them from doing that. This action costs the person some freedom. This other action costs someone else some money. What is our authority for doing each of these things? Have we stepped on someone's toes or have we done what is right according to the law?

In addition to the letter of the law, there is the issue of the spirit of the law. It goes to the purpose and intent of the law. Many hold that it is better to comply with the spirit of the law than to obey the letter of the law. There are times when having to comply with the letter of the law gets in the way of accomplishing the spirit of the law. Mother Teresa was considering taking over a vacant tenement building in New York and converting it to a shelter to house the homeless. There were so many city codes and regulations to comply with, including outfitting the aging building with modern elevators, that the expense of rehabilitation was prohibitive. No laws were broken, but no homeless were housed, either.

The law is to be servant to society, to the people. It is to order our lives and make them better. There are times, however, when society becomes servant, even slave to the law. In these instances, the benefits of the law are not conferred upon the people. The people are deprived of them. Nevertheless, it is incumbent on the property manager to know the laws and to obey them, in spirit and according to the letter. The intent is that by obeying the law in the letter and in the spirit, lessors and lessees will receive all that is coming to them. Consider the following areas of legal compliance.

# AMERICANS WITH DISABILITIES ACT (ADA)

The Americans with Disabilities Act (ADA) was passed by Congress in 1990. It is about inclusion. It requires any business or public facility to be accessible to everyone, including those with disabilities. A disability is defined as a physical or mental impairment that substantially limits one or more of an individual's major life activities such as performing manual tasks, caring for oneself, walking, seeing, hearing, speaking and working. The law includes state and federal government buildings such as city halls, libraries, office buildings and post offices. Businesses in the private sector that are open to the public are considered public accommodations and must also comply with the ADA. Included in the list of private sector/public accommodation properties would be shopping centers, hotels and motels, concert halls, churches, professional offices, gas stations, retail stores, places of education, public display or collection, public gathering, exhibition, entertainment and office buildings.

The Americans with Disabilities Act Accessibility Guidelines (ADAAG) provide standards to be observed in the design, construction and alteration of buildings that come under the jurisdiction of the ADA. The guidelines address such particulars as reach ranges and space allowable, protruding objects, parking and passenger loading zones, ramps, stairs, elevators, platform lifts, doors and windows. They specify how rest rooms are to be arranged with heights for urinals, lavatories and mirrors, arrangement and configuration of toilet stalls, drinking fountains, water coolers and shower stalls.

According to the ADAAG, alteration means "a change to a building or facility made by, on behalf of, or for the use of a public accommodation or commercial facility, that affects or could affect the usability of the building or facility or part thereof. Alterations include, but are not limited to, remodeling, renovation, rehabilitation, reconstruction, historic restoration, changes or rearrangement of the structural parts or elements, and changes or rearrangement in the plan configuration of the walls and full-height partitions. Normal maintenance, reroofing, painting or wallpapering, or changes to mechanical and electrical systems are not alterations unless they affect the usability of the building or facility."

The ADAAG directs that all buildings and facilities that come under the jurisdiction of the ADA must have an accessible route for all persons, including the disabled. This means "a continuous unobstructed path connecting all accessible elements and spaces of a building or facility. Interior accessible routes may include corridors, floors, ramps, elevators, lifts and clear floor space at fixtures. Exterior accessible routes may include parking access aisles, curb ramps, crosswalks at vehicular ways, walks, ramps and lifts."

Of particular interest to income property owners and managers, the ADAAG defines a dwelling unit as "a single unit which provides a kitchen or food preparation area, in addition to rooms and spaces for living, bathing, sleeping and the like. Dwelling units include a single family home or a townhouse used as a transient group home, an apartment building used as a shelter, guest rooms in a hotel that provide sleeping accommodations and food preparation areas, and other similar facilities used on a transient basis." The ADAAG guidelines do not imply that the unit is used as a residence.

General exceptions are made to the requirements of the ADA under the following circumstances. "In new construction, a person or entity is not required to meet fully the requirements of these guidelines where that person or entity can demonstrate that it is structurally impracticable to do so. Full compliance will be considered structurally impracticable only in those rare circumstances when the unique characteristics of terrain prevent the incorporation of accessibility features. If full compliance with the requirements of these guidelines is structurally impracticable, a person or entity shall comply with the requirements to the extent it is not structurally impracticable. Any portion of the building or facility which can be made accessible shall comply to the extent that it is not structurally impracticable. Accessibility is not required to (a) observation galleries used primarily for security purposes; or (b) in non-occupiable spaces accessed only by ladders, catwalks, crawl spaces, very narrow passageways, or freight (non-passenger) elevators, and frequented only by service personnel for repair purposes; such spaces include, but are not limited to, elevator pits, elevator penthouses and piping or equipment catwalks."

Accommodations must also be made in the area of communication. A disabled person must have access to telephones, intercoms and buzzers to be able to communicate with people in the facility and out of the facility.

Many facilities leased by tenants and managed by property managers come under the jurisdiction of the ADA. The property manager must identify those properties and inform the owner as to what is required. The professional property manager will not be a legal expert in the administration of the ADA, but should consult one in order to ensure that the details of the law are carried out.

The lessor or lessee may be responsible for the required alterations. The parties must come to agreement and the arrangement should be stipulated in the lease contract.

# FAIR HOUSING LAWS

Initial Fair Housing Laws are established with the advent of the United States Constitution and the Bill of Rights. Fair Housing Laws were further defined by the Civil Rights Act of 1866, which states in part that, "All citizens of the United States shall have the same right in every state and territory, as is enjoyed by white citizens thereof, to inherit, purchase, lease, sell, hold and convey real and personal property." The frame of reference provided by "white citizens" was the only meaningful standard to express the intent of the legislators in 1866.

The U.S. Supreme Court upheld the Civil Rights Act of 1866 in the case of *Jones v. Mayer*, 1968. Alfred Mayer was a real estate broker in Chicago. Jones was an African-American buyer who claimed he was not given the same opportunity to view and buy homes as white prospects. Mayer *steered* Jones to segregated black neighborhoods and failed to show him the same homes as white buyers of similar financial qualifications.

The Fair Housing Act (technically known as Title VIII of the Civil Rights Act of 1968) further prohibits discrimination in the sale, lease or financing of housing based on race, color, sex, religion, familial status, disability or national origin. In the United States, people can live where they choose to live. The only qualification is financial.

There are many ways a property manager could violate Fair Housing Laws. Care must be taken to avoid the following offenses.

## Refusing to Rent

Refusing to rent to a prospective tenant for reasons of race, color, sex, religion, marital status, familial status, disability or national origin is illegal. The issue of familial status is defined as having at least one member of the family under 18 years of age or the  presence of a pregnant woman. It addresses the issue of children and it is illegal to discriminate against a family because of the presence of children. The only exception to the familial status antidiscrimination provision of the law is those developments that are designated for residents 55 years of age and over. A new amendment to this provision requires that such a complex have at least one person 55 or older in 80% of its units, that management state specifically that the housing is intended for older persons, and that such policies are consistently followed.

A prospective tenant with a disability also cannot be discriminated against in rental housing. Again, a disability is defined as a physical or mental impairment that substantially limits one or more of a person's major life activities. It includes areas of walking, talking, seeing and hearing. For the most part, landlords are not required to make alterations to their structures but must allow the disabled to do so and can require that the structure be returned to its original condition upon vacancy. However, according to Amendments to the Fair Housing Act adopted in 1988, a residential building of four or more units ready for occupancy after March 1991 must provide access for the disabled.

Owners and managers could discriminate in these areas and hide their unlawful practices. Sometimes it's difficult for a tenant to know why he or she was refused, or to prove discrimination if it occurred. Local Fair Housing Councils and other advocacy groups often use *testers* to gather evidence of violation of Fair Housing Laws. One would-be tenant in California approached an apartment building to look at an apartment and had the door slammed in her face as soon as the landlady saw her. The prospective tenant happened to be black. She also happened to be a Los Angeles County deputy sheriff. A co-worker of the deputy sheriff  then approached the landlady with the same results. The local Fair Housing Council sent two testers to the apartment building and the landlady showed similar behavior. The commission found racial discrimination and awarded the prospective tenant $10,000 and imposed a $10,000 civil penalty for "outrageous conduct."

No one has the right to refuse another person a place to live because of who they are. A landlord known to the author refused tenancy to a family because the parents didn't speak English. Teenage children did, but the landlord was concerned that if something happened when the children weren't home, he wouldn't be able to communicate effectively with the parents. Though nothing came of the refusal to rent, the landlord was fortunate. The language people speak is intimately tied to national origin and ethnicity. It would have been difficult for the landlord to deny discrimination against the would-be tenants because of who they are.

# Steering

Steering is just what it sounds like—directing people to certain locations. It involves steering people into those locations based on the characteristics on which we may not discriminate—race, color, sex, religion, familial status, marital status, disability or national origin.

If someone comes to our office looking for a house or apartment and they are of a certain ethnic background, we do not have the right to assume that they want to live in a segregated part of the community occupied only by members of their own ethnicity. Many people have deliberately chosen integrated neighborhoods so that their children would have the benefit of a diverse cultural influence. This was the essence of the case of *Jones v. Mayer*, 1968, as cited before. Remember, people can live where they want to live and they have the right to understand all of their options so they can make their own choices.

Property managers and real estate agents and brokers are on the front lines of implementing the Fair Housing Laws. We must not be guilty of perpetuating bigotry and prejudice by steering people into neighborhoods where we think they belong. This can be done deliberately with intent to harm, or it can be done inadvertently because of our own assumptions and biases. Either way it is unlawful and we must make every conscious and professional effort to be certain we give everyone equal opportunity and choice.

A prospect should be qualified financially before it is determined what properties will be shown to him or her. The property manager or agent should also listen extensively to the desires of the prospect so they can be matched with an appropriate property according to the qualities they want and their ability to pay. Then the property manager or agent should show the same properties to that prospect as they would for any other prospect of the same qualifications and preferences. Remember, this is a color-blind profession and we have the opportunity to open doors for people that they have every constitutional right to receive.

A *Prospect Equal Service Report for Rentals* provided by the National Association of Realtors has been reproduced on the following page. The form documents the sequence the property manager followed to serve the prospective tenant. Considerations such as whether or not the prospect desired information about housing for older persons, what locations were requested, properties shown and services provided, whether an application was offered to the prospect and whether or not it was returned help provide guidelines for service and documentation of non-discrimination.

## Figure 16-1    Prospect Equal Service Report

### PROSPECT EQUAL SERVICE REPORT

Rentals

Date:                    Agent:                                                              Office:

#### PROSPECT INFORMATION

| Name: | Name: |
|---|---|
| Address: | Address: |
| Home phone:          work phone: | Home phone:          work phone: |
| Race: * | Race: * |

\* For Affirmative Marketing purposes. Information on prospect race is sought to assist in the monitoring of the firm's commitment to equal professional service. Article 10 of the NATIONAL ASSOCIATION OF REALTORS® Code of Ethics states: **REALTORS® shall** not deny equal professional services to any person for reasons of race, color, religion, sex, familial status, handicap, or national origin. REALTORS® shall not be parties to any plan or agreement to discriminate against a person or persons on the basis of race, color, religion, sex, familial status, handicap, or national origin.

| Prospect came to us as a result of | Prospect is ___ current tenant ___ previous tenant | ___ Ad (source) | ___ For rent sign | ___ Referral (source) | ___ Other |
|---|---|---|---|---|---|
| Prospect preferences | possession date | rent range | size and type of unit: # bedrooms other features: | | |

**Does prospect desire information regarding Housing for Older Persons?**
*If so, is any member of prospect's household over 55?*

**Prospect requested locations:**

#### SERVICE PROVIDED - PROPERTY SHOWN

**Did the prospect initially request information on or ask to view any specific property(ies)?**

| If yes, list address for each request, include street address, unit #, and community. | Rent | Deposit | Was unit shown? | If shown, prospect's comments and preferences. If not, why not. | Application offered? |
|---|---|---|---|---|---|
|  |  |  |  |  |  |
|  |  |  |  |  |  |

**Did you offer to put the prospect on a waiting list for any property requested?**

If so, indicate which properties

**Were other properties offered to the prospect?**

| List properties offered or shown. Include community, address, & unit #. | Rent | Deposit | Was unit shown? | If shown, Prospect's comments and preferences. If not, why not. | Application offered? |
|---|---|---|---|---|---|
|  |  |  |  |  |  |
|  |  |  |  |  |  |
|  |  |  |  |  |  |

| Were qualifying questions asked prior to application? If yes, indicate information obtained | ___ Income | ___ Employment | ___ Current Rent | ___ Other |
|---|---|---|---|---|
| Was an application offered to the prospect? | Did the prospect complete and return the application? Keep application on file for reference | | | |

Application and credit check fees quoted to prospect

Disposition, contact dates and comments:

*Use the back of this page to list additional information, including other properties shown.*

# Discrimination in Terms or Conditions of Lease

It is unlawful to discriminate in the terms or conditions of a lease based on race, color, sex, religion, familial status, marital status, disability or national origin. As a property manager it may be your personal experience that you will have more difficulty with a single male tenant than with a married couple or family. The single male tenant may play loud music, have parties, not take good care of the rental unit, not be as considerate of his neighbors and have women over at all hours of the night, but you cannot create separate conditions for his tenancy. You cannot require a co-signer or a larger deposit because he is a single male. You may be exactly right in your anticipation of trouble, but you must still treat all prospective tenants by the same terms and conditions

You cannot set different prices for the renting of an apartment to people of different races. Some would choose to do this to discourage certain races from applying. Others would actually expect to receive more for being willing to accept a certain race. Some would advertise a higher price but reveal only to their preferred racial group that they can pay less. The danger of this, of course, is not attracting as many qualified prospects because of overpricing. The same price must be offered to all, regardless of race or other personal characteristics. A bigoted owner might not see the problem since the property *is* available. It is not sufficient that it is available. The point is there must be no impediment placed in the way of any racial group.

You cannot say that white people can have pets and black people can't. You can make restrictions on pets if you want to, but they must apply equally to all people.

You cannot set one limit on the total number of occupants you'll accept in a unit and apply that to Hispanics, and set a more liberal limit for people of another ethnic group. Again, it is a valid restriction out of concern for wear and tear, but it must be applied even-handedly.

Requirements and restrictions are the prerogative of ownership and property managers. The prudent management of a real property asset demands it. But requirements and restrictions cannot favor one group and slight another. Equal opportunity is the name of the game.

## Discrimination in Advertising

It is illegal to make statements in advertising that would serve to discriminate based on race, color, sex, religion, familial status, marital status, disability or national origin. Advertising that discouraged or turned people away based on these characteristics would violate Fair Housing Laws. It is a violation of law to advertise in such a manner and it is a violation of law to implement one's rental policies in that manner. Phrases to be avoided would include the following.

- "No Catholics"

- "Whites only"

- "Singles only"

- "No singles"

- "No children"

- "No gays"

- "Single white female preferred"

- "Couples must show proof of marriage"

- "No wheel chairs allowed"

- "No Asians, Blacks or Hispanics"

- "No single males"

Fair Housing Laws provide that all people, regardless of the above characteristics, have equal rights to fair housing opportunities. People can live anywhere they choose to live, so long as they can afford it.

## False Statements of Availability

A cowardly way of trying to discriminate against people is to lie about the availability of a property. "Sorry, it's already rented" may sound like the sure-fire way out for a bigoted landlord, but it is one of the excuses that is easily verifiable. The would-be tenant could double check by having a friend inquire. Fair housing advocates could easily document such false statements.

## Interference

There are many ways a bigoted person might try to interfere with a person exercising his or her constitutional rights in choosing a place to live. One way would be to try to intimidate the prospective tenant or owner into not occupying the chosen property. An example of this occurred recently where a black family was having a home built in a middle-class tract of homes. As they came by one day to inspect the progress, a white neighbor living next door to their new house came outside draped in a confederate flag. The white man asked the black man if he planned on moving into the house. The black man affirmed that he did. The white man assured him that he would be the worst neighbor he ever had.

The intimidation worked. The black family, having two children, decided they did not want the trouble that was promised by the unreasonable neighbor. The white man's interference kept them from living in their chosen neighborhood.  One consolation to this sad act was that the white man received 21 months in federal prison for his actions. Sadly, even upon reflection, he could not figure out what he had done wrong.

The property manager is a real estate professional and should be informed of the laws that pertain to Fair Housing. He or she should also be committed to the ideals behind the laws and operate in a spirit of fairness and equality, helping others to exercise their own choice and gain the full benefits of The Fair Housing Act.

## Consequences

Consequences for violating Fair Housing Laws are serious and may be implemented at the federal level, as well as in state and local jurisdictions. Penalties will fall to ownership and to the real estate professional in violation of the law.

For the real estate professional, consequences are likely to manifest in three possible scenarios.

### DISCIPLINE

If the professional is licensed with one's respective state department of real estate, or is a member of a professional association, discipline is a likely result of discrimination. It could mean  having a license suspended or revoked, being fined, and having membership in an association suspended or revoked. The individual may also be required to take extra courses in the area of fair housing to decrease the likelihood of ever erring in the same manner again.

### CIVIL DAMAGES

The real estate professional who acts in such a way as to deprive an individual of his or her civil rights to fair housing may be sued for actual damages. Damages or injunctive relief may also be sought from the owner of the property, requiring him or her to follow through and rent or lease the property to the prospect if it is still available.

### CRIMINAL SUIT

If the real estate professional is involved in a conspiracy to deprive an individual of rights to fair housing, he or she may be prosecuted by the U.S. Attorney General to enforce the Federal Open Housing Law. Complaints would have to be filed with the U.S. Department of Housing and Urban Development within one year of the occurrence of the discrimination.

## Prevention of Discrimination

The professional property manager should strive to eliminate all forms of discrimination in one's practice. This can be accomplished by taking the following actions.

(1) Tap into current information on Fair Housing Laws, including updates and amendments. This can be done through local apartment associations and fair housing advocate groups. Make sure you're informed.

(2) Designate a fair housing specialist in your office, fixing responsibility on that person to stay informed and train other staff members in policies, procedures and changes.

(3) Adopt a policy of fair housing practices for your office. Post the Equal Housing Opportunity logo and poster as depicted on

this page and commit to living up to its ideals. Prepare a one-page statement of your policies and sign it, posting it in a prominent location in your office for all to see.

(4) Emphasize objective criteria that will determine who is accepted as a tenant and who is rejected—criteria such as rent-to-income ratio and credit record. Have a checklist of such criteria to indicate exactly what the basis was for acceptance or rejection of a tenant.

(5) Keep individual records in each file so you can guide your actions and see what you have done. This attention to detail will also help you defend yourself should false accusations be brought against you.

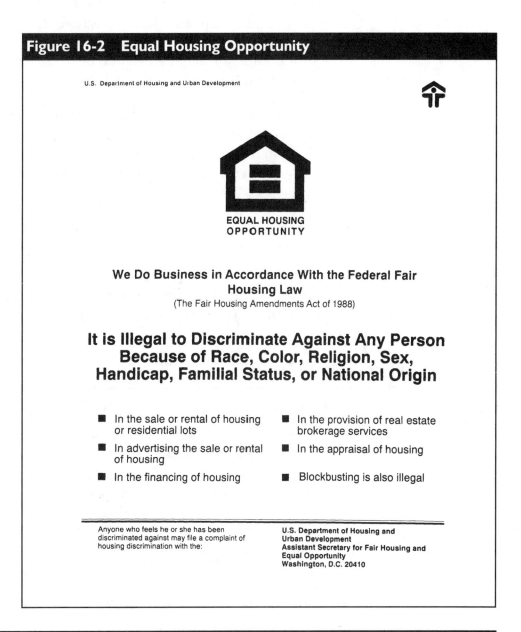

**Figure 16-2   Equal Housing Opportunity**

U.S. Department of Housing and Urban Development

**EQUAL HOUSING OPPORTUNITY**

**We Do Business in Accordance With the Federal Fair Housing Law**
(The Fair Housing Amendments Act of 1988)

**It is Illegal to Discriminate Against Any Person Because of Race, Color, Religion, Sex, Handicap, Familial Status, or National Origin**

■ In the sale or rental of housing or residential lots

■ In advertising the sale or rental of housing

■ In the financing of housing

■ In the provision of real estate brokerage services

■ In the appraisal of housing

■ Blockbusting is also illegal

Anyone who feels he or she has been discriminated against may file a complaint of housing discrimination with the:

**U.S. Department of Housing and Urban Development
Assistant Secretary for Fair Housing and Equal Opportunity
Washington, D.C. 20410**

# THE PROCESS OF EVICTION

The eviction process is precisely defined to protect the rights of a tenant. If procedures are not followed exactly, the landlord may have to start the process over again, losing a lot of time and money. Many feel that the process is skewed to the advantage of the tenant, so precision in following the correct steps to remove a tenant must be followed.

A professional eviction service points out that tenants more than 10 days late in paying the rent bring their obligation current less than 20% of the time. Evictions in Small Claims Court take an average of 65 to 90 days to complete. Lock-out techniques and self-help evictions can subject the landlord to damages and countersuits. If there are appeals by the tenant, bankruptcy or third-party claims to possession, these events create further complexities in the process and require more legal expertise. It is recommended that competent legal guidance be followed in the eviction process. This is no time for fooling around.

While we are in need of professional legal advice to carry out an eviction to be sure we are complying with all the requirements of a particular jurisdiction, it is beneficial to know the basic steps of the process and to understand the concept behind each step.

## Unlawful Detainer

The most expedient eviction process in most jurisdictions is the unlawful detainer action. Final results can happen quicker than with other court procedures if all steps are followed correctly.

## Three-Day Notice

The three-day notice to pay or quit is the first step in the eviction process by unlawful detainer. It is the notice that is generally given if the tenant is not paying rent. Since the tenant is already delinquent in the paying of rent, a 30-day notice is not required. One three-day notice must be served in person to each tenant named in the notice. All adults living in the rental unit should be named in the notice, even if some are not mentioned in the lease. If not, third party claims of possession may arise later to further delay the process. This is a common mistake landlords make. If you don't know the names of all parties in possession, one attorney advises naming them as *Doe I*, *Doe II*, and so forth. At least then their possession of the unit has been acknowledged. If it becomes impossible to serve each party in possession in person, the posting and mailing method may be used. The notice is posted on the door of the rental unit and mailed to each tenant named in the notice. This is affectionately known in the industry as the "nail and mail" method.

---

**Figure 16-3    Three-Day Notice to Pay or Quit**

## NOTICE TO PAY RENT OR QUIT

TO: _____
All residents (tenants and subtenants) in possession (full name) and all others in possession

WITHIN THREE DAYS after the service on you of this notice, you are hereby required to pay to the under-

signed or_____, his authorized agent, the

rent of the premises hereinafter described, of which you now hold possession amounting to the sum of

_____ dollars ($ _____)

enumerated as follows:

$ _____ Due From _____ 20 _____ To _____ 20 _____

$ _____ Due From _____ 20 _____ To _____ 20 _____

$ _____ Due From _____ 20 _____ To _____ 20 _____

OR QUIT AND DELIVER UP THE POSSESSION OF THE PREMISES.

The premises herein referred to are situated in the city of _____ ,

County of _____ , State of California, designated by the number

and street as _____ , apt. _____ .

YOU ARE FURTHER NOTIFIED THAT, the owner/landlord does hereby elect to declare the forfeiture of your lease or rental agreement under which you hold possession of the above-described premises and if you fail to perform or otherwise comply, will institute legal proceeding to recover rent and possession of said premises which could result in a judgement against you including costs and necessary disbursements together with treble damages as allowed by law for such unlawful detention.

DATE: _____     _____
OWNER  /  AGENT

---

## Thirty-Day Notice

A 30-day notice is served in the same manner as a three-day notice to initiate an unlawful detainer action. It is used typically in situations where the tenant is not delinquent in payments, but a fixed period lease has expired or a landlord sold the unit and the buyer wanted to move in on a certain date. If money is due, the landlord is not obligated to accept anything less than payment in full. If he or she accepts a partial payment, the three- or 30-day period must begin over again. This is one tactic a tenant can use to stall for time.

### Figure 16-4 Declaration of Service

-PROOF OF SERVICE-

I served the within:

1. Name: _____

2. Person with whom left: title or relationship to person served:

   _____

3. Date and Time of Delivery: _____

4. Date of Mailing: _____ Place of Mailing: _____

5. Address, City and State (when required, indicate whether address is home or business): _____

   _____

6. Manner of Service (Check appropriate box):

   [] A. PERSONAL SERVICE: By handing a copy to the person served.

   [] B. SUBSTITUTED SERVICE: By leaving a copy at the dwelling, house, usual place of abode, of the person served in the presence of a competent member of the household, at least 18 years of age, who was informed of the general nature of the papers: and thereafter mailing (by first-class mail, postage prepaid) a copy to the person served at the place where a copy was left.

   [] C. SERVICE POSTING: By posting a copy at a conspicuous place on the dwelling, house, usual place of abode pursuant to Section 1162(3); thereafter mailing (by first-class mail, postage prepaid) a copy to the person served to the posted address. At said time and place, _____

   could not be found nor could a person of suitable age or discretion be found on the premises. At said time I was over the age of 18 years.

I declare under penalty of perjury that the foregoing is true and correct.

Executed on _____ 20 ___, at _____ California.

_____
(signature of declarant)

_____
(type or print name of declarant)

_____
(type or print address)

_____
(phone number)

## Declaration of Service

To verify service of the three- or 30-day notices, the server can execute a *Declaration of Service Notice to Resident(s)/Tenant(s)* (**Figure 16-4**). This notice declares under penalty of perjury that the declarant served notice to the tenant in the manner specified in the document, either in person or by the mail and post method. It also states that the declarant is willing and able to testify to such in court if necessary. Such a notice documents the service process and firms up the case for the landlord.

## File Unlawful Detainer Action

The next step in the unlawful detainer action is to appear in the court of appropriate jurisdiction and file the unlawful detainer action against the delinquent tenant. The filing will require verification of a valid rental agreement between lessor and lessee, and documentation of the proper serving of a three-day or 30-day notice. When the appropriate number of days have expired without the tenant responding, the landlord may file the unlawful detainer action in court.

The court will then issue a summons which must be hand delivered to each tenant. The summons informs the tenant that he or she has been sued for unlawful detainer, the case number of the lawsuit, the court name and address, and the time allowed for the tenant to respond if they wish to defend themselves. Attached to the summons is a  copy of the complaint against them. Since most of the time an unlawful detainer action is brought for not paying rent that is due, there is usually not much of a defense, and most tenants do not respond at this time. If the tenant does not respond, the court may enter a judgment against the tenant for the relief demanded in the complaint, which could result in the garnishment of wages or taking of money or other property requested in the complaint, as well as eviction.

If the tenant does respond to the complaint, the landlord bringing the unlawful detainer action should seek a court date as soon as possible. This usually takes several weeks to accomplish.

As to the hand delivery of the summons and complaint, if this cannot be accomplished due to evasive actions on the part of the tenants, the landlord may be able to post the summons and complaint and mail to each tenant. It is important that all tenants in possession, even if not named in the lease, be named in the complaint and served with the summons. This will prevent them from coming forth later and stalling the process of eviction. If the landlord has to resort to mailing the summons to the tenants, service may not be effective until 10 days after the mailing and the tenant will gain another five days in which to respond. These processes and how they are carried out determine the efficiency of the eviction process.

Let's assume that the summons and copy of the complaint have been properly served. There was either no response from the tenant or an inadequate defense. A judgment is rendered against the tenant for the delinquent amount plus court costs and attorney's fees if allowed in the lease agreement. The landlord also receives the right to recapture the premises with a writ of execution. This gives the U.S. Marshal's Office the authority to evict the tenant. They will serve the tenant with a five-day notice to vacate. If the tenants have not vacated by that time, they will be escorted from the premises. At this late stage, even the most obnoxious tenant usually leaves without a fight. The marshals always win.

About all that is left to resolve at this point is the condition of the rental unit and any personal property that may have been left behind. If the rental unit is trashed beyond what the security deposit will cover, damages can be documented and an additional judgment can be sought. Collection, however, would require diligent pursuit and would be possible only if the ex-tenant is working.

If personal property remains, it should be inventoried in the presence of the marshal. The landlord should file a Notice of Right to Reclaim Abandoned Property and send a copy to the tenant's last known address. In most jurisdictions if there is no response after a specified number of days, the landlord can dispose of the property. If the property is worth less than $300, he or she can dispose of it and keep the proceeds. If the property is worth more than $300, a public sale must be held and the landlord keeps only the amount of the cost of storing and selling the merchandise. Any additional proceeds would go to the local jurisdiction, such as the county.

To save the landlord time and money, it is important that the proper legal steps be followed each time an eviction is necessary. Professional advice and services can be invaluable for this process, and passes the torch of responsibility to that party.

## Figure 16-5   Notice to Vacate

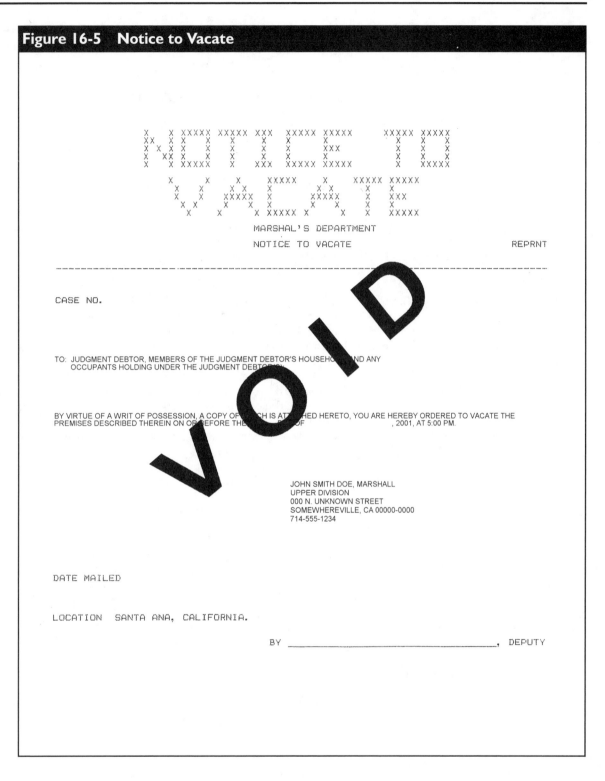

MARSHAL'S DEPARTMENT

NOTICE TO VACATE                                                    REPRNT

CASE NO.

TO:  JUDGMENT DEBTOR, MEMBERS OF THE JUDGMENT DEBTOR'S HOUSEHOLD AND ANY
     OCCUPANTS HOLDING UNDER THE JUDGMENT DEBTOR(S).

BY VIRTUE OF A WRIT OF POSSESSION, A COPY OF WHICH IS ATTACHED HERETO, YOU ARE HEREBY ORDERED TO VACATE THE
PREMISES DESCRIBED THEREIN ON OR BEFORE THE        DAY OF                       , 2001, AT 5:00 PM.

JOHN SMITH DOE, MARSHALL
UPPER DIVISION
000 N. UNKNOWN STREET
SOMEWHEREVILLE, CA 00000-0000
714-555-1234

DATE MAILED

LOCATION   SANTA ANA, CALIFORNIA.

BY _____, DEPUTY

**Figure 16-6   Notice of Right to Reclaim Abandoned Personal Property**

# Notice of Belief of Abandonment

TO: _____

TENANT(S) IN POSSESSION OF THE PREMISES AT:

_____
Street Address

City of _____ , County of _____ , California.

This notice is given pursuant to Section 1951.3 of the Civil Code concerning the real property leased by you at the above address.  The rent on this property had been due and unpaid for 14 consecutive days and the lessor/landlord believes that you have abandoned the property.

The real property will be deemed abandoned within the meaning of Section 1951.2 of the Civil Code and your lease will terminate on _____ , 20 __ , a date not less than 18 days after the mailing of this notice, unless before such date the undersigned receives at the address indicated below a written notice from you stating both of the following:

(1)  Your intent not to abandon the real property;

(2)  An address at which you may be served by certified mail in any action for unlawful detainer of the real property.

You are required to pay the rent due and unpaid on this real property as required by the lease, and your failure to do so can lead to a court proceeding against you.

DATE: _____

_____
LESSOR (SIGNATURE)

_____
LESSOR NAME (PRINT)

_____
ADDRESS

_____

# ENVIRONMENTAL AND SAFETY ISSUES

Much attention has been given in the last 20 to 30 years to environmental and safety issues as they affect the use of real property. Federal laws, of course, have jurisdiction in all states and the professional property manager must be familiar with them. It is important also that the property manager investigate the state and local laws that pertain to his or her area. When federal and state or local laws differ, the more stringent laws must be obeyed. In doing so, all of the regulations will be honored.

Consider the following laws that were enacted by Congress that impact the environmental area.

## The National Environmental Policy Act (NEPA)

NEPA was passed in 1970 and requires that an environmental impact statement be prepared and released prior to any federal action that would affect the environment. Environmental impact reports are also required by some state and local governments for private developments. The Environmental Protection Agency (EPA) was established with NEPA to lead the way in the nation's attempt to deal with pollution problems.

## The Clean Air Act

The Clean Air Act was passed in 1970 and requires the EPA to establish national standards for clean air. The EPA designates how many particles of each pollutant can be present in the air. Factories and power plants will have to be concerned with the amount of emissions they allow into the air. The EPA publishes guidelines called the National Emission Standards for Hazardous Air Pollutants (NESHAP), must reading for managers of industrial property.

## The Clean Water Act

The Clean Water Act of 1972 is comprised of amendments to the original Clean Water Act of 1948. The objective is to prohibit the discharge of pollutants into our natural waters and to create bodies of water that are clean enough to swim in and for fish to live in. The EPA reports that we are making progress since the date of enactment.

## Superfund

The Superfund law is officially known as The Comprehensive Environmental Response, Compensation and Liability Act (CER-CLA) of 1980. It is called "Superfund" because it establishes two trust funds to help finance the cleanup of properties that have been impacted by the release of hazardous wastes and substances. The Superfund Amendments and Reauthorization Act of 1986 (SARA) enables the federal government to place a lien on property subject to cleanup action. Unlike most government liens, the Superfund lien is subordinate to established senior liens.

## The Toxic Substances Control Act (TSCA)

The TSCA was passed in 1976 and allows the EPA to determine which substances are hazardous to the health of human beings or the environment, and to establish controls on the testing and use of such substances.

## The Asbestos Hazard Emergency Response Act (AHERA)

AHERA was passed in 1986 and amended the TSCA. It requires all public schools to be inspected for the presence of asbestos and to remedy the problem if it is likely to be hazardous to people's health. Many times the proper disposal of hazardous substances such as asbestos or polychlorinated biphenyl (PCBs) is expensive. Lessors and lessees, whose responsibility it is to dispose of these items, sometimes take shortcuts to save money, resulting in further pollution and danger to human health. The property manager must be clear on proper procedures and on what steps lessors and lessees are taking.

 The laws governing the protection of the environment and human health and safety are many. It is the responsibility of the professional property manager for the sake of the environment, the value of the property and the health and safety of concerned people, to see to it that laws governing environmental issues are followed. Research with property associations and environmental associations including the EPA as well as legal counsel will ensure that the property manager is aware of all necessary laws.

When the environmental laws are understood, it is necessary from a leasehold standpoint that responsibilities be fixed with the lessor and/or lessee. In an industrial property, it is reasonable to expect the lessee who creates any hazardous waste to be responsible for properly disposing of it. In residential property, the tenant has the right to expect that an environment safe from hazardous substances will be provided. Both parties should understand what the laws require of them and what their responsibilities are under the lease.

# LANDLORD/TENANT RELATIONS

Another area of law for the property manager to be aware of is landlord/tenant relations. Property managers should always know where they stand in the law. Do they have the right to require the tenants to park their cars off the property? Do they have the right to tow their cars away? Do they have the right to evict? Do they have the right to restrict their behavior? Can the property manager be sued for taking a certain action?

Many times the landlord/property manager gets better results by using psychology and garnering cooperation than insisting on the letter of the law. If the property manager is *right* but loses money for the owner due to property damage, it is a Pyrrhic victory. It goes back to the days of the Roman Empire when Rome won a bloody battle, but the cost of victory wasn't worth it. It would have been better to withdraw, to compromise or even give in. Sometimes discretion *is* the better part of valor.

In large residential complexes, tenants sometimes form tenant groups. They approach management with a spokesperson and make requests regarding many issues. Open lines of communication are a helpful tool for the property manager in these kinds of situations. When legal action must be taken, so be it. But a spirit of cooperation and teamwork will always accomplish far more than force.

# HOMEOWNERS' ASSOCIATIONS

Sometimes a property manager is involved in managing a development that is governed by a homeowners' association. When this is the case, the property manager will have to be acquainted with a number of sets of regulations.

## Covenants, Conditions and Restrictions (CC&Rs)

CC&Rs govern the property owners and place restrictions on what they can do while living in the development and to their units. Restrictions could be in the form of a covenant or a condition. A covenant is a promise to do or not to do something. Violation of it can result in an injunction compelling compliance. A condition, if violated, can result in forfeiture of the property.

Some typical restrictions found in CC&Rs regulate the type of screen door an owner can place on the unit, prohibit a resident from installing a basketball hoop above the garage door and prevent an owner from installing a patio cover. One long-time resident of a condominium complex was severely injured in an automobile accident. After spending several months in the hospital, she returned home, permanently bound to a wheel chair. Because her two-story condominium didn't have a bedroom on the first floor, she wanted to build a room addition. The board of directors of the homeowners' association rejected her request and rightfully so. A big part of the value in the development is attributed to the conformity of the units. If residents were allowed to add on and modify their units as they wished, a hodge-podge effect would result and values would plummet. Sad as it is, the only recourse the resident has is to sell her unit and buy a new home more suitable for her current circumstances.

## By-Laws

By-laws are rules and regulations adopted by the association that govern the association, stipulating what it can and cannot do. As the residents have to follow the rules of the CC&Rs, so the association has to follow the mandates and procedures of the by-laws.

## Federal and State Laws

These laws regulate tenancy and rights and interests in property. In one retirement community with a homeowners' association, a man over 55 married and brought his wife into the development to live with him. The wife was not yet 55. The development was a stock cooperative where owners own a share of stock in a corporation with the right to occupy a certain unit. The owner drew a new grant deed, establishing himself and his new wife as joint tenants in the condominium. Some of the older women who lived in the development complained about the younger wife using the pool since she was not yet 55 and apparently turned more heads than they did. To further complicate matters, the husband died. Tenancy laws say that the husband's interest automatically terminates and reverts to the wife. CC&Rs said that the wife can't be an owner-occupant in the development since she is not yet 55. The homeowners' association compromised and allowed the wife to remain in the development (and even use the pool) but she would not receive the shares of stock in her name until she turned 55. Recent amendments to the "housing for older persons" laws would have resolved the problem, requiring only that at least 80 percent of the housing in a development be occupied by at least one person 55 years of age or older.

# CONCLUSION

There are so many activities, rights and functions related to the ownership and use of real property. The professional property manager directs many of these activities, rights and functions. All must be done under the authority of the law. It is a big responsibility not to be taken lightly. Consult with professional associations, colleagues and legal counsel whenever there is a question as to what to do. The extra care you take to be sure of your decisions will pay great dividends in time and money later on.

# QUESTIONS

1. Law is established in society to:

    a. protect the rights of lessees

    b. be a servant to society

    c. protect the rights of lessors

    d. all of the above

2. The Americans with Disabilities Act (ADA) applies to:

   a. government buildings

   b. businesses in the private sector that are open to the public

   c. churches

   d. all of the above

3. A disability as incorporated in the ADA is defined as:

   a. a physical impairment that prevents an individual from working

   b. a physical or mental impairment that substantially limits one or more of an individual's major life activities

   c. a sensory impairment that inhibits one's ability to hear, see or speak

   d. none of the above

4. The Americans with Disabilities Act Accessibility Guidelines (ADAAG) provides standards to be observed in the:

   a. design, construction and alteration of buildings that come under the jurisdiction of the ADA

   b. choice of location for a public accommodation facility

   c. cost of construction of a public accommodation facility

   d. all of the above

5. According to ADAAG, normal maintenance of a building:

   a. is never considered an alteration

   b. is an alteration

   c. is not an alteration unless it affects the usability of the building

   d. none of the above

6. General exceptions to the requirements of the ADA for new construction are granted under the following circumstances:

    a. when the owner can demonstrate that compliance is too expensive

    b. when the owner can demonstrate that it is structurally impractical to comply

    c. when the owner can demonstrate that compliance is inconvenient

    d. no exceptions to the requirements of the ADA are ever granted

7. Accessibility to public accommodation facilities under the ADA is required in all of the following areas except:

    a. observation galleries used primarily for security purposes

    b. lobbies

    c. restrooms

    d. meeting rooms

8. The ADA was passed in what year:

    a. 1970

    b. 1990

    c. 1995

    d. 1965

9. Fair Housing Laws ensure that:

    a. separate but equal housing be made available to all people

    b. all people get to live where they want to

    c. prejudice and bigotry in the U.S. will be eliminated

    d. all people in the U.S. have an equal opportunity to choose where they will live

10. Under the Fair Housing Laws of the United States, the only qualification for an individual to live in a particular location is:

    a. acceptance by neighbors

    b. the appeal of the location

    c. financial

    d. personal characteristics

11. In the landmark case of 1968, real estate broker Alfred Mayer was found guilty of discrimination against his buyer, Mr. Jones. Specifically, Mr. Mayer was guilty of:

    a. steering
    b. blockbusting
    c. mayhem
    d. duress

12. Under Fair Housing Laws a landlord is forbidden to refuse a prospective tenant for all of the following reasons except:

    a. race
    b. religion
    c. ability to pay
    d. familial status

13. Under Fair Housing Laws a landlord can have different requirements for different classes of tenants in which of the following categories:

    a. deposit amount
    b. number of occupants
    c. co-signer
    d. none of the above

14. Which of the following would be violations of Fair Housing Laws:

    a. refusal to rent
    b. discrimination in advertising
    c. false statements of availability
    d. all of the above

15. Consequences of violating Fair Housing Laws for a real estate professional could include:

    a. discipline
    b. civil damages
    c. criminal charges
    d. all of the above

16. Prevention of violation of Fair Housing Laws:

    a. is attainable by a concerted effort of education and procedures
    b. is not always possible
    c. applies only to real estate agents
    d. none of the above

17. The first step in the eviction process for a delinquent tenant is to:

    a. post and serve a three-day notice
    b. file a three-day notice
    c. post a summons
    d. turn off the electricity

18. Occupants in possession but not named in the lease:

    a. need not be named in an unlawful detainer complaint
    b. cannot by law be named in the unlawful detainer complaint since they are not named in the lease
    c. must be named in the complaint to avoid delays later
    d. have to leave with the official lessees anyway when the marshal evicts them

19. Environmental cleanup issues:

    a. are always the responsibility of the lessor
    b. are designated for responsibility in the lease
    c. are always the responsibility of the lessee
    d. are resolved by the city or county

20. The management of developments governed by homeowner associations is a complex task. The property manager must take into account which of the following sets of regulations:

    a. CC&R's
    b. bylaws
    c. federal and state laws
    d. all of the above

# ANSWERS

1. *d*
2. *d*
3. *b*
4. *a*
5. *c*
6. *b*
7. *a*
8. *b*
9. *d*
10. *c*
11. *a*
12. *c*
13. *d*
14. *d*
15. *d*
16. *a*
17. *a*
18. *c*
19. *b*
20. *d*

# Glossary

**Accountant:** A person who supervises the keeping of financial records pertaining to properties being managed. Generally more qualified than a bookkeeper.

**Accredited Residential Manager (ARM):** A property management designation offered by the Institute of Real Estate Management (IREM).

**Accredited Management Organization (AMO):** A property management designation offered by the Institute of Real Estate Management (IREM) to property management companies that meet prescribed high standards.

**Administrative Assistant:** A position that assists any of the executive or middle management personnel in the achievement of their job objectives.

**Agricultural Land:** Land used for farming purposes, including growing crops and raising livestock.

**AH&MA:** The American Hotel and Motel Association, the only trade association representing the lodging industry.

**AIDA Formula:** In marketing, a formula for writing an ad that is designed to get maximum results. A=Attention, I=Interest, D=Desire, A=Action.

**Airport Hotel:** A lodging accommodation to meet travelers' needs at the beginning or end of a journey. The modern ones include conference rooms, fitness centers and restaurants.

**All-Suite Hotel:** A hotel offering full suites to its guests similar to a one- bedroom apartment.

**Americans with Disabilities Act (ADA):** A law passed by Congress in 1990 requiring any business or public facility to be accessible to everyone, including those with disabilities.

**Americans with Disabilities Act Accessibility Guidelines (ADAAG):** A document which provides standards to be observed in the design, construction and alteration of buildings that come under the jurisdiction of the ADA.

**Annual Net Income:** Also called net operating income, the amount of income left from an income-producing property after all expenses have been deducted.

**Asbestos Hazard Emergency Response Act (AHERA):** A law passed by Congress in 1986 which amends the Toxic Substances Control Act (TSCA). It requires all public schools to be inspected for the presence of asbestos and to remedy the problem if it is likely to be hazardous to people's health.

**Asset Manager:** An executive who oversees the firm's real estate resources, setting goals and strategies with ownership interests. Also called a portfolio manager.

**Assignment:** Regarding a lease, a new tenant takes the place of the original tenant, taking possession of the property and responsibility for the lease agreement, making payments directly to the landlord.

**Assistant Manager (Hotel):** The manager who relieves the general manager of selected duties and interfaces with department heads.

**Back-End Ratio:** The ratio of all fixed debt, including housing expenses, to gross income.

**Back-of-the-House:** Operations of the hotel business that are preparatory in nature and take place behind the scenes, out of the view of guests.

**Balance Sheet:** A report showing the assets of a business, the liabilities, and the net worth.

**Band of Investment:** A method of determining the capitalization rate in which the return demanded by investment money in various positions is calculated and combined.

**Banquet Director:** The person in charge of all physical aspects of a banquet.

**Bed & Breakfast Inn:** A lodging accommodation generally converted from a large house or hotel with personal service to offer a pleasant get-away experience.

**Bell Captain:** The second-ranking job in the service department in charge of the bellhops.

**Bellhop:** A service assistant in a hotel to usher guests to their rooms, carry baggage and offer other personal services.

**Bookkeeper:** A person who keeps financial records on properties being managed.

**Building Engineer:** A position that inspects the structured components and the permanent systems of a building to ensure safety and compliance with all government regulations.

**Business Cycle:** The constant fluctuation of levels of income, employment and the amount of goods and services produced in a given fiscal year.

**Buyer's Market:** A stage in the real estate market in which the ready, willing and able buyer is in the minority and is in control of the market. A time of oversupply and decreased demand. Prices decline during this stage of the cycle.

**By-Laws:** Rules and regulations that govern the activities of a homeowner's association.

**Capacity:** Legitimate legal status to enter into a contract (not mentally incompetent nor under-age), one of the legal essentials of a valid contract.

**Capitalization Rate:** The desired rate of return on an income producing property expressed as a decimal or percentage indicating the relationship between the value and the income.

**Cash Flow Statement:** A report showing cash flow after distribution for various categories of expense.

**CC&Rs:** Covenants, conditions and restrictions placed on certain types of real property which limit the activities of owners.

**CERCLA:** The Comprehensive Environmental Response, Compensation and Liability Act, a law passed by Congress in 1980. Establishes two trust funds to help finance the cleanup of properties that have been impacted by the release of hazardous wastes and substances. Commonly known as superfund.

**Certified Apartment Maintenance Technician (CAMT):** A designation offered by the National Apartment Association (NAA).

**Certified Apartment Manager (CAM):** A designation offered by the National Apartment Association (NAA).

**Certified Apartment Property Supervisor (CAPS):** A designation offered by the National Apartment Association (NAA).

**Certified International Property Specialist (CIPS):** A property management designation offered by FIABCI-USA.

**Certified Leasing Specialist (CLS):** A designation offered by the International Council of Shopping Centers (ICSC).

**Certified Manager of Community Associations (CMCA):** A designation offered by the Community Associations Institute (CAI).

**Certified Marketing Director (CMD):** A designation offered by the International Council of Shopping Centers (ICSC).

**Certified Property Manager (CPM):** The most advanced property management designation offered by the Institute of Real Estate Management (IREM).

**Certified Shopping Center Manager (CSM):** A designation offered by the International Council of Shopping Centers (ICSC).

**Classified Ad:** A small ad designed to give basic information.

**Clean Water Act:** A law passed by Congress in 1972 to prohibit the discharge of pollutants into our natural waters.

**Clerk:** A position in a hotel devoted to the detailed attention to one or more specific functions, such as reservations or floor activities.

**Commercial Property:** A property where commerce is conducted, such as an office building or retail shopping center.

**Common Interest Developments (CIDs):** Real property developments that include common interests and shared common areas.

**Community Apartment Project:** One type of CID in which the owner has an undivided interest in the land with the exclusive right to occupy a particular unit.

**Community Center:** A retail center anchored by a small department store and supported by up to 50 smaller stores. At least 5,000 households are usually needed to support a community center.

**Comparison:** A method of determining the capitalization rate by looking to the operational capitalization rate of similar properties in the area.

**Compliance Clause:** A clause in a lease designating which party is responsible for complying with various laws.

**Concierge:** An employee in a large hotel who makes special arrangements for guests, such as procuring theater tickets.

**Condition:** A limiting restriction in the ownership of real property, the violation of which could cause the owner to lose title or have his or her estate modified in some way.

**Condominium:** A structure for either residential, industrial or commercial use whereby the owner owns the interior airspace of the unit plus an undivided interest in the common areas.

**Consideration:** Anything of value, one of the essentials of a valid contract.

**Convention Hotel:** A large hotel designed to accommodate thousands of guests for attendance at conferences.

**Covenant:** A promise or assurance set forth in a written agreement allowing or disallowing certain activities on the part of the owner.

**Damage or Destruction Clause:** A clause in a lease detailing how the partial or total destruction of the property would be handled between the parties to the lease.

**Default Clause:** A clause in a lease setting forth the lessor's remedies in the event of a default by the lessee.

**Demographics:** The study of statistics relating to populations, especially in the areas of demand for certain types of real estate.

**Depression:** A rare stage in the business cycle following a recession characterized by extremely high unemployment and very little purchasing power.

**Discrimination:** Violating someone's right to fair housing opportunity on the basis of who they are, such as characteristics of race, color, sex, religion, familial status, marital status, disability or national origin.

**Display Ad:** A large, expansive ad that may use graphics and pictures to tell a more complete story.

**Door Attendant:** An employee in a large hotel who assists guests through entrances and exits and keeps foot traffic moving.

**Double Net Lease:** An arrangement whereby the tenant pays the rent, utilities, property taxes, special assessments and insurance premiums.

**Downtown Hotel:** An older hotel with a downtown location.

**Economic Rent Increase:** An increase in rent prompted by a shrinking supply of comparable rental units in an area and the ability of tenants to afford the increase.

**Economics:** Related to real estate, a study of the factors that cause people to prosper and create a viable demand for real property.

**Effective Gross Income:** Also known as adjusted gross income, the income actually collected after deducting for collection losses.

**Elevator Operator:** Nearly obsolete, an employee in a large period hotel who adds authenticity and keeps traffic moving.

**Environmental Protection Agency (EPA):** A federal agency established in 1970 to ensure the enforcement of the National Environmental Policy Act (NEPA).

**Escalation Clause:** A clause in a lease that allows for rent increases based on the occurrence of a certain event.

**Estate:** Ownership arrangements that tell the types and duration of interests that an individual has in real property.

**Estate at Sufferance:** A situation where a tenant has come into possession in a lawful manner but has stayed beyond the prescribed duration of the agreement hostile to the owner's wishes.

**Estate at Will:** A tenancy agreement that endures as long as both parties are willing. It can be terminated unilaterally.

**Estate for Years:** An arrangement by which the tenant takes possession on a particular date and will remain in possession until a particular date. It could be for any period of days, weeks, months or years.

**Eviction:** The legal process by which the tenant is removed from the property due to violations of terms of the lease.

**Executive Manager:** An executive who oversees the entire operation of a property management firm.

**Express Warranty:** An obligation to a tenant created by a promise made by the lessor or lessor's agent that caused the tenant to enter into the lease.

**Facilities Management Administrator (FMA):** A property management designation offered by the Building Owners and Managers Institute (BOMI) with emphasis on the management of a commercial facility.

**Fair Housing Laws:** Laws originating in the United States Constitution ensuring all persons the fair opportunity for housing of their choice in the United States.

**Fair Labor Standards Act:** A law enacted during the depression regulating certain aspects of labor that the lodging industry feels is in need of revision.

**FDIC:** The Federal Deposit Insurance Corporation, a federal agency which insures depositors in banks and savings and loan associations to protect their deposits in case of bank failure.

**FHA:** The Federal Housing Administration, established in 1934 to insure certain types of home loans, protecting the lender and allowing a small down payment from the borrower.

**Fief:** Rights in the land that become heritable.

**Financial Analysis:** A study of the property's income producing performance and potential.

**Forms:** Documents that provide written evidence of agreement, activity, policy and responsibility.

**Freedman:** In medieval times, a status of citizenship that would allow a person to own land.

**Freehold Estates:** Ownership rights and interests that may continue until the death of the owner and possibly pass on to his or her heirs.

**Front-End Ratio:** The ratio of all housing expenses to gross income.

**Front-of-the-House:** Operations of the hotel business that deal directly with guests.

**General Ledger:** A report showing an accounting of all debits and credits going through the business bank account for various periods of time.

**General Maintenance Workers:** Refers to workers in various trades hired from time to time to keep a building running smoothly.

**General Manager (Hotel):** The top manager in charge of all departments of a hotel.

**Graduated Lease:** Sometimes called a step-up lease, usually a long-term lease with an escalation clause allowing for a rent increase based upon the occurrence of a certain event.

**Green Properties:** Hotels that participate in the AH&MA's environmental management program.

**Gross Lease:** An arrangement whereby the tenant pays the rental payments only and the landlord pays all of the expenses.

**Guest Ranch:** A housing accommodation providing a unique vacation experience for a guest who participates in ranch life.

**Homeowners' Association:** An association formed by homeowners for their mutual benefit.

**Hotel:** A commercial establishment built solely for the purpose of accommodating travelers.

**Housekeeper:** An employee in a hotel who cleans and stocks the guest rooms.

**Industrial Property:** A property where products are manufactured or assembled. The conducting of industry.

**Lawful Object:** The purpose, object and operation of the contract is legal, one of the essentials of a valid contract.

**Lease:** A written agreement by which possession of the property is transferred and the stream of income is secured.

**Leasing Agent:** An agent who secures qualified tenants for leases on residential, commercial or industrial property.

**Less Than Freehold Estates:** Leasehold interests.

**Liability Indemnity Clause:** A clause in a lease holding landlords harmless from the actions of their tenants.

**Lord:** In earlier times, a regional supervisor of a large piece of land.

**Maintenance Clause:** A clause in a lease designating which party is responsible for maintenance of the property beyond normal wear-and-tear.

**Maintenance Supervisor:** A position responsible for maintenance of buildings in his or her charge. This person hires workers and supervises all maintenance activities.

**Management Plan:** A plan for future management based on financial reports and projection accepted by ownership.

**Market Analysis:** A study which gives an understanding of the economic factors operating in the local marketplace related to the subject property.

**Market Rent:** Based on a survey, what the competition is receiving in rent for similar space with similar amenities.

**Market Survey:** A report generated by software comparing the subject property in various categories of performance to competing properties in the area.

**Mega-Center:** An oversized shopping center that attracts shoppers from hundreds of miles around. Also called a super-mall.

**Middle Managers:** Property managers who are involved in hands-on activities that implement the decisions of owners and upper management.

**MIMO Form:** The move in, move out form, detailing inventory and initial condition of rental space, and inventory and condition upon move-out.

**Moratorium:** A temporary prohibition against building in certain areas to control the rate of development.

**Motel:** A hybrid of motor-hotel, a housing accommodation in outlying areas for middle-class America. Located along major highways, it gives easy access to lodging to those traveling by automobile.

**Motor Camps:** Chains of campgrounds designed to accommodate motorists and recreational vehicle drivers.

**Multi-Family Units:** Residential structures intended to house more than one family unit, such as duplexes or apartment buildings.

**Mutual Consent:** A meeting of the minds, one of the essentials of a valid contract.

**National Apartment Leasing Professional (NALP):** A designation offered by the National Apartment Association (NAA).

**National Environmental Policy Act (NEPA):** A law passed by Congress in 1970 that requires an environmental impact statement to be prepared and released prior to any federal action that would affect the environment. This is also required by some state and local governments for private improvements.

**Neighborhood Center:** A retail center supported by a thousand or so households, usually anchored by a grocery store and supported by a dozen or so other compatible stores.

**Net Lease:** An arrangement whereby the tenant pays the rental payment plus certain agreed upon expenses.

**Net Operating Income:** Also called net annual income, the amount of income left from an income-producing property after all expenses have been deducted.

**On-Site Manager:** A property manager who lives on-site, handles day-to-day activities, and interacts with tenants on a regular basis.

**Operating Budget:** A basic tool of the property manager to help in planning.

**Operating Expenses:** Expenditures necessary to the operation of an income-producing building that are subtracted from effective gross income to arrive at net operating income.

**Page:** An employee in a hotel who delivers a message or summons a guest.

**Paired Sales Analysis:** Matching up two properties that are identical in all respects except for one variable. Determines the value of that variable in the marketplace.

**Percentage Lease:** An arrangement whereby the tenant pays a percentage of gross receipts and/or a minimum flat amount.

**Period Hotel or Inn:** A hotel or inn that conveys the essence of a particular period of time in history.

**Periodic Tenancy:** Tenancy from period to period, such as a month-to-month tenancy.

**Planned Unit Development (PUD):** A development in which each owner owns his or her own housing unit and land, and has an undivided interest in common areas with other owners.

**Porter:** A baggage handler.

**Portfolio Manager:** An executive who oversees the firm's real estate resources, setting goals and strategies with ownership interests. Also called an asset manager.

**Post-House:** An inn accommodating travelers in the 1600s.

**Professional Community Association Manager (PCAM):** An advanced designation offered by the Community Associations Institute (CAI).

**Project Operating Report:** A report that breaks income and expenses down into specific categories and matches them to budget objectives.

**Projection:** An anticipated operational income and expense statement projected into the future to aid in planning.

**Property Analysis:** An on-site inspection and study of the subject property so that the entire physical plant is thoroughly understood.

**Property Management:** The practice of real estate that manages and preserves the real property assets of another person.

**Property Supervisor:** A property manager who is responsible for several properties and supervises the on-site managers of those properties.

**Prosperity:** A stage in the business cycle when unemployment is low and consumers have a lot of purchasing power.

**Public Accommodation Property:** A privately owned property where the public has certain rights, such as a hotel or office building.

**Quiet Enjoyment:** The right of a tenant to be undisturbed.

**Real Estate:** Originally, the king's land. Today, a term that refers to real property.

**Real Estate Cycle:** A fluctuation of supply and demand in real estate affected by the state of the business cycle and resulting in various levels of activity for building, lending, purchasing and leasing real estate. The cycle swings between the extremes of a buyer's market and a seller's market.

**Real Property Administrator (RPA):** A property management designation offered by the Building Owners and Managers Institute (BOMI).

**Real Property Manager (RPM):** A property management designation offered by the Building Owners and Managers Association (BOMA).

**Recession:** A stage in the business cycle when production has surpassed demand resulting in unemployment and declining prices.

**Recovery:** A stage in the business cycle when consumers once again buy goods at reduced prices, increasing demand in relation to supply.

**Regional Center:** A large retail shopping center (sometimes called a mall) with half a dozen major department stores along with 100 to 200 general merchandise and specialty shops. Customers are drawn from as far as 50 miles and comprise 50,000 to 150,000 households.

**Regional Manager:** A property manager who works for a large property management company and oversees the work of property supervisors or on-site managers.

**Registered Property Manager (RPM):** A property management designation offered by the International Real Estate Institute (IREI).

**Rent Control:** A local ordinance prohibiting rent increases on certain types of property.

**Residential Property:** A property where people reside, including single family residences, condominiums and apartment buildings.

**Restriction:** A limitation on the use of a property by the owner. May be private (as in a deed or declaration of restrictions) or public (as in zoning).

**RevPAR:** Revenue per available room, a statistic followed in the lodging industry.

**Risk Manager:** A property manager who evaluates complex issues—sometimes global issues—to protect the value of real estate assets.

**RTC:** The Resolution Trust Corporation, established by the Federal Government in 1989 to help failed savings and loans liquidate real property assets.

**Scheduled Gross Income:** All of the income a property is scheduled to produce.

**Seller's Market:** A stage in the real estate market in which demand is greater than supply—more buyers than sellers—and prices rise.

**Serfdom:** In medieval times, a status that was insufficient to allow a person to own land.

**SFR:** A single family residence. A house that is intended to be occupied by one family.

**Single Net Lease:** An arrangement whereby the tenant pays the rent plus utilities, property taxes and any special assessments on the property.

**Skyscraper:** Tall steel-framed structures that originally housed mostly office buildings.

**Special Purpose Properties:** Properties that are designed to meet unique purposes within a community, such as—but not limited to—mini-storage facilities and mobile home parks.

**Standard Operating Procedures (SOP):** Standard procedures that are followed for efficiency whenever specified regularly occurring events take place.

**Steering:** Directing people to specific locations for housing accommodations, depriving them of choice, a violation of Fair Housing Laws.

**Step-up Lease:** Sometimes called a graduated lease, usually a long-term lease with an escalation clause allowing for a rent increase based upon the occurrence of a certain event.

**Stock Cooperative:** A development in which a corporation is formed for the purpose of holding title to improved real property.

**Strip Center:** A small retail center located in the suburbs, containing half-a-dozen to a dozen stores of various kinds.

**Subletting:** The process by which the original tenant gives up use or possession of all or part of the property but receives payment from the sub-lessee and remains fully responsible for the entire lease payment to the landlord.

**Suburban Hotel:** A lodging accommodation within driving distance of the downtown area of a large city, designed to attract business clientele.

**Suburbs:** The area within driving distance of a city's downtown.

**Summation:** A method of determining the capitalization rate in which various risk factors are weighted and combined.

**Super-Mall:** An oversized shopping center that attracts shoppers from hundreds of miles around. Also called a mega-center.

**Superfund:** Officially known as the Comprehensive Environmental Response, Compensation and Liability Act (CERCLA), passed by Congress in 1980. Establishes two trust funds to help finance the cleanup of properties that have been impacted by the release of hazardous wastes and substances.

**Superintendent of Service:** The person in a hotel who supervises all front office service personnel.

**Supply and Demand:** A basic economic principle in which the greater the supply of an item, the lower its value. When an item is scarce in relation to demand, the value is high. Applies to real estate and all commodities.

**Syndicate:** A group of individuals formed for the accomplishment of some business purpose such as a corporation or limited partnership.

**Systems Maintenance Administrator (SMA):** A property management designation offered by the Building Owners and Managers Institute (BOMI) with emphasis on supervision of systems and personnel.

**Systems Maintenance Technician (SMT):** A property management designation offered by the Building Owners and Managers Institute (BOMI) with emphasis on the technical maintenance of various systems such as heating and air conditioning.

**Three-Day Notice to Pay or Quit:** The initial notice given to a tenant to begin the eviction process.

**Three I's Formula:** An application of sound human relations principles when handling the impending removal of a tenant from the property. (#1) Interaction (#2) Incentives (#3) Intimidation.

**Timeshare:** A specialized type of resort property whereby owners purchase the right to occupy the space for a certain period of time during the year.

**Tourist House:** A lodging accommodation offered in a private home enjoyed by guests on bus or auto tours seeking to economize.

**Toxic Substances Control Act (TSCA):** A law passed by Congress in 1976 which allows the EPA to determine which substances are hazardous to the health of human beings or to the environment.

**Triple Net Lease:** An arrangement whereby the tenant pays the rent, utilities, property taxes, special assessments and insurance premiums; and takes responsibility for repairs and maintenance.

**Unlawful Detainer Action:** An action filed in court in an eviction process requiring the tenant to respond within five days.

**Urbanization:** The clustering of people around big city areas for work and living.

**Use Clause:** A clause in a lease designating which parties are authorized to use the property and for what purpose.

**VA:** The Veterans Administration, providing benefits to qualified veterans including the VA loan guaranteed by the VA and offering low or no down to the borrower.

**Vacancy Factor:** Money lost due to vacancies and other collection losses, usually expressed as a percentage of scheduled gross income.

**Valet:** An employee in a large hotel who receives, parks and retrieves a guest's automobile.

**Variance Analysis:** An analysis of reports provided by software programs offering explanation for variances from the budget.

**Vassal:** A person who received a fief from a regional lord.

**Washroom Attendant:** An employee in a large hotel who ensures the cleanliness and supplies of restroom facilities.

**Writ of Possession:** A document that is executed at a default hearing authorizing the sheriff's office to evict the tenant.

# INDEX

**INDEX**

**INDEX**

**INDEX**